REGNUM EDINBURGH 2010 SERIES

Witnessing to Christ in a Pluralistic World

Christian Mission among Other Faiths

REGNUM EDINBURGH 2010 SERIES

The Centenary of the World Missionary Conference of 1910, held in Edinburgh, was a suggestive moment for many people seeking direction for Christian mission in the twenty-first century. Several different constituencies within world Christianity held significant events around 2010. From 2005, an international group worked collaboratively to develop an intercontinental and multi-denominational project, known as Edinburgh 2010, and based at New College, University of Edinburgh. This initiative brought together representatives of twenty different global Christian bodies, representing all major Christian denominations and confessions, and many different strands of mission and church life, to mark the Centenary.

Essential to the work of the Edinburgh 1910 Conference, and of abiding value, were the findings of the eight think-tanks or 'commissions'. These inspired the idea of a new round of collaborative reflection on Christian mission – but now focused on nine themes identified as being key to mission in the twenty-first century. The study process was polycentric, open-ended, and as inclusive as possible of the different genders, regions of the world, and theological and confessional perspectives in today's church. It was overseen by the Study Process Monitoring Group: Miss Maria Aranzazu Aguado (Spain, The Vatican), Dr Daryl Balia (South Africa, Edinburgh 2010), Mrs Rosemary Dowsett (UK, World Evangelical Alliance), Dr Knud Jørgensen (Norway, Areopagos), Rev. John Kafwanka (Zambia, Anglican Communion), Rev. Dr Jooseop Keum (Korea, World Council of Churches), Dr Wonsuk Ma (Korea, Oxford Centre for Mission Studies), Rev. Dr Kenneth R. Ross (UK, Church of Scotland), Dr Petros Vassiliadis (Greece, Aristotle University of Thessalonikki), and coordinated by Dr Kirsteen Kim (UK, Edinburgh 2010).

These publications reflect the ethos of Edinburgh 2010 and will make a significant contribution to ongoing studies in mission. It should be clear that material published in this series will inevitably reflect a diverse range of views and positions. These will not necessarily represent those of the series' editors or of the Edinburgh 2010 General Council, but in publishing them the leadership of Edinburgh 2010 hopes to encourage conversation between Christians and collaboration in mission. All the series' volumes are commended for study and reflection in both church and academy.

Series Editors

REGNUM EDINBURGH 2010 SERIES

Witnessing to Christ in a Pluralistic World

Christian Mission among Other Faiths

Edited by

Lalsangkima Pachuau and Knud Jørgensen

First published 2011 by Regnum Books International

Regnum is an imprint of the Oxford Centre for Mission Studies
St. Philip and St. James Church
Woodstock Road
Oxford OX2 6HR, UK
www.ocms.ac.uk/regnum

09 08 07 06 05 04 03 7 6 5 4 3 2 1

British Library Cataloguing in Publication Data
A catalogue record for this book is available from the British Library

ISBN: 978-1-506476-04-9

Typeset by Words by Design (www.wordsbydesign.co.uk)

The photo on the cover shows 'Christ Temple' at the Tao Fong Shan center for dialogue, spirituality and studies in Hong Kong. The center and the Christ Temple were built in the 1930s as a meeting place for Buddhist monks from China and Christians. The center functioned in that manner until the beginning of World War II. Today the center, with its Chinese and Buddhist architecture, continues to be a place of dialogue between people of living faiths.

This volume has been sponsored by the
Areopagos Foundation in Norway and Denmark

Distributed by 1517 Media in the US and Canada

Contents

FOREWORD

Kirsteen Kim

From the start 'study theme two' was one of the most challenging of the nine study themes of the Edinburgh 2010 project. The general topic of interfaith issues in mission was bound to be important in the preparatory research and in the conference discussion, especially because when the themes were first identified, in 2005, it was just four years after 9/11. But in this very contentious climate, is mission an appropriate response?

In 1910 the 'world religions' paradigm with which we are familiar today was not yet established. Delegates to the World Missionary Conference in Edinburgh generally understood that Christianity was 'the world religion', the only truly universal religion which was the fulfilment of all other religions, and to which they would eventually submit. A century or so later when the term is applied to Christianity it is to say that the Christian faith is 'a world religion' – one among several deemed worthy of the name. Textbooks differ as to whether there are five or six or sometimes more 'world religions'. Each is given a logo and they are taught from an apparently neutral position as independent and autonomous systems of equal worth and bearing no fixed relation to one another. The religions are variously perceived to be in conflict or competition, or to offer complementary paths of life.

Over the last one hundred years different Christian churches have wrestled with this new perception and have found various ways of expressing the uniqueness or distinctiveness of Christianity, and its relation to the other religions, but without religious domination. These solutions have been variously expressed in terms of Christian apologetics and theologies of religion. On the ground situations of religious pluralism – familiar for centuries in many parts of Asia and Africa but a recent development for many in Europe and the Americas – have afforded opportunities for experiments in interfaith dialogue and cooperation. New ways are being sought to address intractable conflicts which are exacerbated by religious differences. In some situations Christian majorities have been challenged to make room for other faiths while in other places Christian minorities have insisted on religious freedom.

Its recent colonial legacy, including the negative approach towards other traditions at Edinburgh 1910, has led many Christian scholars of religion and interfaith practitioners to eschew the word 'mission'. The distinctive contribution of Edinburgh 2010 was to insist that Christian mission has a place in a pluralistic world, even in the tense post 9/11 situation. This book of the work of study theme two is notable in reclaiming the practice of mission, in the sense of witness to Christ, as an appropriate, justifiable and considered response to the presence of other faiths.

Having re-learnt what the Orthodox have long known and Pentecostal movements have more recently experienced – that the Christian church has a unique identity and God-given task in the world to witness to Christ, this important book also highlights another insight of Orthodox theology and Pentecostal conviction – that the church witnesses as part of the economy of the Holy Spirit. Christian witness is joining in the work of the Christ-like Spirit of God who blows to vivify and sanctify the whole creation. On the one hand this pneumatological approach expands both the scope of mission – to include the redemption of the whole creation – and also the partners of mission – to include even those of other faiths who share the same spirit. On the other hand, it delimits mission to witnessing to Christ and it precludes attitudes and actions in mission that are incompatible with the love of Christ. By dealing mainly in position papers from different church perspectives and case studies of several different religious traditions in a variety of global contexts, *Witnessing to Christ in a Pluralistic World* graphically illustrates what it means to do mission among other faiths today in the (self-sacrificing) power of the Holy Spirit. It ties this not to a grand theory of everything but to the particular witness of Jesus Christ incarnated among us.

The editors and the conveners of study theme two are to be congratulated in bringing together a wide variety of contributors and facilitating such a useful and stimulating discussion of the continuing imperative of Christian mission among other faiths.

Prof. Kirsteen Kim, PhD
Professor of Theology and World Christianity and
Director of Programmes in Theology and Religious Studies,
Leeds Trinity University College, UK

INTRODUCTION

Lalsangkima Pachuau and Knud Jørgensen

The present volume comes from the preparatory study works of theme number two (or "theme two" as popularly termed), namely "Christian Mission among Other Faiths" of "Edinburgh 2010," the centenary celebration of the World Missionary Conference of 1910. Edinburgh 2010 had *Witnessing to Christ Today* as its main theme which was subdivided into nine themes (or sub-themes). Nine study groups were organized around the nine themes to do preparatory studies on each theme with participants and input from all the Christian families and all parts of the world. The approach of the studies was expected to be inclusive of both theoretical and practical, with perspectives drawn from academic and practice-oriented viewpoints.

The core study group of theme two began with a small number and expanded eventually. The group was led by co-conveners Lalsangkima Pachuau, Asbury Theological Seminary, USA (Presbyterian, India) and Niki Papageorgiou, Aristotle University of Thessaloniki (Orthodox, Greece) together with Knud Jørgensen, Areopagos, Norway (Lutheran, Denmark/Norway) who also represented the Study Process Monitoring Group of Edinburgh 2010. Other members of the group were Michael Biehl of Missionsakademie, University of Hamburg (Lutheran, Germany), Eunice Irwin of Asbury Seminary (Christian and Missionary Alliance, USA), and John Azumah, London School of Theology (Presbyterian, Ghana).

Each study group was asked to prepare a 10,000 word summary essay on the theme considering the followings:

1. Identify some *key questions and items* which are of global importance within the area of your study theme.
2. Highlight some general *historical achievements and developments* in your study area since 1910 till today.
3. Give some *illuminating and telling regional case studies* and examples which illustrate major trends and challenges in your area of study.
4. Identify *key priorities* for global Christianity concerning the future of Christian mission in the 21st century in the area of your study theme.
5. Identify *strategic recommendations* which you propose for being listened to and communicated.

6. Find creative ways to meaningfully translate findings into formats that can motivate Christians involved in mission at grassroots level.
7. Include discussion questions that will facilitate use of the publication in peer discussions.

To do justice to this set of expectations and to respond to public enthusiasm surrounding the Edinburgh 2010 conference, the core study group decided to invite contributions from scholars and missional practitioners on the theme.[1] To be both theologically and ecclesiologically representative and to be inclusive of missiological issues and approaches to all the major religions, the invitees were asked to be concise and representative. Thus, the core group wrote the summary essay on the theme and organized a corporate study by inviting other essays from carefully selected scholars and leaders. While the summary essay has been published together with the works of other study groups in *Edinburgh 2010 Witnessing to Christ Today*, edited by Daryl Balia and Kirsteen Kim (Oxford: Regnum, 2010), early versions of the essays in the present volume were made available electronically at the Edinburgh 2010 website. These essays served as resources and background materials for the study process on the theme. The quality of the essays and the uniquely diverse theological and ecclesiological traditions represented convinced us of the value of this publication. The summary essay by the core group has been reproduced here to serve as an introduction.

In inviting inputs and contributions of thinkers and leaders, it was thought that position papers and case studies from a variety of persons with various backgrounds and experiences would be most appropriate and benefitting. The position papers include reflections on the theme from the different ecclesiastical and confessional traditions. They include: Roman Catholic, Greek Orthodox, Ecumenical, Evangelical, Pentecostal, and Seventh-Day Adventist. None of the essays were, however, meant to represent these traditions, but were done by scholars and practitioners from the traditions. Among the case studies are articles on Christian mission among Muslims, Hindus, Buddhists, Jews, new religious movements and folk or primal religions. As far as possible, we try to have voices from the different theological confessions or missiological approaches for each religious tradition. We hope the rich variety both in approach and theological representation would serve as a stepping stone for the future of

[1] We are aware of the imbalance between male and female contributors. Women contributors include those who have written on the Pentecostal and the Orthodox perspectives and one of the writers on mission and primal religion. The editors have tried hard to have more women contribute but several declined. The reason why men predominate in this discussion could be that women are often excluded from leadership in religions and their approach to dialogue is therefore at a more personal and grassroots level.

theology of religions. We operate with a conviction that theology of religions is the heart of missiology.

In the study of the theme we have explored ways of witnessing to Christ while acknowledging the religious and cultural plurality of a world experiencing a resurgence of religious beliefs and an escalation of conflicts. We have therefore explored the theological meaning of religious plurality reflecting on how it bears on Christian soteriology and missiology and addressed questions of conversion, proselytism, dialogue and encounter. These issues are reflected in the chapters of this book.

We believe that the relationship of Christian faith and mission to other living faiths is the core issue in contemporary missiological thinking. In a world where plurality of faith is increasing in importance and in terms of geographical spread, insights on this plurality are highly needed to strengthen our ability to better understand our own faith and the faith of others. In this manner we shall be equipped for a meaningful and open encounter with others, and we shall, perhaps in a small manner, pave the way for peace among women and men of good will.

The encounter between religions is not something new. Different religious beliefs and practices have lived and clashed as long as history has been recorded. In the same way the history of Christianity is a story of encounters with other faiths and other lords. Such encounters are seen in the Pauline testimony to one God and Lord, the apologists' defense of the Christian faith against idolatry, Christian life in the Eastern Mediterranean in the midst of Islamic domination, the adjustment of Christians to the onslaught of the Ottoman Turks in the Middle Ages, the challenge to the Renaissance from Jewish communities and from Islamic philosophy. To most Christians in the global South and East, the encounter with other religions has been a daily experience for generations. In the West, living in a pluralist society is still something new and threatening wherefore the West sorely needs to learn from the experiences of the global South.

Even though religious diversity is not new, there has for the last 15-20 years been an upsurge in the discussion and in the theological literature on theologies of religions and on Christian mission among other faiths. One reason is probably the 'discovery' in the West of other religions living in its own midst and neighbourhood. It may in our view rightly be claimed that no other issue in Christian mission is more important and more difficult than the theologies/theology of religions. We believe this will remain the major missiological challenge for mission in a new century.

To some religious pluralism has come to mean 'religious relativism'. To the post-modern mind, it is inconceivable for one particular tradition to claim itself as the source of ultimate truth and salvation. The influence of this thought has been increasingly felt among Christians. This view of Christian faith in the midst of other faiths is fairly new. The diversity of religions should be affirmed as something good in a rainbow era. That the Christian gospel is for all in a universal sense is easily agreed upon among

Christians, but when the 'particularity' of Jesus Christ becomes clear from reading Scripture, both the modern and post-modern mind tend to re-interpret this to mean that other religions may be equally true. To claim the opposite is no longer tenable to most people, including many Christians. There is probably a plethora of reasons for this, but a major factor, we believe, is a modern worldview that moves faith from the public to the private arena.

This book is, *inter alia,* trying to grapple with this issue, but its contributions do not merge into one harmonious voice of unity. We, the editors, want our readers to know where we stand on this. The Edinburgh 2010 celebration in June issued a 'Common Call' to which this study process also made its contribution. Emerging from the discussion of our theme in the conference, the Common Call states:

> Remembering Christ's sacrifice on the Cross and his resurrection for the world's salvation, and empowered by the Holy Spirit, we are called to authentic dialogue, respectful engagement and humble witness among people of other faiths – and no faith – to the uniqueness of Christ. Our approach is marked with bold confidence in the gospel message; it builds friendship, seeks reconciliation and practises hospitality.

As editors we agree with this statement, and we also found helpful another well-known statement from the Mission and Evangelism Conference of the WCC in San Antonio in 1989 which said:

> We cannot point to any other way than Jesus Christ; at the same time we cannot set limits to the saving power of God.[2]

We appreciate this tension, and do not attempt to solve it.

The theological viewpoints of the editors need not be shared by, and has not been imposed on, the contributors. As said above, the contributors come from various traditions and faith confessions.

Following the essay by the core group, the first part brings together 'Position Papers on Various Ecclesial Traditions' with the intention of showing the breadth of views across denominational and confessional lines. To the reader this may prove valuable since it opens the windows of our often enclosed ecclesiological rooms. At the same time it provides platforms for listening and dialoguing about theology of religions within Christian traditions. These essays show, in our opinion, that there is more common ground for such a conversation than many of us are aware of.

The position papers are followed by two bridging thematic chapters, namely 'Evangelism and Apologetics', and 'Theologies of Religions'. Both of these themes represent principal issues in the conversation about Christian mission among other faiths. Thus they provide an underpinning for the third part of the book.

---

[2] Fredrick R. Wilson, ed. *The San Antonio Report – Your Will be done: Mission in Christ's Way* (Geneva: WCC Publications, 1990), 32.

The third and major part of the volume features a series of case studies presenting the topic of Christian mission in conversation with the major living faiths, with new religious movements and with primal religions. These case studies unfold the missiological and practical issue of Christian mission among other faiths. For several of the topics we have gathered contributions and, so far as possible, divergent views from two or three persons, also to have a geographical and confessional spread. The reader will note that some of the authors of these case studies are critical of using the term 'mission', and even more so 'conversion', as we relate and dialogue with people of other faiths, while other contributors feel that the term adequately expresses their concern. This will often have to do with how we understand 'mission'. As editors, we look at 'mission' as *missio Dei* in which we participate by witness (*marturia*), thereby mirroring the overall theme of Edinburgh 2010 'Witnessing to Christ Today'. This *marturia* will then find expression in '*kerygma'* (proclamation), '*diakonia'* (service) and '*koinonia'* (community and fellowship). This understanding provides space for various understandings of mission, but it does underline that this book, in all it diversity, is about 'Christian Mission among Other Faiths'.

Lalsangkima Pachuau and Knud Jørgensen
June 2011

CHRISTIAN MISSION AMONG OTHER FAITHS[1]

The Edinburgh 2010 Study Group

A Centennial Historical Background

'How should we relate with and witness to people of other faiths?' This appears to be the most crucial missiological question facing Christians at the end of the twentieth century. While some go to the extent of consultative relations with the adherents of other faiths (under such rubrics as 'wider ecumenism'), others look for peaceful manners of communicating the meaning of Christian faith with the intention of persuading (or converting) them to the faith. We shall identify a few crucial milestone-themes in the development of Christian missiological thought on this topic between Edinburgh 1910 and Edinburgh 2010.

Edinburgh 1910 and Fulfilment Theory

Among the eight topics of the commissions in 1910, two of them – Commission I and Commission IV – had 'non-Christian' in the titles. While Commission I does not really deal with 'non-Christian' as such, Commission IV relates the missionary message to non-Christian religions. Among the eight commissions, the responses to the questionnaire generated by Commission IV were considered to be the best and the commission attracted the 'disproportionate attention' of scholars in the succeeding decades. The Continuation Committee of Edinburgh 1910 seriously considered publishing the responses, but abandoned the attempt with 'reluctance' says Brian Stanley.[2] As the commission's report says, the focus was not on non-Christian religions per se, but on studying 'the problems involved in the presentation of Christianity to the minds of the non-Christian peoples.'[3] Though veiled by the reigning Western optimism and victorious spirit, it was one of the early serious empirical works on other faiths. A questionnaire containing eleven questions was distributed to

---

[1] Daryl Balia & Kirsteen Kim, eds. *Edinburgh 2010. Witnessing to Christ Today* (Oxford: Regnum Books Internatinal, 2010). 34-60.

[2] Brian Stanley, *The World Missionary Conference, Edinburgh 1910* (Grand Rapids and Cambridge: William B. Eerdmans Publishing Co., 2009), 245.

[3] World Missionary Conference, Edinburgh 1910, *Report of Commission IV: The Missionary Message in Relation to Non-Christian Religions* (Edinburgh and London: Oliphant, Anderson, & Ferrier, 1910), 1.

missionaries working among non-Christians around the world, and 187 responses were received.[4] The dominant theology of religions in Commission IV is 'fulfilment theology,' and the missionary task was concluded to be a humble enquiry and identification of '"points of contact" in non-Christian religions', using them 'to draw adherents of other faiths toward the full revelation of truth found in the Christ ….'[5] The fulfilment idea is seen to be apostolic (or biblical) as the report explains:

> We can see how the whole Apostolic view grew out of the twofold endeavour of those first missionaries of the Church to meet what was deep and true in the other religions, and to guard against the perils which arose from the spell which these earlier religions still cast upon the minds of those who had been delivered from them into the larger life of the Gospel.[6]

Since the theology of fulfilment caters more to the so-called 'high religions', other religious traditions, generally categorized as 'animistic', did not fit the theory so much. But the relatively small survey materials on primal (or 'animistic') religious traditions (27 responses of which 16 were missionaries in Africa[7]) provided helpful material for later scholarship in the field.[8]

Continuity or Discontinuity

The fulfilment theology at Edinburgh 1910 continued to be the dominant approach for much of the first half of the twentieth century. It was largely on the broad basis of the fulfilment idea that the emerging challenge of secularism was responded to in the Jerusalem meeting of the International Missionary Council in 1928, and in the influential 'Laymen's Inquiry' published in 1932 as *Rethinking Missions*. The latter proposed a radical departure for missionary motive and stirred much debate. It criticised the missionary denouncement of other religions, invited the missionaries to be co-workers with people of other faiths, and advocated that 'the primary duty' of a missionary should be presentation 'in a positive form his [sic] conception of the true way of life and let it speak for itself.'[9] It was this radical redefinition of the missionary's work in relation to other ('non-Christian') religions that set the next major theme in motion – that of

---

[4] Stanley, *The World Missionary Conference*, 235. Only three of the 11 questions dealt specifically with the nature and characters of other religions. These are questions 2, 6, and 8.

[5] Stanley, *The World Missionary Conference*, 212.

[6] World Missionary Conference, 1910, *Report of Commission IV*, 215.

[7] Stanley, *The World Missionary Conference*, 235.

[8] See J. Stanley Friesen, *Missionary Responses to Tribal Religions at Edinburgh, 1910* (New York: Peter Lang, 1996).

[9] William Ernest Hocking (ed.), *Rethinking Missions: A Laymen's Inquiry after One Hundred Years* (New York and London: Harper & Brothers Publishers, 1932), 40.

continuity or discontinuity – at the Tambaram (Madras, India) meeting of the International Missionary Council in 1938.

A Dutch missiologist and a former missionary to Indonesia, Hendrik Kraemer, wrote a preparatory text for the meeting, *The Christian Message in a Non-Christian World*. Written in seven weeks,[10] this 450-page book was not easy to understand. While the thesis of the book may simply be stated as 'discontinuity' and not 'continuity', the manner by which Kraemer came to the point is complex and easily misunderstood. Against many false allegations later on, Kraemer showed a deep respect for all non-Christian religions saying, 'the non-Christian religions are not merely sets of speculative ideas about the eternal destiny of man,' but are 'inclusive systems and theories of life';[11] and the Christian attitude to them 'has to be essentially [a] *positive* attitude.'[12] However, Kraemer made a great departure from the Edinburgh 1910 search for 'points of contact'. He said that such a search for 'points of contact' is 'a misguided pursuit',[13] and he argued that God's revelation in Jesus Christ was 'absolutely *sui generis*' and could not be related to other religions. As Wesley Ariarajah rightly states, 'The revelation of Christ, in his [Kraemer's] view, directly contradicted all human religious life and wisdom',[14] and thus there cannot be continuity from non-Christian religions to Christianity. O.V. Jathanna summarises Kraemer's view in the words, 'the Christian faith is radically different from all other religions in that it is radically theocentric, even as a soteriological religion'.[15]

Kraemer's book, his presentation in the conference, and the follow-up writings, stirred long debate. So polarized was the discussion that while James Scherer of the United States calls Kraemer's book 'the most famous book about mission theology of all time,'[16] for C.F. Andrews, a missionary in India, it was to be dropped '"unceremoniously" into the waste paper basket'.[17] The conference affirmed Kraemer's main point while opposing his idea of radical discontinuity. It says,

---

[10] Veli-Matti Kärkäinen, *An Introduction to the Theology of Religions* (Downers Grove, IL: IVP, 2003), 181.

[11] Hendrik Kraemer, *The Christian Message in the Non-Christian World* (London: International Missionary Council, 1938), 102.

[12] Kraemer, *The Christian Message*, 104.

[13] Kraemer, *The Christian Message*, 134.

[14] Wesley Ariarajah, *Hindus and Christians: A Century of Protestant Thoughts* (Grand Rapids, MI: William B. Eerdmans Publishing Co., 1991), 66.

[15] O.V. Jathanna, *The Decisiveness of the Christ-event and the Universality of Christianity in a World of Religious Plurality* (Frankfurt: Peter Lang, 1981), 94.

[16] James A. Scherer, *Gospel, Church, & Kingdom: Comparative Studies in World Mission Theology* (Minneapolis, MN: Augsburg Publishing House), 17.

[17] C.F. Andrews quoted by T. V. Philip, *Edinburgh to Salvador: Twentieth Century Ecumenical Missiology* (Delhi: ISPCK, 1999), 194.

> …we believe that in Him [Christ] alone is the full salvation which man [sic] needs.… We do not think that God has left Himself without witness in the world at any time. Men [sic] have been seeking Him all through the ages. Often this seeking and longing has been misunderstood. But we see glimpses of God's light in the world of religions, showing that His yearning after His erring children has not been without response.

In the succeeding discussions, it became clear that even those who follow Kraemer's discontinuity position do not necessarily agree with its radical nature. Lesslie Newbigin, for instance, while agreeing with Kraemer's discontinuity theory in general, does not agree that there is total discontinuity.[18]

Dialogue in the Pluralistic Context

By 1988, when the World Council of Churches (WCC) organised the fiftieth anniversary of the International Missionary Council's Conference in Tambaram, it was clear that the ecumenical church had moved on from Kraemer. The main theme had become dialogue in the pluralistic context. Proponents of dialogue in Protestant ecumenical circles introduced their case by opposing Kraemer's position. In WCC circles, no one did more than Stanley J. Samartha to introduce the concept of inter-religious dialogue as he transformed his position as Study Secretary of the Word of God and Living Faiths of Men into the Director of the sub-unit on Dialogue with People of Living Faiths and Ideologies between 1968 and 1971.[19]

In this movement toward a dialogical approach, the WCC followed Vatican II developments in the Roman Catholic Church. The Vatican Council posited an affirmative posture not only toward non-Catholics, but also to non-Christian religions. In its document *Nostra Aetate*, Vatican II states that the Catholic Church is not opposed to anything 'true and holy' in other religions. This was seen by many as a major departure from its traditional position. Theologies of religions such as Karl Rahner's 'anonymous Christian' theory and Raymond Pannikar's 'unknown Christ of Hinduism' followed up Vatican II in paving the way for a new and positive attitude to other religions. Asian Christian leaders and thinkers in religiously pluralistic neighbourhoods took the lead in this venture.

Interfaith dialogue, as it was introduced from the early 1970s, was a controversial subject matter, or it was treated so. Proponents such as Samartha insisted that any motive to convert the dialogue partner of another religion is unacceptable. The dialogue partner is to be treated with respect

---

[18] Joe M. Thomas, 'Continuity, Discontinuity, and the Finality of Christ: A Theological Essay on the Thought of Lesslie Newbigin and Hendrik Kraemer', *Dharma Deepika: A South Asian Journal of Missiological Research* 29/1 (January – June, 2009), 28.

[19] See Stanley J. Samartha, *Between Two Cultures: Ecumenical Ministry in a Pluralist World* (Geneva: WCC, 1996), 38-75.

and should be received with openness. Any claim for superiority by Christians is considered an impediment for the practice of dialogue. Interpreted this way, many feared dialogue was a way of compromising their Christian faith, and thought that it rendered Christian mission meaningless. Along with dialogue came a controversial relativistic theology called 'pluralistic theology', which affirmed the salvific validity of different religions. Some pluralists were of the opinion that interfaith dialogue can happen only through pluralistic theology, thus confusing dialogue with pluralistic theology. Mission, for pluralistic theologians, has to be confined to what is morally just, dialogically possible and resulting in the common liberation of humanity, all of which aspects can be shared with people of other faiths.[20] Samartha, for instance, defines mission as 'God's continuing activity through the Spirit to mend the brokenness of creation, to overcome fragmentation of humanity, and to heal the rift between humanity, nature and God'.[21] In a gathering in 1986, pluralist theologians described themselves as those who 'move away from insistence of the superiority or finality of Christ and Christianity toward recognition of the independent validity of other ways'. They described this as 'the crossing of a theological Rubicon'.[22]

Closely tied to the question of plurality and dialogue is the validity of religious conversion as a change of religion from one to another (inter-religious conversion). While most pluralistic theologians either minimize or question the validity of inter-religious conversion, conversion remains one of the most important self-defining topics for Evangelicals. It was on this issue that dialogue and evangelism or dialogue and mission were often set in tension. The tension has now been largely resolved in most Christian circles. As the ecumenical effort to forge 'a code of conduct on conversion' affirmed in 2006, 'while everyone has a right to invite others to an understanding of their faith, it should not be exercised by violating others' rights and religious sensibilities'.[23]

Dialogue was confused with pluralistic theology, and continued to be treated by some with suspicion for quite some time. Other Christians came to interpret interfaith dialogue differently. As early as in the mid 1970s, Evangelical leader and thinker John R.W. Stott discussed 'dialogue' favourably as a mode of Christian mission. Drawing from the examples of the famous missionary to India, E. Stanley Jones, who practised

---

[20] See, *inter alia*, Paul F. Knitter, *Jesus and the Other Names: Christian Mission and Global Responsibility* (Maryknoll, NY: Orbis Books, 1996), 108-153; S. J. Samartha, *One Christ – Many Religions: Toward a Revised Christology* (Maryknoll, NY: Orbis Books, 1992), 162-175.

[21] Samartha, *One Christ – Many Religions*, 170.

[22] John Hick & Paul F. Knitter (eds), *The Myth of Christian Uniqueness: Toward a Pluralistic Theology of Religions* (Maryknoll, NY: Orbis Books, 1987), viii.

[23] World Council of Churches, 'Toward a Code of Conduct on Conversion' (draft), available at www.oikoumene.org (accessed August 5, 2009).

'roundtable' conference as 'dialogue with Hindus', and Bishop Kenneth Cragg's work as 'dialogue with Moslems', as well as Bishop David Sheppard's work on 'dialogue in industrial Britain', Stott advocated a true Christian dialogue as a way of doing Christian mission.[24] In the decades following Stott's work, other Evangelical Christians have spelled out an Evangelical theology of religions. While some have discussed the issue mainly in the new pluralistic context of the West, others such as Timothy Tennent have dealt with the issue in connection with the non-Christian religious faiths.[25] The recent works of Pentecostal theologians such as Veli-Matti Kärkkäinen[26] and Amos Yong[27] have clearly signalled that theology of religions, with dialogue and witness in the pluralistic world as the core subject-matter, has come of age. In the Catholic Church, post-conciliar documents such as *Redemptoris Missio* (1990) and *Dialogue and Proclamation* (1991) seek to both correct what are perceived to be theological errors in interreligious issues and to connect the plural context with the church's faith.[28] Since the joining in 1961 of a large number of Orthodox Churches in the WCC, the Orthodox tradition has also contributed significantly in reshaping Christian missiological thought. Its pneumatological perspective of communion of the entire creation with God and theological-anthropological understanding of *theosis* or deification makes the Orthodox missiology a true invitation to the life of the triune God.[29]

The plurality of religions has now been accepted as the fact of life. Christian mission cannot be conceived without acknowledging the plurality of religions and the demand for a dialogical mode of existence and way of

---

[24] John R.W. Stott, *Christian Mission in the Modern World* (Downers Grove: IVP, 1975), 58-81.

[25] See Timothy C. Tennent, *Christianity at the Religious Roundtable: Evangelicalism in Conversation with Hinduism, Buddhism, and Islam* (Grand Rapids, MI: Baker Academic, 2002).

[26] Kärkäinen, *An Introduction to the Theology of Religions*.

[27] See Amos Yong, *Discerning the Spirit(s): A Pentecostal-Charismatic Contribution to Christian Theology of Religions* (Sheffield: Sheffield Academic Press, 2000).

[28] See William Burrows (ed.), *Redemption and Dialogue: Reading* Redemptoris Missio *and Dialogue and Proclamation* (Maryknoll, NY: Orbis Books, 1994); John Paul II, *Redemptoris Missio* 'On the Permanent Validity of the Church's Missionary Mandate' (1990); Pontifical Council For Inter-Religious Dialogue, 'Dialogue and Proclamation: Reflection and Orientations on Interreligious Dialogue and the Proclamation of the Gospel of Jesus Christ' (1990). Documents available at www.vatican.va.

[29] Petros Vassiliadis, Niki Papageorgiou, George Kondortha & Nikos Dimitriadis, 'Mission among Other Faiths: An Orthodox Perspective', a position paper submitted to Study Group 2, Edinburgh 2010 (2009), available at www.edinburgh2010.org.

witnessing. Christians must treat people of any faith and no faith with genuine respect in their act of witnessing to the gospel.

From Geography to Scenarios

The developments described above occurred in a world which has dramatically changed during these last hundred years. Without using the term, the participants of the Edinburgh conference had envisioned a globalization of Christian faith, but, even more so, of Christendom. Their understanding of 'ecumenical' (*oikumene* – the whole inhabited world) referred to the sphere of the Christian domination. The success of Christian mission would be the conquest of the 'non-Christians' in the form of an expansion of the territory of the Christian nations onto the whole globe and thus the fulfilment theory for some implied the vision that eventually all other religions should vanish.

During the decades after the Edinburgh conference a multiplication occurred of churches, denominations, movements and confessions, such as Evangelical, charismatic, Pentecostal. In the same period the nascent Ecumenical movement became acutely aware that beyond the Protestant mission movement there were other and often much older churches living and witnessing to Christ in various cultures. Today we realise that among the various dialects of the Christian faiths, there are different understandings and hence different ways of analysing the missionary and religious situation in the world. Some Christians see regions or other religious groups under the shadow of sin or evaluate human activities in the light of the last judgment. Others emphasise the realm of spirits or powers and principalities fighting with or against God. Again others analyze the globe in social, political, economic terms and relate their faith response to what they conceive to be the challenges of the local situations and global tendencies. These are debates among Christians with differing world views which in some cases conflict with each other. For instance, while some Christians fight for liberation,[30] others call for evangelism of individuals. The debates, however, unlike at Edinburgh 1910, today cut across geographical boundaries and occur at the same time in various places and contexts. There they carry with them a former history of relating, as in the case of Christian and Muslim faiths as opposing forces; this lingers in the background of actual relations of Christians and Muslims.[31] The debate on

---

[30] The recent consultation on 'Christian mission among other faiths' at Bangalore repeatedly addresses liberation and fighting for justice (2.5.6) and violence (5.6) in the context of mission. 'Report cum Statement of the consultation at the United Theological College, Bangalore, India, 2009. Towards Edinburgh 2010. A Consultation on "Christian Mission among others Faiths"'. Papers available at www.edinburgh2010.org.

[31] J. Azumah, 'Christian Mission and Islam', position paper submitted to Study Group 2, Edinburgh 2010 (2009), 2-3, available at www.edinburgh2010.org.

how to perceive the world and how to account for the presence of other faiths was opened towards the close of the twentieth century among Christians. It raises questions as to how we should understand Christian mission among other faiths: as a mission to non-Christians, as a mission among other faiths, or witnessing to Christ in the context of contemporary challenges in the mutually edifying fellowship of 'neighbours of living faiths and ideologies'.[32]

These different Christian attitudes coexist along with those of adherents of other faiths and along with new religious movements which have sprung up after the Edinburgh meeting in 1910 and still continue to come into being. Although estimates of numbers vary, there is general agreement that the Christian faith globally has the largest number of adherents, followed by the Muslim faith and Hinduism. The next group in size is that of 'non-religious people', by which David Barrett and his team understand persons without formal or organised religious relations, including agnostics, freethinkers, humanists and secularists. Two points however are noteworthy with regard to the numbers relating to Christianity. Firstly, in spite of all the many forms of mission the percentage of Christians in the world population did not significantly change during the last hundred years. Secondly, Christianity – in almost all its forms – has grown significantly in the global South and this growth has taken place primarily in the postcolonial period.[33]

From a sociological point of view the truly global religions are Christianity and Islam. They cross ethnic and national frontiers and are inculturated in various cultures and peoples. Other world religions like Hinduism and Buddhism are strong and dominant in their regions of origin and among migrating Hindus and Buddhists living in Diaspora communities.[34] Buddhism as a missionary religion, and in various forms, has attracted some Westerners, and new religious movements growing out

---

[32] 'Report cum Statement, Bangalore', 8.

[33] D. B. Barrett et al., 'Missiometrics 2008: Reality Checks for Christian World Communions', *International Bulletin of Missionary Research* 32 (2008), 27-30.

[34] The term 'transnational' names these movements which are crossing frontiers and cultures but are not global in the sense of being present everywhere. In the context of our theme 'transnational' applies especially to local ethnic-religious Diaspora communities which are however in constant relation to their home communities. S.L. Pries, *Die Transnationalisierung der sozialen Welt. Sozialräume jenseits von Nationalgesellschaften* (Frankfurt/M.: Suhrkamp Verlag, 2009), 16. Aghamkar submitted a position paper on an Indian Christian attempt to relate to Indian migrants residing in the US by revisioning the Hindu Diwali festival. Aghamkar, 'A Christian Diwali: Contextualizing Witness as Celebration with the Hindu Community', paper submitted to Study Group 2, Edinburgh 2010 (2009), available at www.edinburgh2010.org.

of Hindu traditions have found new adherents.[35] An awareness that the history of religions has not yet come to an end is one aspect of our theme 'Christian mission among other faiths'.

The contexts in which these attitudes towards and conceptions of the others occur is often described with the term *globalization*, which is a complex concept. For the sake of our discussion we focus on globalization as a specific constellation of global relations and strategies affecting or even dominating local circumstances. Goods and international funds move freely around the globe but their trading is concentrated in only a few places in the world[36] and the consequences affect other places in diverse ways. (Bio-) technologies and also military technologies, which have become so threatening in the last decade, are produced in certain countries but put to use or even imposed on the other side of the globe where they are used to create economic or technological domination. Migration is a world-wide phenomenon; migrants move to selected places where only a few (and well educated) are welcomed, whereas the mass of the migrants who have left their homes because of economic threat are searching for a better life which the receiving societies are unwilling or unable to provide.[37] Information technology is globally present but causes a digital divide excluding those who have not more effectively than frontiers. These examples demonstrate that globalization is a power constellation and generates new hierarchies and dependencies or oppression[38] and marginalization, and in some cases offers new opportunities and liberating interrelations.

To sum up, human life in the globalized world is not de-territorialised. Conflicts and violence, military action, famine and floods, affluence and poverty are concentrated in particular places on the globe with a shocking regularity over time. Seen critically in a non-Western perspective, globalization still knows a geography and therefore centres of powers[39]. Most of these are still localised in the global North; the present power centres are, however, no longer so clearly co-extensive with one geographical region since new power centres have come into being in the global South and East. Nor are they any longer co-extensive with the

---

[35] See Ole Skjerbaek Madsen, 'The Church's Encounter with New Spiritualities', a position paper for Study Group 2, Edinburgh 2010 (2009), available at www.edinburgh2010.org).

[36] Pries, *Transnationalisierung*, 29.

[37] T. Prill, *Global Mission on our Doorstep. Forced Migration and the Future of the Church* (Münster: Monsenstein & Vannerstadt, 2008).

[38] The 'Report cum Statement, Bangalore' cautions against the mammonization of structures and relations (6) and greets chances to work together in issues like environmental issues or in fighting HIV/Aids (7).

[39] S. Randeria & A. Eckert, (eds), *Vom Imperialismus zum Empire. Nicht-westliche Perspektiven auf Globalisierung* (Frankfurt: Suhrkamp Verlag, 2009).

former power centres of Christianity because new power centres have emerged outside the North.

Scenarios

It is especially at the cross-sections of global and local powers that the questions of identity have become burning issues for national states, ethnicities, cultures, and also for religions. Against this background we shall look at 'Christian mission among other faiths', not by comparing, contrasting, or relating the Christian religion to other religions as was done in the report of Commission IV at Edinburgh 1910. Individuals or groups need to formulate their answers to these challenges. The challenges interact with and influence each other, compete and in many cases clash. To understand 'Christian mission *among other faiths*' means to perceive Christians as believing human beings among other believing and non-believing human beings, sharing, facing, or opposing each other in specific situations in which they live their faith and draw on their respective traditions. This aspect is captured by what the Pontifical Council for Inter-religious Dialogue termed 'dialogue of life',[40] meaning that Christians and churches exist among other believers, among those who oppose religion altogether or feel they have moved beyond it. Christian mission witnesses to the incarnated Christ, and the faith thus finds expression, or is inculturated, in a 'diapraxis' (see below). To become a Christian should not mean to change one's culture and thus to alienate oneself from those among whom one is living.

The dynamics of the meetings of the world religions are not only defined by their faiths, theologies, world views, and spiritualities. Local and/or global factors play an important role: Which faith group constitutes a majority or the marginalized? Are the practitioners allowed to act openly in their societies and is mission permitted? Transgressing the geographical and Protestant vision of Edinburgh, we today include the insights and approaches of churches and traditions which were not present in 1910, including some of the oldest churches in the world and some of the numerically strongest strands of Christianity (Orthodoxy, Roman Catholic, and Pentecostal). Their approaches in mission, and more specifically to mission among other faiths, come into view.[41] Mission is the task of the

---

[40] See Pontifical Council for Inter-Religious Dialogue and the Congregation for the Evangelization of Peoples, 'Dialogue and Proclamation' in Burrows, *Redemption and Mission*, 93-118, especially 104.

[41] See position papers for Study Group 2, Edinburgh 2010 on confessional approaches to mission among other faiths, available at www.edinburgh2010.org: Vassiliadis et al., 'Mission Among Other Faiths. An Orthodox Perspective'; Harold A. Netland, 'Christian Mission among Other Faiths: The Evangelical Tradition', position paper submitted to Study Group 2, Edinburgh 2010 (2009), available at www.edinburgh2010.org.

local churches, but what some call 'reverse cross-cultural mission' is going on at a large scale today. The missionaries of today may come from South Korea and work in Afghanistan or China or come from Ghana and work in Germany or Finland. Even where mission is not conceived in an ecumenical manner those who are in mission cannot overlook others being in mission.

Against this background a number of scenarios come to mind which characterize challenges of the present and the near future for 'Christian mission among other faiths' because they call for specific forms of missionary engagement in the contact with members of various faith communities. The way they relate to each other in multi-ethnic or plural situations may reach from opposition, which may eventually lead to violence or oppression of the others, to a dialogue of communities and individuals, or to a relativism in the guise of pluralism which dissolves any faith into a mere personal persuasion. Thus believers of various faith communities are forced to recognise to what extent their own religious perception of the situation and the motivations for their actions or their power aspirations contribute to the local constellation. This means that a dialogue of life is incomplete without a dialogue of faiths. Christian mission among other faiths has to be specific to the context Christians share with believers of other faiths.

PLURALISM, MULTI-ETHNICITY, MULTI-CULTURAL SOCIETIES

Globalization has brought nations and cultures into closer contact, and Christian mission faces pluralism in various forms. Migration is one of the main reasons for the co-existence of different religions and faith groups within one region. The challenge to all faith communities today is to shift from tolerating a factual pluralism to a concept of religious pluralism which transcends earlier concepts like the fulfilment theory or the criteria of difference or continuity. In some regions of Africa and Asia, religious, ethnic, and cultural pluralism has always been a characteristic of society and has fostered concepts of more fluid or multiple identities. Some of the postcolonial societies, however, struggle in this respect. Whereas on a grassroots level believers of different faiths often live peacefully together, the situation changes when in such contexts a religious group identity becomes a political factor, as in some parts of Indonesia where Christians and Muslims clash, or as in India where groups have politicised Hinduism with the result that Christians and Muslims are accused by them of being non-Indians.

Led by politicized or even ethnicized religion, a lack of freedom of religion characterizes many parts of the world today. In some countries Christian believers and their congregations are forced to keep quiet, and any form of mission is judged to be illegal.[42] The main challenge for the

[42] For some hints to reactions, see Azumah, 'Christian Mission and Islam', 4.

Christians in such a situation is probably how to stay faithful and live their faith among other faiths when they are not allowed to become publicly visible, or to receive new believers, and are constantly under suspicion for being 'unsafe' citizens. Pressure leads Christians to leave regions like Iraq, where churches and Christian communities are vanishing. We also note that other faith communities may perceive their existence in predominantly Christian cultures and nominally pluralist cultures along similar lines. Christian mission in such contexts has often been accused of being a colonial force. It is imperative to promote an understanding of mission as witnessing to Christ, meaning that Christians live together with those of other faiths. The fruitfulness of theologies of religion for such contexts will have to be proved by whether they help Christians to interpret the plurality of religion in relation to pluralism in social and political life.[43]

URBANIZATION

One scenario of growing importance is urbanization. Currently more than fifty percent of the world population and approximately fifty-eight percent of the world's Christians live in urbanized areas. We recognise an urban scenario in the metropolises of what used to be the first world, but the fastest growing cities are in Asia, Africa, and Latin America. It is estimated that in 2050 between 75-80 percent of the world's population will live in urban centres or regions, which also will comprise the majority of the Christians of the world. The hope for (better) economic opportunities will often, for the migrants, result in the loss of supportive community structures, a break-down of relations and of the extended family system, and possibly a weakening of values. Global religions, ideologies, new forms of living one's faith, new religious movements and cults emerge or re-arrange the balances in the communities or influence worship and bring new challenges of syncretism. A loss of identity and search for survival in the new context are also spiritual challenges which force people to reformulate their faith and identity. On the other hand, urban regions offer the possibility to integrate into new networks along old lines of adherence or to radically reformulate one's faith.

Urbanization is one aspect of migration, taking place both within countries and regions as well as being a global phenomenon. Approximately 175 million people or three percent of the world's population are estimated to be on the move worldwide. Compared to 1910, when migration was mainly of European peoples to their colonies, migration from the North has declined. The countries of origin of people on the move today lie mostly in Asia, Africa, South America and Eastern

[43] See for instance, H. Ucko, 'Christian Mission among Other Faiths', against V.-M. Kärkkäinen, 'Theologies of Religions. A Position Paper', both papers submitted to Study Group 2, Edinburgh 2010 (2009), available at www.edinburgh2010.org.

Europe, and the receiving countries are mostly in the global North,[44] although the countries hosting the highest percentage of migrants are oil-producing countries (Arab Emirates, Kuwait), and Asia hosts the largest refugee population.[45] Migration can be a transitory state in life or a definite change. Although reasons to migrate often are hunger, war, natural catastrophes, and lack of economic opportunities, the vast majority of people affected by these threats stay in the regions struck.[46] Migration is part of globalization but most countries have highly restrictive legislation which places migrants in the receiving countries in a situation of being tolerated but most often considered illegal. Migrants may find in their faith a resource for survival which will strengthen the cultural-linguistic expression of their faith as their identity. Faith, origin, and the search for a future, for identity and dignity blend together, and therefore this scenario is important for our theme.

Marginalized Aboriginal and Indigenous Peoples

At the opposite end of a global map of such scenarios are the aboriginal and indigenous peoples. An estimated 300 million belong to this group and are concentrated in seventy countries on all continents. Despite their unique cultures they share a specific blend of ethnic, cultural, economic, political, and religious identities which distinguish them from the surrounding dominant societies and the national states of which they are considered citizens. Many aboriginal cultures retain stories of being assigned geographical locations on the earth. They respectfully embraced many of the customary laws they inherited from their ancestors who, they believe, received these directly from the Creator. These remain binding upon all descendents as a covenant sign of the group's response to the gifts of the Creator. They mark their right relationship to the cosmic and to one another, and define how they relate to their environment and people beyond the confines of their community. Through these the people live with structure, order and certainty. In the history of mission we see how entire peoples became Christian, and then struggled with how to reconcile their identity with the new faith, and also with how to relate their community sense and constitutive exclusion lines to an understanding of being part of a universal church. Most of the Christians in the global South today originally came from these primal religious and cultural traditions.

---

[44] Jehu J. Hanciles, 'Migration and Mission: The Religious Significance of the North-South Divide', in Andrew Walls & Cathy Ross (eds.), *Mission in the Twenty-first Century: Exploring the Five Marks of Global Mission* (London: Darton, Longman and Todd, 2008), 118-29

[45] Prill, 'Global Mission', 32, 35.

[46] An estimated overall migration stock of 175 million in 2000 against a figure of 975 million alone suffering from hunger. See www.welthungerhilfe.de/hunger_spezial.html.

The life and environment of aboriginal peoples are endangered today. The traditional religion, or a revitalised version, cannot always help to ensure survival. For instance, where religion is linked to land and the land is taken away in the name of modernization or the development of the nation-state, these groups do not only become homeless or displaced, but also become rootless peoples without a future. The globalized world does not easily tolerate enclaves, and in many cases the dominant societies are not willing to recognise the rights of these communities.[47] Christian mission among aboriginal peoples must ask how Christians and Christian churches will be engaged in fighting for their rights. And how they should relate to them in witnessing to Christ. Are they willing to recognise how aboriginal or indigenous peoples which have become Christian may enrich Christian faith by their ways of inculturation?[48]

INFORMATION TECHNOLOGY, CYBERSPACE AND VIRTUAL REALITIES

The advanced electronic communication systems are offering new channels for communication transgressing the medium of written text by including records of spoken word, sound and image. They even offer new forms of co-presence and interaction and thus formulate new challenges and opportunities for mission. Since the last decade of the twentieth century, groups or individuals adhering to different religions have globally and locally been using the internet for propagating their beliefs.[49] Virtual space and communication via the worldwide web can create interactive transnational communities of reference which ensure a presence also where the religion in question is not found. Classic traditions and their institutions, organisations, groups, individuals, and cults populate cyberspace in order to influence individuals. Through the internet, traditions or beliefs reach far beyond the actual region of their presence, and can therefore create a kind of globalized consciousness for their adherents. Such global interaction can affect their perception of the actual situation and influence the actions they take locally. Where access to the

---

[47] An interesting example for a different approach to an originally indigenous religion by W. Abimbola, *Ifá Will Mend Our Broken World: Thoughts on Yoruba Religion and Culture in Africa and the Diaspora* (Roxbury, MA: Aim Books, 2003).

[48] See for instance, M. Vargas, 'A Neopentecostal Experience of Bolivian Aimara people', unpublished paper submitted to Study Group 2, Edinburgh 2010 (2009), available at www.edinburgh2010.org; or G. Chamorro, *Auf dem Weg zur Vollkommenheit. Theologie des Wortes unter den Guaraní in Süd-Amerika* (Exegese in unserer Zeit, 11), (Münster: LIT Verlag, 2003).

[49] See for example, Gary Bunt, *iMuslims: Rewiring the House of Islam* (Chapel Hill: University of North Carolina Press, 2009); J. Kwabena Asamoah-Gyadu, '"Get on the Internet!" Says the LORD': Religion, Cyberspace and Christianity in Contemporary Africa', *Studies in World Christianity* 13 (Dec 2007), 225-242; Kirsteen Kim, 'Ethereal Christianity: Reading Korean Mega-Church Websites', *Studies in World Christianity* 13 (Dec 2007), 208-224.

internet is available on a broad basis a multitude of presentations of faith and religion coexist separated from the physical church or group in which they are based, which makes it difficult to 'discern the spirits'. Also websites for interreligious dialogue and mutual cooperation have sprung up. This scenario is very influential, especially among youth in the West and in the technologically advanced sectors of Asia.

Conclusions

The scenarios presented are not the only ones which could be described. But through them we see clearly the global spread of Christian faith, and they help to identify present and future challenges to the global Christian faith community. A hundred years after the Edinburgh conference these scenarios testify to the shift from distinguishing between a Christian and a non-Christian world to recognising a global world. Christians and people of other faiths face an enormous diversity of global and local expressions of Christian faith and ways of witnessing to Christ. In this context we propose to reflect on our theme more from the perspective of the other. A theology which recognises the dignity of human beings as created by the one God cannot deny such dignity and respect to others; it will therefore want to honour their faith. Not religions, but human beings meet and share, ignore or enrich one another, clash and fight. Phenomena like religiously tainted violence and fundamentalism are not best approached as if they were caused by religion or mission. They are better understood as attitudes of human beings engaging in conflicts in which they activate their religious convictions and power aspirations to understand their situation and to search for possibilities to act and to change it.

Perspectives and Hermeneutical Reflections

Because Christians believe that what God has done in Jesus Christ is good news for all, Christians are called to share the good news in the power of the Spirit. This is the *raison d'être* for mission. This mission takes the concrete form of witness (*martyria*). Mission is therefore to share one's faith and conviction with other people, inviting them to discipleship, whether they adhere to other religious traditions or not. Such sharing is to take place with confidence and humility.[50] Our faith is about discovering grace in the cross and resurrection of Jesus Christ. Vulnerability is therefore how we encounter the others, without forgetting the faith we are stewards of.

---

[50] Notto R. Thelle, 'Mission to Buddhists?', Position Paper, submitted to Study Group 2, Edinburgh 2010 (2009), 9, available at www.edinburgh2010.org.

Dialogue, Witness and Mission

Mission is what the church is sent to *be* – *koinonia*, community, presence, nearness, worship. Mission is what the church is sent to *do* – *diakonia*, care, service. Mission is what the church is sent to *say* – *kerygma*, proclamation of the gospel, dialogue, apologetics. The overriding concept is that *mission is witness to others about the gospel. Martyria* is the sum of *kerygma*, *koinonia* and *diaconia* – all of which constitute dimensions of witnessing: 'We are using a missiological hermeneutic when we read the New Testament as the testimony (witness) of witnesses, equipping other witnesses for the common mission of the church'.[51]

Dialogue is, in this perspective, part of what we are sent to *say* and thus a key expression of witness. Dialogue means witnessing to our deepest convictions, whilst listening to those of our neighbours in a two-way exchange. Without such commitment to others dialogue becomes mere chatter, in the same manner as it becomes worthless without the presence of the neighbour. This emphasis on 'neighbour' further means that we cannot dialogue with, or witness to, people if we from the outset resent their views. The scenarios presented above describe how all of us live in a multi-religious setting, in situations where coexistence with believers of other faiths is part and parcel of our daily life (even though the power relations among people may be very asymmetric). Christian theology must therefore be a theology of dialogue[52]. And it must be a theology of inculturation and contextualization – in conversation with and listening to the local context and its culture and religion. Contextualization is not an alternative to mission, but a specific way of being in mission. In the same way dialogue is not an alternative to mission, but a specific way of being in mission.

Dialogue is only possible if we proceed from the expectation of meeting God who has preceded us and has been relating to people within the context of their own culture and conviction. God is there before we come (Acts 17) and our task is not to bring God along, but to witness to the God who is already there. We therefore take off our shoes as we approach men and women of other living faiths. Dialogue is a way of taking seriously that all humans are created in God's image. The other is always 'you' – someone that I listen to because there is something valuable to listen to from any human being created in the image of God. In the same manner I too share with others what is on my heart – what I have seen and heard and touched with my own hands (1 John 1:1-2).

The theologian Walter Brueggemann uses the term 'othering' to remind us of the importance of not seeing the religious other as a counter-object but rather 'the risky, demanding, dynamic process of relating to one that is

---

[51] Darrell Guder, *The Continuing Conversion of the Church* (Grand Rapids, MI: Wm B. Eerdmans, 2000), 53-55.

[52] David J. Bosch, *Transforming Mission. Paradigm Shifts in Theology of Mission* (Maryknoll, NY: Orbis Books, 1991), 483-84.

not us'.[53] In a similar manner some Orthodox theologians advocate making the 'other' a partner.[54] To evolve such a mindset, Kärkkäinen says, Christian churches and congregations should be encouraged and empowered to initiate patient training and education with regard to such issues as:

- Raising the awareness and importance of interfaith engagement, which means venturing outside one's own safety zone and making oneself vulnerable.
- Helping deal with our fears of the other that often include not only the generic fear of the 'stranger' but also the tendency to 'demonize' others' religion and beliefs
- Facilitating the study of another religion in order to gain a more accurate portrayal of another person's beliefs and sensitivities, including the capacity to interpret the meaning of rites and rituals.[55]

Another metaphor for 'othering' is that of 'hospitality', a concept that we know from Scripture as well as in various cultural contexts, and which is used in a WCC document from 2006. The metaphor is here used as the hermeneutical key to a Christian understanding of dialogue with others.[56]

Just as *martyria* expresses itself in dialogue, it also encompasses *diakonia* and *koinonia*. Dialogue aims at joining hands. At a personal and relational level a dialogue relationship carries with it a concern for the welfare of my sister and brother in terms of being a neighbour. In the larger context – in the community with Muslims, Hindus, Buddhists and others – dialogue has to do with reducing the images of hostility of one another, developing relationships across the barriers of faith, race, gender and cultural background, and stimulating common action for the sake of society. This is often called *diapraxis* (bringing together dialogue and praxis). There is a growing need for such diapraxis, especially in the form of community-oriented dialogue. It is important to meet neighbours, colleagues and groups in the community with an attitude of sharing and listening. In that way we can get to know each other better, create friendships and relationships across barriers of ethnic, cultural, social, political and religious differences. Joining with others of different background in community projects for peace, human rights, social activities, health improvement, political freedom and democracy is an important aspect of being in dialogue with others.

---

[53] Walter Brueggemann, *The Covenanted Self: Explorations in Law and Covenant* (Minneapolis, MN: Augsburg Fortress, 1999), 1.

[54] Vassiliadis, 'Mission among Other Faiths'.

[55] Veli-Matti Karkkainen, 'Theologies of Religions'.

[56] 'Religious Plurality and Christian Self-understanding', preparatory document for the World Council Of Churches Assembly, Porto Alegre, 2006. See also Ucko, 'Christian Mission among Other Faiths'.

Dialogue is *a basic way of life* because Christians share life and contexts with neighbours of other faiths. This implies that they establish dialogical relations so that there is hope of mutual understanding and fruitful co-existence in multi-religious and pluralist societies. If it is a basic way of life, then the arena for dialogue cannot be limited to the media, the public sphere and scholarly discussions and debates. Rather dialogue has to do with family, working place and neighbourhood. A very high percentage of people in the West have never had a conversation about faith with people of another faith. Dialogue here is therefore a matter of creating meeting places and using opportunities.

Dialogue is no a substitute for mission or a hidden form of mission. Mission and dialogue are not identical, neither are they so opposed to one another. One can be committed to dialogue and to Christian witness at the same time: 'We affirm that witness does not preclude dialogue but invites it, and that dialogue does not preclude witness but extends and deepens it'.[57] The Christian faith cannot surrender the conviction that God, in sending Jesus Christ into our midst, has taken a definite course of action and is extending to us forgiveness, justification, and a new life which, in turn, calls for our response in the form of conversion.[58]

Christian Mission in a Pluralist World

The scenarios above have described aspects of the pluralist and multi-religious global setting. An essential point of entrance into a Christian view on how to relate to this global context is the WCC statement at San Antonio in 1989: 'We cannot point to any other way of salvation than Jesus Christ. At the same time we cannot set limits to God's saving power....We appreciate this tension, and do not attempt to solve it'.[59]

Living in a plural context has for centuries been the daily experience of most of the world. Accepting to live in a pluralist world implies that mission will not attempt to 'conquer' the world in any religious or other sense. Pluralism is the context of Christian mission among other faiths. The claims of rationalism have, in Western culture, left people with a heritage that gives priority to the world of facts in the public realm while faith and values belong to the private sphere. In the private sphere Western culture has accepted pluralism. The Christian faith, together with other religions and religious worldviews, has been relegated to this sphere where pluralism reigns in a growing jungle of religiosity and individualised values. One consequence is that we have lost the concept of Christian faith as *a public truth*; that is, as a truth that relates to all of us and which has importance for

[57] World Council of Churches, *The San Antonio Report* (Geneva: World Council of Churches, 1990).
[58] Bosch, *Transforming Mission*, 1991, 488.
[59] WCC, *The San Antonio Report*.

society and community.[60] This development may be acceptable for religious views and for new spiritualities which view themselves as attaining to an esoteric *gnosis* in closed circles. For the Christian faith it is different: The Christian faith is a confession of Jesus Christ as Lord, not only my Lord or the Lord of the church, but the Lord of creation. This confession cannot be relegated to the sphere of the individual, and it cannot accept that there is more than this reality – the reality over which Christ is Lord.

Christians do not accept being relegated to the private sphere. However, where Christians express this conviction or act accordingly, they accept that in the public space their voice is one voice among others because they are committed to pluralism. The missionary theologian Lesslie Newbigin calls this *committed pluralism*, in contrast to *agnostic pluralism*.[61] Agnostic pluralism has renounced any talk about knowledge and truth in relation to faith. Committed pluralism, on the other hand, takes other worldviews seriously and dares to raise questions about the other's faith.

We enter the dialogue on the basis of our own belief or confession – and recognise that others will do the same. This stance implies that truth is to be found in a life of discipleship to Jesus Christ as he is known through a life lived in the community of disciples, in faithfulness to the tradition about him, and in openness to all truth which may be discovered in history. Our commitment is to a historic person and to historic deeds. Without these events, our faith would be empty. There need not be any dichotomy between 'confessing Christ' and 'seeking the truth'. As we meet the other, we expect to hear and learn more of truth. Granted, we shall interpret these new truths by means of the truth we have already committed our life to. Our encounter with Christ through Scripture and faith represents our ultimate commitment. And we expect that our neighbour will have his or her faith commitment.

There will be many different answers to the question of Christian understanding of other faiths:

- Other religions and ideologies are wholly false; non-Christian religions are the work of the devil and demonic cunning
- Other religions are a preparation for Christ (which the gospel fulfils; this was the view of Edinburgh 1910; cf. section 1 above); there are essential values in other religions
- An understanding, emphasised by Orthodox theologians, of the presence and work of the Holy Spirit in creation, culture and religions[62]

---

[60] Lesslie Newbigin, *Foolishness to the Greeks* (Grand Rapids, MI: Wm B. Eerdmans, 1986), 21-41.

[61] Lesslie Newbigin, *The Gospel in a Pluralist Society* (Grand Rapids, MI: Wm B. Eerdmans, 1989).

[62] Kirsteen Kim, *The Holy Spirit in the World. A Global Conversation* (Maryknoll: Orbis, 2007), 51-52.

- The Roman Catholic view of the world religions as concentric circles (with the Catholic Church as the centre). The architect was Karl Rahner who furthermore viewed non-Christian religions as the means through which God's salvation in Christ will reach those who have not been reached by the gospel ('anonymous Christians')
- The view that religions are worlds in themselves, with their own structures and worldviews. They face in different directions and ask different questions. The gospel relates differently to Islam than it does to Hinduism or Buddhism. And the differences are for real. Other religions are not a sort of reduced copy of Christianity or simply echoes of Christianity's own voice[63].

The view of those who collaborated to write this paper is that religions are ambiguous responses to divine revelation. Within every religion, also in Christianity, there is a dark side, but Christians will also recognise 'revelation' in all of them, particularly in terms of creation. Christians may cautiously claim that every part of the created world and every human being is already related to Jesus (cf. Paul's speech on Areopagos where the presence of the altar for the unknown God implies that God is already there). Everything was made through the Logos, he is the life of all, and he is the light that gives light to every man. Christians will recognise the presence and work of Jesus not only within the area where he is acknowledged. In every human there is not only a moral consciousness (Rom 2:14-15), but also a religious consciousness.[64] This does not imply that everything is light; both Scripture and experience make it clear that there is also darkness, but the light shines in the darkness. And this light will also shine in the lives of all human beings: The Christian confession does not imply that we should deny the reality of the work of God in the lives and thoughts and prayers of men and women outside the Christian church. Neither do we deny the dark side of religion – every religion including Christianity – but this dark side does not prevent us from seeing the light of God in the lives of men and women who do not acknowledge him as Lord.

For Christians the cross of Jesus exposes our rejection of God and our sin – *and* God's way of meeting this rejection. The power of God is hidden on the cross *sub contrarie specie*, Luther said; that is, under its contradiction. Christians believe that what looked like defeat turned out to be victory. This historic deed – the turning point of history – 'stands throughout history as witness against all the claims of religion – including the Christian religion – to be the means of salvation….religion is not the

[63] Bosch, *Transforming Mission*, 485.

[64] Terrance L. Tiessen, *Who Can Be Saved? Reassessing Salvation in Christ and World Religions* (Downers Grove & Leicester: Inter-Varsity Press, 2004), 107-110.

means of salvation'[65]. At the same time the cross becomes *the master clue* for Christians in our common search for salvation. And it is along the same way that we wonder whether we who follow Christ, can be saved apart from all who have not yet had the opportunity to respond to the gospel.

> The church, therefore, as it is *in via*, does not face the world as the exclusive possessor of salvation, nor as the fullness of what others have in part, the answer to the questions they ask, or the open revelation of what they are anonymously. The church faces the world, rather as *arrabon* of that salvation – as sign, first fruit, token, witness of that salvation which God purposes for the whole.[66]

There is in the Good News *a scandal of particularity* in the way God relates to the world. It is this scandal of particularity that we meet in the Christ revelation. At the same time we cling to God's 'amazing grace' and the confidence that this grace is sufficient for us and all other creatures. So there is a '*wideness in God's mercy*'[67] where the narrow boundaries of the church are widened through what in Orthodox theology is called, 'the economy of the Spirit'.[68] Down through history we find theologians who have spoken about God's work in the world and the possibility of salvation beyond explicit Christian faith:

- Justin Martyr believed in *logos spermatikos*, or seed-bearing word, by which he affirmed the seed of the revelation in Christ in existing cultures.
- Clement of Alexandria proposed that God had given the law to the Jews and philosophy to the Greeks.
- Irenaeus, like his contemporaries, assumed that the gospel had been taken throughout the world by the apostles. Had he known otherwise, he would still have been optimistic about the salvation of the unevangelized since Christ's incarnation implied for him a recapitulation of the history of fallen humanity, and since people will be judged according to the privilege of revelation that they have received.
- *Lumen Gentium* from Vatican II states that 'those also can attain to everlasting salvation that through no fault of their own do not know the gospel of Christ or His Church, yet sincerely seek God…'.[69] Even in the more strict declaration *Dominus Iesus* (2000) it is emphasised that 'the salvific action of Jesus

---

[65] Lesslie Newbigin, *The Open Secret* (Grand Rapids, MI: Wm B. Eerdmans, 1978), 200.

[66] Newbigin, *The Open Secret*, 203-204.

[67] Clark H. Pinnock, *A Wideness in God's Mercy: The Finality of Jesus Christ in a World of Religions* (Grand Rapids: Zondervan, 1992).

[68] Vassiliadis, 'Mission among Other Faiths'.

[69] Vatican II, *Lumen Gentium*, 'Dogmatic Constitution on the Church' (1963), §16. Available at www.vatican.va.

Christ…extends beyond the visible boundaries of the Church to all humanity'.[70]

- Martin Luther rarely spoke about the unevangelized. However, in his commentary on Romans (1515), he writes about those who have not heard the gospel that 'all people of this type have been given so much light and grace by an act of prevenient mercy of God as is sufficient for their salvation in their situation, as in the case of Job, Naaman, Jethro and others'[71]
- The well-known Christian apologist J.N.D. Anderson affirmed the uniqueness of Christ but also affirmed that where the God of all grace has been at work in the hearts of individuals, they too may profit from this grace[72]
- Harold A. Netland, an Evangelical missiologist, encourages Evangelicals to explore the implications of trinitarian theology for our understanding of other religions and advocates a 'dynamic tension between the universality of the triune God and the particularity of the incarnate word…'[73]
- Alister McGrath, a contemporary evangelical Anglican[74], states:

> We cannot draw the conclusion….that only those who respond will be saved. God's revelation is not limited to the explicit human preaching of the good news, but extends beyond it. We must be prepared to be surprised at those whom we will meet in the kingdom of God[75].

In the same manner, as in the San Antonio statement of the WCC mission conference in 1989, we affirm the uniqueness of Christ: Anyone who ever has been, is now or ever will be saved is accepted by God on the grounds of the sacrifice of Christ and our identification or union with him. There is no other ground. To this should, however, be added that God gives to every human being a revelation sufficient to elicit saving faith; no one will be condemned because of lack of revelation. In conclusion, we can

---

[70] Congregation for the Doctrine of the Faith, *Dominus Iesus* 'Declaration on the Unicity and Salvific Universality of Jesus Christ and the Church (2000), §12. Available at www.vatican.va.

[71] Pelikan, Jaroslav (ed.), *Luther's Works* (St Louis: Concordia, 1972), 25:181, quoted in Thiessen, *Who Can Be Saved?* 57.

[72] J.N.D. Anderson, *Christianity and Comparative Religion* (Downers Grove, IL: InterVarsity Press 1970).

[73] Harold A. Netland, 'Christian Mission among Other Faiths'. See also Timothy Tennent, *Theology in the Context of World Christianity* (Grand Rapids, MI: Zondervan, 2007).

[74] See also Alister McGrath, 'Evangelism and Apologetics' (2009), position paper submitted to Study Group 2, Edinburgh 2010, available at www.edinburgh2010.org.

[75] Alister McGrath, 'A Particularist View: A Post-Enlightenment Approach', in John Hick, *et al.* (eds), *More than One Way? Four Views on Salvation in a Pluralistic World* (Grand Rapids, MI: Zondervan Publishing House, 1995), 65-70.

never solve the creative and dynamic tension between being both missionary and dialogical.

Pneumatological Approach

When the Roman Catholic Church accepted the idea that salvation beyond its own boundaries was possible, yet through Christ, it affirmed the Spirit's work elsewhere, leading to greater interest in dialogical engagement with other religions.[76] Dramatic change in the doctrinal position of Roman Catholics raised difficult questions about where and how to locate the work of the Spirit in the religions. Recently, Pentecostal-charismatic scholars began a conversation to identify God's work through the activity of the Spirit and spirits among non-Christians, bringing them to faith.[77] The Holy Spirit's role in other religions raises two issues of significance for Christian mission among other faiths: (1) the relationship of Spirit and spirits in the religions; and (2) primal religion as the basic structure for understanding spirituality in the religions, with Israel's religion as a foundation for Christian witness.

PNEUMATOLOGICAL DIMENSION IN A CHRISTIAN THEOLOGY OF RELIGIONS

The dialogue movement assumes the Spirit's activity mediating witness of the gospel in conversations with people of other religions. A pneumatological approach goes farther to identify dynamic moments when Spirit-induced phenomena happen in individuals and in religions. Kirsteen Kim calls this new area 'mission pneumatology'.[78] Pentecostal scholar Amos Yong seeks evidence of the (Holy) Spirit and the spirits at work in people of other religions, but holds in theological tension Christian orthodoxy and openness. His approach, probing aspects of 'one-Spirit' and 'many spirit' cosmologies, anticipates God's revelation to be present in areas of: the Ultimate powers, the lesser powers, ancestors, nature, human and other spirits in religions or new spiritualities. This approach is along the lines of what may be broadly termed 'discerning of Spirit(s)'.[79] In his method Yong does fresh exegesis of biblical accounts describing persons of other faiths living in proximity to Jewish or Christian communities. He examines language from texts that describe interactions, suggestive of

---

[76] Vatican II awakened the Church to recognize the wider work of the Holy Spirit in the world, leading to ecumenical openness and restoration of relations with other Christian churches; the documents affirmed the 'pre-eminence' of the Spirit's role as the 'principal agent' of the church mission *ad gentes* (John Paul II, *Redemptoris Missio* 'On the Permanent Validity of the Church's Missionary Mandate' (1990), §§21-30. Available at www.vatican.va). Kim *The Holy Spirit in the World*, 146-47.

[77] Works of two authors, Amos Yong and Kirsteen Kim, provide a sample of the new approach: Yong, *Discerning the Spirit(s)*; Kim, *The Holy Spirit*.

[78] Kim, *The Holy Spirit*, 140.

[79] Yong, *Discerning the Spirit(s)*.

witness, to detect the dynamics between the (Holy) Spirit and spirits. Believing a spiritual dimension exists in all religions as well as in Christianity, his immediate concern in mission is to become aware of, yet not accept uncritically, accounts of how people in the religions have spiritual relationship with the powers, their community and their world.[80]

This focused investigation across cultures and religions locates patterns of receptivity and response from people in the religions. Like data may be found in similar religious contexts revealing the nature of the Spirit's witness of Christ. Such pursuit is limited by the Christian belief that we may expect but cannot determine absolutely the work of the Holy Spirit whose task it is to 'testify to Christ and make him known so that people will believe' (John 14-16).

RECOVERY OF PNEUMATOLOGICAL FOUNDATIONS FROM PRIMAL RELIGIONS AND WORLDVIEWS

Primal and aboriginal religions, as described before, have been recovered as a resource for witness. Edinburgh 1910 participants opined that the Christian gospel was unlikely to be readily accepted into Africa because of its strongly held traditional religious beliefs, in which there were no inherent concepts upon which to build the Christian message.[81] A century later African Christians, missiologists and historians argue the opposite, attributing conversion of more than fifty percent of the population of Africa, and much successful spreading of Christianity in the West, largely to the witness of Pentecostal Christians from the global South.[82] Scholars now ascribe the spread of African Christianity to the fact that it became so well adapted to its base of primal religion.[83] The worldviews of primal

---

[80] The terms 'One Spirit' and 'many spirits' distinguish cosmological answers to the question of whether power is concentrated in a single Spirit or many spirits? Amos Yong's discerning of the work of God in 'one Spirit' and 'many spirits' cosmologies allows that the Holy Spirit need not be christologically perceived (Yong, *Discerning the Spirit(s)*, 68), but that criteria for discernment of the Spirit cannot be other than Christological, (Yong, *Discerning the Spirit(s)*, 167). Yong's project fits with Ole Skjerbaek Madsen's investigation of new spiritualities and new religions, where followers have rejected a personal understanding of the Divine or Source. A point of contact in witness, both would agree, should be initially along the lines of what has been received and experienced as truth; the hope is also that the person might recognize the *logoi spermatikoi* within the new spirituality, at least God's Spirit being still present if only identified in the initial dialogue leading to Christ. (Madsen, 'The Church's Encounter with New Spiritualities').

[81] Harold F. Miller, 'Closure for an African Century,' *Occasional Papers* 26 (An oral version of the paper was presented to the annual Mennonite retreat at Limuru, Kenya, Dec 1998) accessed online at: mcc.org/respub/occasional/26closure.html on August 27, 2009.

[82] Philip Jenkins, *The Next Christendom: The Coming of the Global Christianity* (New York/Oxford: Oxford University Press, 2002), 8.

[83] Harold W. Turner, 'The Religious Reactions of Primal Societies to Higher Cultures: A New Field in the History of Religions', A lecture at the Centre for the

people and people of the Old Testament have similarities, and parallels exist between primal religious and Pentecostal groups.

The uniqueness of the primal worldview rests in an inherent belief of indigenous peoples that creation is a living system, a network of spiritual relationships in which they find themselves. Creation is invested with the Spirit that gives life and power to control and guide all things. Amos Yong, writing about the implications of such a worldview to create capacity for a holistic relationship to God, summarises his discussion on the pneumatological theology of creation, speaking of Old Testament scriptures, by saying, 'Most important, the spiritual and the material realms are intertwined both ontologically and epistemologically. Regarding the former, the Spirit both hovers over the waters of creation and gives the breath of life; the human is intimately and intricately connected with the orders of creation'.[84] Both traditional believers and Pentecostals rest their faith on being in relationship with the powers and following the design of creation. This theo-cosmic posture grounds all else. For this reason, pneumatological foundations are basic to Christian witness among other religions, and a starting point is exploring the Spirit(s) dimensions of faith.

The basic religious insight that Christians from primal backgrounds gain is that Christ is Creator God, the Lord of creation. Initially, their worship occurs while encountering the Spirit in creation. Later, after indigenous people accept Jesus Christ as Lord of the new creation, who made salvation possible by restoring harmony to all things through his sacrifice, worship becomes adoring the triune God and pursuing the kingdom of God on earth. If Pentecostal spirituality can be described as a re-emergence of 'primal spirituality' in post modernity,[85] it is well suited to challenge spiritualities of Western Christianity and theistic or cosmic religions because it relates to the creation and the Spirit. The Pentecost narrative is comprehensive, affirming unity in diversity, engaging many traditions but pointing each to a single reality.[86] The Apostle Paul invited diverse people in Athens to

---

Study of New Religious Movements in Primal Religions, Birmingham, United Kingdom, 1986; Gillian M. Bediako, '"All Believers Are Primalists Underneath": Towards a New Appreciation of Old Testament Religion as Primal Religion', a lecture at Calvin College, Grand Rapids, Michigan, July 2007; Andrew Walls, 'Primal Religious Traditions in Today's World', in *The Missionary Movement in Christian History: Studies in the Transmission of Faith* (Maryknoll, NY: Orbis Books, 1996), 119-39.

[84] Yong, *Discerning the Spirit(s)*, 300

[85] Harvey Cox, *Fire From Heaven: The Rise of Pentecostalism and the Reshaping of Religion in the Twenty-first Century*. (London: Cassell, 1996).

[86] Kirsteen Kim, *The Holy Spirit*, 162, paraphrasing Amos Yong's investigation of a 'unity in diversity' theme in the account of Pentecost, describes how '…on that occasion the Holy Spirit is seen to be the ground of personal encounter and of personal identity in community, establishing eschatological reconciliation'. See Amos Yong, '"As the Spirit Gives Utterance": Pentecost, Intra-Christian

consider Christ on the basis that the Spirit's power in creation was from God who made all things, and present in the Son, the risen Christ, whom God has declared as Lord (Acts 17).

Pentecostalism's apologetic is experiential, not merely rational. Pentecostals participate in a persuasive sharing of life in the Spirit. When Christians from the global South living as immigrants in situations of struggle manifest vibrant faith and tenacious hope in God for daily needs, such evident faith challenges secularists. When Western Christians attempted spiritual warfare to reach people with alternative spiritualities they largely failed, but a constructive pneumatological approach may have succeeded because identities are restored through spiritual relationship – a new self-understanding that they are made in the image of God (*imago Dei)* and belong to the people of God.[87] By healing prayers sin is overcome and harmony brought to the community.[88]

The pneumatological approach arose because Christians needed categories and criteria by which to search out the (Holy) Spirit among the spirits in the religions. In Pentecostal churches, spiritual phenomena abound: worship offers immediate access to divine power; signs and miracles happen in response to faith; personal empowerment flows as tongues and ecstasy strengthen daily life; exhortation comes through words of knowledge and wisdom; the Word is spoken by messengers appointed to guide the community.[89] The blessing of wellbeing is felt, the harmony of all creation, while in mystical communion with nature.

POWER ENCOUNTER

The word pair 'power encounter' is fairly recent, but intends to describe an ancient phenomenon: The powerful encounter when two religious worldviews and two religious groupings clash. The prime examples in the Bible include Elijah and the prophets of Baal on Mount Carmel, and Jesus' battle with Satan and his driving out of evil spirits as signs of the advent of the kingdom. Up through the history of the church there are many examples of such power encounters from situations where the Christian faith was crossing cultural and religious boundaries. Examples are also known from the recent and contemporary history of mission. The phenomenon is widespread among indigenous Christians and charismatic and Pentecostal churches in the global South.

Originally the confession of faith according to the Apostles' Creed was prefaced by renouncing the devil and all his works and all his being. This

---

Ecumenism and the Wider *Oikumene*', *International Review of Mission* 92/366 (Apr 2003), 299-314.

[87] Madsen, 'The Church's Encounter with New Spiritualities'.

[88] Marcelo Vargas describes indigenous Christian spirituality among the Aimara people in Bolivia as they are nurtured in the Power of God Church in his article, 'A Neopentecostal Experience of Bolivian Aimara People'.

[89] Vargas, 'A Neopentecostal Experience'.

renouncement is still in use in some churches and is particularly being used at baptism, to ensure and proclaim that the devil has no rights anymore to this infant or adult, who immediately after is marked with the sign of the cross. In this sense baptism is a power encounter, reminding the devil that he has lost the battle on Golgotha on Easter morning. In some settings renouncing the devil also implies the removal and burning of fetishes belonging to the person to be baptised (e.g. in Ethiopia). This biblical image reminds us that faith is God drawing us to himself and thus to turning us away from what can be called demonic in all religions. This reality must follow us into dialogues of religion and particularly in our encounter with religious practices invoking the spirits. The encounter with New Spiritual Movements has again brought this reality home to a Western culture that thought it had got rid of the primitive notion of 'devil'. In the practice of some of these movements, the door to an occult jungle of spirits and 'forces' is made wide open. Often this has resulted in personalities being invaded and in communities being demonized.[90]

Some would say that the matter of power encounter also relates to some of the major destructive forces in the world, such as the use of violence and war to solve conflicts, the oppression of women, discrimination against others (apartheid, casteism, ethno-centrism), and the distortion of sex and sexual abuse.[91]

People of faith must discern and respond to the spirit dimensions of the religions and their environment – although these are conceived in different ways. The new approach widens evidence and introduces vocabulary to facilitate interreligious dialogue on the spiritual level and concerning experience of the Spirit. Mission pneumatology is a helpful and hopeful task.

---

[90] See *inter alia* Madsen, 'The Church's Encounter with New Spiritualities'.

[91] Walter Wink, *Engaging the Powers. Discernment and Resistance in a World of Domination* (Minneapolis, MN: Fortress Press, 1984); Kim, *The Holy Spirit*, 150-6.

Position Papers from Various Churches and Traditions

Protestant Perspectives: Christian Mission Among Other Faiths

Hans Ucko

Recently a friend asked me what I was writing. I said, "An article on Christian mission among other faiths". He said, "Get a life". He didn't have to spell it out. I knew what he meant.

For people of other faiths and most people not affiliated with the church but equally moral and as ethical as church-going Christians, the idea of Christian mission among other faiths is, I would suggest, mostly considered strange, passé and outdated, if not right out arrogant and some would say even a threat to peace in the world. There is however much you object to the contrary, a stain on the concept mission. When stating this, I need to say that mission has also contributed to human dignity, literacy, health and all that we usually say is part of the good life. It is therefore appropriate to define what one means with Christian mission, because it is one dimension alone of mission that is contested. Christian mission is manifold and always has been. Mission is diaconal work, acts of solidarity, partnership and exchange between churches in the North and churches in the South. It is providing technical expertise on health and agriculture, education and advocacy in the so called Third World. Few would contest Christians working with victims of HIV/AIDS. Few would argue against Christians doing what they can to alleviate world hunger or ease the plight of poverty. If this is mission, so be it, provided of course that there is no hidden agenda. But mission understood in the sense of trying to convert people to becoming Christians, does meet with little if any understanding or endorsements from most people outside the Christian fold. It is not only Muslim fundamentalists that set off adverse reactions in society. The 23 young Korean Christians from one of the more evangelical churches in South Korea abducted by the Taliban in Afghanistan in 2007 on what they themselves said was a journey "to practice sharing love", fuelled angry reactions at home and world-wide. It was not only because they did not adhere to warnings not to go on this mission but because it became increasingly clear that there was more to the operation than humanitarian relief. Some of the reactions were quite clear, "Thank you very much; we do not need more religious people stoking the fires of the world. The blazes of conflict are problematic enough as they are. We do not need to add to the conflagration".

But if mission has no hidden agenda but truly is presence through education, solidarity, advocacy and diaconia, there would probably not be many objections among people of other faiths. The question is whether Christians themselves could be satisfied with mission being only diaconia, solidarity, and advocacy. Would it be enough? Or would not Christians want to insist upon that Christian mission in the midst of all its different manifestations is intrinsically about bringing people of other faiths to the Christian faith? Mission is linked to the Great Commission (Mt.28, 18-20) and these verses are traditionally interpreted as being about the conversion of people of other faiths to the Christian faith.[1] It is precisely this interpretation that people of other faiths and people in general would find offensive and unacceptable.

Mission does not have a good pedigree. More often than not concepts such as racism, colonialism and militarism are mentioned as bedfellows of mission. And the concept mission looks as if it is beyond redemption at least in the minds of people of other faiths and people outside the periphery of the church and sometimes, if only implicitly also by Christians themselves. Invited by a Turkish institute for dialogue among Jews, Christians and Muslims, I was asked to address one of three concepts chosen by the hosts as being particularly controversial. The rabbi present was to address the concept of Zionism. The Muslim lecturer was to address the concept of jihad. As the Christian representative I was invited to speak to the topic 'mission'! Zionism and jihad were the illustrious buddies of mission that day. This is a perception of mission that one needs to reckon with and it is present not only among Turkish Muslims.

We carry as Christians with us the heritage of "carrying the Gospel to all the Non-Christian World" and the task articulated by John Mott as "the evangelization of the world in this generation".[2] It is my experience that quite a few Christians feel embarrassed about this heritage. One could affirm the task of mission to provide community in an increasingly atomized world or to be a source of social assistance in economically challenging times. But Christian mission as having a mission among people of other faiths that went beyond diacony, advocacy or solidarity, that it had to do with Christianising the world or making converts among Jews, Muslims, Hindus and Buddhists, would strike many as outlandish and passé. If at all to be considered, slogans or catch-words from Edinburgh 1910 would need to be understood in a very figurative sense to be relevant today.

---

[1] This commanding designation, the Great Commission, for Mt.28, 18-20 programs the reader. The Bible text has nothing of this militant air about it but no one sees or hears this anymore. The discipleship is gone; the soldiers for conversion have entered.

[2] Addresses and Papers of John R. Mott, Volume Five, The International Missionary Council, New York, Association, Press, 1947. 12, 13, 19.

It is obvious that we have to make some distinctions before continuing. There are of course Christians, probably closer to more zealous and conservative expressions within the Christian community that would also today *expressis verbis* say that Christian mission is the conversion of people and that this is precisely the business of the church. The church is nothing if it is not carrying the Gospel to the entire non-Christian world. The church is betraying its Lord and Master if it does not feel that John Mott's words literally apply for this generation and every generation. They have nothing learned and nothing forgotten. There is nothing learned how it came to be that Christian mission became a concept, difficult to redeem. There is no attention paid as to whether the church has anything learned from past mistakes. There are no or few regrets and there isn't anything allowed challenging the understanding of mission among people of other faiths as divinely ordained. What matters is what is written and there is little space for human experience, history and knowledge. One may make oblique references to human mistakes in mission but they do not change divine injunction.

The word 'mission' is not restricted to the Christian world. It is present in various contexts. One is the concept mission as in the mission of the permanent diplomatic delegation representing its government in another country. Although far away from home, it is loyal to it in all respects; it interprets its vision and traditions, it is faithful to its history and it seeks as much as is possible to make sense of the interests and concerns in whatever it does in the country it now resides in. It is living in one country but it is not of that country. Others may say what they want but it is as it is.

But the diplomatic mission makes sense only in relation to the country it resides in. It is not a diplomatic mission on the moon or if it is, it is very lonely. The diplomatic mission even of the most reclusive countries in the world is still eager to establish some kind of relations, explaining its raison d'être. Christian mission cannot be an exception. It is only in relation with people of other faiths that it can make sense of its own mission. By itself it is maybe in splendid isolation but it is not in the real world. A lot of our talk about Christian mission among other faiths is rather preaching to the choir. We speak to ourselves and persuade ourselves that this is the right way to go about it. We formulate new ways of explaining mission in ways that sound so nice, so kind, so overwhelmingly filled with love that not one Christian could ever object to it but it is not among Christians, where it needs to be affirmed.

One of the interesting aspects of the Edinburgh 1910 conference was the questionnaire sent out to missionaries in the field. The responses were often revealing. They told the story about missionaries having been trained to meet with Islam or Hinduism but left them unprepared to meet with Muslims and Hindus. The missionaries were surprised not meeting Islam but Muslims, not meeting Hinduism but Hindus. Some of the perceptions changed among the missionaries and that was all for the better. It was regrettable that these encounters with reality did not more impact the missiological thinking coming out of the Edinburgh missionary conference. The conference ended not on a note of curiosity of what people of other faiths might contribute to the glory of God but on calls for evangelising the world. It is true that the question of religious plurality continued to engage missiological thinking from Edinburgh 1910 and onwards but we need more than treading water today. What is needed in 2010 is that the religiously plural world impacts our missiological thinking, that missionaries are encouraged to listen more to the encounters they have made with people of other faiths than only to the mission statement that has become like a mantra.

It should not be that difficult. Throughout the decades since Edinburgh 1910, missiologists have been trying to push the boundaries towards recognition of religious plurality as God-given plurality. Articulated together with many words about positive Christian witness so as not to scare anyone away from seeing the world as it actually is, the message is there: religious plurality is not a problem to overcome. It is normal that there are Buddhists and Hindus and Christians and Muslims just as it is normal that there are apples and pears and strawberries and lemons. But it seems so difficult and it makes so many pull their theological brakes. The most recent document from the World Council of Churches (WCC) "Religious plurality and Christian self-understanding" was never received by its Central Committee. It received a warning text at the latest Assembly in Porto Alegre in 2006, where it was relegated to being a background document. The Deputy General Secretary himself phrased the warning: "It must be emphasized that the paper does not represent the view of the WCC."[3] And yet the message is so careful in its attempts to speak about religious plurality, every word is brought forth imbued with sentences about the overwhelming and inscrutable majesty of God, the boundlessness of the Spirit, as if trying to justify the audacious claim: plurality is a fact! Listen to the words from the WCC statement:" We are convinced that we have been called to witness in the world to God's healing and reconciling work in Christ. We do this humbly acknowledging that we are not fully aware of the ways in which God's redeeming work will be brought to its completion. We now see only dimly, as in a mirror, for we now know only in part and do not have the full knowledge of what God has in store for us (cf. 1 Cor. 13:12-13).

Many Christians have found it difficult to make sense of, or relate creatively to, the reality of other religious traditions. However, as Christians we believe that the Spirit of God is at work in ways beyond our understanding (cf. John 3:8). The activity of the Spirit is beyond our

---

[3] Religious Plurality and Christian Self-understanding, Document no PB-14. http://www.oikoumene.org/en/resources/documents/assembly/porto-alegre-2006/3-preparatory-and-background-documents/religious-plurality-and-christian-self-understanding.html

definitions, descriptions and limitations. We should seek to discern the Spirit's presence where there is "love, joy, peace, patience, kindness, goodness, faithfulness, gentleness and self-control" (Gal. 5:22-23). The Spirit of God is groaning with our spirit. The Spirit is at work to bring about the redemption of the whole created order (Rom. 8:18-27).

A second understanding of the concept mission, which we use in society, is the mission statement of the market or the company indicating the special task that the company has set before itself to carry out. It sets the tone for the whole company. It interprets the vision and it provides tools for the strategy. There is something here for Christian mission to learn. The company knows that it cannot rely on its vision and mission-statement alone; it needs to take seriously its potential clients, their needs and their world. If there is no market analysis, the company even with the most powerful mission statement is likely to go wrong. Some of the latest insights from the economic recession in our time provide a lesson. The market or the company will in our time of recession need to be even more attentive and transparent in relations with customers. They are today more likely than before to punish the market and its minions severely if they fail to keep their promises. The market needs today more than ever to show it empathizes with consumers' concerns. In our time there will maybe even *mirabile dictu* be a need to move from passion to compassion also in marketing. It is simply not enough today to say 'buy!', even if the mission statement recommends it.

While we usually frown upon comparisons with the market, one should maybe even more than before be attentive to learning from it. It is not enough to say that Christian mission is only different and not comparable. A "market analysis" of Christian mission among other faiths will show that it is not enough with a Christian mission statement.

Some years ago the Office on Interreligious Relations and Dialogue of the WCC in collaboration with the Pontifical Council for Interreligious Dialogue (PCID) and ultimately also the World Evangelical Alliance (WEA) embarked upon a project towards producing 'A Code of Conduct on Conversion', a set of considerations for Christian mission among people of other faiths. An important lesson for Christian theologians involved in the project was to listen to what people of other faiths had to say about Christian mission among them. People of different faiths were invited to a hearing of a couple of days to tell Christians the story of how conversion is looked upon in the Hindu world, the Muslim world, among Jews and Buddhists. Stories about unethical attempts to gain converts, aid-evangelism as well as the role of Christian schools and hospitals were shared. The report provides an interesting testimony. There was unanimity that freedom of religion "connotes the freedom, without any obstruction, to practice one's own faith, freedom to propagate the teachings of one's faith to people of one's own and other faiths, and also the freedom to embrace another faith out of one's own free choice." But the concluding sentence puts it all into context: "At the same time, all should heal themselves from the obsession of converting others."[4] It is simply not enough to refer to a mission statement and its interpretation as if written in stone, even if it is considered holy writ.[5]

100 years after Edinburgh, it is not enough to restate the words of yesteryear, even if they are seen as foundational for the project mission. Any concept of mission that presupposes that people of other faiths are doomed lest they are converted needs to be rethought. Whatever the way of talking about the fate of the other and the reason for mission, less direct, more round-about , the point is that the rationale for mission should have nothing to do with an explicit or implicit judgment of other religious traditions as to their possibility to function as vehicles for salvation, liberation, enlightenment, nirvana, moksha, release, bliss, etc. We need another reading of the Christian tradition, where God is present and not absent among the peoples of the earth, where God is the creator of all and the Incarnation is not limiting the yearnings and visions and hopes and dreams of people. Precisely because the classical reading of our tradition prompted the way of exclusion, we need another reading. The way of rejection and exclusion of the other has been the guiding principle in the history and theology of the church and it affected also its missiology. It began with the Jews and it is still going on in reciprocal exclusions of other churches, let alone other religious traditions. We need a reading of our Scriptures that allows another vision of the other. We need a reading and understanding that allows us to affirm with open and generous hearts that religious plurality is as God-given as any other plurality present in God's creation and that therefore Muslims and Buddhists are in their religious traditions as much striving towards the numinous as any Christian is. "God has been present in their seeking and finding, that where there is truth and wisdom in their teachings, and love and holiness in their living, this, like any wisdom, insight, knowledge, understanding, love and holiness that is found among us, is the gift of the Holy Spirit."[6] It would demand another

[4] Report from the Interreligious Consultation on 'Conversion – Assessing the Reality' Organized by the Pontifical Council for Interreligious Dialogue, Vatican City, and the Office on Interreligious Relations & Dialogue of the World Council of Churches, Geneva.
http://www.oikoumene.org/en/programmes/interreligiousdialogue/current-dialogue/no-50-february-2008/report-from-the-interreligious-consultation-on-conversion-assessing-the-reality.html

[5] The end result of the process was presented in June 2011 as "Christian Witness in a Multi-Religious World. Recommendations for Conduct",
http://www.worldevangelicals.org/pdf/1106Christian_Witness_in_a_Multi-Religious_World.pdf.

[6] Baar Statement: Theological Perspectives on Plurality http://www.oikoumene.org/en/resources/documents/wcc-programmes/interreligious-dialogue-and-cooperation/christian-identity-in-pluralistic-societies/baar-statement-theological-perspectives-on-plurality.html

missiology, which is more consistent with the world-view we have today. The world of Edinburgh 1910 had two worlds: the Christian world *and* the non-Christian world. The theology that supported this missionary geography looked upon other religions as obstacles and threats to the missionary effort of spreading the kingdom of Christ. Our worldview today has had to relinquish the idea that there is only one direction, from the North or the West to the South or the East, from Jerusalem to the rest of the world, etc. We no longer live by 'Roma locuta est, causa finita est'.

Whenever the talk is about Christian mission among other faiths, one is immediately challenged: Is it wrong to become a Christian?? What about the beginnings of the church? Was it not precisely that people, Jews and Gentiles, those foreign to the Gospel, were attracted by it to an extent that they were willing to invest their life in this new way?

I am curious about this need to be affirmed. I will go along but will continue to ask why there is this need. I will say, yes, it is true; people left their old ways and joined the new way. Yes, there is nothing wrong about people of other faiths becoming Christians today. Yes, we should not be "ashamed of the gospel; it is the power of God for salvation to everyone who has faith, to the Jew first and also to the Greek" (Rom.1, 17).[7] But why is it that the detractors of dialogue, those putting up a finger of caution, so often need to be affirmed in their faith? Is the need that Christian mission among other faiths is successful and not contested something that has become a corner stone of a fearful church? We need to get beyond that fear and focus on God's presence and not that we through mission carry God to the world. The spirit of apologetics is devastating and it is often present in the traditional discourse on mission.

It seems to me that a proper celebration of Edinburgh 1910 would be not a strategy for Christian mission among other faiths unless it is formulated in the context of worship, liturgy, silence, meditation, in short not the language of propositions but the language and spirit of veneration and doxology. This is where Christian mission needs to have its centre. The liturgy opens hearts and minds, enables inner attention to the mystery of the narrative, the words of the Bible and gives also the mission discourse another meaning. We should seek to listen in a new way to the narrative, in the form in which the church has formulated it, on the basis of all of scripture and in contemplation of God self. In this way even the mission narrative is linked to prayer and becomes prayer and liturgy.

A new song needs to be sung, where God is praised revealing God self among all the peoples of the earth, even in ways that are contradictory, for ways to serve humankind and all the earth, for possibilities to learn from each other, for ways of being faithful to that which one has received without denigrating the other, for the salutary insight that God cannot be

---

[7] NB this verse does not call for Gospel pride, haughtiness or condescension however well wrapped it may be in theologizing about the other.

fully grasped in any one tradition and that nothing can exhaust God, not even the revelation of God.

PROTESTANT PERSPCTIVES: CHRISTIAN MISSION AMONG OTHER FAITHS: THE EVANGELICAL TRADITION

Harold A. Netland

The title of this essay might well invite questions on at least two fronts: Can we really speak of *the* evangelical tradition regarding other religions? Evangelicals are hardly a monolithic group, and they bicker endlessly over many issues -- including questions about religious others. Moreover, what do we mean by "evangelical" anyway? Does the term have a clearly identifiable meaning today? Fair enough. Nevertheless, with appropriate qualification (not all of which can be done here) I think we can speak of evangelicals as an identifiable group. And in spite of internal disagreements, we can pick out some major themes that characterize evangelical approaches to other religions.

Richard Pierard and Walter Elwell speak of evangelicalism as, "The movement in modern Christianity, transcending denominational and confessional boundaries, that emphasizes conformity to the basic tenets of the faith and a missionary outreach of compassion and urgency."[1] While the roots of evangelical commitments are in the inspired Scriptures and the ecumenical creeds, contemporary evangelicals have been shaped in particular by the Protestant Reformation, Pietism, the Awakenings, the Wesleyan holiness movements, the nineteenth and twentieth century Protestant missionary movements, and response to the multiple challenges of the Enlightenment and the rise of theological liberalism.

Alister McGrath identifies the following as "six controlling convictions" at the heart of evangelicalism:

1. The supreme authority of Scripture as a source of knowledge of God and a guide to Christian living.
2. The majesty of Jesus Christ, both as incarnate God and Lord and as the Savior of sinful humanity.

---

[1] Richard V. Pierard and Walter A. Elwell, 'Evangelicalism', *Evangelical Dictionary of Theology*, 2nd ed., ed. Walter A. Elwell (Grand Rapids: Baker Academic, 2001) 405. The literature on defining evangelicalism is enormous. For a helpful discussion see Timothy Larsen, "Defining and Locating Evangelicalism", in *The Cambridge Companion to Evangelical Theology*, eds. Timothy Larsen and Daniel J. Trier (Cambridge: Cambridge University Press, 2007) 1-14.

3. The lordship of the Holy Spirit.
4. The need for personal conversion.
5. The priority of evangelism for both individual Christians and the church as a whole.
6. The importance of the Christian community for spiritual nourishment, fellowship and growth.[2]

On this understanding, a large portion of Christians today in Asia, Africa and Latin America can be considered evangelicals. It is true that contemporary evangelicalism has been closely associated with twentieth century North American Christianity. American evangelicalism emerged as an alternative to fundamentalism, but especially since 1980 it has become linked with socially and politically conservative agendas. Many non-Western evangelicals have become uncomfortable with the label because of its association with recent American socio-political agendas. It is nevertheless important to recognize that, when defined theologically, large numbers of Christians worldwide are evangelicals and thus that global evangelicalism cannot be limited by factors peculiar to recent North American Christianity.

Two significant markers of international evangelical identity emerged in the twentieth century: the Lausanne Movement and the World Evangelical Alliance (WEA). The Lausanne Movement, guided by the Lausanne Committee for World Evangelization, convened the first and second International Congresses on World Evangelization at Lausanne (1974) and Manila (1989). The Lausanne Covenant, produced at Lausanne I (1974), has become a symbol of evangelical identity worldwide. According to its official website, the WEA is a network of churches in 128 nations representing more than 420 million evangelical Christians. [3]

It is impossible in this brief essay to do justice to the variegated nature of global evangelicalism and the ways in which evangelicals approach religious others. I will highlight some dominant themes in evangelical thought and practice, focusing upon developments in the West and materials available in English.

Evangelicals and Mission

Evangelicals have a deep commitment to evangelism and mission, and thus it is not surprising that perspectives on other religions reflect this concern. We might take John Stott, architect of the Lausanne Covenant, as representative of evangelical understandings of mission. In a seminal 1975 work, *Christian Mission in the Modern World,* Stott said that while mission does not refer to everything that God is doing in the world or that the

[2] Alister McGrath, *Evangelicalism and the Future of Christianity* (Downers Grove, IL: InterVarsity Press, 1995) 55-56.

[3] http://www.worldevangelicals.org/aboutwea. Accessed July 17, 2009.

church is to do, it does describe "everything the church is sent into the world to do. 'Mission' embraces the church's double vocation of service to be 'the salt of the earth' and 'the light of the world'." Central to Christian mission is evangelism, sharing the gospel of Jesus Christ with others. "And the good news about Jesus that we announce is that he died for our sins and was raised from death, and that in consequence he reigns as Lord and Savior at God's right hand, and has authority both to command repentance and faith, and to bestow forgiveness of sins and the gift of the Spirit on all those who repent, believe and are baptized".[4] Similarly, Christopher Wright defines Christian mission as "our committed participation as God's people, at God's invitation and command, in God's own mission within the history of God's world for the redemption of God's creation."[5]

Evangelicals have emphasized the imperative of the Great Commission of Mt. 28:18-20, to "make disciples" of all peoples. Roughly 80% of the world's population professes some religious allegiance.[6] Thus, in "making disciples of all peoples" Christ's followers are to share the gospel with sincere adherents of other religious ways. Evangelism and the call to repent of one's sin and by God's grace, to embrace Jesus as Lord and Savior, with all that this entails, are central components of an evangelical approach to religious others.

The Question of Other Religions

Until quite recently, evangelical discussions of other religions were limited largely to concerns relating directly to evangelism. Evangelical statements from the Berlin Congress on Evangelism (1966), the Wheaton Congress on the Church's Worldwide Mission (1966), the Frankfurt Declaration (1970), and even the Lausanne Covenant (1974) are unambiguous on Jesus Christ as the one Lord and Savior for all humankind and the rejection of soteriological universalism. But they have almost nothing to say about non-Christian religions themselves.

The 1974 Lausanne Covenant, for example, has only two sentences mentioning non-Christian religions, and then only in the context of rejecting syncretism and the idea that Christ's salvation might be available through other religions. Lausanne II in Manila (1989) produced the Manila Manifesto, a document which, echoing the Lausanne Covenant, states, "We

[4] John R.W. Stott, *Christian Mission in the Modern World* (Downers Grove, IL: InterVarsity Press, 1975) 19, 30, 54-55. For a helpful overview of recent evangelical theology of mission see Charles Van Engen, 'Forty Years of Evangelical Mission Theology', in *Mission on the Way: Issues in Mission Theology* (Grand Rapids: Baker, 1996) 127-44.

[5] Christopher J. H. Wright, *The Mission of God: Unlocking the Bible's Grand Narrative* (Downers Grove, IL: InterVarsity Press, 2006) 23.

[6] Joanne O'Brien and Martin Palmer, *The Atlas of Religion* (Berkeley: University of California Press, 2007) 14.

affirm that other religions and ideologies are not alternative paths to God, and that human spirituality, if unredeemed by Christ, leads not to God but to judgment, for Christ is the only way."[7] But the Manifesto gives greater attention to the religiously pluralistic world in which we are to make disciples and it introduces a fresh theme – a call for humility in our witness among religious others.

> In the past we have sometimes been guilty of adopting towards adherents of other faiths attitudes of ignorance, arrogance, disrespect and even hostility. We repent of this. We nevertheless are determined to bear a positive and uncompromising witness to the uniqueness of our Lord, in his life, death and resurrection, in all aspects of our evangelistic work including inter-faith dialogue.[8]

Much had changed since Lausanne 1974, and evangelical leaders, especially in Asia, were insisting that theologians and missiologists give greater attention to issues posed by the renewed vitality of other religions.

By the 1990s there was growing recognition that evangelicals need to think more carefully about the relation between the gospel and the religions. In 1992, 85 evangelical theologians from 28 countries came together in Manila under the auspices of the World Evangelical Fellowship (now World Evangelical Alliance) for a conference on "The Unique Christ in Our Pluralistic World". The resulting WEF Manila Declaration combines a strong commitment to the authority of Scripture and to Jesus Christ as the one Lord and Savior for all peoples with a concern to take seriously the religious realities of our world. The Manila Declaration acknowledges that, "We evangelicals need a more adequate theology of religions"[9]. A year later, veteran evangelical missiologist Ralph Covell observed,

> [Evangelicals] are clear on the uniqueness of Christ and on God's will to save all humanity, but they face the dilemma that most of the people of the world are comfortable in the religion in which they are born. Christ is the unique, but apparently not the universal, savior. When crucial target dates appear -- 1900 and 2000, for example -- they mount new crusades to spread Christ's message universally, but without giving any new, creative thought to the relationship of these efforts to the nagging questions posed by world religions. For the most part, evangelical scholars from the time of the Wheaton Congress on Evangelism (1966) to the Lausanne II International Congress on World Evangelization (Manila 1989) have been satisfied with predictably repeating their basic proof texts on the finality of Christ. Disturbing biblical texts which might nuance their attitudes to other religious

---

[7] 'The Manila Manifesto', in *New Directions in Mission and Evangelization 1: Basic Statements, 1974-1991*, eds. James A. Scherer and Stephen B. Bevans (Maryknoll, NY: Orbis, 1992) 293.

[8] Ibid, 297.

[9] 'The WEF Manila Declaration', in *The Unique Christ in Our Pluralist World*, ed. Bruce J. Nicholls (Grand Rapids: Baker, 1994) 15,

expressions are glossed over, put in footnotes, subsumed under traditional views, or placed in the last paragraph of an article.[10]

More recently, evangelical theologians and missiologists have been developing evangelical perspectives on a range of issues relating to other religions. We will highlight briefly three subjects receiving significant attention.

Salvation

Evangelicals insist that Jesus Christ is the only Savior for all of humankind; reconciliation with God comes only through the person and work of Jesus Christ. But this naturally raises questions about the scope of salvation and how such a particularistic emphasis relates to God's universal salvific will. For evangelicals, this tension has been framed in terms of the destiny of those who do not hear the gospel. There has long been some disagreement among evangelicals on the issue, but the question became especially contentious for North American evangelicals during the 1990s. Evangelicals generally agree that the Biblical witness is clear on the following points: (1) All people are sinners and face God's just condemnation for sin. (2) Salvation -- that is, forgiveness of sin, justification and reconciliation with God, and all that this implies -- is available only on the basis of the sinless person and atoning work of Jesus Christ. (3) No one is saved merely by doing good works or being religiously devout. (4) Salvation is always only by God's grace and must be personally accepted through faith. (5) Ultimately, not everyone will be saved. (6) God is entirely righteous, just, and fair in his dealings with humankind. (7) Both out of a sense of obedience to her Lord and compassion for the lost, the church is to be actively engaged in making disciples of all peoples.

But is it nevertheless possible for those who have never heard the gospel to be saved? Contemporary evangelical responses fall into three broad categories. First, many evangelicals hold that only those who hear the gospel and explicitly respond in faith to the name of Jesus in this life can be saved. Explicit knowledge of the gospel of Jesus Christ is thus necessary for salvation.[11] Many evangelicals regard this as the traditional evangelical

---

[10] Ralph Covell, 'Jesus Christ and World Religions: Current Evangelical Viewpoints', in *The Good News of the Kingdom: Mission Theology for the Third Millennium*, eds. Charles Van Engen, Dean S. Gilliland and Paul Pierson (Maryknoll, NY: Orbis, 1993) 162-63.

[11] See John Piper, *Let the Nations Be Glad!* (Grand Rapids: Baker, 1993); Ronald Nash, *Is Jesus the Only Savior?* (Grand Rapids: Zondervan, 1994); Carl F. H. Henry, *God, Revelation, and Authority*, vol. 6 (Waco, Texas: Word, 1983) 367-69; and *Faith Comes By Hearing: A Response to Inclusivism*, eds. Christopher W. Morgan and Robert A. Peterson (Downers Grove: InterVarsity Press, 2008).

position and it has been prominent in conservative evangelical theologies of mission.

A rather different perspective is that of the "wider hope", which maintains that on the basis of Scripture we can expect that large numbers of those who never hear the gospel nevertheless will be saved. 1992 saw the publication of Clark Pinnock's A *Wideness in God's Mercy* and John Sanders' *No Other Name: An Investigation into the Destiny of the Unevangelized.*[12] Pinnock and Sanders argue that although Jesus Christ is the one Savior for all people and salvation is possible only because of Christ's atoning work on the cross, one need not know explicitly about Jesus Christ and the cross to be saved. They claim that we can thus be optimistic about the salvation of the unevangelized. The writings of Pinnock and Sanders provoked a vigorous – and sometimes acrimonious – debate among North American evangelicals.[13]

Many evangelicals, however, find themselves somewhere between the so-called traditional and "wider hope" positions, convinced that each goes beyond what the Biblical data affirm. Those in this group are willing to admit in principle that God might save those who have never explicitly heard the gospel, but they add that we simply do not know whether this occurs or, if so, how many might be saved in this manner.[14] The clear

---

[12] Clark Pinnock, *A Wideness in God's Mercy: The Finality of Jesus Christ in a World of Religions* (Grand Rapids: Zondervan, 1992); John Sanders, *No Other Name: An Investigation into the Destiny of the Unevangelized* (Grand Rapids: Eerdmans, 1992). A similar view, from a Reformed perspective, is found in Terrance L. Tiessen, *Who Can Be Saved? Reassessing Salvation in Christ and World Religions* (Downers Grove: InterVarsity Press, 2004)

[13] Interestingly, in 1970 J.N.D. Anderson, a highly respected British evangelical, published essentially the same view as Pinnock and Sanders, but his writings were not particularly controversial. See J. N. D. Anderson, *Christianity and Comparative Religion* (Downers Grove, IL: InterVarsity Press, 1970); and Sir Norman Anderson, *Christianity and World Religions: The Challenge of Pluralism* (Downers Grove, IL: InterVarsity Press, 1984). For two decades these were the major evangelical treatment of the relation between Christian faith and other religions. Anderson was regularly invited by evangelicals to speak and write on the subject, expressing a kind of unofficial evangelical perspective on other religions. See Sir Norman Anderson, "The Gospel: A Story to Tell to the Nations", in *Evangelical Roots*, ed. Kenneth Kantzer (Nashville, TN: Thomas Nelson, 1978) 173-83; Anderson, 'Christianity and the World's Religions' in *The Expositor's Bible Commentary*, vol. 1, ed. Frank Gaebelein. (Grand Rapids: Zondervan, 1979) 143-57; and idem, "A Christian Approach to Comparative Religion", in *The World's Religions*, ed. Sir Norman Anderson (Leicester, England: InterVarsity Press, 1975) 228-37.

[14] See, for example, John Stott, *The Authentic Jesus* (London: Marshall Morgan and Scott, 1985) 83; J. I. Packer, 'Evangelicals and the Way of Salvation', in *Evangelical Affirmations*, ed. Kenneth S. Kantzer and Carl F. H. Henry (Grand Rapids: Zondervan, 1990) 121-123; Millard Erickson, 'Hope for Those Who Haven't Heard? Yes, but…' *Evangelical Missions Quarterly* 11 (April 1975) 122-26; David Clark, "Is Special Revelation Necessary for Salvation?" in *Through No*

pattern in the New Testament is that people first hear the gospel and then, through the work of the Holy Spirit, respond in faith to the proclamation of the Word and are saved.

The 1992 Manila Declaration takes up the issue and begins by affirming that, "All salvation in the biblical sense of eternal life, life in the kingdom, reconciliation with God and forgiveness of sins comes solely from the person and work of Jesus Christ." But it leaves unresolved the question of the unevangelized:

> In our modern pluralistic world, many Christians ask: 'is it not possible that there might be salvation in other religions?' The question is misleading because it implies that religions have the power to save us. This is not true. Only God saves. All people have sinned, all people deserve condemnation, all salvation stems solely from the person and atoning work of Jesus Christ, and this salvation can be appropriated solely through trust in God's mercy. The question, therefore, should be rephrased as: 'Can those who have never heard of Jesus Christ be saved?' Old Testament saints, who did not know the name of Jesus, nevertheless found salvation. Is it possible that others also might find salvation through the blood of Jesus Christ although they do not consciously know the name of Jesus? We did not achieve a consensus on how to answer this question. More study is needed.
>
> We did agree that salvation is to be found nowhere else than in Jesus Christ. The truth to be found in other religious teachings is not sufficient, in and of itself, to provide salvation. We further agreed that universalism (that all people without exception will be saved) is not biblical. Lastly, we agreed that our discussion of this issue must not in any way undercut the passion to proclaim, without wavering, faltering or tiring, the good news of salvation through trust in Jesus Christ.[15]

Advocates of all three positions outlined above have been strong supporters of Christian mission and the need for sensitive and appropriate evangelism among followers of other religious ways.

Interreligious Dialogue

Many evangelicals have been suspicious of the term "interreligious dialogue" because of the perception that much of the dialogue associated with the World Council of Churches undermines evangelical theological commitments and evangelism. The 1974 Lausanne Covenant, for example, states, "We also reject as derogatory to Christ and the gospel every kind of syncretism and dialogue which implies that Christ speaks equally through

---

Fault of Their Own? William V. Crockett and James Sigountos, eds. (Grand Rapids: Baker, 1991) 40-41; Christopher J. H. Wright, *What's So Unique About Jesus?* (Eastburne, England: Monarch, 1990) 36-39.

[15] 'The Manila Declaration', 15.

all religions and ideologies."[16] There is no suggestion in the Covenant that there might be appropriate forms of dialogue.

Forms of interreligious dialogue that entail that God's revelation in the Incarnation and the written Scriptures are not definitive or that Jesus Christ in principle is not superior to other religious leaders, or that followers of other religions do not need to be reconciled to God through Christ will be rejected by evangelicals. But there is no reason to hold that such problematic assumptions are essential to interreligious dialogue. Evangelicals are increasingly acknowledging that appropriate forms of interreligious dialogue are an important component of Christian mission today.[17] Interreligious dialogue can serve many positive purposes, including deepening understanding of other religions, enhancing mutual respect, reducing tensions, and fostering ways of cooperating in appropriate ways for the common good.

A particularly significant example of evangelical involvement in interreligious dialogue is provided by the faculty of Fuller Theological Seminary, in Pasadena, California. Doug McConnell, Dean of the School of Intercultural Studies at Fuller states, "Currently the seminary community has formally engaged in dialogues that focus on the Abrahamic faiths – Judaism and Islam – and on groups from which we as evangelicals have either come out of – Catholics – or those who have come from us – Mormons."[18] As part of these efforts, in 2005 Fuller Theological Seminary joined with the Salam Institute of Peace and Justice and the Islamic Society of North America in participating in the Conflict Transformation Program of Dialogue with Muslims and Evangelical Christians, a three year project sponsored by the U.S. Department of Justice. The purpose of the project was "to seek common practices, patterns, and pathways for conflict reduction, resolution, and transformation between faiths as well as to learn how to better resolve differences within our individual faiths."[19] To be sure, not all evangelicals are comfortable with the proactive stance of Fuller Seminary on interreligious dialogue. But increasingly evangelicals, both on nonformal and formal or institutional levels, are building bridges to other faith communities in an effort to defuse religious tensions and establish mutual understanding and respect.

---

[16] 'Lausanne Covenant', 254.

[17] The Manila Manifesto links interreligious dialogue with evangelism as part of our witness. See 'Manila Manifesto', 297.

[18] Doug McConnell, 'Mutual Understanding: An Evangelical Case Study', unpublished paper, 4. Cited with permission of the author.

[19] *Peace-Building By, Between, and Beyond Muslims and Evangelical Christians*, eds. Mohammed Abu-Nimer and David Augsburger, (Lanham, MD: Lexington Books, 2009) xii. As cited in McConnell, 'Mutual Understanding', 5.

Theology of Religions

There are encouraging signs that evangelicals are taking the issues posed by the religious realities of our world seriously and are beginning to develop the contours of an evangelical theology of religions. Veli-Matti Kärkkäinen defines theology of religions as "that discipline of theological studies which attempts to account theologically for the meaning and value of other religions. Christian theology of religions attempts to think theologically about what it means for Christians to live with people of other faiths and about the relationship of Christianity to other religions"[20] The past four decades have seen an enormous amount of literature on theology of religions, most written by Roman Catholics and mainline Protestants.

But since about 1990 evangelicals too have joined the discussion. Gerald R. McDermott has written several books, exploring the doctrine of revelation in relation to other religions as well as suggesting a theological framework for understanding the religions.[21] In addition to *An Introduction to the Theology of Religions*, Kärkkäinen has written a work in which he explores the implications of the doctrine of the Trinity for an evangelical understanding of other religions.[22] Although his proposal is controversial, Amos Yong has developed a creative pneumatological approach to the theology of religions.[23] Timothy Tennent, Winfried Corduan, Chris Wright, Stanley Grenz, D. A. Carson, Ida Glaser, Vinoth Ramachandra, Ajith Fernando, Harold Netland, Charles Van Engen, Ken Gnanakan and Kang San Tan, among others, have all made important contributions to an evangelical theology of religions.[24] The 2002 Annual Meeting of the

---

[20] Veli-Matti Kärkkäinen, *An Introduction to the Theology of Religions* (Downers Grove, IL: InterVarsity Press, 2003) 20.

[21] Gerald R. McDermott, *Can Evangelicals Learn from World Religions? Jesus, Revelation and Religious Traditions* (Downers Grove, IL: InterVarsity Press, 2000); and McDermott, *God's Rivals: Why has God Allowed Different Religions?* (Downers Grove, IL: InterVarsity Press, 2007).

[22] Veli-Matti Kärkkäinen, *Trinity and Religious Pluralism: The Doctrine of the Trinity in Christian Theology of Religions* (Burlington, VT: Ashgate, 2004).

[23] Amos Yong, *Beyond the Impasse: Toward a Pneumatological Theology of Religions* (Grand Rapids: Baker, 2003).

[24] See Timothy Tennent, *Christianity at the Religious Roundtable: Evangelicalism in Conversation with Hinduism, Buddhism, and Islam* (Grand Rapids: Baker Academic, 2002), and Tennent, *Theology in the Context of World Christianity* (Grand Rapids: Zondervan, 2007); Winfried Corduan, *A Tapestry of Faiths: The Common Threads Between Christianity and World Religions* (Downers Grove, IL: InterVarsity Press, 2002); Christopher J. H. Wright, "The Christian and Other Religions: The Biblical Evidence", *Themelios* 9:2 (1984) 4-15; idem, *Thinking Clearly About the Uniqueness of Jesus* (Crowborough, England: Monarch, 1997); S. J. Grenz, 'Toward an Evangelical Theology of Religions', *Journal of Ecumenical Studies* 31 (1994) 49-65; D. A. Carson, *The Gagging of God: Christianity Confronts Pluralism* (Grand Rapids: Zondervan, 1996); Ida Glaser, *The Bible and Other Faiths: Christian Responsibility in a World of Religions* (Downers Grove, IL:

Evangelical Theological Society was devoted to the subject "Evangelical Christianity and Other Religions".[25] Terry Muck and Frances Adeney have produced a groundbreaking work, *Christianity Encountering World Religions*, which combines history with theology and missiology in a creative approach – that of "giftive mission" -- to understanding and responding to religious others in the twenty-first century.[26]

In the days ahead evangelicals need to give careful and creative thought to developing a comprehensive theology of religions that is both faithful to Scripture and reflects accurately the religious realities of our world. Such a framework should explore the implications of Trinitarian theology for our understanding of other religions. In what ways and to what extent are the Father, Son and Holy Spirit present and active throughout creation and human affairs? Here we must navigate carefully the tension between universality and particularity. God's presence and activity are certainly not limited to the church, but neither should we think of the operations of the eternal Logos or Holy Spirit entirely apart from the ministry of the incarnate Son. The dynamic tension between the universality of the triune God and the particularity of the incarnate Word cannot be eliminated.

InterVarsity Press, 2005); Vinoth Ramachandra, *The Recovery of Mission: Beyond the Pluralist Paradigm* (Grand Rapids: Eerdmans, 1997); Ajith Fernando, *Sharing the Truth in Love: How to Relate to People of Other Faiths* (Grand Rapids: Discovery House Publishers, 2001); Harold Netland, *Encountering Religious Pluralism: The Challenge to Christian Faith and Mission* (Downers Grove, IL: InterVarsity Press, 2001); Netland, "Theology of Religions, Missiology, and Evangelicals", *Missiology: An International Review* 33:2 (April 2005) 142-58; Charles Van Engen, 'The Uniqueness of Christ in Mission Theology', in *Landmark Essays in Mission and World Christianity*, eds. Robert L. Gallagher and Paul Hertig, (Maryknoll, NY: Orbis, 2009) 160-75; Ken Gnanakan, *The Pluralist Predicament* (Bangalore: Theological Book Trust, 1992); Kang San Tan, 'Evangelical Missiology From an East Asian Perspective: A Study on Christian Encounter With People of Other Faiths', in *Global Missiology for the 21st Century: The Iguassu Dialogue*, ed. William D. Taylor (Grand Rapids: WEF / Baker, 2000) 295-306. Other significant evangelical works include *One God, One Lord: Christianity in a World of Religious Pluralism*, 2nd ed., ed. Andrew D. Clarke and Bruce W. Winter (Grand Rapids: Baker, 1992); *No Other Gods Before Me? Evangelicals and the Challenge of World Religions*, ed. John G. Stackhouse, Jr. (Grand Rapids: Baker, 2001); *The Trinity in a Pluralistic Age: Theological Essays on Culture and Religion*, ed. Kevin J. Vanhoozer (Grand Rapids: Eerdmans, 1997); and *Christianity and the Religions: A Biblical Theology of World Religions*, eds. Edward Rommen and Harold Netland, Evangelical Missiological Society Series Number 2 (Pasadena, CA: William Carey Library, 1995).

[25] See *Biblical Faith and Other Religions: An Evangelical Assessment*, ed. David W. Baker (Grand Rapids: Kregel Publications, 2004).

[26] Terry Muck and Frances S. Adeney, *Christianity Encountering World Religions: The Practice of Mission in the Twenty-First Century* (Grand Rapids: Baker Academic, 2009).

A comprehensive theology of religions should also develop a more nuanced understanding of "religion". To be sure, Biblical and theological resources are critical for such understanding. But so also are the social sciences – history, anthropology, sociology, and the phenomenology of religions. What is needed are understandings that reflect accurately not only the Biblical witness but also the lived realities of those we refer to as Hindus or Muslims or folk animists. Moreover, religion has much in common with culture, although neither concept can be simply reduced to the other. Evangelical missiology needs to develop the kind of nuanced theological understanding of religion that it has adopted with respect to culture.

Evangelical approaches to religious others will continue to be shaped by the Biblical witness to Jesus Christ as the only Lord and Saviour for all humankind, including devout adherents of other religions. Although Christian mission is certainly broader than merely evangelism and the call to repentance, it must include evangelism as a central element. But the world in which we are to make disciples of Jesus Christ is one marked by the resurgence of traditional religions as well as a bewildering array of new religious movements and spiritualities. It is a post-colonialist world that is acutely aware of the injustices of four centuries of Western imperialism and that believes – rightly or wrongly – that Christianity shares the blame for such injustice. Deeply rooted ethnic, nationalistic and religious tensions erupt in violence, causing many to wonder whether religiously diverse communities can indeed live together peacefully. Religious conversion is increasingly seen as an obstacle to peaceful coexistence. The issues here are complex and require of the Christian proper navigation of two sets of obligations – our responsibilities as disciples of Jesus Christ and as good citizens, both locally and globally. We need to be guided by both the Great Commission (Mt. 28:18-20) and the Great Commandment (Mt 22:35-40). In obedience to our Lord, we are to "make disciples" of all people. As Christ's disciples, we are to love God with our entire being and to love our neighbor – including religious others – as we love ourselves.

Evangelicals must approach Christian mission in today's world with an attitude of humility and repentance for the ways in which Christians have sometimes treated religious others in the past. New models of evangelism and disciple-making that are appropriate for a world full of religious tension and increasingly hostile to evangelism must be developed. The church must show a skeptical world that Christians can be strongly committed to Jesus Christ as the one Lord and Savior for all peoples while also working to promote peaceful relations among religious traditions. Evangelicals must demonstrate through concrete actions that we do accept in appropriate ways the ethnic, cultural and religious diversity in our world. But at the same time, we cannot abandon our commitment to Jesus Christ. So even as we embrace Buddhists and Muslims as fellow human beings created in God's image we must also urge them to be reconciled to God by acknowledging Jesus Christ as their Lord and Savior.[27]

[27] I am grateful to Vinoth Ramachandra, Craig Ott, How Chuang Chua and Doug McConnell for insights that have strengthened this essay. They are not, of course, responsible for any remaining deficiencies.

Roman Catholic Perspectives:

The Evolving Dialogical Identity of the Missional Church Among the World's Religions: A Theological Journey Through the Catholic Teachings

Antony Kalliath CMI

Introduction

The Second Vatican Council reaffirms that "The pilgrim Church is missionary by her very nature"[1]. Indeed mission is constitutive of Christian faith and discipleship. Therefore, being-a- missionary is essentially being-a-Christian. To be a missionary is more an inner call to participate in the *Missio Dei* than an external demand. And this mission dimension of Christian identity makes faith creative and innovative, for faith seeks understanding by responding to the challenges and claims of the context and ethos. Thus faith becomes missional both in its praxis and theory. This missional identity makes the Church ever new and young, its identity organic, its horizons widened and its arena broadened. Owing to this missional existence of the Church, one can discern diverse paradigms and paths of mission in its long journey of two millennia. This legacy will continue for years to come until the 'Reign of God' finally dawns. The most daunting, as well as promising challenge that the Church encounters today is, indeed, the multi-religious context and the prevailing pluralistic ethos in the present globalizing world. Here the substance as well as the style that the Church has to embrace is dialogue. The missional praxis has to become dialogical so much so that the Church has to become dialogical in nature. More than merely a means, dialogue has to grow into the very goal and the celebration of faith. The following discussion is a journey through the various teachings of the Catholic Church on the dialogical mission among religions.

---

[1]II Vatican Council, Decree *Ad Gentes on the Mission Activity of the Church* # 02.

Second Vatican Council's Call for a New Vision and Praxis

To start, Pope Paul VI erected the *Secretariat for Non Christian Religions*[2] in 1964 to emphatically mark the Church's new approach and understanding of the World's religions. Since the Second Vatican Council,[3] dialogue with various religious traditions is positively fostered and has become an inviolable constituent both in theory and praxis.[4] Late Pope Paul VI's D*eclaration on the Relation of the Church to Non-Christian Religions* (1965) gave a decisive momentum to the praxis of dialogue in Christian life. The Pope exhorts that all Catholics engage in "dialogue and collaboration" "with prudence and love" "to recognize, preserve and promote the good things, spiritual and moral, as well as the socio-cultural values found among these men [and women]" (NA # 2).

The theological advocacy of this proactive dialogue with world's religions is discoursed on a broader spectrum of the origin and destiny of human being in the Divine Economy in the Council's new vision. In the Pastoral Constitution *On the Church in the Modern World*, the Council says, "all men [sic] of good will in whose hearts grace works in an unseen way" are recipients of the hope of redemption. It further clarifies, "The Holy Spirit in a manner known only to God offers to everyone the possibility of being associated with this paschal mystery" (GS 22). Elaborating this theological positioning the Council unveils the inclusive "plan of salvation" (LG 16) by saying that all who "fears God" and "does what is right" (LG 9; Act 10:35), "all who strive to lead a good life", "all who acknowledges God the Creator" (LG # 16) and all who live by the dictates of conscience (DH #1)[5] are included in the salvific will of God. Therefore, other religions are not independent or parallel ways of salvation; they are positively incorporated into the plan of salvation. The Council sums up that all adherents of other religions are seeking "in shadows and images" the God who "gives all men [sic] life and breath and all things (Acts 17:25-28) and the Saviour wills all men [sic] to be saved" (1Tim 2:4) (LG 16).

---

[2]It was renamed *Pontifical Council for Interreligious Dialogue* in 1988.

[3]The Second Ecumenical Council of the Vatican, or Vatican II, was the twenty-first Ecumenical Council of the Catholic Church. It opened under Pope John XXIII on October 11, 1962 and closed under Pope Paul VI on December 8, 1965.

[4]This new awareness in the Church is evident in the documents of the Second Vatican Council: *The Dogmatic Constitution on the Church* (*Lumen Gentium*), *The Pastoral Constitution on the Church in the Modern World* (*Gaudium et Spes*), *The Decree on the Missionary Activity of the Church* (*Ad Gentes*), *The Declaration on the Relationship of the Church to Non-Christian Religions* (*Nostra Aetate*).

[5]II Vatican Council, *Declaration on Religious Freedom – Dignitatis Humanae* #1

Magna Carta of Dialogue

The initiative of II Vatican Council's dialogue with World's Religions finds its theological rooting in the encyclical *Ecclesiam Suam*[6] which was published in 1964, just one year before *Nostra Aetate* (1965). While addressing at the conclusion of the Plenary Assembly of the "Secretariate for the Non-Christians" on the 20th year of the publication of the *Ecclesiam Suam* (ES), the late Pope John Paul II described the encyclical as the "*magna carta* of dialogue."[7]

The Encyclical develops a seminal theology of dialogue and explores its sources right in the "mind of God", and situates it on the broader spectrum of salvation itself: "sacred dialogue between God and man [sic]" in history (ES 70); Christ is the archetypal dialogue between the Divine and human, and it should be continued in the Holy Spirit (ES # 71). God has taken "the initiative in the dialogue of salvation": "He hath first loved us"(1Jn 4:10). He/She commenced the dialogue out of love of the world (Joh 3:16). Following God's own example the Church enters into the dialogue out of ardent and honest love. (ES # 72, 73). Since the source and motif of dialogue is God's love, dialogue with World's Religions is primarily theological and soteriological; it is then fundamentally a faith imperative, though it transpires on the social, religious, cultural and political spectrum.

Since dialogue is undergirded in the very mystery of God's love and salvific motif, it is not depended on the merits of human agencies on the one hand, and it cannot set any "limits" and must be inclusive, open and "universal" (ES # 74, 76) and naturally its nature is an ever 'happening event'. It means that it is the "persevering" phenomenon everyday, and it is the historical (ES # 77) constituent of Christian faith. It also characterizes the apostolic mission of the Church; it is a constant endeavour and is inseparable from one's own salvation as well as other's (GS # 80). "Dialogue, therefore, is a recognized method of the apostolate" (ES # 81) as well as the experience of faith. Both have a mutual simultaneity in the Christian life.

Further, the Encyclical dwells on the nature of dialogue. It is the "invitation to the exercise and development of the highest spiritual and mental powers" and "ranks among the greatest manifestations of human activity and culture" (ES #81). It should then be characterized by the meekness and the humility of Jesus' heart (Mt 11:29), and its authority is in virtue of the truth that is affirmed in the process of dialogue, and it is itself an example of virtue of peace, patience, generosity, good will, intimacy, friendship, adherence to the Good and selflessness (ES #81). This way

---

[6]Pope Paul VI *Ecclesiam Suam*, 1964

[7]Pope John Paul II, 'Address at the Conclusion of the Plenary Assembly of the Secretariat for Non-Christians', 3 March 1984, *The Attitude of the Church Towards the Followers of Other Religions*, Secretariatus Pro Non Christianis (Rome: 1984), 3.

dialogue serves "to complete each other [among the different religions]. They encourage us to think on different lines" and "to find better ways of expressing ourselves" (ES 83).

The Encyclical exhorts that the Church of today must take up dialogue with "a great renewal of fervor" in an inclusive "motherly embrace" for its "Catholicity is not an idle boast" but a "mission to foster love, unity and peace among men [sic]" (ES # 93, 94).[8] What is implied is a composite and comprehensive dialogue on a broader perspective "promoting and defending common ideals in the spheres of religious liberty, human brotherhood, teaching and education, social welfare and civil order" (ES # 108). Thus dialogue will window new themes into the holiness and vitality of the Church in her missional existence (GS # 116).

Dialogue, the Praxis of Being Missional

The document of the Vatican's Secretariat for Non-Christian Religions (later called the Pontifical Council of Dialogue), *The Attitude of the Church Toward the Followers of Other Religions* (1984) is an earnest follow-up of the Second Vatican Council's call to "engage prudently and lovingly in dialogue and cooperation" with other religious traditions.[9] It declares that dialogue is an essential part of the Church's mission and the "norm" and "ideal" of the Church's relationship with the world's religions. It explains the goal of dialogue as "mutual understanding and enrichment," and not the change of religion as such (n.03). The mission of dialogue is further explained in the Apostolic constitution *Regimini Ecclesiae:* "To search for methods and ways of opening a suitable dialogue with non-Christians. It should strive, therefore, in order that non-Christians come to be known honestly and esteemed justly by Christians, and that in their turn, non-Christians can adequately know and esteem Christian doctrine and life" (n. 99).

The document shows that *dialogue* has gone deep into the Church's missional existence. It has no other agenda except to *know* and *esteem* the other traditions, and to make the Christian life known. It means that dialogue is "pastoral"(n.06) without any 'hidden agenda'; it should be a new way of being Christian with complementary and exploring mindset in a multi-faith context. Here, the identity of the Church is more a pilgrim community which journeys "forward together with all of mankind [sic] with whom they share the human experience" (n.10). In this sense, dialogue is Church's mission which is the "the commitment to mankind [sic], to

---

[8]This inclusive and open-ended dialogue has to transpire, as the encyclical puts it, in four circles, namely, i. The entire humanity and world, ii. People of World's religions; iii. Ecumenical fellowship of the followers of Christ; iv. Catholic Fellowship. ES # 97-113.

[9]Paul VI *Nostra Aetate*: *Declaration on the Relation of the Church to Non-Christian Religions*, October 1965, #2

social justice, to liberty and the rights of man [sic], and the reform of unjust social structures" (n.12).

Dialogue is therefore understood as a way of seeking truth in a holistic perspective. But the truth should be sought "in a manner proper to the dignity of the human person and his social nature" and in a total respect to human freedom (n.18).[10] "Coercion, or a kind of persuasion" will have to be considered "an abuse of one's right and a violation of the rights of others" (n.18).[11] Dialogue is not for opportunistic tactics but it should spring up from the depth of experience and enquiry. It should emerge from the responsible subjectivity and fidelity to one's life and its aspirations (n.20, 21).

Moreover, life's enquiry into truth is not merely a private affair but a collective journey in which mutual affirmation, reciprocal correction, and fraternal exchange as partners in dialogue is the dynamic, that will only lead to ever greater maturity. Christians must listen to and strive to understand what other believers communicate to us in order to profit from the gifts that God bestows so generously (n.21). Above all, the theological ground of this dialogical existence is to be searched in the Trinitarian mystery of communion and interchange (n.22). This Trinitarian communion in dialogue is further extended and manifested in Christ who enlightens every human being for the mystery of Trinity is revealed in him.[12] And the Holy Spirit who is "the force of life" (see LG 4), "acts in the depth of people's consciences and accompanies them on the secret path of hearts toward the truth" (see also GS 22) (n.24).

Therefore, Christians are called upon to engage in a sincere and patient dialogue with World Religions to learn the treasures the bountiful God has distributed among the nations of the earth (AG 11; cf. AG 41; AA 14, 29) (n.27). Such an engagement with the other faiths can be exercised through multiple layers and ways, namely dialogue of life, dialogue of deeds, dialogue of scholars and dialogue of prayer (ns.29-35). The dialogue at the various layers is not a diplomacy out of socio-political imperatives but primarily a spiritual process of conversion (n.37), which is not imposed but which spontaneously happens in the mutual desire of growth (n.40).

Dialogue in this sense should be incorporated in God's loving plan for every nation (Acts 26:27) and a veritable way to participate in the *Missio Dei.* The Church desires to work with all the faiths to fulfill God's plan (n. 41). The disciples of Jesus engage in dialogue because of the vocation to Christian life. It is indeed a cultural, political and social exercise; but it is much more than this. It is the faith imperative. A tolerant non-involvement of 'I'm OK, you're OK' is not the option. What is entailed is a positive initiative in that dialogue process; it means the dialogue itself has grown as

---

[10]II Vatican Council, *Declaration on Religious Freedom* (*Dignitatis Humanae*), # 3.
[11]*Ibid*, # 4.
[12]See Pope John Paul II, *Redemptor Hominis* (1979), # 8,10,11,13, 14.

a new way of being Christian, or rather, the Church has to become a means of 'dialogue' in the universe of faiths, and thus, a 'welcoming Church.' Dialogue conceived in an ecclesiology of hospitality makes the Church 'missional' rather than missionary. Being missional means open, inclusive, spirit bound, eschatological and trying the future in the vision "abundance of life" (Joh 10:10).

Dialogical Identity

The discourse on dialogue continued honestly and emphatically. Pope John Paul's Encyclical *Redemptoris Missio* (1991) further fathomed and furthered the nuances of dialogue. As the document teaches, dialogue with world's religions is "a part of the Church's evangelizing mission". It is "a method and means of mutual knowledge and enrichment". It is linked to "her mission *ad gentes*" in the composition of "mutual knowledge and enrichment" (# 55). Such a dialogue is not conceived as "tactical concerns or self-interest". The Encyclical sheds light on the tenets and tenor of the dialogue (# 56) as follows:

i) Through dialogue, the Church seeks to uncover the "seeds of the Word (# 56, NA # 2) and "the ray of truth" (NA # 2) found in all religious traditions of the world.
ii) Church should engage in dialogue in a deep respect for everything, for the Spirit blows wherever it wills (*Redemptor Hominis*, 12).
iii) Dialogue is based on hope and love.
iv) Dialogue will thus bear the fruits of the Spirit.
v) Dialogue treats other religions as a positive challenge to discover and acknowledge the signs of the Christic presence and the works of the Spirit.
vi) Consequently, dialogue leads the Church to introspection and to reconstruct her identity in an interfaith context and horizon.
vii) Dialogue will lead her to the fullness of Revelation.
viii) Those engaged in dialogue must be grounded in their own religious traditions as well as open to others.
ix) Humility and frankness for mutual empowerment must be the basic attitude of dialogue.
x) Dialogue, if pursued with docility to the Spirit, leads first and foremost to inner purification and conversion.

In the above mentioned tenor and tenets, dialogue makes the Church a participant in religious pursuits. It offers an immense opportunity, especially through "dialogue of life", to bear testimony to one's own faith as well as to know at a close range the richness of other religions to "build a more just and fraternal society". It is the "path toward Kingdom" in the present multi-faith context. The Encyclical thus conceives dialogue as an open and creative space and visualizes the practice of dialogue a veritable way of building a new identity of the Church in the multi-faith scenario (see # 57).

Dialogue: Proclamation Inter-Gentes

The Declaration of "Dialogue and Proclamation"[13] by the Pontifical Council for Interreligious Dialogue in 1991 shows the Church's firm and irreversible commitment to Dialogue with World's Religions in her missional life. Its point of departure is the positive new awareness and a bold recognition of religious pluralism in the present world of mobility and media. "The World Day of Prayer for Peace" in Assisi, on 27 October 1986 was its backdrop. Its premise is the Evangelizing Mission as conceived in *Redemptoris Missio,* but in a broader scope of integral development, social justice, human liberation (DP #44) and culture (DP 45). It should be admitted that dialogue is visualized in the ambit of proclamation of the Gospel as mandated by the Risen Christ (DP 58). However, proclamation is not seen as a one way traffic in the praxis of dialogue. Dialogue entails openness, receptivity, and tolerance of differences (DP 47). The fruits of dialogue, according to the declaration, are: (i) *Mutual Enrichment* of *all* sides (DP # 9; RM # 55); (ii) *Mutual interrogation* (DP 32); (iii) A call to be "*Purified*" (DP #32), (iv) A call to be "*Transformed.*" (DP # 47); (v) A call to be "*converted*"(DP # 41). There is thus a qualitative shift from *Ad Gentes* (toward the people) to *Inter-Gentes* (among the people) in the understanding of dialogue as espoused in this document. The self-understanding of the Church here is more of a pilgrim community among the pilgrims (DP 36).

It should be mentioned here that the Church is quite conscious of the 'dangers' of dialogue, which frustrate the basis of Christian faith if the dialogical mission is not rooted in the preambles of Christian faith. The Church reminds us that versatility and vitality of dialogue is indeed the faith in Jesus who is the "constant" of the dialogical mission. He, being the radical dialogue between the Divine and Human owing to the Incarnation, is the mandate and referent of dialogical mission. He is the "shore" from which we build bridges of dialogue in the world of religions and religious pursuits. The uniqueness of Jesus is to be searched in its universality, which is realized through the dialogical presence of the Risen Christ through his Spirit, who is ubiquitous and universal. The uniqueness of Jesus is not accomplished through exclusion, but by a dialogical inclusiveness and openness. This is the New Life that the "first fruit of resurrection" witnesses. The faith in Jesus and the salvation accomplished in and through

[13]See, Pontifical Council for Inter-religious Dialogue, *Dialogue and Proclamation* (Rome:1991).

him is, then, the reason and motif of any dialogical evangelization.[14] *Dominus Jesus* quotes the *Lumen Gentium* to drive home the theological reason of the immense hope and promise latent in the missional dialogue: "the unique mediation of the Redeemer does not exclude, but rather gives rise to a manifold cooperation which is but a participation in this one source".[15] The Church, which is the continuation of Jesus' mission, searches its uniqueness by being dialogical, and such an identity is not the given but should be constructed through a dialogical mission (*Dominus Jesus*, ns.16, 17). This way, the Church lives up to its vocation of being *catholic,* which etymologically means 'ubiquitous'. Universality is not a virtual concept but it is uniqueness achieved in ubiquity through a dialogical presence and experience of the "Fullness of Life" achieved in the person of Jesus, the Risen Lord of history and creation.

Dialogue has entered deep into the psyche and consciousness of the Church. The Catholic Church is increasingly pursuing a dialogical path assiduously and consistently. The Church has to become an authentic dialogue to participate in the *Missio Dei* in the present scenario of religious pluralism. There cannot be a turning back. Dialogue is the new experience and the new challenge in the Church's mission, which is ridden with surprises because the agent of Christian mission is the Spirit, which blows wherever and whenever it wills, according to its logic which is beyond human logistics. What is needed, while being engaged in *Missio Dei*, is a radical surrender to the rhyme and reason of the Spirit who reveals the Risen Lord in dialogue of religions.

An Asian Insight

In this context it will be a dismal omission if the contribution of Asian churches with regard to dialogical mission is not briefly dwelled upon. The Special Assembly for Asia of the Synod of Bishops (18 April to 14 May 1998, Vatican, Rome) clearly delineated that dialogue must be the "characteristic mode of the Church's life in Asia" so that Asia participates in the Gospel of Abundance of Life, the very theme of the Asian Synod.[16] The dialogical mission has to be construed in the Asian "spirit of complementarity and harmony" (n.06) and to be practiced in a broader spectrum of "civilization of love" rooted in a theology of communion (n.25). The dialogue must primarily uphold respect to other religions, which is twofold: "respect for man [sic] in his quest for answers to the deepest questions of his life, and respect for the action of the Spirit in man

---

[14] See, Congregation for the Doctrine of the Faith Declaration 'Dominus Jesus' On the Unicity and Salvific Universality of Jesus Christ and the Church (Rome, 2000), n.13.

[15] Second Vatican Council, Dogmatic Constitution *Lumen Gentium*, 62.

[16] The Pope John Paul II, *Ecclesia in Asia* (Rome: Libreria Editrice Vaticana 1998), n. 3

[sic]" (n.20). In this context, the *Ecclesia in Asia* speaks of the imperative of a narrative pedagogy using stories, parables and symbols so characteristic of Asian methodology in teaching" (n.20).[17] Dialogue should be a story-telling, or rather, a "retelling of the story of Jesus through the stories of people".[18] Such a dialogue can vitally take place only in the cultural space because Asian cultures are innately religious. Religious truths are revealed in a culture of stories. Hence dialogical mission in Asia entails enculturation construed in narrative hermeneutics. "Through enculturation the Church, for her part becomes a more intelligible sign of what she is, and a more effective instrument of mission" (n.21).[19] Hence dialogue is not simply a strategy for peaceful coexistence among peoples; the motif of dialogue is to be sought in the Father's dialogue with the world in love through the Son and Holy Spirit. It implies that dialogical mission is grounded in the logic of the incarnation which unveiled the story of Jesus (n.29).

The dialogical mission among Asia's religion is explored with greater depth and breadth in the Asian Bishops' Conferences (FABC). It proposes a 'triple dialogue' to engage in missional dialogue in Asia: Dialogue with "Asian Religions", "Asian Cultures" and "Asian Poor" because these three are inter-related in the Asian scenario.[20] 'Dialogue' has now become the code and call, prowess and panache in the vision and praxis of mission in Asia. Dialogue acquires broader frames and deeper insights in ongoing FABC's deliberations and workshops. It is stated that mission is dialogue. Here dialogue is not meant to win people to an institutional church, but 'to convert people to authentic human values and to deepen and fulfill these values in Christ.[21] Its scope is broadened in terms of integral evangelization, which entails "common-good", "free-community"[22] "promotion of culture, human development and liberation".[23] Such dialogical mission can be engaged in a cultural vision of a "receptive pluralism",[24] which will only respond to the Asian sensibilities so that the Word is incarnated into the Asian genius, and thus the Risen Lord becomes

---

[17] Special Assembly for Asia of the Synod of Bishops, *Relatio post disceptationem, L'Osservatore Romano* (22 April 1998), 15

[18] Antony Kalliath, "Retelling the Story of Jesus Through the Stories of People" Vol.74, No.3 *Vidya Jyoti* (March 2010):55-74

[19] John Paul II, Encyclical Letter *Redemptoris Missio* (7 December 1990), 52

[20] See the Statement of the Asian Bishops' Conference, *Evangelization in Modern Day Asia*, The First Plenary Assembly, Taipei, Taiwan, 27th April, 1974.

[21] Workshop IV: The Gospel, the Kingdom of God, Liberation and Development, International Congress on Mission Manila (7 Dec 1979), n.03.

[22] Fourth Bishops' Institute for Social Action, Antipolo, Manila (4 March, 1978), n.9.

[23] FABC I, Evangelization in Modern Day Asia, 23

[24] The Third Bishops' Institute for Interreligious Affairs on the Theology of Dialogue (Hong Kong, 2-7 Nov 1986), n.16

the inner empowering 'core-experience' in Asian travails towards the "abundance of life" that Jesus has brought.

Towards a Mission of Hospitality in the Eschatological Horizon

To sum up, one would say that Christian mission is not a solitary and private affair but a community witness, because the salvation in Christ is always acquired in and through the community in the Gospel vision. Mission is an invitation to the community of Jesus' disciples. To enter in the universe of faiths the Church should increasingly construct an identity of a welcoming community of pilgrims, which should be dialogical fellowship of mutual empowerment and enlightenment. Hospitality was one of the missional praxis of the early Christianity. Paul exhorts the Romans to "practice hospitality" (Rom 12:13). In the letter to the Hebrews, we note a step further, "hospitality to the strangers" (Heb13:2). This practice of 'welcoming' is a sequel of Jesus' practice of Kingdom ministry.

Jesus is frequently shown offering hospitality: his ministry runs through the great feeding miracles and climaxes in the Last Supper. 'Table' has become a dialogical spectrum where Jesus often shared the Good News. His table fellowship generated an inclusive space in which he formed his disciple community of people from various creeds, class and caste. Again, all his healing ministries powerfully embody God as the host of humanity. Some of the Gospels conclude with the risen Christ cooking breakfast for his disciples on the shore of the Sea of Tiberias (Joh 21:9-14). Moreover, he seeks and rejoices hospitality. He is a frequent guest of "tax collectors and sinners" and what eventually turns out is that Jesus becomes the host (rather than king) of his Kingdom of God, to which all of them are welcomed (Luke 24:30-31). Jesus says, hospitality is the "better portion" of a disciple (Luke 10:42).). In the episode of Emmaus story, Jesus, the guest ultimately becomes the host through "breaking the bread" (Luke 24:30-31). The parable of the last judgment (Mt 25) poignantly points to how the "breaking of the bread" evolves into "breaking of the Word". Praxis of mission among the religions is to be enacted in a "Welcoming –Church" in which a community of disciples is formed irrespective of creed or class. The Jews, the Greeks, Pagans, slaves (1Cor 12:13), the Hindus, Muslims, Buddhists and Dalits are all equal citizens of the reign of God. As Deutero-Isaiah says, we have to 'widen the space of our tent' (Is 54:2), especially in the present world of migration and mobility, in which what we have is a heterogeneous community of multi-faith and multiple belonging. In today's world of cultural plurality, it is only through the praxis of dialogue that we can build up a 'welcoming-ecclesia' which can only be a missional Church.

This widening of the 'tent' to practice hospitality is possible when we engage in a mission in the eschatological horizon which we find in Deutero Isaiah and in Jesus' understanding of the coming Kingdom. The Kingdom of God (*Malkuth Yahweh*) that is formed from a verbal noun is an organic and processing reality. It extends to the future and even beyond the future. This dynamism can be sustained only through dialogical hospitality. At this point I would like to draw from Derrida's postmodernist line of argument. He pitches his advocacy of 'uncontaminated presence' for which he stands for the 'deconstruction' of the closed systems and their totalizing policies. His call for 'deconstruction' of the "grand narratives" is not destructive and negative, but quite creative in the sense that it engenders a new space of creativity in which one can practice, as he says, "pure-hospitality" uncontaminated by ideologies and systems. The hallmarks of this 'hospitality' are democracy, social justice and gratuity. And the 'other' has an inviolable place in this hospitality. To elaborate his thinking, he relies on a platonic term '*khora*' which seems quite relevant when we engage in a dialogical mission in the eschatological vision.

Khora is not a threshold of transition to the higher realm but a 'medium' or a 'space' which dissolves our neat logic of 'either/or' into 'neither/nor' (as distinct from 'and/and'). It is a 'non-place' which liberates human consciousness from the totalizing influence of systems and de-centres grandiose systems and brings about a basic openness in human subjectivity. It is a space of resistance towards exclusive categories as well as of universal politics, and of the possibility of crossing the borders of one's identities, religious, cultural, political. He says that religions, especially revealed religions, operate within the logic of exclusion. Whereas, the notion of *khora* is a narrative space in which one can engage in a secularized religiosity which he loves to call 'messianicity', not 'messianism' found in religious books.[25] This secularized 'messianicity' leads to a new religiosity of 'unconditional hospitality', and engenders a new religious discourse of gratuity both at inter and intra-religious dialogue. It means that mission among religions is not a project in the time scale and range but a vital movement towards New Heaven and the New Earth (Is 66:22) when "God will be all in all" (1 Cor 15:28).

---

[25]See, Derrida, Jacques, 'Force of Law: The Mystical Foundation of Authority', in *Deconstruction and the Possbility of Justice*, ed by D. Cornell, M. Rosenfeld and D.G. Carlson (New York: Routledge, 1992).

ROMAN CATHOLIC PERSPECTIVES:
MOVING TOWARDS A GLOBAL MISSION

Carmelo Dotolo

The missionary movement today is experiencing a period of change. It is not just about changing models in the theory and practice of mission; it is the acknowledgement that mission is an *event* that renews itself through dialogue with the world, culture and society. The need for sincere dialogue, in fact, is one of the most significant signs of the times, showing how mission is called on to operate a constant process of discernment, so that it can meet the demands of men and women of our times. This entails the strength to identify a *new paradigm*. It is no accident that mission today is becoming increasingly *global*. It must live within the confines of the different cultures, within geographical spaces that are becoming ever closer in the struggle for a worldwide ethics, in the meeting with other religions. Mission is the place where humanity invokes the right to life and to better quality in relationships.

This framework requires a redefinition of the objectives of missionary reflection and practice. It is no longer a case of thinking, reflecting and operating within the context of a Christian society or of aspiring to a form of Christianization which, for many, appears like proselytism. Rather, the focus should be on promoting *processes of liberation and salvation according to the criteria of the Kingdom* proclaimed and practiced by Jesus and by the first Christian communities.

Missions and the Signs of the Times

To maintain that the theology of mission is engaged in rethinking its identity, with respect to both theoretical reflection and pastoral practice, is nothing new. It could not be otherwise, because it is a specific aspect of the Christian event to consider oneself constantly a part of the historical process, which means translating the innovations introduced by the Gospels into the lives of men and women who are searching for the meaning of life. The importance of enculturation, therefore, is a characteristic trait of the mission of the Church. The Church looks at the rhythmic flow of time with the attention of one whose task it is to account for the revelation as the sign that directs the course of history in a different way.

Yet it is also known that the relationship between the Gospels and culture, the Church and the world, is not the result of a humanitarian *marketing* operation, or a rebalancing act within a system of religious, political and cultural forces. Instead, it is the laborious development of a relationship between the project of the Kingdom and the human being's desire to build a more dignified and better world in which to live. Therefore, no mission can be conceived without an appropriate focus on the signs of the times. Today the issues that rise from the different visions of life, humankind and the world require genuine intentionality of mission.

This is the groundwork for understanding the creative tension that animates the self-understanding of missiology, regardless of whether a change of paradigm is taking place or the dynamics of evangelization are being overhauled. The history of the 20th century does not just bring to the fore the paradoxical appeal of the Christian project, but also lifestyles, models of thought, and ethical criteria that, inspired by the *kerygma*, challenge horizons as we know them; demanding project-making autonomy and decision-making freedom. In this state of affairs, the indication of a crisis of the Christian message is not marginal, because it affects the capacity of Christianity to build its own future and, consequently, its missionary capability. The question, therefore, concerns the problematic nature of certain ways of translating the meaning of mission and its legitimacy, in relation to the assumption that every culture and religion contains a response to the concerns of humankind. The reason lies in the complexity of the new 'areopagoses' or market places. In particular, we are faced with a cultural plurality that highlights the importance of *alterity* and of *difference*. We are at a delicate and crucial crossroads: pluralism represents the cultural atmosphere of our times, the vital context in which stable convictions, ingrained principles and criteria capable of generating consensus and mobilization are all mixed up. The impact is not indifferent compared to certain *standards* of evangelization and pathways of pastoral training or to the interpretation of certain philosophical and theological categories. In short, today, no theological and missiological reflection is possible without the perception of the claims of pluralism and without understanding certain trajectories that affect the possibility of announcing the Gospels. Pluralism is modifying the *structures of plausibility* of culture, revealing the face of a necessary relativism, which, at the same time, is not separate from an aggressive relativism, which seems to translate *anything goes* into a theorem. At the same time it has changed the way in which we look at the role and meaning of the religious experience within the context of human existence. What counts is the indication of a religious meaning appropriate to the needs of the human person. The reflection on pluralism and mission should be viewed against the backdrop of these issues.

Missiology and Alterity

A significant aspect of alterity is the religious universe, with its multiplicity of languages, rites, and ethical codes. Most people now accept the fact that the religious experience is no longer indifferent to culture. Humans give shape to their experience by means of signs, symbols and models which belong within a certain context (whether geographical, economic or religious), and according to the rules of *historical memory*. This selects, passes on and develops the cultural elements of the past so that they can be reprocessed and delivered to the future by both individuals and society as a whole, including the risk of altering these elements. Now, the understanding of culture and the focus on interculturality – as a dimension of evangelization – require that we make an effort to interpret the *meanings* that humankind has woven and the *core symbols* around which culture is organized. Among these, *religion* emerges as the constituent element of the system; some would even go so far as to say the foundational element or, in any case, of decisive importance for culture, to the point that interpreting religion is understanding culture, and vice versa. Regardless of the various positions and interpretations with respect to the religious dimension, it presents itself as a form of knowledge producing action and hope; as the assertion of an original order that embraces humankind and the world and supports and brings light into life.

Despite this, it is precisely in the interpretation of religion that pluralism has assumed a leading role. It has become the key issue of the current missiological reflection and practice, starting from the core issue of the Christological understanding of revelation.[1] This claim, however, constitutes an embarrassing stumbling block for the standard-bearers of pluralism in the dialogue of religion. The reason for this is the surprising peculiarity of the incarnation which shows the previously unseen dimension of both God and humans. Yet that which constitutes an obstacle and a problem could represent the condition for a respectful and authentic encounter with the other religions. The advent of Jesus Christ has given Christianity both the opportunity for and the necessity of experiencing the relationship with the other religions as a free gift of the innovation represented by the combination of the revelation of God and the singular story of Jesus Christ.

It is precisely the singularity of the story of Jesus Christ that interprets the universal nature of Christianity and allows an open attitude to every culture and religion. This means that the universal nature of the revelation of God – expressed in the historical concreteness of Jesus Christ – is not a religious *a priori* but a given, an event that belongs to history and which allows a different assessment to be made of religious pluralism. Therefore, it is based on this event, and on the encounter with the other revelations,

[1] Cf. C. Dotolo, *Un cristianesimo possibile. Tra postmodernità e ricerca religiosa*, (Giornale di Teologia, 324: Brescia: Queriniana 2007).

that we can grasp the pathway inaugurated by God's project of salvation. The novelty introduced by Christianity consists in the fact that the revelation has achieved its peak in God's historical communication and giving of himself through his son, Jesus Christ. This is the claim of the revelation and the promise of God which has already been realized in the Paschal mystery, but which is yet to come (already and not yet). This *not yet* condition is unquestionably a part of God's plan, but it is also up to the human being's free decision to make the truth that is Jesus Christ its own. From this perspective, Christ and the Holy Spirit are related to the universal history of humankind, albeit in differing degrees. This means that the Christian revelation is not just an event that gives space to the other and sets him free, but it is also open to the future, as the manifestation of his most intimate reality.

A possibility emerges based on this: the Christian message, in its opening to the anthropological universal, is capable of collaborating with the other religions to rethink their respective identities, within the context of a mutual dialogue that aims not at eliminating them, but at pointing the way to a more fruitful overall unity, outside each one's fence. In other words, one can grasp – in the opening up of religions to the Mystery – a possible call to meet up with the innovation inherent in the Christological revelation, at a time in which the message and the practice of Jesus encourage one to rethink the meaning and form of the religious experience. With his style of life, he wants us to explore our lives in a significant way. Jesus Christ carries within him *something more*, because he is a person who reveals and saves, starting from the claim of being the truth of both God and humankind. It is precisely this claim which we must face up to and measure ourselves on.

It is unthinkable, therefore, for mission to place between brackets the uniqueness of Jesus Christ, in which the Church experiences its tension *ad gentes* and the very reason for its existence in history. The Church's witness is called to a *qualitative mission*, to be a critical and propositional interpreter of the values of the Gospels. It is precisely in the pedagogical attention to evangelization, as an announcement and as the transformation of history, that we can understand the increasingly urgent need of a pastoral catechesis capable of tackling the challenge of pluralism.

The Creative Tension of the Mission

Pluralism, after all, is a *chance* for the missionary movement, because it invites people to perceive alterity and diversity as a possible meeting place and a space for solidarity. The evangelizing mission of the Church, therefore, exercises a *creative tension*. It springs from the need to state afresh the question that Jesus asked of his disciples: *"Who do you say I am?"* (Matt 16,15), to discover – in the form of the *agape* as the total gift – a style of announcing the Gospels that correlates, albeit critically at times, the reality of the Christian message and the reality of the religious traditions. At the same time, however, it highlights how the alterity of the Gospel highlights a process of enculturation of faith, through the acceptance of the models and paradigms of the cultures which it penetrates. The prospective is to create opening *questions* and to offer a value to the salvation process already under way, with a focus on the human condition, with its aspirations, expectations and suffering. In the Gospel message there is a potential *unicum* of *humanization* which gives the Church the boldness to offer an alternative model, capable of making the Earth more hospitable and humankind a more livable community. It is for this reason that the Christian community, as a sign of a countercultural lifestyle, can exercise a critical role with respect to the obvious dehumanization of humankind and the instability introduced by globalization. If the objective of mission is to announce the singular revelatory nature of Jesus Christ and to humanize, in accordance with the values of the Kingdom, then we can identify the following elements:

a) *The religious factor* is decisive in helping people grasp the transcendent meaning in history, the closeness of God, who invites every man and woman to freedom, justice and salvation. Faced with the temptation of a religion made for its own use and consumption, or a religion incorrectly focused on mere mental and physical well-being, it is expedient to teach people a style of faith that focuses on liberation. Spirituality itself must become a criticism of every false spiritualism. This is where the ecumenical dialogue between the religions fits in.

b) *The social factor*. The missionary proclamation must constantly focus on and aim at discovering the other, without whom no genuine experience of growth and collaboration is possible. It is necessary to re-iterate a sensitivity that is already a part of the current missionary practice: attention to the poor, minorities (immigrants, women, young people, etc), people who live with concrete material needs and with the need to be listened to. In particular, it is necessary to be able to live and promote an *intercultural style*.

c) *The cultural dimension*. We should not be naive: there is a cultural, scientific, mass media world, the presence and influence of which is significant for perceiving and interpreting reality. Whether right or wrong, it is through these channels that models of behaviour and ethical values are passed on, which then condition the day-to-day lives of many people. To interact with these new opinion-making and trend-setting worlds means to identify new strategies and tasks (ministries) capable of modifying certain ideas and practices of the missionary movement.

The Importance of Dialogue

Mission, therefore, is openness to dialogue. We can grasp the signs of the Spirit in the different religious traditions and the plurality of cultures. This is why a dialogic spirituality in the world of religious pluralism requires a *confessional humility* that is capable of fuelling equality between the parties and enhancing the convinction that the other is a gift that can enrich us. This horizon is a fixed point in magisterial and theological reflection. The importance of dialogue, as a style and a tool for an open meeting, constitutes one of the key issues of rethinking the mission of the Church in relation to the other religions. The encyclical *Redemptoris Missio* by John Paul II (1990) and the documents issued by the Pontifical Council for Interreligious Dialogue – *Dialogue and Mission* (1984) and *Dialogue and Proclamation* (1991)[2] – emphasize that dialogue should permeate the existence of believers and communities: religions have played and still play 'a providential role in the divine economy of salvation' (*Dialogue and Proclamation,* n. 17), and the opening up to the faith of the other implies the capacity to share his vision of the world, with a sympathy that is prior to understanding. One's belonging cannot constitute an obstacle, nor determine the relevance of the interpersonal encounter, just like our convictions must be set aside when they are inadequate for understanding the other. This is why the ecclesial communities must experience the style of the dialogue within mission, which basically means 'to transform that humanity from within, making it new' (*Dialogue and Proclamation*, n. 8). If dialogue can produce mutual knowledge and enrichment it is because it makes us able to change, to experience the event of *conversion* as an opening up to the meeting with truth, which the Spirit donates when accompanying any meeting that wants to go to the heart of the problem. It is obvious, however, that the style of the dialogue requires us to rethink the way we consider and experience religion, because where religious experience is insensitive towards the search of a reliable meaning of life, when it violates the dignity of men and women, resorting to unbending and fundamentalist positions, it loses its truest purpose: that of promoting freedom and the exercise of the common good. It is no accident that where there is no *religious freedom*, as stated in the Declaration *Dignitatis humanae*, then one of the decisive preconditions – dialogue itself – is no more.

Therefore, the following two points are important:

a) *The dynamics of interculturality.* A decision that can no longer be postponed concerns the *dialogic meeting of cultures*, despite the objections that intercultural dialogue is the harbinger of a certain cultural relativism. To meet with a different culture is an event that can enable people to come face to face with a different way of thinking, which can, at times, if not often, be radically different. Yet we cannot neglect this aspect if we wish to dialogue in a responsible manner on the questions of life. Therefore, we

---

[2] See Pontifical Council for Interreligious Dialogue, *Dialogo Interreligioso nell'insegnamento ufficiale della Chiesa Cattolica dal Concilio Vaticano II a Giovanni Paolo II (1963- 2005)*, edited by F. Gioia, (Vatican City : LEV: 2006).

should not be surprised to learn that *interculturality* does not just mean welcoming the other; it also creates a conflict in understanding because it leads towards the construction of a new form of civil coexistence. Within these coordinates Christianity aims at building a new culture, capable of focusing on dignity and on rights, especially of those who are excluded and marginalized as a result of imperialist policies.

b) *Ecumenism and interreligious dialogue*. Religions must learn how to cooperate in the construction of a new world of rights and duties. This requires a great degree of maturity. The principle of religious freedom and equality is no longer sufficient although it is still decisive. We need a new style of cooperation between states and religions. It is true that, in the profound crisis of recent years, the forceful demand for an identity and symbols in which one can recognize oneself, has boosted religious membership and religious values. The focus on the social, cultural and political dimension of religion, however, should include all the religions; otherwise there is a risk of recreating ideological blocks and discrimination between strong and well-rooted religious groups and new religious movements, religious minorities and other religions. This highlights the importance of rediscovering the ecumenical tension and interreligious dialogue as a means for creating the conditions for acceptance and discussion with respect to functional goals within a more just society, more attentive to the needs of everybody.

An Orthodox Perspective: Moving Among Other Faiths

Petros Vassiliadis, Niki Papageorgiou and Nikos Dimitriadis

The overall approach of the Eastern Orthodox Church to people of other faiths grows out of her theology. The importance of theology, nevertheless, does not necessarily mean surrender to a "theology from above". After all, as St. Maximos the Confessor has insisted, a theology without action is a theology of the Devil. There are three distinctive characteristics of the Eastern Orthodox theology which determine the Church's attitude toward the other religions: her *ecclesiological* awareness, the *pneumatological* dimension of her understanding of the Holy Trinity, and her teaching of *theosis*.

The Orthodox Church – without setting aside her conviction that she is "the One, Holy, Catholic and Apostolic Church", and her task to witness to the whole Gospel to the whole world; without forgetting that her Lord Jesus Christ is "*the* way, *the* truth and *the* life" (Jn 14:6) – humbly believes that although she is the authentic bearer of the apostolic tradition, she is only a simple servant in the "mission" of the Triune God. This conviction is the result of the "economy of the Holy Spirit". According to this dimension of Trinitarian theology – for centuries marginalized in the West – the Holy Spirit, the *"Spirit of Truth,"* which leads us to the *"whole truth"* (Jn 16:13), *"blows wherever He/She wills"* (Jn 3:8), thus embracing the whole of cosmos.

The Orthodox, therefore, believe that God uses not only the Church, but many other powers of the world for his mission for the salvation of humankind and the entire creation. With this contribution the theological vision becomes wider, and the missionary task transcends to new, previously unimaginable areas of action: the emphasis is no longer placed on mere proselytist activities, but on full scale conversion of both the Christian evangelizers, and those to whom the witness is rendered. In this way, a total transformation occurs and the implementation of God's Rule becomes a reality, since, according to the biblical *Magna Carta* (Mt 25), God judges humanity with criteria other than the conventional religious ones. With the "economy of the Spirit" the narrow boundaries of the

Church are widened, and the cultural (and religious) superiority syndromes give place to a "common witness" and a humble "inter-faith dialogue".

However, the Orthodox never dissociate the "economy of the Spirit" from the "economy of Christ/the Word", her Pneumatology never overshadows Christology; rather it is conditioned in a dynamic way by Pneumatology. Defining *missio Dei* on the basis of John 21, the Orthodox believe that God in his own self is a life of *communion,* and that God's involvement in history (and consequently our missionary task) aims at drawing humanity, and creation in general, into this communion with God's very life. This ultimate expression of *koinonia* and love through this kind of "inter-faith" encounter is transferred to the whole world, not as dogmas or ethical commands, but as a communion of love.

This openness toward the faithful of other religions is also reinforced by the unique Orthodox anthropology, developed especially by the Byzantine Orthodox theologians of the second millennium, and expressed in such terms as *theosis* or *deification.* This Orthodox theological doctrine is the result of the Christian doctrine of *incarnation;* it was a further elaboration of the *justification by faith* notion, and St. Athanasius' famous dictum: "God became man, so that human beings may become gods (acquire *theosis*)". According to this dynamic theology the human nature in the Orthodox Byzantine tradition is not a closed, autonomous entity (as it was believed in the post-Augustinian western Christianity, which was trapped by the static dichotomy of "nature"-"grace"), but a dynamic reality, determined in its very existence by its relationship to God. Guided by a vision of how to "know" God, to "participate" in His life, and, of course, to be "saved" neither by an extrinsic action of God nor through the rational cognition of propositional truths (contrary to the medieval scholastic views), but by "becoming God", this soteriological notion is much more inclusive to non-Christians than the old conventional exclusivist mission theology of Western Christianity. Together with the *relational* understanding of the "social" (Cappadocian) Trinity, the Orthodox permanent task of *theosis* – a task, but at the same time a "given" at God's creation of humans in His "image" – is neither a neo-platonic return to an impersonal One, nor a replacement of the biblical (Pauline) *justification by faith,* but a true continuation of the biblical expressions of life "in Christ" and "in communion of the Holy Spirit".

This *pneumatological* and *deification* understanding of mission has nothing to do with *syncretism*. Those who believe in the importance of inter-faith dialogue, mainly on the basis of the "economy of the Spirit" – and the Orthodox also on the basis of the anthropology of *deification* – insist that the mutual respect and peaceful relations and co-existence with faithful of other beliefs (or even non-believers) do not by any means lead to the naïve affirmation that *all religious are the same*. On the contrary, the dialogue and the co-operation are necessary, exactly because the various religious traditions are different and promote different visions of the reality.

In inter-faith dialogue the encounter between religions (i.e. between *faithful* of different religions) is understood as an "encounter of mutual commitments and responsibilities" towards the common goal of humanity, to restore communion with God, and thus restoring the rule of God "on earth as it is in heaven".

This kind of Christian witness does not aim at the creation of a new "pan-religion", or a new "world religion", as it is quite naively claimed by ultra-conservatives from all Christian confessions, but would inevitably lead to a "communion of faithful from different religious traditions". After all, this is the ultimate goal of the divine economy, as it is clearly stated in Scripture (cf. Eph 1:10, Col 3:11 etc).

This endeavor not only decreases the enmity and the hostilities between people of different religions; it is also a call to the faithful to engage strongly in social development. Above all it makes the "other" a partner in mission, not an "object" of mission. Viewing the faithful of other religions as co-workers in God's mission, the Christian *synergetically* assists in the realization of the work of the Holy Spirit for a new world order, a new world economy based on the biblical truth that the "land belongs to the Lord" and caring for the "fullness of life", i.e. a global communion of love, which transcends his/her personal as well as cultural and ethnic *ego*. The common Christian witness unceasingly promotes the salvific power of God through Jesus Christ, but does not obliterate God's dynamic involvement through the Holy Spirit into the whole created world. It is a useful means to carry out the unity within a more and more divided world.

The place of Orthodoxy, as all preeminent Orthodox theologians insist, is not on the margin of history, but at the center of social change, as a pioneer agent in the reconciling work of the Holy Spirit. Mission is conceived by the Orthodox as a response to the call of the Triune God for a common journey and a participation in the love of God. Hence the importance it gives to a *martyria-mission* – which extends even to *martyrdom* – and to the doxological praise of God in liturgy. For the Orthodox, the liturgy is not only a springboard for mission (that is why they call it *liturgy after the liturgy* – which can also mean that mission is *a liturgy before the actual liturgy),* but a proleptic manifestation of God's Kingdom and an offering and thanksgiving for the *oikoumene,* in fact, for the entire world, regardless of religious convictions.

If one surveys the diverse religio-cultural contexts of various Eastern Orthodox Churches (but also the non-Chalcedonian Oriental Orthodox Churches) one can observe that there is a long history of peaceful co-existence between Orthodox and people of other religions. When the Crusaders in the Middle Ages launched that dreadful campaign to liberate the Holy Land, they accused the Orthodox of "being too tolerant toward the Muslims".

The Indian example is even more telling, certainly deserving special mention. India is the home of major religions like Hinduism, Buddhism,

Jainism and Sikhism, and despite this there is no historical incident of any real conflict between Christianity and the other faiths. The life and historical memory of a genuinely Indian and Oriental Church like the Malankara Orthodox Church, for instance, would illustrate the peaceful co-existence and good relations between Christianity and other religions in India. Ironically the Orthodox in India experienced oppression and persecution for the first time in their history, not from Hindus or Buddhists but from the colonial Portuguese Christian (Roman Catholic) authorities in the 16th century. And in addition, this colonial Western Catholic mission divided the Indian Church which was one and united until that time.

Indian Christianity maintained naturally the uniqueness of its Orthodox faith while in social and cultural matters it was fully inculturated in the indigenous Indian context. Furthermore, the profound philosophical-spiritual-ethical context of Hindu, Buddhist and Jain religions provided support for the spiritual-ethical ethos of the Orthodox Christianity. There had always been a dialogue of life and an underlying, though not always articulated, feeling of fraternity, mutual respect and a sense of common ground between Orthodox Christianity and the major religions of India. The old "western" aggressive "mission paradigm" with its brutal and intolerant attitudes (from the Roman Catholic and the Protestant missions) did a lot of harm in India. As a consequence, in recent years many contemporary Indian theologians attempt to draw from the wealth of the Indian philosophical and spiritual tradition and the long legacy of mutual respect and openness experienced by the Orthodox presence.[1]

[1] The last two paragraphs were added by the Oriental Orthodox theologian, Fr. K.M. George who also subscribes to the theological argument of the rest of the chapter.

A PENTECOSTAL PERSPECTIVE:
CHALLENGES, CONTRIBUTIONS AND COMMITMENT OF PENTECOSTALS IN MISSIONARY WORK AMONG OTHER FAITHS

Julie C. Ma

Introduction

From the beginning of the twentieth century the modern Pentecostal movement has been primarily a missionary movement. Its exponential growth and global expansion in diverse forms attest to this. Its expression is found not only among Pentecostal churches such as the Assemblies of God and the Zion Church in South Africa, but also in almost every church tradition in the world today. Pentecostals have traditionally concentrated on evangelism and church planting as their missionary work since its inception.

At the same time there have been signs of changes in the Pentecostals' mission engagement. Shifting their mission paradigm was needed because of rising needs in society. Although the emphasis on proclamation with the resultant establishment of local congregations remains strong, the scope of mission engagement now includes what is called diakonic dimension, or care for the needy in society. And there is no doubt that such a change in mission attitude and engagement is viewed as a positive development in inter-church and inter-religious relations.

In order for us to identify unique challenges that Pentecostals face from other religious communities, it is important to probe what makes Pentecostals assume their distinct missionary approaches. For example: From what theological resources do they draw their motivation for its unique perspective of mission? I will briefly look at several areas of Pentecostal mission engagement with social issues beyond its traditional evangelism and church planting;[1] and I will present Pentecostal's unique challenges in mission particularly in relation to other religions. This study has one main question to ask: What is the Pentecostals' unique challenge

[1] Wonsuk Ma, 'The Spirit and Mission: Two Ripples of Pentecostal Mission', *Lausanne World Pulse* (Http://www.lausanneworldpulse.com/themedarticles.php/925, April 4, 2008)" calls this the second ripple of Pentecostal mission.

and contribution to inter-religious relations while they continue their commitment to Christian mission?

Theological Motivation for Pentecostal Mission

Out of several commonly identified theological capitals of Pentecostal mission, two are discussed here: pneumatology and eschatology.

Baptism of the Holy Spirit

Although the exact language used in reference to the work of the Holy Spirit differs, the role of the Holy Spirit in motivating believers in mission has commonly been held. For example, William Seymour, the leader of the Azusa Street Mission, made it clear that the experience of the Holy Spirit, especially baptism in the Spirit, was not the end in itself but a means to mission: "Now, do not go from this meeting and talk about tongues, but try to get people saved."[2]

Although the Holiness branch of early North American Pentecostalism linked the baptism in the Spirit to the sanctifying work of the Holy Spirit, an increasing number of later Pentecostals interpreted this unique experience of the Holy Spirit as empowerment of power for mission based on Acts 1:8. Charles Parham, the other Pentecostal pioneer who predated Seymour, even advocated that tongues were a missionary language, supernaturally equipped by the Holy Spirit to expedite the end-time harvest.[3]

Urgency of Christ's Return as Motivation for Missionary Urgency

This missionary movement rooted in its emphasis on the Holy Spirit's empowerment was augmented by temporal urgency. *The Apostolic Faith*, the publication of the Azusa Street Mission, provides several enlightening glimpses of the early Pentecostal eschatological paradigm. Here is one example:

> There is no man at the head of this movement. God himself is speaking in the earth. We are on the verge of the greatest miracle the world has ever seen, when the sons of God shall be manifested, the saints shall come singing from the dust (Isaiah 26:19) and the full overcomers shall be caught up to meet the Lord in the air: The political world realizes that some great crisis is at hand,

---

[2] Quoted in Stanley H. Frodsham, *With Signs Following: The Story of the Latter-Day Pentecostal Revival* (Springfield, MO: Gospel Publishing House, 1946), 38.

[3] James R. Goff, Jr., *Fields White Unto Harvest: Charles F. Parham and the Missionary Origins of Pentecostalism* (Fayetteville: University of Arkansas Press, 1988), 15-16, 72-75. See also J. Roswell Flower, 'Editorial', *The Pentecost* (August 1908), 4; quoted in Gary B. McGee, *This Gospel Shall Be preached,* vol. 1 (Springfield, MO: Gospel Publishing House, 1986), 45-46.

> the scientific world, the religious world all feel it. The coming of the Lord draweth nigh; it is near, even at the doors.[4]

At least two elements of the day contributed to this eschatological urgency. The first is a pre-millennial version of the last days, commonly held among the Holiness branches of North American evangelicalism. The return of the Lord coincides with the rapture of his church before the seven years of tribulation. An unprecedented missionary work, or a 'great harvest' will precede this historical climax, and the special endowment of spiritual power found its theological justification. For this reason, the contemporary advent of the Spirit was popularly called the 'latter rain' in contrast to the original outpouring of the Spirit recorded in Acts 2. The second is the general mood of the age as the clock ticked toward the new century.[5]

Social Engagement in Pentecostal Mission

In general, evangelical mission has expanded the scope of its mission engagement to include the social dimension. The most visible turning point is the adoption of the Lausanne Covenant, which declares proclamation and social service as 'partners' of mission.[6] Although the exact relationship between the two and the issue of priority have been hotly discussed since the Lausanne Conference in 1974, evangelicals steadily explore various social issues as part of their mission agenda, and they include poverty, social injustice, children at risk, disaster relief and others.[7]

Pentecostals, partly riding this change in evangelical mission thinking and practice, and partly with the waning expectation of, and emphasis on, the imminent return of the Lord, began to expand their mission scope. Recently a handful of Pentecostal missiologists formulated a theological

---

[4] 'Pentecost Has Come' *The Apostolic Faith* 1:1 (Sept. 1906), 1. See also 26 in article, Grant McClung, 'Try To Get People Saved: Azusa "Street Missiology"' in *Azusa Street and Beyond*, ed., Grant McClung (Gainesville, Florida: Bridge-Logos, 2006), 1-26. It explains, *The Apostolic Faith* was published from the Azusa Street Mission by William J. Seymour and Florence Louise Crawford. Five thousand copies of the first issue were distributed. Only thirteen issues were published from Los Angeles before Crawford moved to Portland, Oregon, to establish with the Apostolic Faith movement in the Northwest. The last issue was dated May 1908.

[5] Vinson Synan, *The Spirit Said 'Grow': The Astounding Worldwide Expansion of Pentecostal and Charismatic Churches* (Monrovia, CA: MARC, 1992), 39-48. See also Julie Ma, 'Pentecostalism and Asian Mission', *Missiology: An International Review* 35:1 (Jan 2007), 23-37.

[6] It is found in various places, for example, on http://www.lausanne.org/covenant.

[7] For a passionate plea to evangelicals to incorporate 'justice' issues, see, for example, Ronald Sider, *Evangelicalism and Social Action in a Lost and Broken World* (London: Hodder & Stoughton, 1993).

basis for such mission engagement, sometimes with the encouragement of 'radical evangelicals.'[8]

Teen Challenge

The ministry of Teen Challenge grew out of the burning vision of David Wilkerson, an Assemblies of God pastor, to bring transformation to troubled youths. The brutal murder of an innocent man by eighteen teen gang members was headline news for months. This incident challenged Wilkerson to seriously expand his view of mission to address social issues such as this. In 1957 Teen Challenge was born in New York as a residential drug rehabilitation program, and today it has become one of the world's most successful drug recovery programs. The life-changing impact of the ministry has been popularized through *The Cross and Switchblade*, both in print and in a movie.[9]

The genius of the ministry lies in its duplicability in various forms and in diverse socio-cultural contexts. Since the first Teen Challenge training center pioneered in Rehrersburg, Pennsylvania in June of 1962, other centers opened in Chicago, Boston, Dallas, Philadelphia, San Francisco, and Los Angeles. These new Teen Challenge ministries were pioneered by people who had read *The Cross and the Switchblade*, or from just a simple visit to a Teen Challenge center. Today Teen Challenge operates the international ministry known as Global Teen Challenge across many countries.[10]

In 1976, the federal government funded a research project that confirmed that over 70% of the graduates of Teen Challenge are maintaining a drug-free life.[11] It makes Teen Challenge one of the most successful programs to free people from drug addiction.

Calcutta Mercy Ministries

A missionary couple, Mark and Huldah Buntain, came to Calcutta in 1954 with their one-year old daughter. Calcutta was a desperate city crowded with around 18 million people, 80% of who lived in slums. There were 1,000 people to every toilet and 5,000 to every drinking fountain. Hulda Buntain later recalled her early impression of the city:

---

[8] 'Brussels Statement on Evangelization and Social Concern, produced by the Brussels Consultation of the Division of Foreign Missions of the Assemblies of God', *Transformation* 16:2 (1999), 41-43.

[9] 'Mass Murder of a Teen-age Gang in New York', Life Magazine (Feb. 24, 1958), 30-31. Vol. 28 (2008), 5.

[10] David Batty and Ethan Campbell, *Teen Challenge*: *Assemblies of God Heritage*, Vol. 28 (2008), 17, 19.

[11] David Batty and Ethan Campbell, *Teen Challenge,* 17.

> ...Clapboard hovels, street vendors, beggars, half-naked children, and an estimated 40,000 human rickshaws fill the roads. Epidemics do not discriminate, snatching the lives of young and old. Cholera, Typhoid, Tetanus, and more keep hospitals and mortuaries busy.[12]

The Buntains lived for 40 years where the poverty, diseases and dangers threatened every life including theirs. Their commitment and love for the suffering Indians motivated them to carry on a feeding ministry for 20,000 women and children each day. Besides, they were involved in educating 10,000 children, managing a hospital that thousands rely on for survival, and planting churches in far-flung villages. These works continued even after Mark's death, through the courage of Huldah.

Other Social Works

Pentecostal churches have also been involved in other social ministries such as caring for HIV/AIDS patients, sex workers, prisoners and others. Sam Mugote, senior pastor of Deliverance Church in Uganda and his associates have trained small groups of 10-15 people in hundreds of churches in HIV/AIDS pastoral care. It is estimated that more than 7,000 AIDS patients and their families were ministered to by these trained workers.

In Bangkok and Calcutta, several Pentecostal churches and mission groups are involved in ministry among sex workers. Often industry agents and syndicates approach the parents of girls who are normally between twelve and thirteen years old with an offer of a cash advance and with a promise of good jobs in large cities for their daughters. However, almost without exception, they are taken to brothels to be sold to the sex industry. Hope Church in Bangkok, for example, began a residential school in partnership with a Swedish Pentecostal church to minister to women rescued from prostitution or a sex slave market.[13]

Pentecostal Mission Among Other Faiths: The Reflective Level

As briefly mentioned, Pentecostal mission was fueled by two theological sources: pneumatology and eschatology. With the waning of eschatological urgency that once drove Pentecostal mission, such requires a serious revisioning of its mission basics. This process of theological revision will also afford Pentecostals an opportunity to identify their theological

---

[12] Huldah Buntain, *Woman of Courage* (Tyndale House Publishers: Wheaton, Illinois, 1984), 22.

[13] Donald E. Miller and Tetsunao Yamanori, *Global Pentecostalism: The New Face of Christian Social Engagement,* (Berkeley: University of California Press, 2007), 121-122.

traditions which may hinder their peaceful coexistence with people of other faiths.

What is Mission?

It is not just Pentecostals who have recently been challenged with this fundamental question. The century-old crusade model shares its ethos with the western colonial past with Christendom ideology. For Pentecostals, 'witnessing' is the most popular description of Christian mission, and they base this on the model of the book of Acts.

Several suggestions have been made for Pentecostal mission to rethink its mission basics. The first attempt is to explore the biblical basis of Pentecostal mission in a broader theological platform than narrowly defined pneumatological missiology based on Acts 1:8. Two examples may suffice to illustrate this possibility. An Asian Pentecostal theologian proposed such a basis in the book of Genesis, particularly the role of the Spirit of God in creation theology.[14] Setting the goal of mission as the restoration of God's creation intent, it can open Pentecostal mission to a much wider horizon, including social engagement and environmental issues. At the same time, the role of the Spirit of God, or the Holy Spirit in creation, its maintenance and transformation, is at the center of mission reflection. The second example came from a renowned Pentecostal New Testament scholar. Gordon Fee proposes the theology of God's kingdom as a suitable ground for Pentecostal mission.[15]

As a movement of the socially and economically poor, the movement began as a religion of transformation and this story has been replicated all over the world since then.[16] One such example is the theological bases for the Latin American Child Care, which has not only provided quality Christian education to many economically deprived children, but also contributed to the transformation of numerous societies throughout Latin America.[17] Such scholarly reflection covers many 'new' mission areas, and

---

[14] Wonsuk Ma, 'God's Creation: The Source for Mission in the Spirit', in *Med Kristus til Jordens Ender: Festskrift til Tormod Engelsviken,* eds., Kjell Olav Sannes, Egil Grandhagen, Terje Hegertun, Knud Jorgensen, Kristin Norseth, Rolv Olsen (Tronheim, Norway: Tapir Akademisk Forlag, 2008), 65-76.

[15] Gordon D. Fee, "The Kingdom of God and the Church's Global Mission," in *Called and Empowered: Global Mission in Pentecostal Perspective*, eds., Murray A. Dempster, Byron D. Klaus and Douglas Peterson (Peabody, Massachusetts: Hendrickson, 1991), 7-21.

[16] For the social upward mobility, which Pentecostalism created among the poor mass in Latin America, see David Martin, *Tongues of Fire: The Explosion of Protestantism in Latin America* (Oxford UK and Cambridge MA: Blackwell, 1990), 77-78.

[17] Douglas Petersen, *Not By Might Nor By Power: A Pentecostal Theology of Social Concern in Latin America* (Oxford, UK: Regnum, 1996), 199-200.

all engaging with social issues, including gender issues, ecumenism, ecology and others. The accumulation of such studies will be an important resource in revisioning and articulating the holistic understanding of Pentecostal mission.

Pentecostal Theology of Religions

Fundamentally Pentecostals have an extremely simplistic understanding of non-Christian religions: they are territories of evil spirits. Their extreme dualistic worldview quickly divides their world between godly and evil, and every domain of evil is a spiritual battleground. The warfare language recently developed by the Third Wave advocates is an outgrowth of this simplistic Pentecostal worldview.[18] With such an orientation and almost militantly aggressive evangelistic mode of mission, other faiths are easily demonized and almost never viewed as neighbours able to coexist with Christians in the same community.

When asked if the Holy Spirit operates outside of the church, an immediate response, without thinking, will be an affirmative 'No.' This is understandable as Pentecostal understanding of the fullness of the Spirit is still another stage beyond the work of the Spirit in regeneration. This naturally confines the sphere of the Spirit's work within the church among believers. This narrow understanding of the Spirit keeps Pentecostals from seeing an equally active role of the Spirit in creation for example, and this will require a close look at the Old Testament evidence.

Only recently, a serious academic inquiry was made by a young Pentecostal scholar. Pentecostal engagement with other religions at the theological level boils down to its unique pneumatological tradition. As in the case of the definition of mission, a pneumatological theology of creation, that is, a focused attention to the role of God's Spirit in creation may provide an important framework where the Pentecostal understanding of religions can be placed.

> ...Pentecostal intuitions regarding a world that is infused with the presence of the Spirit who has indeed been poured out on all flesh can not only reform, reshape, and renew our thinking about the nature of the material world and its relationship to God the creator but also to orient us to live appropriately in a world that is alive with the activity of the Spirit of God. Most importantly, because of the saving work of God includes redemption of the cosmos.[19]

[18] For example, C. Peter Wagner and F. Douglas Pennoyer, eds. *Wrestling with Dark Angeles: Toward a Deeper Understanding of the Supernatural Forces in Spiritual Warfare* (Ventura, CA: Regal Books, 1990) contains a useful interaction between Third Wave advocates and evangelicals.

[19] Amos Yong, 'The Spirit, World Pentecostalism, and the Renewal of Theology and Praxis in the 21st Century', *Journal for the Interdisciplinary Study of Pentecostalism Charismatic Movement*, 8:1 (2009), 15.

When Pentecostals are confronted with the question of the Spirit's operation outside of the church, they will immediately suspect the agenda of religious pluralism. Even if Pentecostals are finally persuaded that God's Spirit in creation is at work, including in every living thing, social unit and even cultures, Pentecostals know only too well that the next argument will be whether the Spirit also works in other religions. Their missionary impetus will further shut down any door of dialogue. It will require a more conducive and trusting environment for them to be able to see for themselves that the Holy Spirit is at work before regeneration through various channels, and this will help them see that the Spirit indeed works outside of the church. At the same time, Pentecostals will not compromise their firm conviction that there is no other name given than Jesus for salvation (Acts 4:12), and this has made them a powerful missionary people. Pentecostals also presents clearly a view of truth in religious pluralism.[20]

In this seemingly dialectic situation, Wolfhart Pannenberg's approach may be useful: working with the common dominant theme of universal truth. However, he also recognizes that there is a clash of "ultimate truth" presented by each religion against others. He, therefore, sharply opposes the older approach to the study of religions in which there was a search for a "common essence." [21] His risk may be then "placing all theological principles on the open market of public accountability."[22] For him, "a 'truth' that would be simply my truth and would not at least claim to be universal and valid for every human being could not remain true even for me. This consideration explains why Christians cannot but try to defend the claim of their faith to be true."[23]

One promising group of Pentecostal thinkers in inter-religious relations may be young Pentecostals in the global South, who live and practice their faith in daily interaction with people of other religions. With a more holistic worldview, they may be more open to a wider scope of the Spirit's presence and work.

---

[20] Veli-Matti Karkkainen, 'Doing Christ's Mission in the Pluralistic Context of Asia: A critical Dialogue With Some Asian Christologies', in *Asian Church and God's Mission: Studies Presented in the International Symposium on Asian Mission in Manila, January 2002*, eds., Wonsuk and Julie Ma (Manila: OMF Literature INC, 2003), 109-126.

[21] W. Pannenberg, *Anthropology in Theological Perspective* (Philadelphia: Westminster, 1985), 15.

[22] Carl E. Braaten, 'The Place of Christianity among the World Religions: Wolfhart Pannenberg's Theology of Religion and the History of Religions', in *The Theology of Wolfhart Pannenberg: Twelve American Critiques with an Autobiographical Response*, eds., Carl E. Braaten and Philip Clayton (Minneapolis: Augsburg, 1988), 287-312.

[23] Pannenberg, *Anthropology in Theological Perspective*, 15.

Potential Areas of Cooperation with Other Faiths

This section will sample several areas where Pentecostals develop their mission practice where cooperation with other religious groups is possible.

Disaster Relief

Disasters such as an earthquake are a common human challenge regardless of religious orientation. As the very human existence is threatened, the mobilization of every possible resource and immediacy of action are critical. In such an emergency situation, every religion has a unique value in promoting human well-being and flourishing regardless of cultural, religious or political orientations. Also most religions teach the virtue of altruism and self-sacrifice for the sake of others. With this commonality, and in the face of dire and large scale needs, religious groups and civic organizations are called on to cooperate with one another to maximize their contribution to the alleviation of human suffering.

Although such a situation provides a more likely opportunity for cooperation between other religious groups, it still takes many efforts in order to cross the religious divide. In the case of the tsunami crisis in eastern Indonesia, Muslim authorities had strict rules for Christian relief organizations to prevent any Christian evangelistic activity. However, after an initial period of relationship building, the efforts of Christian organizations were not only appreciated, but also sought after.

Poverty and Economic Injustice

Poverty has been the most pressing issue in the developing countries, the majority of whom happen to be in the traditional 'mission field.' International market economy usually puts small scale farmers and producers in the non-western world in a disadvantaged position in the sharing and distribution of the profits of their products and labor. Here is a painful reality:

> Coffee in Uganda represents 70-85% of foreign exchange earnings; few buyers for their products resulting in less competition; an imbalance in information between buyers and sellers: buyers are more aware of market trends; changes in technology and fashion swings; weak representation in the World Trade Organization, the G8 group of countries; reduction in Lower Income Countries' state capacity to plan, bargain and regulate on behalf of small producers. This all requires ethical guardians to fill the watchdog vacuum.[24]

[24] Chris Sugden, 'Fair Trade and Christian Mission: An Overview of Further Steps in Christian Witness in International Trade', *Transformation* 17:3 (July-September, 2000), 118.

There have been a variety of approaches to the issue, but the fair trade initiatives have gained momentum since the 1960s. Such an approach may serve as an example for possible inter-religious cooperation, as each religion has a global network of communities. Such structures can be used to create a grassroots movement to address unfair and discriminatory international trades. Pentecostals and various religious groups can join hands together to engage in the market in order to help those who are deprived to have a fairer share.[25] There is a Christian response called Traidcraft established in 1979 and similar programs are found in many places. Often a community of farmers in a developing area consists of different religious orientations, and a cooperative work is essential for the initiative to succeed.

Environmental Issues

This is one global issue that threatens everyone regardless of race, religion and economic status. Even at a local level, various civic and religious groups have to work together to find ways to protect our environment. It is important to remind ourselves that often Christians are blamed for today's environmental crisis. Lynn White, for example, argues, 'We shall continue to have a worsening ecological crisis until we reject the Christian axiom that nature has no reason for existence but to serve man [*sic*].... Christianity...insisted that it is God's will that man [*sic*] exploit nature for his proper ends.... Christianity bears a huge burden of guilt.[26] White's thesis has been criticised by both historians and theologians, but it has had a broad influence and has been much repeated.[27] Pentecostals and other religious groups should not stay silent. They need to bring awareness of our misconception that 'whatever the discoveries of science, whatever the rate at which we multiplied as a species, whatever the changes we made to our seas and landscape, we have believed that the world would stay much the same in all its fundamentals.'[28] Religious groups have also been guilty of leaving environmental issues to the hands of politicians and scientific communities. It is important for religious communities to raise a common voice for advocacy and proper action to protect the environment from further damage.

An open gold mine operation brought serious environmental damage to mountain villages in the northern Philippines, including dust, disappearance

---

[25] Chris Sugden, 'Fair Trade and Christian Mission', 118.

[26] L. White, 'The Historical Roots of Our Ecologic Crisis', *Science* 155: 1204-1207 (1967), 21.

[27] For example, Francis Schaeffer reprinted White's essay in its entirety in his Pollution and the Death of Man, London: Hodder & Stoughton, 1970, commenting favourably on it.

[28] This Common Inheritance: Britain's Environmental Strategy. Cm 1200. London: HMSO, 1990.

of water, trees and chemical pollution. Mostly animists, and some Christians including Catholics, the villagers fought a David-Goliath war with a huge multi-national company. With no government support, they approached a Pentecostal pastor to lead their cause. He quickly began to form a leadership group including various religious leaders. After a steady campaign, the government finally intervened and upheld the villagers' demand for an environmentally friendly operation. In the course of this struggle, various groups brought their unique resources, including expertise in education, governmental links, and even places and hospitality, for meetings.

Inter-religious cooperation is possible when at least two conditions are met: 1) a common issue that affects the whole community; 2) the common agenda without political element; and 3) religious groups with openness to different views and orientations and without a proselytizing agenda. There may be other fruitful areas for such cooperation, including children at risk and health issues such as HIV/AIDS.

Conclusion

In a realistic term, two things need to be mentioned as a way of conclusion. The first is openness. By definition, Pentecostals have chosen an extremely narrow theological and practical path. They are sometimes blamed for converting other Christians into their form of faith, not to mention people of other faiths. It is not just a matter of attitude, but more seriously a matter of theological belief, articulated or assumed, which drives one's action. For example, in an Islamophobic western environment, a meaningful reflection and action is hard to come by. For this reason, the role of emerging Pentecostal minds in the global South becomes essential. The second is action: with the entrepreneurial spirit of Pentecostal mission, various creative attempts can be devised and implemented, perhaps at a local level in the beginning but slowly expanding to a wider level.

In spite of much pressure that Pentecostals may feel to revise their thoughts and actions, there should be a clear self-understanding that Pentecostals are to remain uniquely Pentecostal in their belief and practice. They are not called to become someone else. Only then can Pentecostals offer their unique understanding of other faiths and their approach for peace, reconciliation and cooperation for the common good.

An Adventist Perspective: Mission to World Religions and Contemporary World Views

Ganoune Diop

Introduction

Trajectory

This essay is written with two objectives: one, to delineate the scope and content of the good news that is shared with adherents of world religions and philosophies; second, to point out the rationale for the need to develop an understanding of the inner logic of each world religion and worldview in order to present the gospel in a way that resonates with their own categories and core values while preserving the integrity of the biblical message.

The following assumptions have informed our approach: Each world religion is a unique world of thoughts irreducible to common grounds with other world religions and philosophies. While building bridges of understanding is necessary, and while respecting and honouring the dignity of every human being are incontrovertible components of biblical faith, uncritical generalizations of commonalities between world religions and philosophies tend to downplay the claims of Jesus Christ and do not do justice to the unique contributions claimed by each world religion and philosophy.

For example, if for the purpose of cordial interfaith relations one uncritically assumes without further clarification that Abraham is a common figure among monotheistic religions, one such shortcut deprives each monotheistic tradition of its unique perspective. The figure and functions of Abraham are delineated variously and for different reasons and purposes in each monotheistic religion. To say that all monotheistic religions are religions of the book is not very helpful, because each one of them defines revelation concerning both the revealer and the revealed, from different perspectives.[1] Strictly speaking, Christianity is not the religion of a book but rather of a person, Jesus Christ.

---

[1] See Jacques Ellul, *Islam and Judéo-christianisme*, (Paris: Presses Universitaires de France, 2006).

Moreover, even to postulate that Jesus Christ is a figure common to Christians and Muslims creates difficult interpretive issues. For Christians who worship Jesus, to hear people of other faiths say they respect Jesus while carefully stripping Him of allusions to his divine identity creates uneasiness in reference to their claims. Even the assumption that theological or ecclesiological concepts can be used and applied to people of other faiths without critical thinking may present some pitfalls. Words are caught in specific webs of ideas that provide boundaries for their intelligibility. Words extracted from their biblical roots and contexts, when provided with new settings where relations to other categories create new trajectories other than what the biblical writers intended, cannot form the basis of intelligent interfaith relations. Careful contextual studies, not just background studies, provide safeguards against transgressing the boundaries of meaning and significance specific to words or concepts usage in context. Blending belief systems creates entirely new systems depriving thereby each system of its uniqueness, coherence, and claims. Moreover, people who blend religions are not immune to being exclusivist in their claims.

Genuine respect for adherents of world religions, therefore, requires allowing them to define their religions on their own terms. Authentic dialogue takes place on the platform of openness to difference. Significant contributions from a Jewish world of thought have considerably enriched the conversation.[2] Truthfulness therefore, in relating to people of other faith traditions is the best platform for genuine encounters. Faithfulness to the content of biblical revelation is a safeguard against syncretistic alliances. In this respect, Lamin Sanneh pointed out that truth claims need not be "discontinuous with the demands of interfaith conversation."[3]

Presuppositions

First, except for radical agnostic positions, each world religion or philosophy provides a diagnosis of the human condition and predicament. Our assumption is that the biblical Christian faith offers a comprehensive diagnosis of human condition. Corollary to this premise, we postulate that in the Bible we do find a comprehensive solution to human problems, an antidote to all the woes, evils and sorrows that plague human existence.

Second: The good news as it relates to the person of Jesus Christ and in its comprehensive and multifaceted expressions as found in Judeo-Christian Scriptures is not the focus of the scriptures and traditions of other world

---

[2] Jonathan Sacks, *To Heal a Fractured World: The Ethics of Responsibility* (London, New York: Continuum, 2005), 32.

[3] Lamine Sanneh, quoted by George R. Sumner, *The First and the Last: The Claim of Jesus Christ and the Claims of Other Religious Traditions* (Grand Rapids: Eerdmans, 2004).

religions and philosophies. This absence justifies the necessity for mission to all peoples.

Third: All followers of Jesus Christ have been entrusted with a commission to confess and testify to the sovereignty of Jesus Christ in the totality of their lives. From an Adventist perspective, in consonance with the principles of the Reformation (Christ alone, Scripture alone, grace alone, faith alone and all glory to God) the commission to share the good news goes together with loyalty to the whole chain of biblical truths. Adventists further see this mandate as twofold: first, the proclamation of the everlasting good news in the context of the Three Angels' messages just prior to the Second Coming of Jesus Christ, and second, the restoration of a whole chain of biblical truths, understood as being the whole purpose of God. Key to these foci are justification by faith or participation in the benefits of Christ, truth as found in Scripture in reference to the understanding of who God is, who we are as humans, and truth in reference to the whole purpose of God for His creation which culminates in the establishment of his kingdom of righteousness, peace, justice, and everlasting fellowship in love.

The Ultimate Criteria for Evaluating World Religions and Relating to their Adherents

The Seventh-day Adventist mission endeavours are predicated upon two criteria for evaluating, for understanding, and for reaching out to adherents of world religions and philosophies, whether for cooperation for the betterment of human existence, whether for dialogue purposes to erode misunderstanding, or for testifying to Christ in creative ways.

Jesus Christ

The ways world religions and philosophies relate, consider, or ignore Jesus Christ, inform us not only on how to assess the validity of their claims but reveal pathways in regard to how to testify to Christ in meaningful ways to them. How they consider the revelation of God in Jesus Christ and His mission of salvation ultimately reveals the degree of their contributions to the need of humankind and creation as a whole.

From the perspective of the Apostle Paul, all thoughts are tested, measured, and brought captive to the obedience of Jesus Christ (2 Co. 10:5). This remains, for Adventists, the best way to do justice to an authentic assessment of world religions and philosophies.

In world religions, although one finds sympathetic portrayals of Jesus Christ, either his prerogatives are usurped or his dignity diminished.

Nevertheless world religions contain gems of truth or even hints or signposts pointing to Jesus. These are tools to build bridges. Despite the fact that the fullness of the revelation of Jesus Christ is not found outside the Bible, doctrinally and morally world religions express a deep longing for Christ because he is the desire of the ages and the fulfillment of all the promises of God, according to the Bible (2 Corinthians 1:20).

A significant declaration of a key figure in Adventism, Ellen G. White, is a fitting place to sense the pulse of key aspects of an Adventist view of non-biblical World religions. She states without equivocation that non-biblical world religions though they had great teachers, they all rob their adherents from genuinely contemplating the face of Jesus Christ. She states that "It is the gospel of the grace of God alone that can uplift the soul. The contemplation of the love of God manifested in His Son will stir the heart and arouse the powers of the soul as nothing else can." [4]

The Christian testimony consists in sharing with adherents of world religions and philosophies the claims of finality and sufficiency of the salvific revelation of God in Jesus Christ. The claims of Christ to provide a comprehensive solution to human predicament are the clear testimony of New Testament writings, especially the statement according to which he is the light of the world, the way, the truth, and the life, the bread, and the door, the resurrection. All these metaphors are indications of His unique divine status. The New Testament logic is predicated upon the fact that it takes God to reveal God, to forgive offenses against God, to cause humans to participate in the life of God, and be adopted as children of God.

Jesus' divine prerogatives are the reasons why he cannot be confined or ultimately accommodated to any human religious or philosophical category. There is something about him that always escapes the confines of our categorizations. The wineskins of world religions do not seem to be able to contain Him. All figurations always fall short. Religious, cultural, social, nationalist frames of reference cannot define Him. He was more than Jewish and Israelite. He belongs to all peoples. Social and political arenas are too circumscribed to specific places and people to do justice to His universal cause, claims and cosmic order. Religions that begin as quests from below cannot comprehend or fathom one from above. With Christ there is always something that exceeds and even transcends the boundaries of human perception, knowledge and experience. Words cannot adequately define Him. He is the creator of language and initiated communication (see the prologue of the Gospel of John).

The foundation of the edifice of the Christian witness is the revelation of God of communication and fellowship in love; a triune God. This experience of God distinguishes the Christian faith from any other religious of philosophical tradition. The Trinity unites all Christian despite the different emphases various denominations focus on. Adventists, grounded on this confession of faith, emphasize the part of God's story according to which the same God who has come and has dwelt among human beings

---

[4] Ellen G. White, *The Desire of Ages: The Conflict of the Ages Illustrated in the Life of Christ* (Mountain View, CA: Pacific Press Publishing Association, 1940), 478.

will come a second time to bring a closure to the intrusion of evil, sin and suffering. He is coming to restore a world of peace, justice, righteousness, eternal fellowship in love, gratitude, and everlasting joy.

With the first Advent, a new reality had dawned: the presence and will of God mediated through sanctuaries, temples, holy places or through intermediaries such as prophets, priests, kings, wise persons, found fulfillment in the revelation of the Jesus Christ. His person crystallizes what God had to say or show.

Divine Revelation in Scripture

The Revelation of God in Jesus Christ is corroborated by His revelation in Scripture. The criterion for truth about God, human beings, the world and its destiny within the overarching purpose of God is the written revelation of God's character and will in Scripture.

To assess how conformed is a world religion to the content of Scripture becomes an incontrovertible tool. A given religion's concept of God, of human beings, of sin, salvation, and eternal destiny exposed to Scripture will reveal its veracity or lack thereof. In the midst of competing ideologies, the role of Christian Scriptures is critical in shaping Christian worldview, ethical and moral choices and the development of godly character. [5]

> That Word, cherished in the heart, will yield to the student a treasure of knowledge that is priceless. Its ennobling principles will stamp the character with honesty and truthfulness, temperance and integrity.[6]

A holistic view of the Bible informs a holistic view of mission: one that affects all aspects of life more specifically living for the glory of God in whatever the follower of Christ is engaged in. This is an enactment of the reformation principle *Soli Deo Gloria.*

---

[5] Ellen G. White, *Our High Calling* (Washington DC, Review and Herald Pub. Association, 1961), 31,"There is no book the perusal of which will so elevate and strengthen the mind as the study of the Bible. Here the intellect will find themes of the most elevated character to call out its powers. There is nothing that will so endow with vigour all our faculties as bringing them in contact with the stupendous truths of revelation. The effort to grasp and measure these great thoughts expands the mind. We may dig down deep into the mine of truth, and gather precious treasures with which to enrich the soul. Here we may learn the true way to live, the safe way to die. A familiar acquaintance with the Scriptures sharpens the discerning powers, and fortifies the soul against the attacks of Satan. The Bible is the sword of the Spirit, which will never fail to vanquish the adversary. It is the only true guide in all matters of faith and practice.

[6] White, *Our High Calling*, 1961:31.

A Biblical Perspective on Human Predicament and Antidote

The way human predicament is presented in the Bible is multifaceted. It is personal and internal, the heart is desperately wicked and incurable (Jeremiah 29). It is familial and societal: all relations and relationships are affected by sin, self, and Satan. It is environmental and ecological: Nature sighs and yearns after liberation, after the revelation of the children of God (Romans 8:18-25). Human struggle against evil has also cosmic proportions. Evil spirits are depicted as participating in the woes that affect people and nature. Our existential predicament affects and encompasses the whole of reality. This is the reason why there is a need to heal the whole of reality. The awareness for this need is discernable in the way New Testament authors approached sharing the good news.

The Apostle Paul provides us with a model for how evangelism can be conceived. As an evangelist he proclaimed, testified, and was determined to do all he could to persuade his audiences or those who read his writings to believe in Jesus the messiah and to be reconciled with God. In First Corinthians 9:16 The Apostle Paul states:" For if I preach the gospel that gives me no ground for boasting. For necessity is laid upon me. Woe to me if I do not preach the gospel."

Near the end of his life, in a farewell speech, Paul reveals that there is something he was very intentional about, that is, to declare the whole purpose of God. He says twice in his farewell discourse to the Elders of Ephesus gathered in Miletus, that he did not shrink from declaring to them the whole purpose of God (Acts 20:18-32).

The whole purpose of God is complete redemption, complete restoration, complete healing or salvation, comprehensive solution to multifaceted existential problems.

A Holistic Approach to the Issue of Salvation in Scripture

Each religion or worldview is characterized by an inner-logic that assures its coherence and relevance for its adherents. Even though "no religion is explicable in terms of a single inner logic because "religions are always eclectic systems in which several inner-logics are at play,"[7] In the case of world religions, to discern the human predicament they attempt to solve is a place from which to explore their inner-logic.

From a biblical perspective the purpose of God is to lead humans to the knowledge of His person and to salvation (1 Tim 2:3-4). The knowledge of God is mediated through Jesus Christ and salvation is the comprehensive liberation of humans for fellowship with God in a restored creation.

The perspective of Salvation in terms of liberation from all alienations and restoration of fellowship with a God of love, Himself initiator and

---

[7] Will Deming, *Rethinking Religion: A Concise Introduction*, (New York: Oxford University Press, 2005), 96-97.

involved in the atonement of humans' sins, is unique to biblical Christian faith. Salvation along with a plethora of words and concepts associated with it is the core of the good news as expressed through Scripture. It is a comprehensive and multifaceted antidote to all human ills, predicaments, and evils.

To appreciate the uniqueness and comprehensive nature of the good news as presented in Scripture, one needs to look at the problem(s) world religions and philosophies claim to have identified and offer a cure for:

> Different religions offer differing diagnoses and cures…The diagnosis that a particular religion articulates asserts that every human person has a basic nonphysical illness so deep that, unless it is cured, one's potential is unfulfilled and one's nature cripplingly flawed. Then a cure is proffered. The diagnosis and cure assume (or, if you prefer, entail) the essential structure of a religion's view of what there is, at least insofar as what there is has religious importance.[8]

There are as many diagnoses and cures as there are religions and philosophies.

However, the good news can only be good enough if it addresses all the ills of human existence. If a person has several illnesses, finding one or two or a few cures to his or her diseases would not be good news enough. All his or her diseases have to be addressed and cured.

In other words, a comprehensive solution has to be found. Evidently, the claim to provide this comprehensive solution is not unique to the Christian faith. Nonetheless, by providing a diagnosis of human problems that is part of a cosmic issue, the Bible opens a much bigger window. The foundation for the whole edifice of the Christian faith is that Jesus is Lord and Savior not just of a group among humans or even all humans but of the whole cosmos and the whole of reality.

The impact of evil upon the human heart is addressed at length and comprehensively in the Bible. An inescapable diagnosis of the problem of all humans is that the heart is desperately wicked (Jeremiah 17:9). The heart has become the seat of evil intent and source of bad actions and behaviour. Total depravation of human heart marks the life of every individual. Despite calls to wash one's heart in order to rid it from evil thoughts (Jer. 4:14), improvement is not enough as the prophet Ezekiel argues. There is a need of a new heart (Ezek. 18:31; 36:26).

Beyond the gift of a new heart, the good news is inseparable from the whole purpose of God which is complete redemption, complete restoration, complete healing or salvation, comprehensive solution to multifaceted existential problems. The concept of everlasting good news indicates its comprehensiveness. This is a key aspect of what Adventists understand as everlasting good news.

---

[8] Keith E. Yandell, *Philosophy of Religion: A Contemporary Introduction*, (New York: Routledge, 2005), 23.

In the context of Revelation 14, the good news is first of all the good news about God Himself. He is the creator, the judge, the redeemer, the one who deserves the glory, worthy to be worshipped. This world is not therefore a product of chance. The good news is also about grace: Giving God the glory implies thanking him about the grace and peace he gives. He is a gracious God. The core of what Jesus brought is articulated in terms of grace and truth (John 1:17). From the point of view of human beings, this everlasting good news is predicated upon a series of bad news. Looking at the first chapters of the book of Genesis the following motifs further developed throughout Scriptures surface: Sin and its consequences, curse and its manifestations, death and its symptoms, ultimate abandonment and second death. Salvation consists in the reversal of this bad news.

What is needed therefore is restoration of fellowship with God, atonement for sin, forgiveness, cancellation of the curse, restoration of life strength and healing, fullness of life at physical, intellectual, emotional, spiritual, social, and cosmic levels: a complete restoration of justice, righteousness, and peace.

The good news is about God's purpose to reverse the plight, dislocation and difficulty of human existence. Life in the world the way it is experienced has its plethora of tragedies. God throughout the Bible promises something better; the promises of the fulfillment of His purposes nurture hope among those who wait on the Lord for ultimate deliverance.

The good news is ultimately a reversal of all negative and harmful realities detrimental to peace, justice, righteousness and the reign of God. These foundational themes and motifs constitute the history of redemption, which is the subject matter of Scripture. For Adventists who take into consideration that the Scriptures testify of Jesus (John 5:39), Jesus also embodies the good news. He is the demonstration of God's love (John 3:16), became sin (2 Co 5:21), a sacrifice for sin. He bore the curse (Gal 3:13), experienced the abandonment of the Father. He became the righteousness of God (1 Co. 1:30). He brought grace and truth (John 1:17). He overcame death, and delivers from fear and captivity. He embodies God's rule. He is God's sanctuary among human beings, the Word of God who became flesh and dwelt among us.

World religions and philosophies though not aware of it are deeply searching for him. For indeed He is the yes of God: all the promises of God are yes in Him (2 Co 1:20).

The Ultimate Goal of Mission: Sharing the Revelation of the Triune God

The climax of God's self revelation is the descent of the Son. Jesus comes from where everybody wants to go. Among world religions Mahayana Pure Land Buddhists wants to go to a Pure Land where there is no sorrow. Muslim traditions elaborate on an alleged single night journey the Qur'an alludes to, according to which the prophet Muhammad mystically was granted ascension to seven heavens. The Sufis Muslims desire to cleanse their heart from all dross in order to journey to God.

The essence of the Christian witness is the acknowledgement of a simple yet profound truth: Jesus Christ is Lord. He is God from God. God highly exalted Him, and bestowed on Him the name which is above every name, that at the name of Jesus every knee should bow, of things in heaven, and things in earth, and things under the earth. And that every tongue should confess that Jesus Christ is Lord, to the glory of God the Father (Phil 2:9-11).

The above confession of faith and several others including those in reference to the Holy Spirit have prompted Christians to believe and to formulate with great care that God is one in essence but three in persons.

This revelation distinguishes Christianity from other religions. It is the stepping stone for further revelations on the nature and character of God.

> The doctrine of the Trinity is the highest achievement of Christian Theology. It is the central claim of the faith, in which all other elements find their center. Like the keystone at the top of a Gothic arch, it could only be put in place after lengthy and painstaking labor; yet without it the entire vault would eventually collapse. Many of the difficulties that Christian theologians have faced, as they have attempted to shore up various structures of the faith over the past several centuries can be traced in part to the faulty construction (or in some cases, the complete absence) of this all-important keystone.[9]

The Adventist emphasis is on the part of God's story according to which the same God who came and dwelt among human beings will come a second time to bring a closure to the intrusion of evil, sin, and suffering. He will come to complete the fulfillment of God's kingdom of peace, righteousness and justice, everlasting fellowship in love, gratitude and eternal joy.

The essence of fellowship is indeed participation in Trinitarian life. Mission consists in sharing the revelation of the Triune God and is an invitation to join God's cosmic family.

Conclusion

Each world religion has an inner logic. Finding this inner logic by means of the identification of the diagnosis a religion offers of human problem (s) and the solution (s) they propose to their adherents along with the values attached to them and the taboos they reject, helps to better understand and relate to these people. Creative interfaith and mission endeavours focus on similarities and common ground between faith traditions. Theological reflections focus on discerning the distinctive characteristics of each world

---

[9] David S. Cunningham, *These Three are One: The Practice of Trinitarian Theology*, (Malden, MS: Blackwell, 2000), 6, 7.

religion and philosophy in order to find out the inner-logic and raison d'être. From an Adventist perspective, correct theological insights function as safeguards against possible drifting into syncretism. One has to keep in mind that similarities should not dissimulate the profound differences and at times unbridgeable distances between world religions and biblical Christian faith. Biblical Christian faith is unique in its view of God, human nature, salvation, and human destiny. To create a platform to share God's story, character and purpose as revealed in the Bible, it is necessary to mingle with people of other faiths or philosophies, to learn about their worlds and words, to actively search for redemptive analogies fully aware that similar words or concepts used belong to webs of words and ideas that tell different stories. Effective witnessing takes at times paths where truth and errors are so woven that prayer to have discerning minds becomes vital.

Adventists are at a crossroad of world mission. Adventism has much in common with many faith and philosophical traditions. Because of an uncompromising commitment to Scripture which testifies to Jesus Christ, and as an eschatological movement, Adventists point to the Coming One all hearts are deeply yearning to see. They invite all to an exodus in preparation to meet Him for an everlasting fellowship.

THEMATIC PAPERS

Evangelism and Apologetics

Alister E. McGrath

Apologetics is about giving reasons for faith. It is about showing people that Christianity makes sense; that becoming a Christian does not mean committing intellectual suicide, or abandoning what is best in a culture or existing worldview. Apologetics aims to deal with barriers to faith, giving reasoned and thoughtful replies which allow our audience to appreciate the full appeal and coherence of the Christian faith. In particular, it is about setting out the full attractiveness of Jesus Christ, so that those outside the faith can begin to grasp why he merits such serious consideration. This means offering a vision of reality which is rationally, relationally, morally, and imaginatively compelling.

In a highly perceptive essay published in 1965, the Oxford theologian and New Testament scholar Austin Farrer (1904-68) argued that faith needed to be seen to be reasonable if it was to gain cultural acceptance.[1]

> Though argument does not create conviction, the lack of it destroys belief. What seems to be proved may not be embraced; but what no one shows the ability to defend is quickly abandoned. Rational argument does not create belief, but it maintains a climate in which belief may flourish.

Farrer's essay was written to mark the death of the great Oxford apologist C. S. Lewis (1898-1963) two years earlier. Farrer used his essay to reflect specifically on the reasons for Lewis's remarkable accomplishments and success as an apologist. Farrer argued that this achievement reflected Lewis's unusual ability to offer "a positive exhibition of the force of Christian ideas, morally, imaginatively, and rationally." This is a fine summary of Lewis's approach from a sympathetic and informed critic, which is useful in helping identify Lewis's particular gifts, and how they came to resonate with the public mood.

I believe that these reflections must play a role in our strategic planning for the future, following through on the agenda of Edinburgh 1910. Although Farrer's point was made in connection with western culture during the late 1950s and early 1960s, it has much wider application to your reflections. Farrer has observed that Christianity is easily dismissed when it can be portrayed as a cultural outsider; as something that tramples

[1] Austin Farrer, 'The Christian Apologist'. In *Light on C.S. Lewis*, edited by Jocelyn Gibb (London: Geoffrey Bles, 1965), 23-43; Quote at 26.

over and devalues traditional and deeply embedded cultural values. While Farrer focuses primarily on the implications of the cultural perception that Christianity is irrational, his analysis is easily extended to the perception that it is dull, oppressive, culturally western, or the preserve of fanatics.

Apologetics is often presented as a technique for winning arguments. As the noted Catholic apologist Avery Dulles once put it, "the apologist is regarded as an aggressive, opportunistic person who tries, by fair means or foul, to argue people into joining the church."[2] Some apologetic manuals seem to believe that the essence of apologetics is what amounts to verbal manipulation, intellectual bullying, and moral evasion. But it shouldn't be like this.

Western apologetics is still dominated (especially among older male North American writers) by rationalist approaches, which focus on winning arguments. There is an urgent need to break away from this approach, for two reasons. First, it is wedded to a modernist way of thinking, which lost its cultural dominance in the west a decade ago, and fails to connect with postmodern trends in culture, especially among younger people. Second, the New Testament itself sees the appeal of the Christian faith as transcending reason, involving an appeal to the heart and the imagination, rather than abstract argumentation. I hope you will move beyond this, and not lock evangelism into the past.

Theology and Apologetics

So what role does theology play in apologetics? I want to suggest that theology plays a major role in responsible apologetics, in two distinct ways. First, by insisting that we set apologetics in its proper context; secondly, by allowing us to appreciate the richness of the gospel, and identifying what the best "point of contact" might be for the gospel in relation to a given audience.

The first theological issue concerns the need to see apologetics and evangelism as rooted in God – first, in the realities of the gospel, and secondly, as nourished and sustained by God's grace and spirit. We must move away from technique-based approaches, looking instead to developing a vision of God which both inspires and informs our outreach. Avery Dulles is one of many writers to express concern about theologically-deficient approaches to apologetics. He writes: "numerous charges are laid at the door of apologetics: its neglect of grace, of prayer, and of the life-giving power of the Word of God."[3] It is a powerful point, which must not be ignored. Rational persuasion cannot convert. We are dependent on the grace of God. If people are blinded by the "spirit of the age", divine grace is needed to heal them. This is something that we all

---

[2] Avery Dulles, *A History of Apologetics* (New York: Corpus, 1971), xv.

[3] Dulles, *History*, xv.

know to be true; yet somehow, it often seems to get overlooked. We must recall the famous words of John Newton, in his hymn *Amazing Grace*:

> 'Twas grace that taught my heart to fear,
> And grace my fears relieved;
> How precious did that grace appear
> The hour I first believed.

The point is obvious: it is God's grace that illuminates and ultimately converts. We, as apologists, have a role within this process; it is an important role, but one that must never become a barrier to the operation of God's grace.

Going Beyond Rational Argument

Apologetics engages the mind, the heart and the imagination. We impoverish the gospel if we believe it only impacts upon the human mind, and neglect the impact of the gospel on all of our God-given faculties. One of the most significant critics of a purely rationalist approach to apologetics is the great eighteenth-century American Puritan theologian Jonathan Edwards (1703-58). For Edwards, rational argument has a valuable and important place in Christian apologetics. But it is not the sole, and perhaps not even the chief, resource of the apologist. As he pointed out, the real basis of evangelical transformation is an apprehension of divine glory.[4]

> Great use may be made of external arguments, they are not to be neglected, but highly prized and valued; for they may be greatly serviceable to awaken unbelievers, and bring them to serious consideration, and to confirm the faith of true saints… [Yet] there is no spiritual conviction of the judgment, but what arises from an apprehension of the spiritual beauty and glory of divine things.

Edwards' argument is significant, and merits close consideration. For the heart of his analysis is that arguments do not convert. They may remove obstacles to conversion and support the faith of believers, but in themselves and of themselves they do not possess the capacity to transform humanity. Instead, we must aim to convey or bring about "an apprehension of the spiritual beauty and glory of divine things". Apologetics is about capturing our imaginations with glimpses of glory, not simply persuading our minds with impressions of rationality.

This allows us to set aside a series of misconceptions. We are not called upon to argue people into the kingdom of God by rationalist logic, or aggressive rhetoric. The task of the apologist is to bring people to a point at which they can catch a glimpse of the glory of God; or, to use Edwards' phrase, gain "an apprehension of the spiritual beauty and glory of divine things". This insight is liberating. It reminds us once more that apologetics

---

[4] Jonathan Edwards, *Treatise on the Religious Affections* (New Haven, CT: Yale University Press, 1978), p 307.

is not about manipulative human techniques, but about the grace and glory of God. But it also raises the question of how we can appreciate the glory, wonder and joy of the gospel to be appreciated – a point to which we now turn.

Theology informs apologetics, enabling the apologist to have a full and firm grasp of the richness of the gospel, and hence an understanding of which of its many facets might be the most appropriate starting point or focus for a given audience. We cannot hope to present the totality of the gospel in a single address. We have to start somewhere. Theological analysis very often enables us to identify the most helpful starting point. This is not about reducing the gospel to a single point; it is simply a tactical judgment about where to begin. The rest can and should follow. Yet the decision about where to start is often the most crucial judgment an apologist must make, and it is essential that it is informed by a thorough knowledge of both the gospel itself and the audience that is to be addressed.

Let me share an image with you that I first developed twenty years ago and have often found helpful in thinking about the role of theology in informing apologetics.[5] One of the most famous experiments in English scientific history was carried out by Isaac Newton in his rooms at Cambridge in the late seventeenth century. He found that passing a beam of white light through a prism "decomposed" the white light into the colours of the rainbow. All those colours were already present in the beam of white light; the prism merely separated them out, and allowed them to be seen and appreciated individually.

Theology can be thought of as acting like that prism, enabling us to identify and appreciate the individual elements of the gospel. The apologetic importance of this insight is immense. It means that we can conduct a theological analysis of the gospel, and identify which of its many aspects may relate particularly well to a specific audience. Different people have different needs and concerns. One aspect of the gospel may interlock with one group of needs, while another may match up with others. To appreciate this point, let us return to look briefly at a central theme of the Christian faith – the meaning of the cross.

I am sure that I do not need to remind you that it is impossible to summarize the immensely rich and complex message of the cross in a few words.[6] Indeed, one of the great delights of theology is that it offers us the opportunity of reflecting deeply (and at leisure!) on the full meaning of the

---

[5] It can be found in Alister E. McGrath, *Bridge-Building: Effective Christian Apologetics* (Leicester: Inter-Varsity Press, 1992); US edition, *Intellectuals Don't Need God and Other Modern Myths* (Grand Rapids, MI: Zondervan, 1993).

[6] For some excellent attempts, see John Stott, *The Cross of Christ* (Leicester: Inter-Varsity Press, 1985); Charles E. Hill and Frank A. James (eds), *The Glory of the Atonement: Biblical, Historical and Practical Perspectives* (Downers Grove, IL: Inter-Varsity Press, 2004).

great themes of the Christian message, such as the cross of Christ. Yet it is important to note that a number of aspects can be identified within that message – each of which has particular relevance to certain groups of people. If we pass the "word of the cross" through a theological prism, we find, in the first place, that it has many components, and, in the second, that each relates particularly well to a specific audience. Let me give you a few examples.

One great theme of the gospel is that the cross and resurrection of Jesus Christ free us from the fear of death. Christ has been raised from the dead, and those who have faith will one day share in that resurrection, and be with him for ever. Death is no longer something that need be feared. We celebrate this supremely at Easter. This great message of hope in the face of suffering and death is crucial for us all. Yet it has a special relevance to those many people who wake up in the middle of the night, frightened by the thought of death.

Another great theme of the cross is that of forgiveness. Through the death of Christ, real forgiveness of our sins is possible. This helps us to understand that our redemption is both precious and costly. Yet it also helps us appreciate the relevance of the gospel to a particular group of people – those who are burdened by guilt. Many feel that they can hardly continue living on account of that guilt. Theology identifies one of the many facets of the gospel which has especial relevance to those people. Those sins can be forgiven, and their guilt washed away.

I trust that these points are so obvious that they do not require elaboration. The critical point is this: theological analysis must be followed by cultural discernment, as the apologist identifies those aspects of the gospel which are most likely to resonate with the audience being addressed, and works out how best to communicate, illustrate, and embody them. Theological analysis is essential to good apologetics; yet it is not sufficient. It may lead to the proclamation of the gospel in terms that either fail to connect with the cultural context, or which presents Christianity in such a way that it needlessly violates cultural norms of rationality or social acceptability.

Cultural Translation: The Importance of the Audience

Apologetics is audience-specific. To illustrate this, we shall consider some speeches in the Acts of the Apostles, each of which show a clear and principled statement or defense of the gospel in terms adapted to the cultural situation of their respective audiences.

Peter to the Jews (Acts 2) An excellent example of an apologetic address aimed at a Jewish audience is provided by Peter's Pentecost sermon (Acts

2:14-36).[7] The audience is Jewish; Peter therefore cites an authority which carries weight with this audience – the Old Testament. Peter's apologetic is directly related to themes which were important and comprehensible to a Jewish audience. Peter demonstrates that Jesus meets the specific expectations of Israel by appealing to authorities (here, prophetic passages in the Old Testament) which carried weight with his audience, while using language and terminology which would readily have been accepted and understood by his audience. Note in particular his specific reference to Jesus as "Lord and Christ". No explanation is offered, nor was it necessary. These were theological terms that were familiar to his audience.

Paul to the Greeks (Acts 17). Peter's sermon on the Day of Pentecost contrasts sharply with Paul's apologetic address at Athens – the famous "Areopagos speech". This Greek audience had no knowledge of the Old Testament, nor would they see it as carrying any weight. Paul thus opens his address to the Athenians with a gradual introduction of the theme of the living God, allowing the religious and philosophical curiosity of the Athenians to shape the contours of his theological exposition.[8] The "sense of divinity" present in each individual is here used as an apologetic device. What the Greeks held to be unknown, possibly unknowable, Paul proclaims to have been made known through the resurrection of Christ.

Paul to the Romans (Acts 24). Finally, we may note an apologetic address to a Roman audience. The most important speeches in Acts to deal with Christianity in the eyes of the Roman authorities are found in Acts 24–26. Recent studies have stressed the way in which these speeches conform to patterns which were well known in the legal proceedings of the period.[9] In his point-by-point refutation of his accusers in Acts 24:10–21, Paul follows the "rules of engagement" laid down by Roman legal custom. Paul thus argues along lines that carried cultural weight and intellectual plausibility in engaging this audience.

These early apologetic speeches and sermons point to the need to relate the same gospel to different audiences, who possess different ways of thinking, different core cultural values and beliefs, different criteria of evidence and rationality, and different aspirations. The challenge you face is to correlate the gospel with these cultural realities.

---

[7] For detailed studies of this major text, see the classic study of Robert F. Zehnle, *Peter's Pentecost Discourse: Tradition and Lucan Reinterpretation in Peter's Speeches of Acts 2 and 3* (Nashville, TN: Abingdon, 1971). Although dated in some respects, the work remains an important analysis of the text itself and its underlying strategy.

[8]See Bertil Gartner, *The Areopagus Speech and Natural Revelation* (Uppsala: Gleerup, 1955). Once more, this work offers many important insights, even if scholarship has moved on somewhat since then.

[9]See Bruce W. Winter 'Official Proceedings and the Forensic Speeches in Acts 24–26', in B. W. Winter and A D. Clarke (eds), *Ancient Literary Setting* (Grand Rapids, MI: Eerdmans, 1994), 305–36.

As a Reformation scholar, I have always been impressed by the early Protestant insistence that the gospel must be proclaimed and taught in a language that is understood by ordinary people. If the gospel is proclaimed in a language that our culture cannot understand, or using a medium that it cannot access, then the church has failed in its mission. It is just about as realistic as sending evangelistic tracts written in English to an unchurched people who, in the first place, speak French and in the second, cannot read. Good theological analysis does not necessarily lead to appropriate cultural communication!

Conclusion

In this paper, I have emphasized two points:

1. The need to reflect theologically on the gospel, to ensure that we have appreciated its many elements and aspects;

2. The need for cultural reflection, *initially* on which of these aspects are best adapted to the context we are engaging, and *subsequently* on how best to articulate, conceptualize and embody these themes in this specific situation.

Theologies of Religions

Veli-Matti Kärkkäinen

The Many Dimensions of Interfaith Encounters

The recent document "Religious plurality and Christian self-understanding,"[1] reminds us of the most prominent challenge the Christian Church faces in the beginning of the third millennium:

> Today Christians in almost all parts of the world live in religiously plural societies. Persistent plurality and its impact on their daily lives are forcing them to seek new and adequate ways of understanding and relating to peoples of other religious traditions …
>
> All religious communities are being reshaped by new encounters and relationships.… There is greater awareness of the interdependence of human life, and of the need to collaborate across religious barriers in dealing with the pressing problems of the world. All religious traditions, therefore, are challenged to contribute to the emergence of a global community that would live in mutual respect and peace.

While not a new challenge – just think of the calling of our forefather Abraham from the polytheistic Ur of the Chaldees or the walk of St. Paul around the altar to the "unknown god" in Athens – the intensity and urgency of the interfaith challenge today is unprecedented. Whereas in the past, other religions were "out there," in today's world with mass communication, increased migration, sophisticated technology, as well as a general mindset that celebrates diversity, religious encounters happen as much in our very neighborhoods as in "mission fields" or other exotic locations.

While Christian theology has always paid some attention to theological issues regarding interfaith encounters, particularly during times of heightened tensions such as those in North Africa with Islam in the seventh century or when new opportunities were looming large such as with the neo-Hindu Reform's interest in Christ in nineteenth-century India, only in recent decades has this topic risen to the center of reflection. Religious plurality is not only a sociological, cultural, and political challenge, as

---

1 'Religious plurality and Christian self-understanding', # 2, 3. http://www.oikoumene.org/en/resources/documents/assembly/porto-alegre-2006/3-preparatory-and-background-documents/religious-plurality-and-christian-self-understanding.html

much as it is all of that; it is also a deeply theological issue: "Our theological understanding of religious plurality begins with our faith in the one God who created all things, the living God present and active in all creation from the beginning. The Bible testifies to God as God of all nations and peoples, whose love and compassion includes all humankind."[2]

Technically called Christian theology of religions, this discipline attempts to account theologically for the meaning and value of other religions, particularly in missionary and other encounter situations. Theology of religions is the Christian Church's reflection on the meaning of living with people of other faiths and the relationship of Christianity to other religions.

Theology of religions, however, is more than theology and doctrine. It has everything to do with our attitudes, mindset, love, ability to relate to the Other, and so forth. In other words, thinking and loving, reflection and relating both matter. In fact, they are all indispensable. One error is to concentrate solely on theological and doctrinal analysis. Anyone who has lived in multifaith environments knows from experience that people of faith meet at the personal level which may foster mutual understanding, coexistence, and the feeling of neighborhood or misunderstanding, suspicion, and even conflict. Another error, similarly critical, is to bracket out all theological issues for the sake of alleged "dialogue" – be it the doctrine of the Trinity in relation to Muslims, the question of the ultimate religious end in relation to Hindus, or the issue of human personality/self in relation to Buddhists. This mistaken approach can also take the form of focusing exclusively on religious collaboration in socio-political and ecological improvement to the exclusion of any doctrinal conversations.

Attempting a balanced approach, it is necessary to seek out resources at various levels of interfaith encounters. Naming them levels of "dialogue," Stanley J, Samartha of India distinguishes (1) Dialogue of Life, in which participants are more concerned with issues that pertain to daily living and common values; (2) Dialogue of Action, which involves common work for justice and shared concerns such as HIV/AIDS and the cause of the poor; (3) Dialogue of Experience, which concerns daily spiritual experience and expressions; and (4) Dialogue of Experts, which is interested in theology and philosophy of the faith traditions.[3] All these levels feed both mutual understanding and a missionary encounter.

The Diversity of Christian Responses

While all Christian churches today acknowledge the urgency and challenge of interfaith issues, Christian theology does not speak in a uniform way. In

---

[2] 'Religious plurality and Christian self-understanding', # 27.

[3] Stanley J. Samartha, *One Christ, Many Religions: Towards a Revised Christology* (Maryknoll, NY: Orbis, 1991), 88.

order to properly orient the discussion, it is useful to map out the kaleidoscopic diversity of views across ecclesiastical traditions and theological persuasions. This makes the theology of religions discourse also an intra-Christian ecumenical conversation and learning process.

The most common way of trying to make sense of the maze of Christian responses to other religions is the threefold typology of Exclusivism, Pluralism, and Inclusivism. Exclusivists hold that salvation is available only in Jesus Christ and that a personal response of faith is necessary. On the other end of the spectrum, for Pluralists other religions are legitimate means of salvation. In the pluralistic mindset, there is a rough parity between religions, and therefore, there are many ways to God, more or less equal. The mediating group, Inclusivists, hold that while salvation can only be found in Christ, its benefits have been made universally available even to those who have not heard the gospel. In other words, the inclusivist view maintains that among the saved there might be a great number of people from other faiths who never heard of Christ but for whom Christ died and who in some way or another were already "turning" to the God of Bible by following the light given in the structure of their own religion and trying as best as they could to follow moral precepts.

The exclusivist option, in one form or another, has been by far the most common view among Christians and missionaries throughout Christian history. It was not until the advent of modernity in the eighteenth century that serious doubts were targeted against that confidence. Currently, the conservative segment of Christianity most strongly sticks with the traditional exclusivist position. From the perspective of the whole worldwide Christian church today, though, the largest group of Christians belong to the inclusivist camp because that is the official position of the Roman Catholic Church as defined by Vatican Council II in the 1960s. Differently from the Pluralisms, that view is strongly Christocentric in its insistence that salvation can only be found in Christ. At the same time, unlike Exclusivism, Inclusivism opens the door of salvation to many who never heard the gospel. While pluralistic forces are vocal in the academia and among the specialists, Pluralisms have not gained much following among ordinary believers and clergy, let alone missionaries. Among the mainline Protestants and Anglicans, a negotiation is underway between traditional Exclusivism and (Catholic-type) Inclusivism.

The Dynamic Tension

Without unduly simplifying a complex set of issues, it can be said that the main question of theology of religions culminates in the negotiation of two basic biblical affirmations. The first is the foundational biblical teaching according to which God "wants all men [and women] to be saved and to come to a knowledge of the truth" (1 Tim 2:3). A number of biblical passages such as John 3:16 speak of God's universal love and desire not to forsake anyone. Balancing this principle of the "optimism of salvation" is another equally strong biblical conviction, namely, that "Salvation is found in no one else, for there is no other name under heaven given to men by which we must be saved" (Acts 4:12). Another way of expressing this principle of the "particularity of salvation" is John 14:6: "I am the way and the truth and the life. No one comes to the Father except through me." The way one negotiates this seemingly simple dialectic has everything to do with one's theology of religions.

The biblical materials concerning the early church's view of other religions and other gods are scarce. What can be said safely is that the first church adopted the Jewish monotheism (based on Deut. 6:4) and held to the universality of God's person and nature, as well as the common origin and destiny of all people (Acts 17:28). At the same time, an intensive, intentional evangelization of all people is evident, both toward Jews and Gentiles.

The dynamic tension between the dark picture of humanity in Romans 1 and the affirmation of the relative value of religiosity in Paul's Athens address in Acts 17 brings home the complex nature of the continuity and discontinuity with regard to (other) religions. Early Christian theology followed this dynamic line. While taking for granted the superiority of the Christian faith and the need to proclaim Christ as the only Savior, at times the Fathers showed a limited openness towards other religions, and often welcomed non-Christian philosophical insights. This dynamic is aptly illustrated in the title of a recent book by the Canadian Baptist Clark Pinnock, *A Wideness in God's Mercy: The Finality of Jesus Christ in a World of Religions* (1992) and elaborated by the late Jesuit missionary theologian Jacques Dupuis in his discussion of the implications of Romans 1 and Acts 17:

Discontinuity places the stress on the radical newness of Christ and his resurrection and by contrast sees the ancient world as darkness and sin. That is the viewpoint of Rom 1. The continuity, on the contrary, underlines the homogeneity of salvation unfolding according to God's plan. It is the viewpoint of Acts 17, which, where the religion of gentiles is concerned, presents a Greek world waiting for the unknown God and prepared by its poet-theologians to meet him.[4]

Trinitarian Faith as the Christian Criterion

The most foundational tenet of faith for all Christian churches is the trinitarian confession of Father, Son, and Spirit. The one God of the Old Testament, *Yahweh*, is the Father of Jesus Christ who came to save us in the power of the Spirit. As much as the confession of the Triune God may

[4] Jacques Dupuis, *Toward a Christian Theology of Religious Pluralism* (Maryknoll, NY: Orbis, 1997), 50.

be a stumbling block to interfaith encounters particularly with our Muslim brothers and sisters, that confession cannot be compromised even for the sake of dialogue. At the same time, it doesn't have to be the first topic to be discussed either!

Trinity determines the Christian view of Christ as well. Only when Christ is confessed as truly divine and truly human, following the ancient symbols (creeds) of faith confessed by all Christian churches, can the Christian doctrine of the Trinity be maintained. Making Jesus merely an ethical teacher (as in Classical Liberalism) or only one "Incarnation" among others (as in extreme Pluralisms) – an embodiment of the Deity a.k.a. Hindu *avataras* – not only truncates the confession of the Trinity but also the biblical understanding of Christ.

Many problems in theologies of religions derive from a less than satisfactory conception of the Trinity. A typical pitfall is the pluralistic "theocentric" effort to replace Jesus as *the* Way for the more elusive concept of God at the "center" to whom many "ways" lead. In a healthy trinitarian faith, Father and Son presuppose each other and can never be set in opposition. A similarly appealing error is the turn to the "Spirit" which hopes to get around the centrality of Jesus and Father and makes the work of the Spirit independent from that of Father and Son. According to classic trinitarian faith, the works of the Trinity in the world (*ad extra*) are indivisible: in everything that the Father does, the Son and Spirit are involved as well, and vice versa.

Similarly failing are approaches to other religions and mission that have a tendency to minimize the church and only speak of the kingdom of God and the building of the kingdom as the only goal. That is to fail to recognize the fact that the kingdom, the rule of God, is in itself a trinitarian process: The Son comes in the power of the Spirit to usher in the Father's righteous rule, graciously allowing the community "instituted" by Christ and "constituted" by the Spirit (Orthodox John Zizioulas) – the People of God, the Body of Christ, the Temple of the Spirit – to participate in its coming. Of course, the kingdom is far wider than the church; but the church serves as the sign, anticipation, and tool of the coming rule of God.

If the Triune God is the Creator of the world, it means that, on the one hand, there is some kind of preliminary knowledge and awareness of God among all people who have been created in the image of God and that, on the other hand, all such knowledge, rather than being a human invention, has its source in the God of the Bible. As the early Apologist Justin Martyr taught us, the "seeds" of the *Logos* (the Word), as a result of the Spirit's universal presence, can be found in all cultures and religions. The human being as the image of God is "open" to receive revelation wherever truth – even partial and in broken form – can be found in the world and religions.

This is not to minimize the necessity of God's full self-revelation in Christ, communicated to the peoples of the world through the missionary proclamation of the gospel. On the contrary, it is to give glory to the Triune

God who has already made preparations for the announcement of salvation in Christ. The Bible contains numerous examples of "pagan saints" who knew something – at times, even quite a lot – about God even though they had never yet received God's (special) revelation.

"Salvation Belongs to God"

Theology of religions discourse has tended to focus too much on the question of the access to salvation of people in other faiths. On the one hand, the pluralistic views tend to compromise the uniqueness of the offer of salvation in Christ by making all faiths legitimate avenues of salvation. This is a statement in conflict with both Christian and other religions' convictions. Christian tradition has always attributed salvation only to Christ. Followers of other religions would be offended to hear Christians tell them that their own faith does not offer any unique vision of salvation. On the other hand, the impression from Exclusivism is that there is a tendency to open up the door of salvation as little as possible. This works against the all-embracing love of the Father, the all-penetrating presence of the Spirit, and the universal salvific effects of the Son.

The Christian Church has not been given the "keys" to unlock the Book of Life to know – let alone determine – who will be saved and who not. "It is … humility that enables us to say that salvation belongs to God, God only. We do not possess salvation; we participate in it. We do not offer salvation; we witness to it. We do not decide who would be saved; we leave it to the providence of God. For our own salvation is an everlasting 'hospitality' that God has extended to us. It is God who is the 'host' of salvation."[5]

The Church has been given the simple twofold message, namely, that Jesus is the Savior and that the church is sent even to the ends of the earth to preach the gospel of Christ. Let the Church be faithful in that belief and mission.

"'Othering' with Grace and Courage"

Borrowing from the biblical scholar Walter Brueggemann, I make the term "other" a verb to remind us of the importance of not seeing the religious Other as a counter-object but rather "the risky, demanding, dynamic process of relating to one that is not us."[6] In the "dialogue of life" and "of experience," what matters is the capacity to listen to the distinctive testimony of the Other, to patiently wait upon the Other, and make for him or her a safe space. Similarly, that kind of encounter gives the Christian an

[5] 'Religious plurality and Christian self-understanding', # 47.

[6] Walter Brueggemann, *The Covenanted Self: Explorations in Law and Covenant* (Minneapolis: Augsburg Fortress, 1999), 1.

opportunity to share the distinctive testimony of the love of God. In order for that kind of mindset and attitude to evolve, Christian churches and congregations should be encouraged and empowered to initiate patient training and education with regard to issues such as the following:

- Raising the awareness and importance of interfaith engagement which means venturing outside one's own safety zone and making oneself vulnerable
- Helping deal graciously and in a determined way with our fears of the Other that often includes not only the generic fear of the "stranger" but also the tendency to "demonize" others' religion and beliefs
- Facilitating the study of another religion in order to gain a more accurate portrayal of other persons' beliefs and sensitivities, including the capacity to interpret the meaning of rites and rituals

An important aspect in the process of "othering" is to resist the tendency, so prevalent in secular societies of the Global North and in many forms of religious pluralisms, to draw the Other under one's own world-explanation and thus deny the existence and possibility of genuine differences among religions. It is an act of insult rather than a sign of tolerance to tell the believer of another faith that against his or her own self-understanding no real differences exist in beliefs, doctrines, and ultimate ends.

When the Other is allowed to be Other in his or her own distinctive way, a genuine interfaith encounter has the potential of facilitating both the receiving and giving of gifts. One of the Christian gifts is the sharing of an authentic, personal testimony to Christ, the Lord and Savior, with a view to inviting people of other faiths to submit their lives to the God of the Bible. At the same time, the Christian receives the twofold gift, namely, learning about the Other and at times learning more about one's own faith in the mirror of another faith. This is what the Roman Catholic Gavin D'Costa calls the Holy Spirit's "invitation for mutual engagement."[7]

With this in mind, Christians, along with representatives of other faiths of good will, should do their best to help governments and other authorities to secure a safe, noncoercive place for adherents of religions to present their testimonies without fear. The late missionary bishop Lesslie Newbigin reminded us of the fact that while for Christians the gospel is a "public truth," it has nothing to do with a desire to return to the Christendom model in which the state seeks to enforce beliefs. That should be unacceptable to all religions. In a truly pluralistic society, decision for beliefs can never be a matter of power-based enforcement. When Christians, Muslims, Hindus, Buddhists, Sikhs, Confucians, and followers of other faiths can without fear

---

[7] Gavin D'Costa, *The Meeting of Religions and the Trinity* (Maryknoll, NY: Orbis, 2000), 109-17.

and threat meet each other in a free "marketplace" of beliefs and ideologies, genuinely missionary encounters are also possible.

A powerful metaphor that has been adopted by many contemporary discourses on interfaith encounters is that of "hospitality," a concept well represented in the biblical canon as well as in various cultural contexts. The above-cited ecumenical document "Religious plurality and Christian self-understanding" reminds us that "In the New Testament, the incarnation of the Word of God is spoken of by St. Paul in terms of hospitality and of a life turned towards the 'other' [Phil. 2:6-8]."[8]

Dialogue, Mission, and Tolerance

The recent Catholic interreligious document titled "Dialogue and Proclamation" encapsulates in few pregnant sentences a holistic understanding by listing the principal elements of mission in terms of Christian "presence and witness; commitment to social development and human liberation; liturgical life, prayer and contemplation; interreligious dialogue; and finally, proclamation and catechesis." The document stresses that "Proclamation and dialogue are thus both viewed, each in its own place, as component elements and authentic forms of the one evangelizing mission of the Church. They are both oriented towards the communication of salvific truth."[9] In other words, interfaith dialogue includes and makes space for both proclamation with a view to persuasion by the power of truth and love and to dialogue with a view to facilitating mutual understanding, reconciliation, and harmony.

For the representatives of those religions that are missionary by nature such as Christianity and Islam, any dialogue engagement also provides a legitimate opportunity to try to persuade the other parties of the supremacy of one's own beliefs. Bishop Newbigin tirelessly reminded us that Christian faith – or any other missionary faith – that is not eager and willing to share its deepest convictions in the hope of being able to convince the Other, does not really believe in the truthfulness and value of its faith!

In order for the dialogue to be meaningful it takes both commitment to one's own beliefs and openness to listen carefully to the Other. A true dialogue does not mean giving up one's truth claims but rather entails patient and painstaking investigation of real differences and similarities. The purpose of the dialogue is not necessarily to soften the differences among religions but rather to clarify both similarities and differences as well as issues of potential convergence and impasse. A successful, fruitful

---

[8] 'Religious plurality and Christian self-understanding', # 27.

[9] 'Dialogue and Proclamation', by the Pontifical Council for Inter-Religious Dialogue (May 19, 1991), # 2. http://www.vatican.va/roman_curia/pontifical_councils/interelg/documents/rc_pc_interelg_doc_19051991_dialogue-and-proclamatio_en.html (accessed 4/4/2009).

dialogue often ends up in mutual affirmation of differences, different viewpoints, and varying interpretations.

The contemporary secular mindset often mistakenly confuses tolerance for lack of commitment to any belief or opinion. That is to misunderstand the meaning of the term *tolerance*. Deriving from the Latin term meaning "to bear a burden," tolerance is needed when real differences are allowed. Tolerance means patient and painstaking sharing, listening, and comparing notes – as well as the willingness to respectfully and lovingly make space for continuing differences.

A religiously pluralistic environment and society calls for tolerance that makes room for differences and facilitates mutual missionary enterprises as long as those arise from the self-understanding of each religion.

CASE STUDIES

Mission Among Muslims: Christian Mission and Islam

John Azumah

Edinburgh 1910: Convictions and Commitments

Certain convictions and motivations were the driving forces of the Edinburgh 1910 Missionary Conference. As part of the ground rules, theological issues and their potential for controversy and division were downplayed. Nevertheless certain key theological convictions remained the driving force of the conference. Firstly, there was no debate in the minds of the participants that 'Christianity is the final and absolute religion.' The missionary task was 'not primarily that of proving, but communicating the Gospel's truth.' Secondly, there was the conviction that mission was the business of the (Western) Church and its missionaries. All of the mission agencies that sent out missionaries were located in the West and the rest of the non-Western world was considered "the mission field". This is understandable as Western people were, at the time, the representative Christians. The 'missionary conscience was assumed' and the conference was to be a 'gathering of missionary specialists' united in their commitment and passion for the Great Commission in Matthew 28: 19-20. [1]

Thirdly, mission was understood primarily in soteriological terms: as saving the souls of individuals from eternal damnation. Or in cultural terms: as introducing people from the East and the South to the blessings and privileges of the Christian West. And in ecclesiological terms: as the extension and expansion of particular denominations.[2] The main task the conference committed itself to was 'to exchange views on the ways and means' for 'a triumphant advance of Christianity abroad.'[3] The stated aim of Commission 1V was 'to study the problems involved in the presentation of Christianity to the minds of the non-Christian peoples.' Lurking behind without mentioning by name was "fulfillment theology" as participants repeatedly quoted Matthew 5:17 ("…I have not come to abolish … but

---

[1] David Kerr, 'Towards 2010: Centenary of Edinburgh 1910', a paper from Commission VII, 'Missions and Governments' (2010), available at http://www.towards2010.org/downloads/t2010paper07sum.pdf.

[2] See David J. Bosch, *Transforming Mission* (Maryknoll, NY: Orbis, 1991), 389.

[3] Charles Clayton Morrison, "The World Missionary Conference", published shortly after the conference in the *Christian Century*, July 7, 1910, 1-2

fulfill…") to make the point that all other religions were in some sense preparations for the Gospel. World evangelization as the main motivation was to be achieved through assessments of the "points of contact", i.e. "the good" in other religions for the presentation of the gospel, on the one hand, and moral, intellectual, and social differences, on the other hand, between Christianity and other religions.

In their quest for "points of contact", the reports concentrated on what missionaries on the field perceived as the highest ideals of other religions. This was a major departure from what demonization and summary dismissal of other faiths as purveyors of falsehood. Responding to criticism that the Commission ignored the less estimable aspects of these religions (thus running the risk of romanticizing them), the vice-chairman of Commission IV, Robert Speer, pointed out that 'we should do as we would be done by.'[4] The Commission in its quest for points of contacts was faced with serious challenges when it came to primal religions and Islam. African Traditional Religions (ATRs), for instance were considered collectively as a 'backward and childlike sort of religion' with little or nothing that could be considered as high ideals, which, in turn, meant that ATRs offered minimal, if any, points of contact with Christianity. In a similar vein, the overwhelming majority of missionaries working in Muslim contexts questioned the *praeparatio evangelica* in relation to Islam. Temple Gardiner in particular argued that it was 'so transparently absurd to take this attitude towards a faith which explicitly says it came to supersede the original revelation of Jesus and to destroy the current religion of Jesus.'[5] In other words, he was pointing out the fact that Islam regards itself as fulfilling and superseding Christianity.

Mission among Muslims: A Brief Historical Recap

Islam and Christianity are the two main missionary religions in the world. From the time of Muhammad, the Prophet of Islam, with the exception of the persecuted minority who fled Mecca and sought asylum in Christian Abyssinia in 615, Muslims encountered Christianity from a position of authority and strength. As Muslims conquered vast Christian territories from the seventh century, there came moments of intellectual discussions on matters of religious truth between Muslims and Christians. This pattern can be traced from Muhammad's discussion with a group of Christians from Najran in 630, to discussions between Christian clergymen and Muslim rulers in the 9th and 10th century. Throughout these periods up to the crusades, the material produced for in-house Christian consumption bore the marks of a polemical approach to Islam with the purpose of

[4] Kerr, 'Towards 2010: Centenary of Edinburgh 1910'

[5] Brian Stanley, *The World Missionary Conference: Edinburgh 1910, (Grand Rapids: Eerdmans, 2009)*, 228.

preventing Christians from converting to Islam whilst the material meant for Muslim readership demonstrated a more conciliatory approach. St John of Damascus (675-753) and The Catholicos Timothy I (728-850), are representative of these two approaches.

As Muslim conquests and rule took a strangle hold over Christian populations, 'circumstances [became] such that it took considerable tenacity, often a kind of hopeless doggedness, to remain Christian'[6], let alone to propagate Christianity. After the crusades in the Middle Ages, with the exception of a few individuals, the exchanges between the Muslim orient and Christian occident were in the main based on mutual suspicion, contempt and hostilities until European colonial expansion and missionary enterprise in the nineteenth and twentieth centuries.[7] Despite what Muslim scholarship will have the world believe, the colonial political interest did not always coincide with those of the missionaries. In sub-Saharan Africa, Islam, with the patronage of the colonial powers, made more advances during colonial rule than it did in more than ten centuries of its previous presence. For instance, the Muslim population in Africa rose from 34.5 million at the beginning of colonial rule in 1900 to 145 million by the early 1960s when Africa was slipping out of European colonialism. [8] In most cases colonialism obstructed Christian missions to Muslims. The British declared areas such as Northern parts of Ghana, Nigeria and Sudan as "mission-proof" and banned Christian mission in those areas.

In places like nineteenth and twentieth centuries India, the situation was different. Missionaries had the freedom to do mission among Muslims. Missionaries like Henry Martyn (1781-1812) preached without any hindrance. During the 1910 Edinburgh conference, Commission IV reported that 'workers among Moslems in India all testify that their (Moslems') attitude towards Christ and his people is more friendly and favourable than it was a generation ago.'[9] Nevertheless, on the whole, the missionary enterprise in India amongst Muslims was unsuccessful. This was put down to the approach adopted by the missionaries. True to their pessimism and protestations during the Edinburgh 1910 conference regarding points of contact between Islam and Christianity, the missionaries working amongst Muslims in the Indian sub-continent took a more confrontational and polemical approach to Islam. J. S. Trimingham aptly describes the approach in the following words:

> [T]hey would admit nothing good [in Islam] and gave a dogmatic presentation of Christianity. They thought that it was their work to attack and break down the Islamic religious system, and their method was developed

[6] Kenneth Cragg, *The Call of the Minaret*, (Maryknoll, NY: Orbis, 1985), 307.
[7] See J. M. Gaudeul, *Encounters & Clashes: Islam and Christianity in History, I Survey* (Rome: I. S. A. I., 2000).
[8] Lamin Sanneh, *Translating the Message* (Maryknoll, NY: Orbis, 1992), 88.
[9] Charles R. Watson, 'The World Missionary Conference at Edinburgh and Islam', in *The Moslem World*, Vol. 1, No. 1 (Jan. 1911), 60

> accordingly (sic). They sought to prove to the Muslim by argument and controversy that Christianity was better, and to force an intellectual assent. They failed, for they were fighting on the Muslim's own ground.[10]

As a result, the Indian sub-continent produced some of the most outstanding Christian/Muslim apologetic and polemical literature in the history of the encounters but few converts! Around the mid twentieth century, missionaries were starting to get frustrated by the negligible numbers of converts. An Anglican bishop, Timothy Olufosoye, writing about the situation in The Gambia exclaimed in a report: 'we've toiled all night and caught nothing', a quotation that was also the favourite passage amongst missionaries like Samuel Zwemer who spent more than 38 years (1890-1929) in Egypt and Saudi Arabia.[11] These reports somehow led to what J. T. Addison called 'the almost uniform reluctance of the Christian Church' to do mission amongst Muslims.[12]

Shifting Convictions and Commitments

As pointed out above, during the Edinburgh 1910 conference, the main theological prism through which the nature and practice of mission were viewed was the "fulfillment theology". Today, however, the dominant theological prism is the "pluralist theology" as propounded by people like John Hick, Paul F. Knitter, J. S. Samartha and others.[13] The pluralist view holds that all (the great) religions are equally valid paths of salvation. The confidence and conviction in Christian truth claims are questioned and mission is no longer taken for granted. The argument is that since all religions are equally valid paths of salvation there should be no need to seek to convert Muslims to Christianity and therefore the Great Commission now needs radical redefinition.[14] It is considered arrogant and imperialistic to seek the conversion of people of other religious traditions.

In the post-colonial era, Christian mission in general and mission to Muslims in particular have therefore come under severe criticisms.

---

[10] J. S. Trimingham, *The Christian Approach to Islam in the Sudan* (London: OUP, 1948), 45-6.

[11] Martha T. Frederiks, *We have Toiled all Night: Christianity in The Gambia 1456-2000*, PhD Thesis, University of Utrecht, 2003.

[12] James Thayer Addison, *The Christian Approach to the Moslem: A Historical Study* (New York: Colombia Univ. Press, 1942) 34

[13] Among others, see John Hick and Paul F. Knitter, eds., *The Myth of Christian Uniqueness: toward a pluralistic theology of religions* (Maryknoll: Orbis Books, 1987); Paul F. Knitter, *No Other Name? a critical survey of Christian attitudes toward the world religions* (Maryknoll: Orbis Books, 1985); Samartha, *One Christ, Many Religions: toward a revised Christology* (Maryknoll: Orbis Books, 1991).

[14] For a survey of these positions see Paul F. Knitter, *One Earth Many Religions: Multifaith Dialogue and Global Responsibility,* (Maryknoll NY, Orbis Books, 1995) And John Hick, *God has Many Names* (Philadelphia, Westminster Press, 1982).

Conversion is indeed a controversial issue especially in such places as India and the former communist countries of Eastern Europe, prohibited by law in Muslim countries and punishable by death in mainline Islamic teaching. Some leading Christian scholars and clergy contend that exclusivist claims and the mission they inspire have bred a 'Christian superiority complex that supported and sanctified the western imperialistic exploitation of what was called the 'Third World.'[15] Muslim scholars and activists have also been unrelenting and scathing in their attacks against Christian mission. Muhammad Rasjidi characterises Christian mission in the Indonesian context as the 'exploitation of the weak by the powerful, of the poor by the rich, of the undeveloped by the developed, of the common man by the clever elite'.[16]

At a consultation in 1976 between Christian and Muslim scholars in Switzerland on the nature and history of Christian mission and Islamic Da'wah, a resolution was passed, under strong Muslim pressure, calling for the suspension of Christian mission in Islamic societies in order 'to cleanse the atmosphere of Christian-Muslim relations'.[17] Many argue that mission poisons interfaith relations and is therefore inappropriate in a pluralistic context and that it should be replaced with interfaith dialogue. One of the many criticisms leveled against the late Pope John Paul II was that he actively encouraged evangelism while at the same time calling for dialogue with people of other religions.[18]

As a result of attacks and criticisms against mission, the few Christians and mission organizations operating in Islamic contexts do so under a veil of secrecy, or so they think, clandestinely. The Insider Movements in Islam is a typical example of clandestine missions among Muslims. As a strategy, new believers are required to remain within the mosque and the Muslim community, and, in some cases, missionaries are required to take Muslim names and observe the pillars of Islam.[19] For these mission groups, undercover mission is the only way around threats from fundamentalists Islamic groups, laws against conversions in Muslim countries and to escape the critical eye of a google-ized world and the liberal secular media and

---

[15] John Hick, 'The Non-Absoluteness of Christianity', in *The Myth of Christian Uniqueness*, 18

[16] Muhammad Rasjidi, "The Role of Christian Missions: The Indonesian Experience", in *Christian Mission and Islamic Da'wah*, 80

[17] Reference to the conference statement of a Christian-Muslim Consultation organized by the World Council of Churches in Chambésy, Switzerland, in 1976 in *Christian Mission and Islamic Da'wah: Proceedings of the Chambésy Dialogue Consultation* (Leicester, The Islamic Foundation, 1982), 100-1.

[18] See Byron L. Sherwin & Harold Kasimow (Eds), *John Paul II and Interreligious Dialogue* (Maryknoll NY: Orbis, 1999).

[19] The *International Journal of Frontier Missions* has several articles on the Insider Movements with regard to Buddhists and Hindus, as well as Muslims. See especially Vol. 24, focused on "insider movements," available at <www.ijfm.org/archives.htm>.

academia. The practice of mission in Islamic contexts has therefore undergone radical, and some have argued, unethical revisions as a direct result of the criticism and attacks.

The World Council of Churches, which is a direct outgrowth of the Edinburgh 1910 Conference, issued a document in November 2000 entitled *Striving Together in Dialogue: A Muslim-Christian Call to Reflection and Action* from a Christian-Muslim dialogue meeting in the Netherlands. In this document, the WCC talks of 'a new understanding between Christians and Muslims' and talks of a 'change' made possible as Christians in the West 'were willing and able to rethink their relations with Islam and the Muslim world.' This change includes 'the critical re-examination of Christian mission and the awareness of increasingly being pluralist societies -- some formerly "Christian" -- account primarily for a new call to dialogue.'[20] It is fair to say that the WCC has no clear position when it comes to mission amongst Muslims.

Mission and Dialogue: Locating our Discussion

To start with, it is important to note that the debate as to the appropriateness of conversion is wholly targeted at Christian missions. Islam is a missionary religion and Muslims are engaged in da'wah, but so far, no scholarship or calls are directed at the suspension of Islamic da'wah. Furthermore, as someone from the Majority South, it is important to me to locate the present discussion on the nature and practice of mission within its liberal Western Christian context. Tom F. Driver makes this point unashamedly in the following words: 'It will be the better part of wisdom to acknowledge, even to stress, that the whole discussion about "religious pluralism," as it is represented in this book [*The Myth of Christian Uniqueness*], belongs to Western liberal religious thought at the present time.' Driver asserts that pluralism is a demand laid upon Western Christianity, as a result of a history, which has largely been one of 'universal colonialism.'[21]

Christendom's legacy of anathematization, damnation, excommunication and even extermination of dissenters, as well as slavery, colonialism, the two world wars and the enlightenment in Western Europe, all combine to provide the historical and intellectual context for the present discourse on the nature and practice of mission. These have combined to produce an inherited guilt complex acutely felt in the West. Added to this legacy is the fact that the phenomenon of religious plurality is fairly new in the West as compared to Africa and Asia. Similarly, to a very large extent,

---

[20] http://www.oikoumene.org/en/resources/documents/wcc-programmes/interreligious-dialogue-and-cooperation/interreligious-trust-and-respect/striving-together-in-dialogue.html (accessed 27/07/09)

[21] Driver, 'The Case for Pluralism', in Hick and Knitter, *Myth of Christian Uniqueness*, 207.

the religious 'other' in the West are immigrants, whereas in Africa the religious 'other' are blood relations and fully fledged citizens. The implication of all these factors is that the questions posed by religious plurality to Western Christianity are not necessarily the same as those for African Christianity.

Mission Redefined and Reclaimed

From the Majority South perspective, calls for the suspension or radical redefinition of missions will be viewed as misplaced for the following three reasons. Firstly, mission, properly understood is God's business and not the Church's business. Those who attack and call for the suspension of mission do so with the understanding that mission is the Church's activity. However, from the second half of the last century, the understanding of the nature of mission has changed dramatically. The concept of *Missio Dei*, attributed to Karl Barth, means mission is understood as deriving from the very nature of God. Mission is not an activity of the Church but an attribute of God. God is a missionary God. There is a Church because there is mission, not vice versa. *Missio Dei* is about God the Father sending the Son, and God the Father and the Son sending the Holy Spirit, and the Father, Son and the Holy Spirit sending the Church into the world.[22] The Church is therefore birthed out of mission and missionary by *calling* not by nature. This is a significant departure from the understanding in 1910 that mission was the activity of the Church. If mission is God's and the world, including Muslim societies, is God's, then it follows that the Muslim world cannot be exempted from Christian mission.

Secondly, since the second half of the last century, the demographics and the very *nature* of Christianity itself have changed from what it was in 1910. The point has been made that in 1910 Western people were the representative Christians. From the post-colonial and post-missionary era, i.e. the mid 1960s onwards, 'the map of the Christian Church, its demographic and cultural make-up, changed dramatically.' Christianity exploded in the most unlikely places, given the least consideration by missionary specialists who gathered in Edinburgh in 1910, such as in Africa. Andrew Walls notes, 'After a Western phase that lasted several centuries, the Church has a new shape, a new ethnic composition and a new cultural orientation.'[23] The face and very nature of Christianity are different today from what they were in 1910. As Lamin Sanneh points out, even though African Christianity is riddled with all kinds of ills and corruptions;

> [it] has not been a bitterly fought religion: ... no bloody battles of doctrine and polity; no territorial aggrandizement by churches; no jihads against

[22] Bosch, *Transforming Mission*, 389

[23] Andrew Walls, 'The Great Commission 1910 – 2010', cited from, www.towards2010.org

> infidels; ... The lines of Christian profession have not been etched in the blood of enemies. To that extent, at least African Christianity has diverged strikingly from sixteenth- and seventeenth-century Christendom.[24]

The shift of Christianity to the global South has implications for the discourse about the practice of mission general and mission to Islam in particular. Western missionaries might have taken the seed of Christianity to the rest of the world, but the practice of mission today is largely the responsibility of world Christianity, which, unlike Christendom, is striking in its lack of political clout and imperialist ambitions. The "mission field" has changed and so has the missionary force whose ranks are now filled predominantly by Asian (Korean), African and Latin American Christians.

Indeed there is now what some are calling "reverse mission", mission undertaken by Christians from the global South to formerly Christian heartlands of the West, not through Home Mission Boards, but migration. It is now an established fact that about half of all churchgoers in London are black.[25] A feature writer in the British *Guardian* newspaper declared in near exasperation that as the city of London, 'the cynical capital of the unbelieving English ... continues to be Africanised, so it is being evangelized'.[26] Charges of imperialism and the powerful exploiting the weak leveled against Christian mission are therefore simplistic. Christian mission to Muslims is taking place more in Africa and Asia and carried out by Africans and Asians rather than Westerners. It is therefore imperialistic for Western theologians to call for its suspension and lack of knowledge of the nature of Christian missions today or sheer propaganda for Muslims to label it imperialistic.

It is crucial for Muslims to recognize the changing face of Christian mission in the twenty-first century borne by the Church from the global South. Which means instead of continuing to flog the dead donkey in western Christianity, Muslims have to engage with world Christianity and their understanding of mission. For majority world Christians, mission to the Church is like water to a fish. Worship and witness, profession and proclamation to the Church in the global South are like breathing-in and breathing-out. Christians from the global South have no option but to remain committed to God's mission to their Muslim neighbours and relations.

Thirdly, as we have pointed out already, Islam and Christianity are the only two world religions that have missions at the heart of their faith. Christian missions to Muslims in this context should go beyond the making of converts. As the only two missionary religions, it is in the interest of

---

[24] Lamin Sanneh, *Whose Religion is Christianity?* (Grand Rapids: Eerdmans, 2003), 39.

[25] Philip Jenkins, *The Next Christendom: The Coming of Global Christianity* (Oxford: OUP, 2007) 104.

[26] Leo Benedictus, 'From the Day We're Born Till the Day We Die, It's the Church', *Guardian*, Jan 21, 2005.

adherents of both traditions to have an open discussion on mission itself. In such conversations, the point has to be made that there can be no mission unless there is freedom of religion and that there is an inherent contradiction between mission or da'wah and criminalization of change of religion. As Kenneth Cragg puts it: 'A true understanding of freedom, as freedom of movement of mind, demands that the option should exist' and 'freedom of belief must include freedom of disbelief'. This is so important, Cragg believes, because;

> Freedom of conscience has an absolute value that transcends all special pleading. We are not seeking such changes primarily for the benefit of potential converts. Nor should thoughtful Muslims resist them for the sake of deterring such converts.'[27]

A belief system that denies freedom of disbelief is a prison, and no self-respecting faith wants to be a prison. My own understanding of mission as propagation or evangelism and dialogue is that while the former is primarily concerned with a change in the belief of the other, the latter is primarily concerned with a change in perceptions of and attitude towards the other. The two cannot be mutually exclusive and are equally vital in any genuine pluralistic context.

Christian mission in an Islamic context should therefore involve open and consistent conversations on religious freedom instead of missionaries behaving like drug traffickers or terrorist operatives constantly devising clandestine and underhanded ways of operation. Timothy Tennent is right in observing that the clandestine behaviour that has characterized Christian mission to Muslims in the last couple of decades is unethical and damaging to the credibility of Christians, breeding further distrust towards Christian mission. I share Tennent's counsel that: 'A more open witness in a straightforward, but contextually sensitive way seems to hold the greatest promise for effective and ethical Christian penetration into the Muslim world.'[28]

Doing Mission God's Way

Christian mission in general (mission to Islam included) is not only about the Great Commission in Mathew 20:19-20. It is also about John 20:21: 'As the Father has sent me, I am sending you.' If mission is God's business and the church only called to partake in it, then mission must be done God's way. Doing mission God's way, in my view, involves *stepping up*; *stepping out*; and *stepping in*. Christian mission starts with a call from God and a response from us. We need to *step u*p in response to God's call to

---

[27] Cragg, *The Call of the Minaret*, 306-11

[28] Timothy Tennent, 'Followers of Jesus (Isa) in Islamic Mosques: A Closer Examination of C-5 "High Spectrum" Contextualization', in IJFM, 23:3 (Fall 2006), 113

mission. This is very important with regards to mission to Islam as there are fewer and fewer missionaries venturing into that context. Abraham had to step up in response to God's call to leave his homeland to an unknown place. While the Western Church may be spending all its time debating missions, Christians from the global see stepping up to mission to Islam as a natural expression of their faith.

The second point is the need to *step out*. The very act of creation as recorded in Genesis 1 and 2 is an act of God stepping out. In Philippians 2:6 Paul talks of the humility of Christ; 'who, though he was God, did not demand and cling to his rights as God'. 2:7 'Instead, he emptied himself, taking on the very nature of a slave. He became like human beings, appearing in human form'. In other words, God in Christ stepped out of his very being, his very nature. This is very important in mission within an Islamic context. Christianity has to be taken out or stripped of its Western cultural trappings if Christian mission is to regain credibility in Muslim context. Mission is about expending the self not extending the self, which was the driving motivation at Edinburgh 1910.

Doing mission God's way also involves *stepping in*. It is about going into a different culture, learning a different language rather than teaching others one's language and imposing one's culture on others. This was the Pauline missionary model: 'To the Jews I became like a Jew, to win the Jews. To those under the law I became like one under the law (though I myself am not under the law), so as to win those under the law' (1Cor. 9:20). In mission to Islam therefore, Christians are called to step out of their comfort zones in order to step into unfamiliar and even strange areas. In Christ, God did not only step out, but stepped into our humanity. Mission to Islam therefore has to be incarnational and sacrificial. Mission is not only being prepared to "dirty" ones hands, but, like clay pots bearing treasure, it involves being prepared, and in some cases, meant to be broken. Doing mission God's way in an Islamic context therefore is about stepping out in confident vulnerability.

Finally, in carrying out God's mission in an Islamic context, Christians should bear in mind how the Lord Jesus himself chose to be remembered. 'And he took bread, and when he had given thanks he broke it and gave it to them, saying, "This is my body which is given for you. Do this in remembrance of me"' (Luke 22:19). It is significant that of all that he accomplished during his time on earth, Jesus chose the brokenness of his body, his crucifixion and death for his own memorial, rather than his miracles or exaltation. That Jesus chose to lay power and fame aside and even to allow his own body to be broken in order to heal a broken world is what makes him unique and makes Christian mission imperative in a broken world. By his example, Jesus is teaching us that it takes a cross to fix a broken world not a crown! Christ as a person, rather than a dogma, should form the core of Christian witness. And, 'as long as Christ is Christ, and the Church knows both itself and him, there will be a mission to Islam.'[29]

[29]Cragg, *Call of the Minaret*, 305

Mission Among Muslims:
Christian Mission, Faith and Theology in the Context of Islam

Charles Amjad-Ali

This paper is written for fellow Christians, co-labourers, friends and comrades in the *ecclesia dei*, who are committed to the *regnum dei* and *missio dei*. It is written not to praise Islam, nor to abuse it, but rather to talk of a neighbour who, in recent years, we have loved to hate and hated to love. Instead of following the great command 'our neighbour as ourselves',[1] we have brazenly broken both this command and that of not bearing false witness.[2] We have pointed out the speck in our neighbours' eyes, yet ignored the beam in our own.[3] We cannot afford to condemn others as sinners, and forget our own sinfulness, especially in the context of Reformation Christianity, for one of its central doctrines is *simul iustus et peccator* (simultaneously righteous/justified/just and sinner). Therefore to understand the current character of mission to, and in the context of, Islam, and the reality of the Christian-Muslim encounters, we need to do a quick survey of some important theological, historical and contemporary issues.

Of all religions of the world, historically it is Islam that has most thrust itself onto the consciousness of Christianity as 'the other'. Unfortunately, we have usually responded to this 'other' in negative terms. It is clear that we need a new theological and missiological discourse for new relationships, which are between our particular idea of what it means to be Christian and the acknowledgement that we live in a world of fundamentally plural values that are generated by multiple religious systems. In this context we must make sure that we do not sacrifice those elements which are critically central for Christianity. At the same time we must safeguard that we do not become so provincial that the universal implication of the creation, salvation, and eschatological narrative is lost in polemical and 'evangelical' zeal.

In this context we must acknowledge that the quest for a mission among Muslims is well known for its ultimate failure in spite of the romantic

---

[1] C.f. Mt. 22:39.

[2] Mt. 19:18; Mk. 10:19; Lk. 18:20; Ex. 20:16.

[3] For full reference to this text see Mt. 7:1-5, esp. v. 3.

statements which define it as a brilliant initial effort.[4] Attempts at reviving and operating in the shadow of these earlier efforts have more recently been questioned in light of the ecumenical agenda of dialogue and relations with people of other faiths. This task has become even more difficult in recent years because of the strong and growing hostility toward Islam in the West.

Islam, of all the major religions of the world, is the only post-Christian faith; however this fact is often forgotten, over-looked, or consciously ignored. This is particularly true in missiological discussions and mission studies, where this historical fact is more or less acknowledged, yet quickly passed over in favour of a theological, rather than historical, chronology. We assert that Islam is, theologically speaking, a pre-Christian religion, as it is still based almost exclusively on the 'law', with its related piety, orthopraxis, etc., and has little, if any, 'grace' in it. Even if this were true, which it certainly is not, the way we assert this observation is based solely on a particular Christian reading of the core of its own faith. Most Christians thus end up using a highly Lutheran orthodox theological grammar, regardless of their denominational background, which conveniently ignores the huge debate within Christianity on the 'third use of the law,' sanctification, piety, orthopraxis, etc., which is repeatedly articulated in various ways by Calvinists, Methodists, Baptists and even Catholics. So there is, at the least, a sleight of hand in our presentation of the Christian position vis-à-vis Islam, if not a conscious distortion of our beliefs and convictions.

Islam treats both Christianity and Judaism intimately as 'religions of the book' and their adherents as the 'people of the book' – i.e., *ahl-e-kitab*. As Christianity sees Judaism as the *praeparatio evangelica* (preparation for the gospel), Islam sees these two religions, particularly Christianity, as *praeparatio Islamica* (preparation for Islam). It sees itself as the abrogation and completion of their witness and praise to the one God. The Qur'an begins with *al-Fatihah* (the Opening), which confesses and praises God as the 'totally other' all powerful Lord of the entire universe (*rab al al'ameen*), and the final judge and sovereign of the day of judgment (*malik-e-yom-al-din*). But the very first verse articulates the intimate way He relates to His creation as *al rehman* (the Compassionate) *al rahim* (the Merciful).[5] This dialectic of total intimacy, and total sovereignty and otherness, is constantly maintained throughout the Qur'an. Yet we tend to overlook this and thus see Islam as a religion of a non-intimate God and of law.

Islam has had a longer-term history of success than Christianity. Christianity did not become a ruling force till the so-called 'conversion' of

---

[4] We are reminded of people like Samuel Zwemer, Henry Martyn, William Muir, James Sweetman, Duncan Black MacDonald, Karl Gottlieb Pfander, etc., who are remembered fondly in this context.

[5] It has been argued that the Arabic tri-literal root *r-h-m* in these two words, which are used at every moment of praise by Muslims, means "the womb."

Constantine around 312, and fully emerges as a world power only after the 16th century. Islam on the other hand begins to display such power immediately after the *hijra* (migration), in its first calendar year of 622, and continue this trend until the 18th century. Since the 1970s, if not slightly earlier, it has been undergoing a revival of its power.

Islam, Judaism and Christianity all emerged from the same part of the world and share a geography and heritage. While the earlier religions, for one reason or another, have lost their original or founding locations, (at least until very recently, when the state of Israel came into being), Islam has continued to strongly maintain its location there over these last 1400 years, even as it has expanded all over the world. Of the Pentarchy of Sees (Antioch, Jerusalem, Alexandria, Rome and Constantinople), all were under Muslims, except for Rome. Almost all the holy places of the Bible are still under Muslim control.

Today the Organization of the Islamic Conference (OIC), the second largest intergovernmental organization after the UN, has 57 member-states across four continents. There are also many countries in which Islam is a large minority, e.g., India, and it is the second largest religion in almost every Western state. The current minority Islamic presence in Europe is usually dated to the post-WWII period, and is tied to the necessity of the reconstruction of a war-devastated Europe. The massive death-toll of those who would normally have been deployed for such reconstruction work engendered this demand for immigrant manpower. Though this understanding of history is accurate in part, it also reflects a convenient amnesia of the history of Islam in Europe. Islam ruled Spain for almost 800 years till 1492, (a date regarded as the beginning of modern colonialism and Catholic missiology). Islam also occupied Eastern Europe during the 15th century Turkish expansion (itself part of Europe), and is still fully present in Albania, Bosnia, and as far north as Chechnya. We are now at least aware of these locations because of the recent crises in post-Soviet Eastern Europe.

Not only is Islam a post-Christian religion, but it has grown proportionately faster than any religion in history, including Buddhism and Christianity, which are the world's other two missionary religions. This political and missionary success is seen by Muslims as a sure sign of God's favour. Muslims today occupy three distinct contexts. The *first* is where Muslims hold an absolute majority, with minimum, if any, non-Muslim minorities, e.g., Saudi Arabia, Iran, Afghanistan, etc. However, even in these highly religiously homogenized places, Islam expresses itself in heterogeneous ways, in terms of piety, practice, theology, doctrine and ethics. This is evident not just in the obvious difference between Shi'a and Sunni, but equally so within these respective communities. In these areas, however, the operational *geist* and *sitz im leben* is and will remain Muslim. Whatever transformation and reconfiguration takes place here will be within the context of that Muslim grammar.

The *second* context is where Muslims, though in the majority, have become 'syncretistic', for lack of a better term. In some cases, this is through the influence of Western politics and ideology, originating under colonialism and/or continuing in the post-colonial period. In some cases other religions inform and contextualize Islam and Muslim life. The two contexts are not highly differentiated moments and effect countries like Indonesia (which is the largest Muslim nation), Pakistan, Bangladesh, Malaysia, Nigeria, Sudan, and Turkey (which turned secular earlier than most other European countries). Not that these contexts are rigid and permanent; there is enough tension and malleability for the fundamentalists to exploit by demanding a return to 'pristine Salafi Islam'.[6] That call, with an appropriate admixture of *ummah*, *Qur'an*, and *shariah*, provides them with a moral status way beyond their numbers and thus produces volatility at regular intervals.

The *third* context is where Muslims are clearly a minority. Despite this minority status, the overall numbers involved are very high. They constitute a substantially larger proportion of the world's Islamic population than the total of Arab-speaking Muslims, and growingly so. It is also the most vulnerable and therefore dynamic and creative part of the Islamic world. It seriously struggles to find meaning in that context, i.e., how to remain Muslim in an overwhelmingly non-Muslim society, with no hope of ever converting the system to fit Islamic normatives. There are subtle differences within this context. For example, in India Muslims make up only 13 percent of the population,[7] but they ruled the region for almost a millennium, and had varying approaches to applying Muslim laws – from its harshest application under the Mughal king Aurangzeb, to a complete syncretisation under Akbar and his famous '*Din-e-Ilahi*' (Religion of God). In the case of Ethiopia, where the earliest Muslim migration took place in 615, Muslims never gained a majority and had to live under Coptic rule. Muslims now have a significant minority presence all over Europe, North America and South Africa, with an ever growing articulation of their faith needs. In each of these contexts Islam/Muslims are treated differently, from the banning of the *hijab* in France, to its protection by the state in the US, to the unquestioning acceptance of ritual Muslim practice in South Africa. What is interesting is that in these contexts also, the 'fundamentalists' demand *salafi* practice, etc., when such a possibility can only be part of

---

[6] According to Ibn Taymiyyah (seen as the godfather of Muslim radicalism), the purity of Islam is represented by the period of the first three generations of Muslims (the *Salafi* period), after which distortion and innovation (*bid`ah*) set in.

[7] Of the 1.2 billion population of India, the CIA's *World Fact Book* estimates (as of July 2009) that 13.4% are Muslim (i.e. 156 million). India is thus the third largest Muslim country after Indonesia and Pakistan, and roughly half of the total population of the Arab-speaking world, which includes a huge number of non-Arabs in the Persian Gulf, 30% non-Muslims in Sudan, and a large number of Christians in places like Iraq, Lebanon, Syria, Jordan, Egypt, etc.

some messianic apocalyptic imagination, with no hope of this happening here and now.

Twenty-first century marks the fifteenth century of Islam, and, as in the 15th century of Christianity, Muslims are rethinking their doctrinal, confessional, ethical, and theological content and parameters. Like the Christian Reformation, they are seriously struggling with some of their centrally held conventional and theological positions. From my perspective, this process began as early as Kamal Ataturk Pasha in 1923. He banned a centralized, politico-ecclesial power nexus under the Caliphate which was in continuity, in one form or another, since the Prophet initiated it in 622 in Medina, and was fully established in 632 after the conquest of Mecca. Suffice it to say here, this politico-ecclesial power nexus was never as simple as we claim it to be within Western Christianity and orientalism, nor as claimed by some of the more conservative Muslims – i.e., that there is no separation of religion and politics in Islam because the office of the Prophet and Caliphate was tied in the same person and continued after him. With the end of the Caliphate in Turkey, that synergy came to an end, and with it ended the whole notion of Islamic *ummah* (catholicity under one rule). This led to the emergence of nationalisms, which already had initial impetus in the Arab tribes' struggle against the Ottomans during WWI. This was no small reforming shift. The post-colonial Muslim nation-states emerged as part of nationalistic struggles against colonial rule, resulting in totally new nations as diverse as Pakistan, Bangladesh, Indonesia, Malaysia, Morocco, Jordan, and the Gulf states, etc. So currently Islam finds itself caught between the ideal doctrine of being a universal *ummah* of shared significance and shared commitments, and hard nationalistic identities which have lead to serious long-term conflicts and continue to produce them even today.

So, despite the dominant 'Clash of Civilizations' paradigm, we should take seriously, both epistemologically and ideologically, the fact that Islam has produced more devastating conflict within itself over the last 60 or so years than it has against the West. A clear example of this internal conflict within Islam is the fact that within only 24 years of its independence from British colonialism, and establishment as a country, the first nation ostensibly created for and with a Muslim identity, i.e., Pakistan,[8] was split apart along ethnic and linguistic lines, resulting in the horrific genocide of Bengalis by Pakistan in 1971. Further, between 1980 and 1988 there was a devastating war between Iran and Iraq, and the West's obsession with Iraq is partially a hangover from that period. All these should be part of the concern for the *missio dei*, witnessing, and proclaiming the gospel of Jesus Christ.

---

[8] Israel being the second nation to be created with such an explicitly religious identity.

Another critical point is that Islam does not make an epistemological separation of religion and politics. This poses a challenge to Western missiology, theology and ethics, because they assume this separation to be universally valid, wrongly I might add. To me, however, it is also clear that Islam, in its earliest formation, did make a hard separation of 'church' and 'state' (not that these institutions had the same expression as they did in Christianity). In the serious study of the content and message of the Qur'an, there has been in recent years an emphasis on the differences between the *surahs* revealed in Mecca and those revealed in Medina, in terms of theology and nuance;[9] however, what is not emphasized or studied, is the fact that the Prophet, after his victory over Mecca in 632, decided not to make it his capital, but returned to Medina as the locale of statecraft.

During the last years of his life, the Prophet sought victory over Mecca. It was the place of his origin, early life, work, marriage, relationships, and the place of his first revelations, call to prophecy, and proclamations. After the stunning victory over a much more powerful enemy – the Quraish – to reclaim the city of his birth, he does not however make it his capital, instead returning to Medina as his capital. This is extremely telling, as is the fact that he never makes Medina the *qibla*. While the Prophet moved the *qibla* from Jerusalem to Mecca as late as 624 (i.e. 12 years after the revelation and 2 years after the migration), to date Mecca remains the *qibla*. The capital shifted to Syria just 29 years after the Prophet's death, then to Baghdad, and from there it kept moving. None of these political capitals, despite high intellectual developments, cultural achievements, architectural wonders, etc., were ever claimed to be the *qibla*.

So while Islam did not make the separation of religion and politics, it did have an early separation of 'church' and 'state'. This gives us critical missiological clues as to how to do our missiology as a part of our political activity, and our political activity as part of our missiological commitment to God while maintaining a hard juridical separation of church and state. Thus we can never give theological justification to a state claiming divine right, or special providence or covenantal relationship. Nor should the church or religious institution be allowed to pass *fatwas* on the state, and how it controls the life of citizens who represent much larger faith expressions than one restricted to the faith of the institutions which pass such *fatwas*, bulls, edicts, etc.

As we examined the missionary practices of the church in the late 20th century, it became clear to us that we have carried out our mission in line with our understanding of empire, power, culture, etc., especially over the last 500 years. That such an approach was always false must be acknowledged as part of the contemporary articulation and practice of mission and missiology. Mission must stem from an understanding of God

---

9 See, for example, Kenneth Cragg, *The Qur'an and the West* (Washington, DC: Georgetown University Press, 2005).

who is not an unmoved mover, or apathetic towards human history, nor a God who sets Godself apart as the Other. Rather we should see this God, especially in the *missio dei*, as the one who has heard the cries of the suffering, who is moved by pathos and has spoken for all the victims of the Golgathas of history (*Vox victimarum vox dei*). This God gets involved in human history and human materiality, and not only comes to us through a kenotic act of incarnation, as the epitome of this involvement, but dies on the cross, which is a foolishness and a stumbling block to the empires and the powers that be. In resurrection, that death is not the end, but the resurrected state still fully bears the marks of that cross, thus we are invited to see and put our fingers in those marks. So to make the incarnation non-contingent, and un-contaminated, is a continuation of the early Docetic heresy, and devalues human history and human materiality as having no worth and no substance. This understanding of God as the moved mover is the context in which the *missio dei*, the *regnum dei*, and the *ecclesia dei* fully come together. So we pray 'thy kingdom come, thy will be done'.

The trouble we have in dealing with the missiological task is our fundamental inability to keep the dialectic of righteousness and sin as part of that effort, and our inability to love the others in general, but Islam and Muslims in particular. It is also our inability to move from old patterns of mission, especially in the context of Islam, where they have failed miserably, and to rethink the understanding of vulnerability as central to mission. Islam as a post-Christian religion asks us to question why the need for Islam emerged and why it was so successful in areas which had been dominated by Christians for some 600 years. What becomes very clear with mission in the context of Islam is that a stencilised missiology which claims that one size fits all, cannot and will not work. Islam has a high level of divergence and requires us to take each of these seriously, while continuing to love as well as to give reasons for our hope. We must not articulate this mission only in terms of Matthew 28, but must ask questions of the significance of mission in light of the *kenosis* in Philippians 2, and the call for reconciliation in 2 Corinthians 5:19-21. We must re-examine *missio dei*, *ecclesia dei*, and *regnum dei* in light of Hebrews 13:12-13 which states,

> Therefore Jesus also suffered outside the city gate in order to sanctify the people by his own blood. Let us then go to him outside the camp and bear the abuse he endured.

Mission Among Muslims: New Faith, Renewed Identity: How Some Muslims are Becoming Followers of Jesus

David Greenlee

From the time of Ubaidallah ibn Jahiz, who in Ethiopia became 'the first Muslim… to discover and embrace the truth'[1] and until recent days, the number of Muslims reported as coming to faith in Jesus Christ was small.[2] Something, however, has changed. That Muslims in significant numbers today are, in a biblical sense, coming to faith in Jesus Christ is no secret.[3]

Given this fact, *why* are more and more of our Muslim neighbours running the risks of 'apostasy' and turning to faith in Jesus Christ? How do questions of personal and social identity affect this process? In this paper I will briefly address these questions, focusing on representative published research and writing mostly from the evangelical Protestant tradition.[4]

Lenses to Clarify our Vision

Conversion is a complex phenomenon we will never fully describe. However, as Paul Hiebert often said, 'We see in part, but we do see' (1 Cor.13:12). Aware of (and intending to avoid) its negative connotations, I will use the word 'conversion' following Andrew Walls: 'the idea of

---

[1] Y. Maximov. 'A History of Orthodox Missions among the Muslims', http://www.orthodoxytoday.org/articles4/MaximovMuslims.php, 29 January 2004.

[2] See, for example, S.H. Griffith, *The Church in the Shadow of the Mosque. Christians and Muslims in the World of Islam* (Princeton: Princeton University Press, 2008) concerning the early centuries of Islam and, regarding Egypt until the mid 20th century, H.J. Sharkey, *American Evangelicals in Egypt: Missionary Encounters in an Age of Empire* (Princeton: Princeton University Press, 2008), 6, 63.

[3] Typical of this open reporting are 'Afghan Convert was Ready to Die', http://news.bbc.co.uk/go/pr/fr/-/2/hi/south_asia/4852426.stm, 28 March 2006 and Linda Pressly, 'Life as a Secret Christian Convert', http://news.bbc.co.uk/2/hi/programmes/crossing_continents/6150340.stm 15 November 2006.

[4] From the Roman Catholic perspective, see J.M. Gaudeul, *Called from Islam to Christ: Why Muslims became Christians* (Crowborough, England: Monarch, 1999) and, at a popular level, G. Paolucci and C. Eid, *Cristianos Venidos del Islam: Historias de Musulmanes Convertidos al Catolicismo* (Madrid: LibrosLibres, 2007).

turning…the specifically Christian understanding of the response to God's saving activity'[5].

Seven 'lenses' can help us reflect on conversion. Like filters that pass only certain colours of light, observing conversion through these lenses draws out aspects lost in the glare of other factors. Valuable as individual images, we should also attempt to recombine them into an enhanced, multi-dimensional whole.

The Psychological Lens

Andreas Maurer, having studied conversion in South Africa, notes that we should look at humans 'holistically as [people] with different needs, all of which play a role in the movement to conversion.'[6] Muslims come to faith in Christ – and Christians turn to Muslim faith – not just for 'religious' or intellectual reasons. Various relational, experimental, mystical, and other motives may push or pull them toward change.

Hannes Wiher, drawing on experience in Guinea, observes that 'the content of every conscience is close enough to God's norms in order to be an initial reference point (Rom. 2:1–16).' If our message is based on issues irrelevant to the local conscience, Wiher warns, it may cause 'misunderstanding in the audience and [represent] a call to accept the culture of the missionary' leading to refusal, or a merely opportunistic, outward change. 'Conversion [that] bypasses the indigenous conscience,' he warns, 'may lead to superficial conformity or to compartmentalized conformity, that is, syncretism.'[7]

The role of dreams in drawing Muslims to faith in Jesus Christ has been frequently reported. Seppo Syrjänen[8] is among the few to move beyond phenomenology and consider psychological aspects of how God works in this way. In the search for meaning and identity, many dreams have a role as the culmination of an inner struggle granting license to do that which is otherwise prohibited. Richard Kronk builds on the thought of Carl Jung who 'upholds the possibility that some dreams have an outside source both

---

[5] A. Walls, 'Converts or Proselytes? The Crisis over Conversion in the Early Church', *International Bulletin of Missionary Research* 28, 1 (January 2004), 2-6.

[6] A. Maurer, 'In Search of a New Life: Conversion Motives of Christians and Muslims', in D. Greenlee (ed.) *From the Straight Path to the Narrow Way: Journeys of Faith* (Waynesboro, GA: Authentic and Secunderabad, India: OM Books India, 2006) 93-106. See also his 'In Search of a New Life: Conversion Motives of Christians and Muslims' (ThD dissertation, University of South Africa, 2006).

[7] H. Wiher, *Shame and Guilt: A Key to Cross-Cultural Ministry* (Bonn: Edition IWG, Mission Academics, Band 10, Verlag für Kultur und Wissenschaft), 367.

[8] S. Syrjänen, *In Search of Meaning and Identity: Conversion to Christianity in Pakistani Muslim Culture* (Vammala: Annals of the Finnish Society for Missiology and Ecumenics, 45, 1984), 132, 137.

in their content and in the occasion of their occurrence.' Dreams are significant because they are 'sources of religious significance for the Muslim... [who] relies heavily upon such to define reality, answer ultimate questions and guide his day-to-day activities'.[9]

These writers complement Jean-Marie Gaudeul who observes that we should not 'overlook the fact that the obscure mechanisms of the human psyche are also subject to divine action... [God] speaks to us in the kind of language we can understand, and it is not surprising if he uses dreams and visions and healings to people who believe in them.'[10]

The Behavioural Lens

Paul Hiebert often reminded us that conversion must involve all levels of culture, including the outer layer of behaviour. There is a danger of deception or misinterpretation, but 'transformed behaviour is... a sign of inner transformation and a testimony to the world of that transformation'.[11]

Observed behaviour in itself attracts others to faith in Christ. Mohammad Hassan Khalil and Mucahit Bilici, unusual as Muslim researchers writing about conversion *away* from Islam, make reference to only one attractive factor of the new faith (along with several negatives), a factor that has to do with Christian behaviour. They quote a Christian priest who never observed a Muslim 'who confessed that he accepted Jesus Christ as his Lord and Saviour' because of theological arguments. Instead, 'it is always through a small deed of brotherly love done by a Christian that the heart of a Muslim is moved'.[12]

Participation is a third part of the behavioural aspect of conversion. Mary McVicker observes that 'while physical and cognitive experiences of Jesus tend to differ according to social, economic, or educational backgrounds of the women, behavioural experience is a significant aspect for most Muslim women growing in relationship to God.' Her point has to do with moving beyond the logical, cognitive level in order to communicate with Asian Muslim women who 'taste *behavioural experience* that impacts their journey of coming to faith'.[13]

---

[9] R. Kronk, 'Non-Literary Personal Revelation: The Role of Dreams and Visions in Muslim Conversion' (MA thesis, Dallas Theological Seminary), 14, 22, 25-26.
[10] Gaudeul, *Called from Islam to Christ*, 225.
[11] Hiebert, 'Worldview Transformation', in Greenlee, *Straight Path*, 29.
[12] M.H. Khalil and M. Bilici, 'Conversion Out of Islam: A Study of Conversion Narratives of Former Muslims', *The Muslim World* 90, 1 (January 2007), 118.
[13] M. McVicker, 'Experiencing Jesus: Reflections of South Asian Women', in Greenlee, *Straight Path*, 133-34.

The Sociological Lens

The sociological lens is broad, and helps us consider groups such as migrants. Hasan Abdulahugli finds that those most open to the Gospel in Central Asia are 'those who have tasted hard economic conditions in traditional villages and have moved to the city, away from the social pressures of family, neighbours, and the mosque and into the freedom and love of Christian communities located in urban areas'.[14]

Mogens Mogensen found 'a pattern that links the conversion of immigrants to Christianity closely to their integration into the Danish society'.[15] Perhaps a negative confirmation of this, Gabriël Jansen, reporting only a handful of Moroccan believers in Christ in the Netherlands, finds that 'integration [into Dutch churches]… has turned out to be a disappointment for many'.[16]

Evelyne Reisacher describes important gender differences between North Africans in France. Women's social status, limitations on freedom, and the impact of rejection by family set them apart from men in coming to and growing in faith in Christ. Further, the women she interviewed perceived that, once having come to faith, women are more resilient and likely to persevere than are men.[17]

Robert L. Montgomery observes that 'the religions that have spread often seem to have offered a resource to leaders or to people as a whole in resisting threats to continued existence'[18] while conversion is less likely when no advantage is perceived. Complementing this thesis, Robert Hefner found that 'With Christianity [Javanese Muslim youth of the 1960s] declared their independence from a village social order that, in their eyes, had brought their families pain and humiliation.'[19] Conversely, as a researcher from the Caucasus wrote about 'not-yet-believing' youth in his country, their 'minds have been blinded to understand the true personality and work of Christ because this knowledge has been limited and distorted

---

[14] H. Abdulahugli, 'Factors Leading to Conversion among Central Asian Muslims', in Greenlee, *Straight Path*, 162.

[15] M. Mogensen, 'Migration and Conversion: The Conversion of Immigrants to Christianity in a Danish Context', in T. Engelsviken and T. Strandenæs (eds), *Mission to the World: Communicating the Gospel in the 21st Century, Essays in Honour of Knud Jørgensen* (Oxford: Regnum Books, 2008), 74.

[16] G. Jansen, 'Reaching Moroccans in Amsterdam (the Netherlands) with the Gospel' (MA thesis, Tyndale Theological Seminary, 2000), 133.

[17] E. Reisacher, 'North African Women and Conversion: Specifics of Female Faith and Experience', in Greenlee, *Straight Path*, 109-23.

[18] R.L. Montgomery, 'The Spread of Religions and Macrosocial Relations', *Sociological Analysis*, 52, 1 (1991), 50.

[19] R.W. Hefner, 'Of Faith and Commitment: Christian Conversion in Muslim Java', in R.W. Hefner (ed.), *Conversion to Christianity: Historical and Anthropological Perspectives on a Great Transformation* (Berkeley: University of California Press, 1993), 116.

over the years and the person of Jesus Christ still remains as [the] "God of Russians"'.

Andrew Bush reports that although there are close friendships between Christian and Muslim students at a Palestinian territories university, these relationships are 'hindered by the perception of the Muslim community that Christians in the West hate Palestinians... [and] Palestinian Christians become guilty by association'.[20] In comparison, Anthony Greenham notes that political instability played only a contributory role in the conversion accounts of Palestinians, and even that in only a minority of cases he analyzed. 'For most of the Palestinians, political instability may be too common a factor in their lives to suggest itself as an avenue for the transforming encounter of conversion.'[21]

Finally, under the sociological lens we consider group conversions and movements. Lowell DeJong describes the need for patience, avoiding pressure to quickly plant a church that almost certainly will be marked by the messenger's culture rather than leading to a culturally imbedded church.[22] This may help avoid problems Mogensen found in a related setting where, 'Almost all the [approximately 500] Fulbe converts still had a strong identity as Fulbe and as Christian Fulbe, but the majority of them had serious problems being accepted by their Fulbe community.' He concludes that this is evidently because 'the primary method of evangelism used among this tribe has been "extraction evangelism"'.[23]

In a tribal setting in West Africa, Dan McVey asked why, after an initial period of significant growth, a movement reached a plateau. 'The single greatest obstacle to church growth among the "Jijimba",' he found, was in clearly 'communicating the concept that one can be a follower of Jesus while maintaining identity as a "Jijimba".'[24]

---

[20] A.F. Bush, 'The Implications of Christian Zionism for Mission', *International Bulletin of Missionary Research*, 33, 3 (July 2009), 149.

[21] A. Greenham, 'Muslim Conversions to Christ: An Investigation of Palestinian Converts Living in the Holy Land' (PhD dissertation, Southeastern Baptist Theological Seminary, 2004), 190-91.

[22] L. DeJong, 'An Insider Movement among Fulbe Muslims', in Greenlee, *Straight Path*, 217, 224-28.

[23] M. Mogensen, 'Contextual Communication of the Gospel to Pastoral Fulbe in Northern Nigeria' (PhD dissertation, Fuller Theological Seminary, 2000), 273, 275, available at http://www.intercultural.dk/index.php?mainid=51&subid=571.

[24] D. McVey, 'Hindrances to Evangelistic Growth among Muslim Background Believer Churches of the "Jijimba" People of West Africa', in Greenlee, *Straight Path*, 211.

The Cultural Lens

McVey's comment leads us into consideration of the cultural lens and with it, the question of how questions of identity – individual and group – affect the process of conversion.[25] Lewis Rambo notes that, 'The more consonant the cultural systems [of messenger and receiver] the more likely it is that conversion will transpire. The more dissonant, the less likely it is that conversion will occur.'[26]

A recent study confirms this point, noting that the reason only a small number of Turks in Germany have 'committed their lives to Jesus Christ' may be many Christians' lack of awareness of 'the multicultural character of the Body of Christ', their conventional forms and traditions 'creating barriers between Germans and foreigners'. Further to this, John Leonard observed in France, that since 'immigrants from the same population [choose] different strategies in acculturation, we cannot take the example of any one group and make it normative for the entire population. The church must develop an approach that values what the immigrant values even if this is not what the church believes are best for the immigrant.'[27] Mogensen reports a similar barrier in northern Nigeria where 'a significant percentage of the Fulbe converts complained that they felt that the Christians did not welcome them in the church during the decision and incorporation phases.'[28]

The German study further observes that 'conversion to the Christian faith does not end in betrayal of the oriental culture [nor] threaten Turkish identity' but, in fact, it holds a high chance for the development of a healthy Turkish or Kurdish identity. This reaffirmed my own finding that a by-product of coming to faith in Christ among young Moroccan men was a heightened, positive sense of national identity.[29]

This question of identity has been increasingly explored in recent research. 'Does one have to go through Christianity to enter God's family?' asks Rebecca Lewis.[30] Far from suggesting religious inclusivism, she along

---

[25] 'Identity' could of course be fruitfully considered through other lenses, such as psychology.

[26] L.R. Rambo, *Understanding Religious Conversion* (New Haven: Yale University Press), 42.

[27] J. Leonard, 'Oasis: An Ethnography of a Muslim Convert Group in France' (PhD dissertation, Trinity Evangelical Divinity School, 2006), 292.

[28] Mogensen, 'Contextual Communication', 270.

[29] D. Greenlee, 'Christian Conversion from Islam: Social, Cultural, Communication, and Supernatural Factors in the Process of Conversion and Faithful Church Participation' (PhD dissertation, Trinity Evangelical Divinity School. 1996), 125-27.

[30] R. Lewis, 'Insider Movements: Honoring God-given Identity and Community', *International Journal of Frontier Missiology* 26, 1 (January 2009), 16-19.

with others such as John and Anna Travis[31] explore ways in which believers in Christ may remain completely faithful to Jesus and to the Bible, yet without unnecessarily rejecting (or giving the perception of rejecting) their families and culture.[32]

Approaching the subject from the perspective of history of religions, cultural anthropology, and Christian theology, Jonas Adelin Jørgensen studied followers of Jesus in Dhaka and Chennai who have not openly become part of the existing churches. Jørgensen supports the authenticity of the faith of these groups, for whom Jesus Christ is central, arguing that 'the practice of the *imandars* (faithful to Jesus) and *bhaktas* (devotees of Christ) could be viewed as new and creative manifestations of Christianity in a global age'. He concludes that 'the resemblance with the larger Christian tradition and community ensures Christian identity. At the same time, the differences enlarge our understanding of what actual and lived Christian life and Christian theology might include in globalized Christianity.'[33]

Kathryn Kraft explored the question of identity among Middle Eastern Muslims who had become followers of Jesus including many who encountered difficulties in integrating into and being identified with the existing churches. She notes that 'for most Muslims, leaving Islam cannot even be conceived of as a possibility. While choosing to follow Christ involves for most... consciously rejecting the Muslim creed, they do not want this to entail rejecting their strong cultural heritage, which is identified as Islamic. The biggest challenge they face in developing a new identity is determining how to continue to be culturally Muslim while following a Christian faith.'[34]

---

[31] J. Travis and A. Travis, 'Appropriate Approaches in Muslim Contexts', in C.H. Kraft (ed.) *Appropriate Christianity* (Pasadena: William Carey Library, 2005), 397-414 and 'Factors Affecting the Identity that Jesus-Followers Choose', in J. Dudley Woodberry (ed.), *From Seed to Fruit: Global Trends, Fruitful Practices, and Emerging Issues among Muslims* (Pasadena: William Carey Library, 2008), 193-205.

[32] The *International Journal of Frontier Missiology* frequently explores this 'identity' question with regard to Buddhists and Hindus, as well as Muslims, who have come to faith in Jesus Christ. See especially Vol. 24, focused on 'insider movements' available at http://www.ijfm.org/archives.htm.

[33] J.A. Jørgensen, 'Global Christianity, Contextual Religious Identity and Local Theologies: Isa Imandars and Khrist Bhaktas in South Asia', *Lausanne World Pulse*, http://www.lausanneworldpulse.com/themedarticles.php/895/02-2008 (February 2008). See also J.A. Jørgensen, *Jesus Imandars and Christ Bhaktas: Two Case Studies of Interreligious Hermeneutics and Identity in Global Christianity* (Studies in the Intercultural History of Christianity, 146: Frankfurt: Peter Lang,) and D. Jeyaraj, *Followers of Christ Outside the Church in Chennai, India* (Mission, 51: Zoetermeer: Boekencentrum, 2010).

[34] K.A. Kraft and Abu Atallah, 'The Lives of Arab Muslims who Choose the Christian Faith', *Mishkan* 54 (2008), 16-24.

How do these followers of Jesus find this new identity? Kraft summarizes that while they

> …generally recognize and feel a sense of commonality with each other, they approach their identity negotiation in a variety of ways. Some reject everything about their past and choose to become fully 'Christian.' These are the individuals who are most likely to break off relations with their former communities. Others consider their faith and their ethnicity to be completely separate and consider themselves to be both Muslim and followers of Christ; some of these sought to be socially indistinguishable from their Muslim neighbours. If pressed, most participants admitted to being Muslim in culture and Christian in creed, although the historical animosity between the world's two largest religions would preclude them from ever calling themselves 'Muslim Christians.' The participants who demonstrated the greatest degree of comfort with a well-developed identity were those who had successfully adhered to a Christian religious identity onto a pre-existing Muslim ethnic identity. Nonetheless, each participant worked through this process in his/her own way, usually using careful analysis and critique of his/her own beliefs and circumstances. They expressed a great deal of identity frustration but also agency to negotiate a new identity for themselves.[35]

The Spiritual Warfare Lens

The spiritual warfare lens (Ephesians 6:12) is especially relevant where 'folk Islam' with its various mystical and at times occult practices is prevalent.[36]

Interested in issues of power, a Norwegian researcher considered Indonesians who had come to faith in Jesus Christ. His findings point to the role of miracles in providing clear answers to genuine needs. They often serve as punctual events in the process of conversion, revealing the divine will and demonstrating the superior power of Jesus Christ over the spirit world. Although his research focus was on issues of power, he found that 'assurance of salvation remains the most significant reason for the conversions, even among those informants who fervently exalt the power aspects of the Gospel.'

The Human Communicator Lens

The process of conversion is intimately linked with divinely-enabled human witness (Acts 1:8). Reinhold Straehler reminds us that 'Holistic ministries or non-verbal ministries alone will not communicate to the Muslim that an alternative world-view is possible for him or her' since

---

[35] K.A. Kraft, 'Community and Identity Among Arabs of a Muslim Background who Choose to Follow a Christian Faith' (PhD dissertation, University of Bristol, 2007), 204.

[36] R. Love, *Muslims, Magic and the Kingdom of God: Church Planting Among Folk Muslims* (Pasadena: William Carey Library, 2000).

'there needs to be some verbal communication or communication via media (audio, visual or print).'[37] As Gabriël Jansen observed, among Moroccans who had come to faith in Amsterdam 'the most prominent shared factor [in witness] appears to be the continued personal friendly contact with one or more individual Christians, and most often with a living, loving Christian group'.[38]

The role of media and the methods of our witness vary and should not be seen in isolation from other factors in the process of conversion.[39] However, as Tobias Rink observes, 'The way in which the gospel is communicated, from the convert's viewpoint, is as meaningful as the content of the presentation.'[40] It may also affect the ability of the new believers to become fruitful witnesses themselves, especially where issues of literacy and orality are involved.

The Lens of God's Divine Role

Christian conversion is initiated and enabled by God (2 Cor. 5:18, Tit. 3:3-7). All of the other factors I have discussed are the ways and means by which he draws us to himself. I limit my comments here to two factors.

Numerous studies refer to the importance of Bible study in the process of conversion. Not all who read the Bible come to faith in Jesus Christ, however, for those who do, personal Bible reading, Bible correspondence courses, observing Luke's Gospel in the form of the *Jesus* film, and chronological Bible storying are reported in many studies as significant factors in the process of conversion.[41]

Finally, Abraham Durán speaks of the 'beauty of Jesus.' We must follow Jesus' own example, 'a gradual approach that will lead people to discern the truth and beauty of Jesus' personality, teachings, and life motivating them to be his followers.'[42] Or, in the words of Jean-Marie Gaudeul, 'The formulas of faith only begin to make sense, either suddenly or little by little, when Jesus has been recognized as one who loves us and saves us.'[43]

---

[37] R. Straehler, Reinhold, 'Conversion from Islam to Christianity in the Sudan' (MTh thesis, University of South Africa, 2005), 103-104.

[38] Jansen, 'Reaching Moroccans', 80.

[39] Greenham, 'Muslim Conversions to Christ', 193.

[40] T. Rink, 'Eine Multidimensionale Methodik zur Analyse von Bekehrungsmotiven' (MTh thesis, University of South Africa, 2006), 126.

[41] See, for example, Greenham, 'Muslim Conversions to Christ', Greenlee, 'Christian Conversion from Islam', and McVicker, 'Experiencing Jesus'.

[42] A. Durán, 'The Beauty of Jesus as an Evangelistic Factor', in Greenlee, *Straight Path*, 274.

[43] Gaudeul, *Called from Islam to Christ*, 52-53.

Summary Factors

How is God at work in drawing Muslims to faith in Jesus Christ through these diverse circumstances? Each person is unique; God's grace is creative. Those Muslims who now follow Jesus came to and live out their faith in many different ways. Prediction and prescription are to be avoided. However, three summary factors are independently referred to by several researchers.[44] Muslims who have come to faith in Jesus Christ usually have:

- Encountered the truth of God's Word;
- Received a touch of God's love through his people; and
- Seen a sign of God's power.

God's mercy is deep; his love is wide. The Gospel is good news – for *all* people! To God be all the glory!

[44] For example, Greenham, 'Muslim Conversions to Christ', 193, D. Smith, 'Looking Ahead', in Greenlee, *Straight Path*, pp 287-88, and Syrjänen, 'In Search of Meaning and Identity', 171-72.

Mission Among Hindus:
The 'Festival of Lights' as a Bridge Between Hindu and Christian Communities

Pramod Aghamkar

Introduction

Diwali or the Festival of Lights is synonymous with the popular Hinduism and embodies its core religious values. No other Hindu festival can keep alive the religion, unite the community or affirm the myths by connecting them to theological truths as *Diwali* does. High popularity of *Diwali* due to religious, communal, and cultural significance is well known around the world.[1] The United States Senate passed a historical resolution in 2007 to recognize *Diwali*, welcoming the Hindu festival.[2]

Worldwide receptivity of *Diwali* can serve as a bridge between Hindu and Christian communities for communication of the Gospel message. Contextualizing *Diwali* demands attention to a number of questions: What is *Diwali*? What theological truths undergird the festival? How might a contextual engagement of these theological truths facilitate better communication of the Gospel--in follow-up and discipleship processes, in worship, liturgy or teaching? This paper examines the form and meaning of Hindu and non-Hindu *Diwali* festivals, delineates Christian *Diwali* celebrated in Dayton, OH, USA and proposes creation of a Christian *Diwali*.

Hindu Demographic, Socio-Economic and Religious Affinities of Asian Indians in the USA

The Asian Indian community is one of the fastest growing ethnic groups in North America. The 1990 census indicated the number (not all Hindus) increased 125 percent during the 1980s. [3] The Sikh community grew to

---

[1] Julia Roberts, London, Nov 4, IANS. *http://www.deccanherald.com/content/110394/julia-roberts-wants-diwali-celebrated.html* (11 March 2011).

[2] Aziz Haniffa, 'Senate also adopts Diwali resolution' *India Abroad* 38.8 (23 November 2007a), A6.

[3] Edwin Scott Gaustan and Philip L. Barlow, *New Historical Atlas of Religion in America* (New York, NY: Oxford University Press 2000).

more than a million by 2002 and probably has doubled today.[4] The growth was 9 to 10 times faster than the general population, and by 2008, the Indian community was numerous enough to be taken seriously by American politicians.[5]

Indian cultural traditions remain strong in the United States. In June 2009, a group of about 25 Hindu professionals gathered in a huge home to talk about the economical situation in America. The home resembled a miniature Hindu centre with huge idols dominating the great room and a separate alter for more deities. The idols [about 4' x 3'] had been shipped directly from India, and the host acknowledged the rightful role in all of the success. Hindu prayers during the meeting vividly reaffirmed the group's commitment to their Hindu identity, while being American immigrants.

Hindu Religio-Cultural Adaptations in the Indian Communities

The Hindu worldview is based on the multiplicity of paths to the One (God), a concept referred in Bhagavad Gita 7:2; 9:23-24.[6] For example, Gandhi considered all faiths valid 'as long as [they] reach the same goal'.[7] The inclusive notion infers tolerance and automatically nullifies exclusivism, thus denouncing proselytisation. Traditional values are held high by the community as an ancient Hindu *dharma* (religion).[8]

In the United States, this worldview is increasingly engaging American culture. Modern missionary Hinduism is shaped by *gurus* and organizations associated with Krishna Consciousness.[9] Yoga and meditational activities show a growing Hindu religious engagement across cultural boundaries. The first Hindu prayer offered to open the US Senate on July 12, 2007 marked a milestone in history.[10] Recently, extreme changes are encountered by the Hindu community as a few transgress strict marriage patterns.[11]

---

[4] Gurmukh Singh, 'A Community of Overachievers' *India Abroad* 33.41 (11 July 2003), M3.

[5] Haniffa, 2008 'Asian community poised to swing US elections' *India Abroad* 39. 2 (10 October 2008), A14-A15.

[6] Swami Sivananda, *The Bhagavad Gita (*Shivanandanagar India: The Divine Life Society, 1995), 85.

[7] M. K. Gandhi, *My God* (Ahmedabad, India: Navajivan Publishing House, 1962), 35.

[8] M.R. Dua, 'Where's our Indian-ness?' *India Abroad* 33.41 (11July 2003), M14.

[9] Correspondent, 'ISKCON devotees on unique trip from Pennsylvania to Mexico' *India Abroad* 33:41 (2003), C1.

[10] Haniffa, 'Senate also adopts Diwali resolution' *India Abroad* 38.8 (23 November 2007), A12.

[11] Sandip Roy, 'My family thought it was an American thing' *India Abroad* 39.42 (17 July 17 2009), M12.

The Pluralism Project lists 723 Hindu temples in the US.[12] Additional Jain, Sikh, and Indian Buddhist centres, however, could increase the number to as high as 1500, based on the growth of the community today. About fifty temples visited by the author exhibit traditional sacred architecture, but show innovative or adaptive patterns of assimilation. *Pooja* (prayer) programs designed to meet the community needs.

An estimated five million people from India and a dozen other Asian countries are now living in the US and celebrate *Diwali*. Normally *Diwali* celebrations draw crowds of around 50,000 in Irving, Atlanta, Chicago, and Boston.[13]

A few Hindu sects incorporate Jesus into their pantheon of deities. The majority of Hindus in non-western countries view Christianity as a foreign religion and its converts as unpatriotic. Antagonism towards evangelistic activities by extremists remains strong.[14]

A creative presentation of the Christian message – by using local festivals and especially parts of *Diwali* compatible with the Gospel – would be well received and improve rapport between the faiths. Any social or household setting could be used, for '[a]t least 80 percent of India's Christian population is estimated to have come to faith via a group decision process'[15]. A shared celebration of *Diwali* between Christians and the Hindu community could open new possibilities for unprecedented effectiveness of the Message.

Form and Meaning of Hindu *Diwali*

Diwali or *Deepavali* – literally meaning a row of lamps – annually falls on a new moon day during the months of *Ashwin-Kartika* (October-November). The five-day celebration begins from the 13th day of the dark half of the lunar month *Ashvina* until the second day of the light half of *Kartika.*[16] The festival includes the following general activities rooted in a number of ancient Hindu myths and traditions.

Day one, *Dhanteras*, or *Dhantrayodashi* is associated with the worship of *Dhanwantari*. He appeared at the churning of the ocean carrying nectar in his hand. Buildings and home entrances are adorned with traditional motifs and auspicious hangings. Hindu families buy gold as a sign of

---

[12] Pluralism Project, *http://www.pluralism.org/resources/statistics/tradition.php#Hinduism* (17 June 2009).

[13] Monika Joshi and Ayoti Mittra, 'Community Braces for Festive Season' *India Abroad* 39.2 (10 October 2008), A48-A49.

[14] Suman Guha Mozumder, 'Christian groups protest Orissa violence outside United Nations' *India Abroad* 39.4 (24 October 2008), A15.

[15] Roger E. Hedlund, *Mission to Man in the Bible* (Madras, India: Evangelical Literature Service, 1985), 228.

[16] Jayant Salgaonkar (Ed), *Kalanirnaya* [Semi Almanac] (Mumbai, India: ABC Prakashan, 2009), 10.

increase and worship five grains on this day. Most worship cattle the day prior or during this period as the symbol of wealth.

The second day is Narak *Chturdashi.* The day preceding *Diwali* Lord *Krishna* killed the demon king *Narakaasura* and rescued 16,000 daughters from captivity. The story conveys his ultimate victory over evil. On the new moon of *Kartik* Lord *Rama,* his wife *Sita* and his brother *Laxamana* returned to the kingdom of *Ayodhya* after vanquishing the evil king *Ravana*. The citizens of *Ayodhya* decorated the city with earthen lamps to welcome Lord *Rama* who is revered as the role model king and husband. This day libations are offered to appease *yama* the deity of death.

The third day is important one for business community and to be devoted to the propitiation of *Laximi*, the goddess of wealth. According to a myth, *Laximi* appeared on the new moon day (*amaavasyaa*) of the month *Kartik* during the churning of the ocean for nectar. It is believed that she loiters through by-lanes and showers blessings. On this day *Laximi* is worshiped along with cash, gold, silver and account books.

Day four is called *Varshapratipada* and marks coronation of the king *Vikramaditya*. According to a Hindu myth, *Krishna* stopped the city of *Gokul* from offering prayers to Lord *Indra* who in anger sent a deluge to submerge the people. Nevertheless, *Krishna* saved the city miraculously. This day is considered the most auspicious day to start any new venture.

Bhau Beej, (*Bahi Tika* in Nepal) observed on day five as a symbol of love between siblings. Sisters offer prayers for brothers with an *aarati* (prayer/praise chants). A brother stands in place of *Krishna* who did the noble deed by killing the demon *Narkasura.* A ritual for a brother's longevity and prosperity includes a special square shaped space drawn on the floor, lined with various designs in corn powder or rice grains. A brother(s) may taste a bitter fruit (*Karith*) from a plate holding a lighted earthen lamp before stepping into the square. The sister(s) put a red mark on the brother(s)' forehead and make clockwise and anti-clockwise signs by hand holding silver and gold coins respectively. After eating sweets, the brother (s) in exchange offer presents as a token of love and promise to care for the sister(s). Those who do not have a brother perform a *pooja* (worship/prayer) to the Moon-God.

Most common in *Diwali pooja* (worship) is *aarati* led by a priest or a family head, which includes singing while a plate with a lighted lamp, incense, turmeric, and red powders is circled clockwise facing a deity. The *pooja* ritual at home includes an offering to *agni* (fire), welcoming, installing, foot washing, and decorating the deities followed by the offering of food, fruits, clothing, or money.

Fresh flowers, specific herbs, and plants including *jhal-phaag* used in the rituals.[17] Orange flags are installed. Lamps are kept constantly burning in front of the family deities. S*hloka* (verses) chants, the ringing of bells

[17] Jhal-phaag: A combination of milk, *ghee* (clarified butter), honey and spices.

and the blowing of conch shells symbolize blessings bestowed. *Prasada* (offered food) is distributed to all.

An interesting custom characterizing *Diwali* in North India is indulging in gambling. It is believed that the Goddess *Parvati* played dice with her husband Lord *Shiva* on this day and decreed that whoever gambled on *Diwali* night would prosper throughout the ensuing year. The tradition of playing cards and rummy with monetary stakes on this particular day continues until now.[18] The proposed Christian *Diwali* will exclude this element.

Non-Hindu *Diwali* Festivals

While the Hindu *Diwali* is based on religious myths, Sikhs, Jains and Neo-Buddhists (not discussed) celebrate *Diwali*, but for different reasons. [19]

Sikh Diwali

The Sikh community celebrates in *Diwali* the story of their struggle for freedom based on history.[20] The foundation stone of the global centre of Sikhism, the Golden Temple called *Har Mandar* in India was laid on *Diwali* day in 1577. *Guru* Hargobind Singh, the sixth Sikh *Guru*, was released from the captivity of a Muslim emperor in India in 1619 with 52 other chiefs. He 'earned the appellation of Bandi-Chhor,' meaning deliverer from prison.[21] The released *guru* arrived at Amritsar on *Diwali* day, the Golden Temple was illuminated with lamps, and the day came to be known as the *Bandi Chhor Divas* (day of freedom). Thereafter, *Diwali* in Sikhism commemorates his triumphant arrival and regards the movement dedicated to justice.[22]

---

[18] Diwali Pooja, *http://www.Diwalifestival.org/Diwali-pooja.html* (18June 2009).

[19] The term Neo-Buddhists refers to converts to Buddhism from low caste community under the leadership of Dr. B.R. Ambedkar in the central part of India since 1956. As untouchables the community followed animism with Hindu ideas of *Diwali*. Post conversion *Diwali* incorporated elements of Buddhism . See B.R. Ambedkar, *The Buddha and His Dhamma* (Bombay: Siddharth Publication 1957). Bhau Lokhande, *Boudhanche San, Utsav ani Mansikta* [*Buddhist Festivals, Celebrations and Manners*] (Wardha, India: Sudhir Prakashan 2009).

[20] Sikh Festivals, *http://www.allaboutsikhs.com/sikh-festivals/the-sikh-festivals-divalibandi-chhorh-divas.html* (18 June 2009).

[21] Brigadier Hardit Singh, '"Guru Hargobindji, His Life and Times." Review Guru Hargobindji, His Life and Times', *Abstracts of Sikh Studies* (October -December 1996), 79.

[22] W. Owen Cole, *The Guru in Sikhism* (London: Darton, Longman and Todd 1982), 26.

According to Sikhs, the *Guru* accomplished these extraordinary things through immense spiritual power.[23] *Guru* Hargobind Singh and martyrs are venerated during *Diwali* by offering incense and flowers. The recitation of *Grantha Sahib* (the Sikh scriptures) and religious discourses are held in *Gurudwaras* (Sikh temples). The celebration includes *Kirtan* (devotional singing), a communal meal, and the distribution of food--all without idolatry.[24]

Jain Diwali

Jains tend to celebrate *Diwali* for mystical reasons and as a reminder to follow in the footsteps of *Tirthankar* (teacher) *Mahavira*.[25] *Mahavira* believed to have attained *nirvana* (eternalness) around 2500 years ago on *Diwali* day. 'A new era started from this day which is called *Nirvana Samvat*, which is in vogue among the Jains.'[26] Celebrations include *pooja*, *aarati*, Jain vegetarian food, new clothes, and decorations in homes by the lighting of clay lamps. Worship of the Hindu Goddess *Laximi* is common among certain Jain groups. A collective *aarati* in Jain temples is followed by food.

Non-Hindu accounts show *Diwali* to be a flexible multi-faceted festival. Hindus celebrate it for myths, Sikhs for historical facts and Jains for mystical reasons. Hindus in Nepal feed dogs and cows in north India to express humane concern for the cattle.[27]

Although neither the form nor the reason of celebration is intrinsically Hindu, Jain, or Sikh, several common principles can be summarized – the truth prevails, light overcomes darkness, and the source of prosperity is supernatural. *Diwali* gives opportunity 'to choose the right path that would lead to a life of purity, divinity, and happiness'.[28] Concern for family and humane treatment of cattle are priorities. Though the principles are 'non-Christian', they are not 'un-Christian'.[29]

---

[23] Sameerjit Singh, *Personal Interview by the Author*, Dayton, OH: Dayton Gurdwara (2009).

[24] Ranbir Singh, *The Sikhs and Their Religion* (Dublin, OH: Sikh Educational and Religious Foundation 1999).

[25] Reshma Chandrakant, *Personal phone interview by the author about Jain Diwali.* 28 July 2009.

[26] Hukamchand Bharill, *Tirthankara Mahavira and His Sarvodaya Tritha* (Bombay: Shri Kundkund Kahan Digambar Jain Tritha Suraksha Trust 1981), 61.

[27] A.P. Nirmal, *'Celebrations of Indian Festivals' Primal World Views* (Ibadan, Nigeria: Daystar Press 1976), 81.

[28] Ashwin Kumar, 'Happy Deepavali'. A Message Script Presented at the Hindu Temple of Dayton, Dayton, OH.2008, 35.

[29] Nirmal, *'Celebrations of Indian Festivals,'* 81-82.

Since the festival of *Diwali* encompasses Hindu, Sikh, Jain, and Buddhist observances with variability, could this lead to a contextualization of a Christian *Diwali*?

A *Diwali* Celebrated by Christians in Dayton (Ohio, USA)

A new celebration of *Diwali* by the Indian Christians of Dayton (OH, USA) began with an idea of incorporating and performing native music for the Indian Diaspora. The founder of Satsang Ministries (the author) took initiative to plan the celebration. His prior experience living among Indian communities in India provided insider's perceptions of the religions represented including the knowledge of the languages, myths, deities, art, *mantras* (chanted prayers), and music. He believes that the celebration of *Diwali* is especially compatible with the message of Jesus, who proclaimed 'I am the Light of the world' John 8:12, and 'you are the light of the world' Matthew 5:14.

Vision:

Create and celebrate a Christian *Diwali*.

Purpose:

To plant Gospel seeds in native soil by using the form and compatible elements from *Diwali*. To break down barriers, begin meaningful friendships, gain trust, and build bridges for the Kingdom.

Communication:

Methods included formal, informal, relational and word of mouth. Orange flyers stated details with artists' names and lead singer's picture. Music was emphasized particularly for the Indian Diaspora. The leader formed a team of Indian believers and church friends to accomplish the task.

Venue:

Neutral venues preferred e.g. fellowship or school halls.

Decoration:

Indian women decorated the hall with clay lamps, souvenirs, handmade paintings, etc. Except for images, almost anything Indian was welcomed. A backdrop with pictures of beautiful lamps, Indian flags, and lighted lamps with flowers on the tables for guests made it festive.

Community:

Involvement by multi faith communities was encouraged. A Hindu leader and a pastor lighted the traditional brass lamp together to mark the beginning of the event. Indian leaders shared stories of *Diwali*. The pastor's role was to welcome attendees and to share briefly the Christian meaning of light, based on the story of Jesus. Indian guests, the pastor, and the main singer received customary flowers. The Indian community felt connected when church people served them tea and refreshments.

Music:

Traditional Indian music and instruments such as harmonium (Indian key board), drums (*tabla*), cymbals, violin, and even *tambora* (stringed instrument) are essential. Artists in Indian attire performed seated on a decorated platform.

Hindi, India's national language and *Ghazal* a well-known music style in India and the Muslim world was chosen. Lyrics closely resembled the poetic wisdom literature in the Bible. The author's brother, Prasad Aghamkar, well versed in the language and in *Ghazal* music, was the main singer. Indian people associate God alone as the source of true wisdom and the communicators of pure wisdom command respect from across social boundaries(1 Kings 10:24; 5:12; 4:34). The missionary implication of wisdom literature in the Bible is very relevant during *Diwali.*[30]

The Message:

The message in songs covered similar points found in the address to people of other religions on Mars Hill (Acts 17). A point of contact established by taking up religious themes from popular Indian songs and poets as did St. Paul 'to engage the Athenian worldview and culture'.[31] Family and socio-cultural issues were mentioned, followed by answers to the deeper concerns (Acts 17:22). Lastly Jesus is presented as the Light through songs written by the singer or converts from India (Acts 17:24).

The singer presented the message gradually without syncretism and refrained from attacking obvious things (Acts 17:23). Love, justice, life, and God were topics used in Christian *Diwali* celebrations in other cities.

The challenges included the idea of Christian *Diwali was* questioned by Hindu antagonists; theological concerns surfaced over decorative iconography and songs with mythic stories requested during the concert. The interfaith nature of the event and wise interaction helped to defuse the situation. Internally, westernized Christians of Indian descent worried that *Diwali* was a non-Christian practice; however, participant observation in the Christian *Diwali* helped to resolve their retrospective concerns.

The annual celebration of *Diwali* in Dayton made possible interaction with hundreds of Hindu friends. In its tenth year, the celebration has multiplied to other cities in partnership with local churches and Indian Christians.

Christian *Diwali* Suggested Beyond Dayton

The next step is to offer suggestions for structuring authentic Christian *Diwali* celebrations on a wider scale. The following suggestions are based on Dayton Christian *Diwali* and the author's experiments elsewhere. He

---

[30] Hedlund, *Mission to Man in the Bible*, 144.

[31] Dean Flemming, *Contextualization in the New Testament: Patterns for Theology and Mission* (Downers Grove, Illinois: InterVarsity, 2005), 75.

believes that Christian *Diwali* can retain much of the form of *Diwali*, while giving the story of Jesus new meaning and a pivotal significance. The Gospel story renders new meaning to theological themes known previously. It opens the door for the Indian community to experience the fulfillment of the Truth in a native way.

The use of native festivals such as *Diwali* can fulfill a fourfold purpose for the Kingdom: Build bridges of friendship, plant Gospel seeds, disciple seekers, and educate Christians.

Vision:

Use native festivals such as *Diwali* for the Kingdom purpose.

Day/Time:

Adapt the same, namely the five days including the new moon day in the month of *Kartik* (October-November) similar to Jain and Sikh communities.

Festivities:

Utilize maximum native elements such as clay lamps, Indian gift articles in colours depicting Christian art, symbolism, and verses to communicate the message. Visual witness to the Jesus story through the Indian motifs is important. Illumination of church buildings and centres during this period would create goodwill. Most importantly, the message is sent that Christians hold a non-separatist stance.

Family Prayer:

Preparation would include taking a holy bath, cooking vegetarian food, white garb and women wearing non-occult ornaments. Christian *aarati* would include the reciting of Psalms while lighting a clay lamp on a platter symbolizing Jesus, oil symbolizing the Holy Spirit as the family learns the Bible together led by the head of the family. *Bhajan* (singing) in native languages while seated on the floor with open Bible in a high place should be normal.

The Christian *Bhau Beej* would include visits by brothers to sisters' homes. Preparation may include a ritual place with the symbol of the cross and the Bible verses on the floor drawn by corn powder or rice grains where the brother(s) sits. A platter with a lamp, oil, flowers, and sweets from sisters will mean prayer for longevity and spiritual growth (Deuteronomy 6: 6-9). Brothers may respond by sharing gifts to their sisters symbolizing a promise to pray.

The new *Bhau Beej* would be very meaningful in follow up and discipleship of new believers in India. Ostracized new Christians would find it timely and deeply meaningful to be incorporated in the native manner in the Body of Christ as brothers or sisters (Matthew 19:29). The *Bhau Beej* based on Biblical promises could give greater value to the step of new believers from Hinduism and make the transition acceptable for their non-Christian relatives. Practicing Indian family values at the festival time could create stronger connections, build bridges and open new avenues for witness into Asian Indian homes.

Corporate Worship:

Church services, recitation, Indian singing, dances, and Bible dramas by the community would be ideal during the public facet of Christian *Diwali* celebrations. Open sanctuaries could welcome all to join to worship for five days. The native style of sitting on the floor, usage of flowers and certain colours without icons would create an inviting space for all. Taking Holy Communion during *Diwali* as a family or in churches could be the culmination of the festival.

Festival of Service:

The church as the community of light could get involved in humanitarian and ecological projects especially during *Diwali* time. Holistic concern would demonstrate the way of Jesus to encounter the forces of darkness, poverty, and injustice. Its purgative potential to redefine the meaning of the light is encompassing. Christian mercy acts communicate that God is concerned with history and nature.[32]

Dialogue and Witness:

Diwali probably is the most natural time for the celebrants to understand the true meaning of light at the deepest level. Gospel roots start mostly in contextual events, words, or actions. Christian *Diwali* activities are not meant to be regimented so much as a shared time of engagement.

Contextualizing festivals and *Diwali* in particular is an effort limited or nonexistent in India. A home festival with an emphasis on the Light and the Word was introduced during the Christian mini mass movements in the central part of India in the mid 20th century. As the author observed, the practice was limited to mission compounds and remains almost untraceable today.

However, Roman Catholic Churches in South India have celebrated *Pongal* (Harvest festival) for a long time. Recently indigenous Protestant groups are encouraging adaptations of *Pongal* and village festivals in South India.[33] These steps hold potential of a move towards making *Diwali* a normal festival for Christians.

Observations

The Christian *Diwali* of Dayton has consistently been able to bring together hundreds of Indian people including friends of Arabic orientation to church halls or campuses at the invitation of Indian Christians. Members of Indian Diaspora especially felt respected by provision of a new interfaith celebration that is positive toward their identity. Additionally, trust and communication level between non-Christian Indians and the Christian

[32] Nirmal, *'Celebrations of Indian Festivals' Primal World Views*, 83.

[33] Ebe Sundar Raj, *Sat Guru Aradhana*. (Mussoorie, India: Nivedit Good Books 2007), 54,103.

community improved. A church lay leader said, 'Being a non-threatening festive event, it provided us a venue to invite non-Christian friends.' Meaning, it would not have been possible to invite them to join traditional Christian meetings. *Diwali* gatherings enhanced meaningful interaction and helped plant Gospel seeds in soils otherwise inaccessible.

A man of Arabic orientation unexpectedly told his Indian friend after a *Diwali* music concert about reading the Bible daily at home (probably secretly). Such a confession is inconceivable in a traditional setting and its Kingdom value cannot be underestimated. Seekers and native new believers tend to retain local practices and customs mostly due to social pressures or out of ignorance. The tension between embedded compatible *Diwali* elements and forms of western Christianity remains. Free adaptation by indigenous believers could lead to spontaneous contextualization with didactic values for contextualizers today.[34]

A fresh study could help missiologists understand how new seekers initiate incorporating Gospel elements while practicing old traditions and how Christian *Diwali* could be assimilated as part of the normal Christian celebration in certain areas. The local churches' involvement renewed their vision for contextualization and follow-up. Possibilities of new dialogues and hospitality ministries to pave the way and soften differences between extremist Indian groups and Christians emerged. The westernized Indian Christians comprehended through participation the missiological implications of almost everything done in *Diwali*. A contextualization team has been trained and willing to embark on the Christian *Diwali* mission, trusting in the Holy Spirit to bring transformation of lives.

The festival of *Diwali* provides the necessary framework, structure, and organic occasion to proclaim Christ as the light of the world. It gives stepping-stones, clues, and redemptive analogies for the cross-cultural witness.[35] Christian *Diwali* is not shifting from radical rejection to wholesale acceptance of a Hindu festival. The process of discarding incompatible elements is not to be minimized. Serious in-depth study of the Word, traditions, and experimentation to acquire insider perceptions are necessary in order how best to adapt the festivals. A contextualizing community of new believers, pastors and lay leaders, must be gathered to critique cultural practices in a hermeneutical process.[36] Christian contextualization is a sacred interaction between the Gospel (story) and the native festivals (myths). The Gospel is as relevant as its contextualization.

---

[34] Pramod Aghamkar, 'Building Church on Holy Ground: Proposals to Contextualize Church Buildings in India' (Ph.D. Dissertation, E.S.J. School of World Mission and Evangelism, Asbury Theological Seminary, 2002).

[35] Hedlund, *Mission to Man in the Bible*, 56.

[36] Paul G. Hiebert, 'Critical Contextualization' *International Bulletin of Missionary Research* 11.3 (1987), 104-112.

Jesus is the key to cast new meaning and give fulfillment to *Diwali* festivals (Hindu, Jain, Sikh or Buddhist).

Concluding Remarks

The Christian *Diwali* in Dayton based on the popular phenomenon was a radical step of willful immersion into native cultures, which includes the conceptual and prevailing ideological world (Matthew 28:18-20). Christian *Diwali* finds its fulfillment only in illustrating, communicating, and heralding the story of Jesus. The Gospel confronts the darkness non-polemically, unites orthodoxy and orthopraxis, and compels balance between celebration and service. The vast arena of contextualization of *Diwali* remains an untapped native tool and demands a drastically changed approach towards it by the Indian church.

Dissemination of the Christian *Diwali* locally and globally with the Kingdom cause is not an option but an obligation. The positive steps would '...allow the faith a chance to start a history of its own in each people and its experience of Christ'.[37] A professional Indian woman, an active member in a temple, said after a Dayton celebration in 2007, 'The last song was very touching and meaningful to us'. She and her scientist husband who plays Indian drums for the Christian *Diwali* referred to the Gospel song. Their response reaffirmed the new meaning communicated by the event – through *Diwali*, the Gospel encountered 'but on the deeper level of the underlying existential realities, 'the hearts'.[38] Innumerable non-Christian Indian friends around the world could willingly join, engage, and respond in similar words if given an opportunity to discover the true meaning of the Light through Christian *Diwali*.

---

[37] David J. Bosch, *Transforming Mission* (Maryknoll, NY: Orbis Books, 1991).

[38] Tiina Ahonen, *Transformation through Compassionate Mission* (Helsinki: Luther-Agricola-Society, Finland, 2003).

MISSION AMONG HINDUS:
WITNESSING CHRIST IN THE COMPANY OF HINDUS

K.P. Aleaz

This paper envisages a perspective that 'Mission to People of Other Faiths' can be reconceived today as 'Witnessing Christ in the Company of People of Other Faiths'. The first section clarifies the significance of this shift of emphasis and submits it to the august participants of Edinburgh 2010 for consideration as a direction for mission-thinking in the days to come. The second and third sections are specifically on witnessing Christ in the company of Hindus. Indian Christian thinkers had and is having numerous dialogues with Hindus and their faith experiences and diverse enriching affirmations of Christian faith have emerged as a result of this and the second section indicates the highlights of a few of these. The third section is on the contributions of a few Hindu witnesses to Christ, specifically Neo-Vedantic understandings and interpretations of Jesus. Finally we provide some concluding observations.

The Rationale for Witnessing Christ in the Company of People of Other Faiths

Understanding the religious experiences of the people of other faiths would enrich our Christian understanding and experiencing of the person and function of Jesus as well as the gospel. With humility we may have to accept that there are certain dimensions of meanings regarding Jesus and the gospel which are unfamiliar or not known to us which can be explained to us by people of other faiths. A deeper meaning of Christ and the Christian gospel may emerge in a process of an inter-religious communication. People from diverse religio-cultural backgrounds will, within and for their contexts, understand the meaning of the gospel.[1]

The hermeneutical process and interpretation is important here. It is the hermeneutical context or the contextual socio-political and religio-cultural realities which decide the content of our knowledge and experience of the gospel. Knowledge is formulated in the very knowing process and understanding the gospel of God in Jesus, and is a continuous integrated non-dual divine-human process. Nothing is pre-given or pre-formulated.

---

[1] K. Aleaz, *Some Indian Theological Reflections* (Kolkata: Punthi Pustak, 2007), 68.

We cannot accept some timeless interpretation from somewhere and make it applicable to our context. Understanding and interpretation belongs exclusively to us and to our context, and there is the possibility for the emergence of new meanings of the gospel in the processes of this.[2] One important aspect of the Asian-Indian context is religious pluralism and we, Christians, are in pilgrimage to progressively integrate the truth revealed to others in our own experience of Jesus Christ. We have a duty to identify the glorious ways in which God's revelations are available to us in other religious experiences which can help us to experience new dimensions of meanings of the gospel of God in Jesus.[3] Rather than evaluating other religious experiences in terms of pre-formulated criteria, it is important for us to allow ourselves to be evaluated by them in our understanding of the gospel. They, in the Holy Spirit, will provide us with new meanings of the person and function of Jesus, rather than we dictate to them always. From a particular understanding of Jesus, we have to come to a universal understanding of Jesus.[4] Universal Jesus belongs to the whole of humanity in the Holy Spirit. Here there is growth and newness in the very conception of the person and function of Jesus.

Here we are challenged to evolve a more comprehensive role for other religious experiences in Christian experience than what has been envisaged in the past. To reduce the role of religions to a liberational praxis is a reductionism. To reduce the interpretation of religions solely in terms of folk tales again would be a reductionism. Of course our focus should be the people, as has been emphasized by the Asian theologians. How the comprehensive religious life of people of other faiths is related to the gospel of God in Jesus is the basic question to be answered in the third millennium.[5]

There is a suggestion here for a relational convergence of religious experiences. An important aspect of relational convergence of religious experiences is mutual conversion. Being born in a religion does not mean that we should die in that religion in the same way as we were born. We can get converted into the true sprit of one's own religion and in that very conversion get converted into another religious experience as well. The faith experience of an Indian Christian is not pre-formulated, but is in a process of formulation through the guidance of Hindu and other religious experiences. Indian Christian theology is a conversion of Christian theology to the Indian religio-cultural context. In the very conversion to Jesus in India, there is a conversion to the religio-cultural context of India,

---

[2] K. Aleaz, *The Gospel of Indian Culture* (Calcutta: Punthi Pustak, 1994), 177-282.
[3] Cf. K. Aleaz, *An Indian Jesus from Sankara's Thought* (Calcutta: Punthi Pustak, 1997).
[4] K. Aleaz, *The Role of Pramanas in Hindu-Christian Epistemology* (Calcutta: Punthi Pustak, 1991), 99-100.
[5] K. Aleaz, *Religions in Christian Theology* (Kolkata: Punthi Pustak, 2001), 183-208.

effecting thus a double conversion which points to the possible relational convergence of religious experiences. Religious conflicts are transcended in such an understanding of conversion.[6]

This points to a perspective in inter-religious relations in which all the religious resources of the world are conceived as the common property of the whole humanity. All religious experiences and traditions are simultaneously ours. We do not have any one particular religious tradition alone as our own and others as belonging to others. All are mine as well as all are for all others. All belong to all. It is a religious perspective in which while remaining in one's own religious faith-experience, one can consider other faiths as one's own, as the common property of humanity, for an increasingly blessed and enriched life. It should be noted that if one is intimately familiar with one's own religious system alone, that is a very religiously poverty stricken condition. Here the affirmation is of an inter-connected identity and uniqueness of each of the religious experiences as our own.[7]

Highlights on Christian Dialogues with Hindu Faith-Experiences

Indian Christian thinkers, some of them converts from Hindu faith, since the second half of 19th c., had numerous dialogues with Hindu faith-experiences out of which they have articulated Christian theological reflections on God and Jesus Christ in diverse ways and these reflections are part of the glorious history of Indian Christian theological heritage. These theological reflections provide us new creative insights regarding the Gospel today. New dimensions of meanings regarding the person and function of Jesus have emerged through these reflections. In terms of these reflections Christians are able to witness Christ in the company of Hindus today. There are interpretations on Trinity as *Saccidananda* as well as on the Christian notion of God as corresponding to *Nirguna* Brahman. Christ is interpreted in diverse ways such as God's appearance in the midst of appearances, embodiment of supreme self-sacrifice, one who has to be placed in Ultimate Reality, who enables us to return to unity and who eliminated *avidya* (ignorance), a case of *vivarta*, as theocentric; as extrinsic denominator (*upadhi*), name and form (*namarupa*), the effect(*karya*) of Brahman as well as the reflection (*abhasa*), pervasion, illumination,

---

[6] K. Aleaz, *Theology of Religions: Birmingham papers and Other Essays* (Calcutta: Moumita, 1998), 339-353.

[7] Aleaz, *Theology of Religions*, 176-180; W. C. Smith, *Faith and Belief*, Princeton: Princeton University Press, 1979, 11; *Towards a World Theology: Faith and Contemporary History of Religion*, (London: The Macmillan Press Ltd., 1981), 4-21; 38-44.

unification and delimitation of Brahman in creation, as *Istadevata*, *Isvara*, *Avatara*, Initiator of new creation and the *True Prajapati*.[8]

To speak of Brahman as Saccidananda means that Brahman knows Himself/Herself and from that self-knowledge proceeds His/Her eternal beatitude. Brahman is related of necessity only to the Infinite Image of His/Her own being, mirrored in the ocean of His/Her knowledge. This relation of Being (*Sat*) to Itself in self-knowledge (*Cit*) is one of perfect harmony, bliss (*Ananda*).The Christian doctrine of God as Trinity has a strong resemblance to the Vedantic conception of Brahman as *Saccidananda*, because in the Trinity the Father's knowledge is fully satisfied by the cognition of the *Logos*, the Infinite Image of his Being, begotten by thought and mirrored in the ocean of his substance and his love finds the fullest satisfaction in the boundless complacency with which he reposes on his Image and breathes forth the Spirit of bliss.[9] *Saccidananda* is communion of the Father, Son and the Holy Spirit. It is in the Father's self-awareness and presence to Himself in the Son, that everything that is has come to be. The Son, as he is representative Son of man, is the representation of the created beings in *Cit*; the created beings awake to Being through the Son. *Ananda*, the Holy Spirit is the expression of love in God, love between God and humans and love between humans.[10] *Nirguna* Brahman corresponds to Absolute Personality and does not mean impersonal, abstract, unconscious Being. It means that the attributes which relate the Infinite to the finite are not necessary to His/Her being. Therefore it rightly corresponds to the Christian notion of God.[11]

Jesus Christ is God's appearance in the midst of appearances. In Christ the absolutely transcendental God serves Himself/Herself from Himself/Herself to produce the appearance and to become appearance.[12] The event of Jesus as Christ has to be placed in the Ultimate Reality.[13] Creation is a case of *vivarta* as Brahman remains unchanged by effecting

---

[8] K. Aleaz, *Dialogical Theologies: Hartford Papers and Other Essays* (Kolkata: Punthi Pustak, 2004), 111-26.

[9] Brahmabandhav Upadhyaya, 'A Vedantic Parable', *Sophia* 4:8 (Aug. 1898), 119; 'An Exposition of Catholic Beliefs Compared with the Vedanta', *Sophia* 4:1 (Jan. 1898), 11; 'Our New Canticle', *Sophia* 5:10 (Oct.1898), 146.

[10] Swami Abhishiktananda, *Saccidananda: A Christian Approach to Advaitic Experience* (Delhi: ISPCK, 1974), 79-80, 82, 88, 91, 95, 97, 98, 176-79, 184-85; *Hindu-Christian Meeting Point. Within the Cave of the Heart* (Bombay/Bangalore: The Institute of Indian Culture/CISRS, 1969), xiv, 80, 96-97.

[11] B. Upadhyaya, 'Notes', *Sophia* 1:2 (June 23, 1900), 7; Johanns, 'To Christ through the Vedanta', *Light of the East* 1:1,(Oct. 1922)-12:7 (April 1934); R. V. De Smet, 'Categories of Indian Philosophy and Communication of the Gospel', *Religion and Society* 10:3 (Sept. 1963), 20-26.

[12] Cf. Carl Keller, 'The Vedanta Philosophy and the message of Christ', *The International Review of Missions* Vol. 42 (1953), 377-89.

[13] J. G. Arapura, 'The Use of Indian Philosophical Traditions in Christian Thought', *The Indian Journal of Theology* 29:2 (April-June 1980), 68-71.

the world and similarly Christ's incarnation is also a case of *vivarta* because when the divine Logos takes unto Himself/Herself the human nature the novelty which follows this actuation is entirely on the side of the human nature.[14] There is a progress possible from 'Christo-monism' to a theo-centric Christology.[15]

Renunciation or Love and Sacrifice which Christ has taught us through his life are similar to giving up duality to find the God behind it. The death on the Cross of Jesus Christ can be experienced and expounded as dying to the body and ego as well as the material world.[16] In understanding the work of Christ people from Hindu background are unable to find meaning in the idea of expiation and juridical justification, rather the function of Jesus is experienced as releasing precious life for humanity and making people his devotees. The role of Christ is not of one that mediates the propitiatory requirement to satisfy a righteous God. Rather, the mediatory potency of Christ is that of a potency of the most decisive paradigm case of radical re-centering and self-knowledge. Jesus' acknowledgement of the divine Self as his true Self was so complete and his re-centering so maximal that in and through his life, death and continuing presence in the faith of the believing community a potency for the self-realization is released.[17] Jesus is the initiator of new creation. Christian faith is not primarily a doctrine of salvation but the announcement of the advent of a new creative order in Jesus. The good news is the birth of Jesus and the problem of the Christian is to reproduce him. Christianity is not a juridical problem but a problem in genetics. There is no gulf between God and human beings. God and human person have met in Jesus; not merely met, but fused and mingled into one. To be Christian is to gain this consciousness and this sense of harmonious blend with the divine.[18] We can understand and experience the person of Jesus as the extrinsic denominator (*upadhi)*, name and form (*namarupa*), effect (*karya*) as well as the reflection (*abhasa*) and delimitation (*ghatakasah*) of God, the Supreme Being (*Brahman*). We can understand

---

[14] R. V. De Smet, 'Materials for an Indian Christology', *Religion and Society* 12:4 (Dec. 1965), 11-13.

[15] S. J. Samartha, *The Lordship of Jesus Christ and Religious Pluralism* (Madras: CLS, 1981), 8-12.

[16] Cf. Kalagara Subba Rao, *The Outpouring of My Heart*, translation into English of his Telugu compositions, ed. By C. D. Airan (Guntur: Shrimathy Parripati Sita Mahalakshmi Satya Narayan, 1964).

[17] D. D. Hudson, 'Hindu and Christian Theological Parallels in the Conversion of H. A. Krishna Pillai. 1857-1859', *Journal of the American Academy of Religion* Vol. 40 (June 1972), 196-205; Christopher Duraisingh, 'Reflection on Theological Hermeneutics in the Indian Context', *The Indian Journal of Theology* 31:3-4 (July-Dec. 1982), 271-5.

[18] Chenchiah, 'Jesus and Non-Christian Faith', in *Rethinking Christianity in India*, ed. By G. V. Job et al(Madras: A. N. Sundarisanam, 1938), 49, 54-55, 58- 60; 'Christian Message in a Non-Christian World. A Review of Dr. Kraemer's Book', in *Ibid.*, pp 16-17,19, 21-24, 26-27, 35-36, 42-43.

and experience the function of Jesus as to manifest the all-pervasive (*sarvagatatvam*), illuminative (*jyotih*) and unifying (*ekikrtya*) power of the Supreme Atman (Being), as to manifest that the Supreme *Brahman* as Pure Consciousness (*prajnanaghanam*) is the Witness (*saksi*) and Self of all (*sarvatma)* and as to manifest the eternally present (*nityasiddasvabhavam*) human liberation.[19] The Fall is our fall into the present mode of consciousness, where everything is divided, centered on itself and set in conflict with others. Sin is alienation from our real Self; it is to fall into a separate, divided self. Redemption-atonement is the return to unity; it is awakening to our true being in the Word. In Jesus the sin which brought a divided consciousness into the world is overcome, and nature and humans are restored to their original unity with God.[20] Hindu faith has the conception of sin as *avidya* i.e., the ascription of a false autonomy to created being. Christ has brought us redemption in the sense that he became the very antithesis of self-assertion taking upon himself all the consequence of human assertion of a false autonomy, even unto death on the cross and drawing the whole creation back to the full recognition of its dependence on its source, the Parent God.[21]

Christ can be conceived as the *True Prajapati* as the Vedas explains to us that *Purusa,* who is later conceived as *Prajapati*, the Lord of creation, sacrificed himself for the *Devas*, i.e., emancipated mortals.[22] The Christ of Hinduism is hidden and unknown. *Isvara* is the unknown Christ of Hinduism. The role of *Isvara* in Vedanta corresponds functionally to the role of Christ in Christian thought.[23] Fundamentally the Hindu doctrine of *Avatara* is akin to the Christian doctrine of Incarnation, the distinctiveness being Christ is the Incarnation of the whole Being of God for all times and he came to redeem the sinners.[24] It has also been pointed out that the place of Jesus Christ in the Hindu religious heritage of India is as one of the *Ishta Devatas* or chosen deities or favorite deities. Hinduism readily grants such a place to Jesus Christ. From the side of a disciple of Jesus what is needed is, he/she must not deny other mediators between God and humans, other experiences of God's presence in the human heart, the validity of other *Ishta Devatas*. Such denials lie outside the positive experience of the

---

[19] Cf. K. Aleaz, *An Indian Jesus from Sankara's Thought, Op.Cit.*; *Christian Thought Through Advaita Vedanta* (Delhi: ISPCK, 1996).

[20] Cf. Bede Griffiths, *Return to the Centre* (London: Fount Paperback, 1978).

[21] Cf. Sara Grant, *Towards an Alternative Theology: Confessions of a Non-Dualist Christian* (Bangalore: Asian Publishing House, 1991).

[22] Cf. K. Aleaz, (comp. & Intro.), *From Exclusivism to Inclusivism: The Theological Writings of Krishna Mohan Banerjea (1813-1885)* (Delhi: ISPCK, 1999).

[23] Cf. Raimundo Panikkar, *The Unknown Christ of Hinduism: Towards an Ecumenical Christophany*, Revised and Enlarged Edition (London: Darton, Longman & Todd, 1981).

[24] A. J. Appasamy, *The Gospel and India's Heritage* (London & Madras: SPCK, 1942), 256-58, 75-93; V. Chakkarai, *Jesus the Avatar* (Madras: CLS, 1930).

Christians and therefore have no validity. As we have the Lord and Saviour Jesus Christ, others have their own Lords and Saviours. The theory of multiple avatars is theologically the most accommodating attitude in a pluralistic setting.[25]

A Hindu Way of Witnessing to Christ

In the Indian Renaissance of 19th and 20th centuries, numerous people of other faiths, especially Hindus, have acknowledged the religious and ethical significance of Jesus for them in diverse ways. Raja Ram Mohan Roy, Keshub Chunder Sen and Mahatma Gandhi are some of the prominent figures among them. Ram Mohan was all for the ethical teachings of Jesus. Keshub was the pioneer in conceiving Trinity as *Saccidananda* in terms of the three functions of the one God. Gandhiji very much appreciated the life of Jesus centered on renunciation and he received enormous inspiration from the Sermon on the Mount for his own life and work.[26] We in this paper shall specially focus upon the Neo-Vedantic way of witnessing Christ.[27]

We can identify a development in the conception of the person of Christ in Neo-Vedanta. The later Neo-Vedantins Swamijis Akhilananda[28], Prabhavananda[29] and Ranganathananda[30] are more emphatic on the role of Jesus as an Incarnation as distinguished from an individual human person. According to them, Jesus is one of the *avataras* or the descents of God, born without *karmas* and above *maya*. An *avatara* has the unique power to transmit spirituality, transform human lives by touch, look or wish, and reveal divinity through transfiguration. There is an important difference even between saints and incarnations. Whereas saints are at first bound souls who later became illumined, the incarnations are the veritable embodiments of divine light and power from the very beginning of their lives. As a divine incarnation, Jesus had much compassion and the power to redeem. Also, as an incarnation Jesus was a *yogi* of the highest type who practiced all the *yogas* namely *karma*, *bhakti*, *raja*, and *jnana*. Jesus as an

---

[25] S. K. George, *Gandhi's Challenge to Christianity*, 2nd Edition (Ahamedabad: Navajivan Publishing House, 1947), 48; S. J. Samartha, *One Christ-Many Religions. Towards a Revised Christology* (Bangalore: SATHRI, 1992), 142-50.

[26] Cf. M. M. Thomas, *The Acknowledged Christ of the Indian Renaissance* (Madras/Bangalore: CLS/CISRS, 1970).

[27] For a detailed study on the subject Cf. K. Aleaz, *Jesus in Neo-Vedanta: A Meeting of Hinduism and Christianity* (Delhi: Kant Publications, 1995).

[28] Swami Akhilananda, *Hindu View of Christ* (New York: Philosophical Library, 1949).

[29] Swami Prabhavananda, *The Sermon on the Mount according to Vedanta,* Second Indian Edition (Madras: Sri Ramakrishna Math, 1979).

[30] Swami Ranganathananda, *The Christ we Adore*, Fourth Impression (Calcutta: The Ramakrishna Mission Institute of Culture, 1969).

incarnation had constant vision of God and through *samadhi* he realized the identity and unity of the individual self with the Supreme Self.

But, we should note that in the earlier Neo-Vedantins like Swamijis Vivekananda[31], Abhedananda[32] and S. Radhakrishnan[33] the emphasis is more on presenting Jesus as an ideal, perfect human person. The difference between a human person and Christ is a difference in manifestation; but as Absolute Being there is no difference between the two. The resources of God which were available to Jesus are open to all and if we struggle as he did, we will develop the God in us. What Jesus does is setting an example, by showing the path of perfection. True, those earlier Neo-Vedantins also had no problem in worshipping Jesus as Divine; as one who reveals the Absolute, as a herald of truth on earth. So we can say that Neo-Vedanta keeps a balance between following the path shown by Christ and worshipping him. Jesus is simultaneously a divine being for us to worship and an ideal for us to imitate.

Though Neo-Vedantic Christology may agree that as a divine incarnation Jesus has the power to redeem, transmit spirituality and transform human lives, but this is realized not in the way the Christian Church conceives the atonement. In Neo-Vedantic view, the Christian doctrines, especially the doctrine of atonement goes against the spirit of Jesus[34]. What Jesus does is to show us the way to become perfect, to show us our true nature which is divine, and to bring us to realization which involves the regaining of the lost selfhood[35]. Death on the Cross[36] signifies dying to the lower self and resurrection means rising to the higher universal

---

31 Swami Vivekananda, *The Complete Works of Swami Vivekananda,* Vol. I-VIII (Calcutta: Advaita Ashrama, 1968-1972).

32 Swami Abhedananda, *Complete Works of Swami Abhedananda* (in ten Volumes) (Calcutta: Ramakrishna Vedanta Math, 1967).

33 S Radhakrishnan, 'Reply to Critics' in *The Philosophy of Sarvepalli Radhakrishnan,* ed. by Paul Arthur Schilpp (New York: Tudor Publishing House, 1952), 807-809; *Eastern Religion and Western Thought*, second Ed. (London: Oxford University Press, 1940), 32, 53.

34 Swami Ranganathananda, *The Christ We Adore, Op. Cit.*, 44-48.

35 Swami Vivekananda, *The Complete Works of Swami Vivekananda, Op. Cit.*,Vols. I, 328, 341, 381, 468; Vol. II, 307, 481; Vol. V, 293; Vol.VI, pp 98-99; Vol. VII, 4, 7, 29, 72, 76, 88-89; Vol. VIII, 141, 190, 262.

36 S. Radhakrishnan, *Eastern Religions and Western Thought, Op. Cit.*, 97, 184, *The Heart of Hindustan*, Madras: G. A. Natesan & Co., 1932, 120; 'Fellowship of the Spirit' (Address at the Centre for the Study of World Religion, Harvard, 1961) in *Radhakrishnan Reader. An Anthology* ed. By Nagaraja Rao et al., Bombay: Bharatiya Vidhya Bhavan, 1969, 468-69; Swami Akhilananda, *Hindu View of Christ, Op.Cit.*, 179,183, 189, 195, 197; Swami Satprakasananda, *Hinduism and Christianity. Jesus Christ and His Teachings in the Light of Vedanta,* St. Louis: Vedanta Society of St. Louis, 1975, 174-190; Bhavani Sankar Chowdhury, *The New Wine of Jesus: Christ Taught Vedanta (*Calcutta: One World Publishers, 1982), 12, 93-95.

Self. The Cross is the expression of spiritual power or soul force through which alone we can conquer evil. The Cross of Christ is the very perfection of the teaching of non-resistance of evil. Resurrection[37] affirms that human person is really spirit. Resurrection means the resurrection of the subtle body made of subtle elements. Above all, it is the affirmation of the Neo-Vedantic Christology that the life, death, and resurrection of Jesus are not so much historical events which occurred once upon a time as universal processes of spiritual life, which are being continually accomplished in human lives. Following the example of Jesus, we can also die and resurrect and Jesus as an *avatara* can of course help us in our endeavour. Thus we may both worship Jesus and follow his path.

Conclusion

Search for insights regarding the life and work of Jesus, the meanings of the Gospel of God in Jesus, is an ongoing process and there is a need for Christians to get help from the religious experiences of people of other faiths for this important endeavour. If in the first eighteen centuries, the search was more or less by Christians alone, since then the search has begun in the company of people of sister faiths. But two hundred years or for that matter even two thousand years are nothing compared to the time ahead of us, ahead of creation. Many more dimensions of meanings of Jesus are yet to emerge. This is only the beginning. Hence the importance of the further contributions of sister faith experiences will continue to emerge.

People of other faiths are not enemies of Christians, rather fellow travelers. Their religions and cultures are no more for destruction of Christian missions; rather they are treasures for the enrichment of the Gospel of God in Christ. Therefore witnessing to Christ hereafter is always in the company of people of other faiths. For this the Hindu faith experiences can take the lead as diverse enrichments have already come from that angle.

[37] S. Radhakrishnan, *Eastern Religions and Western Thought*, *Op. Cit.*, 47,170, 176, 222, 223, 226; Swami Akhilananda, *Hindu View of Christ*, *Op. Cit.*, 79-80, 198, 200, 201, 204, 209-212; Swami Satprakasananda, *Hinduism and Christianity: Jesus Christ and His Teachings in the Light of Vedanta*, *Op. Cit.*, 186-88; Bahrain Sankar Chowdhury, *The New Wine of Jesus. Christ Taught Vedanta*, *Op. Cit.*, 12, 95.

Mission Among Hindus:
Historical Reflections

H.L. Richard

The historical roots of the Hindu-Christian encounter are buried in the uncertainty of traditions about the Apostle Thomas and the gradual growth of a Christian community in South India in the early centuries of the Christian era. Intrigues between Roman Catholic and Protestant missions and this indigenous Christian community are outside the scope of this paper, and little from the documented history of the St. Thomas Christians is of interest in the area of Christian mission among Hindus.

So the history of Christian mission in India is about Roman Catholic and Protestant missions that arrived in India in conjunction with European colonial powers. That mission among Hindus is intertwined with colonial history is an emotionally charged reality that is best faced from the start. There are both Hindu and Christian voices that stigmatize Christian missions among Hindus as an aspect of colonial domination.[1] This simplistic paradigm will not influence this paper.

Colonial realities massively impacted both missionary Christianity and Hinduism. The very term and construct of a world religion called "Hinduism" developed during the colonial era. Standard textbooks on world religions and Hinduism all wrestle with the complexity of "Hindu" as a religious designation, and most call for "contextual specificity" as the generic "Hindu" label is so broad as to be nearly meaningless.[2] Geoffrey Oddie has shown how the consciousness of a Hindu religion developed among Indians in reaction against missionary criticisms of what the missionaries imagined about a monolithic religion called "Hinduism."[3]

Christianity's implication in the colonial enterprise moved a steady stream of disciples of Jesus to seek distance from at least colonial realities,

---

[1] By Hindus, Arun Shourie, *Missionaries in India: Continuities, Changes, Dilemmas* (New Delhi: ASA Publications, 1994) and Sita Ram Goel, *History of Hindu-Christian Encounters* (New Delhi: Voice of India, 1989). For a Christian example, see Dharmaraj 1993.

[2] I am indebted to Richard Fox Young (2002) for the phrase 'contextual specificity' in reference to the many varieties of Hindu religious (and non-religious) thought and practice.

[3] Geoffrey Oddie, *Imagining Hinduism: British Protestant Missionary Constructions of Hinduism, 1793-1900* (New Delhi: Sage Publications, 2006).

and at times from Christianity itself.[4] Thus the disputed nature of Hinduism is not the only complex variable in considering Christian mission among Hindus.

There is no simple way to outline a subject as vast and complex as Christian mission among Hindus, but some arrangement of data is needed. Due to significant differences in approach and in results, this paper will divide the subject according to the social status of Hindus engaged by the Christian mission. The low castes, among which success was significant, will be considered first; the high castes, among whom success was limited and among whom approaches went through various changes, will then be discussed.

It was particularly among the lowest of caste groups, today known as Dalits, that Christianity took root in India.[5] Among a few dozen Dalit peoples, "mass movements" developed whereby over a period of years and decades many thousands professed the Christian faith. R. E. Frykenberg gives a good summary of how these movements developed.

> Only by means of agents through whose efforts that message could be translated into locally understandable idioms that were acceptable and attractive, and only after a period of incubation within a potentially new host culture and community, did such movements explode. Only after the new early converts had absorbed and acculturated the Gospel message, together with new and modern technologies that helped them to transmit their new world view, was there a release of spiritual energy that turned and then transformed whole communities.[6]

John Webster suggests that "the modern Dalit movement began with what Christian missionaries called the mass movements".[7] These movements are responsible for the origins of Christianity as it exists in most of India today and define the events taking place where Christianity is currently growing in India. There is a voluminous and growing literature on these movements, and numerous points of fascination and controversy that can only barely be mentioned in this paper.

---

[4] Examples to be noted further on in this paper include Robert de Nobili, Brahmabandhab Upadhyay, E. Stanley Jones, and Manilal Parekh.

[5] The name *Dalit*, which means the oppressed, is of recent coinage. Other names for these peoples were/are untouchables, scheduled castes, *panchamas*, *harijans*, *pariahs*, etc. The government of India still uses 'Scheduled Castes', a term rooted in a schedule (list) originally drawn up by the British government in the 1920s. There is considerable debate about whether "Dalit" should apply only to the castes on this list, or if it can/should also be applied to the Scheduled Tribes, Other Backward Castes, etc. There is also debate in some circles regarding the validity of counting Dalits among Hindus; this paper takes the traditional view that these are Hindu peoples.

[6] Robert Eric Frykenberg, *Christianity in India: From Beginnings to the Present* (Oxford History of the Christian Church, Oxford: Oxford University Press, 2008), 241.

[7] John C. B Webster, *The Dalit Christians: A History* (Delhi: ISPCK, 1992), 22.

It is now clear that the early Dalit people movements were not about attaining freedom and dignity so much as finding better patronage from influential foreign missionaries. Two quotations will need to suffice in support of this statement, taken from studies in the far north and far south of India.

> There is furthermore no clear suggestion in the sources that the labourers became Christians because they wanted liberty from the caste system as such. Rather, they converted because they believed the new masters would treat them better than the old ones. Likewise, there was no question of the converts looking for greater mobility within Christianity, even though this was what they actually gained in the long run.[8]

> The evidence is that Chuhras, accustomed as they were to patron-client relationships, sought to adopt the missionaries and missions as new, more benevolent patrons. It is equally clear that this was a role that the missionaries did not relish and that they resisted.[9]

This change of faith and patronage on a large scale forced the development of indigenous leadership and indigenous patterns of faith and life. Yet it also almost necessarily included Westernizing tendencies, often quite ironically with locals pressing for Western forms and patterns as they desired distance from their former socio-cultural contexts. Again two quotations will make the point.

> Some in the West would question whether the "Gothic" architecture, with enormous structures and lofty spires pointing heavenward, that congregations at such places as Megnanapuram and Nazareth erected with their own hands, in competition with each other, could truly be seen as "Indian" or "indigenous." The retort made by local leaders was that, as former slaves, Shanars (aka Nadars) were not about to copy the styles of temples used by their former masters and were only too glad to find, adopt, or copy new forms for the expression of their faith in buildings that they had erected for their Christ.[10]

> Paradoxically, Westerners had urged an Indian to indigenize according to Indian paradigms that the Indian believed inappropriate; and the Indian adopted Western dress opposed by Orientalizing Westerners.[11]

---

[8] Henriette Bugge, *Mission and Tamil Society: Social and Religious Change in South India, 1840-1900* (Nordic Institute of Asian Studies. Richmond, UK: Curzon Press, 1994), 163.

[9] John Webster, 'Dalits and Christianity in Colonial Punjab: Cultural Interactions', in Judith M. Brown and Robert Eric Frykenberg, Eds., *Christians, Cultural Interactions and India's Religious Traditions* (Studies in the History of Christian Missions, Grand Rapids:Eerdmans, 2002), 103-118.

[10] Frykenberg, *Christianity in India*, 225.

[11] Susan Billington Harper, *In the Shadow of the Mahatma: Bishop V. S. Azariah and the Travails of Christianity in British India* (Studies in the History of Christian Missions. Grand Rapids, USA: William B. Eerdmans and Richmond, UK: Curzon Press, 2000), 142.

Christian education was a major focus of mission among Hindus, among the poor due to their need for development and among the higher castes as an evangelistic strategy (to be noted further below). Higher level education became a powerful source of Westernizing tendencies in Indian society, and also among the more elite Christians who qualified for higher education. The devolution of missionary authority to national Christians in the mid-twentieth century tended strongly to the advantage of the urban elite Christians, to the detriment of the truly Dalit rural masses of Christians.

The churches that have resulted from the people movements of past generations are thus not closely related to Hindu cultural norms. Christianity is effectively locked out of thousands of Hindu castes and communities in modern India, with ongoing mission work still very much focused on the many and various Dalit people groups. The problem for non-Dalit Hindus is well summarized by Herbert E. Hoefer:

> Christian congregational organisation, modes of worship, names, customs of dress (especially among women), styles of church art and architecture, religious language, eating habits, selection of religious leadership, approaches to religious nurture and propagation, attitudes towards Indian history, and expectations on personal habits often differ significantly from the mainstream of the society. Yet, few will today attempt to defend these differences on the grounds of theological necessity. These practices are simply the developments of the Western missionary tradition over the past several centuries. The effect, however, is the same as that of insistence on beef and pork eating, and on circumcision and Sabbath observance: change of cultural habits along with change of faith.[12]

This continuing issue of the relevance of current (and historic) Christianity to Hindus leads to the discussion of attempts to engage higher caste Hindus with the message of Christ. Often this is what is in mind in discussions of Christian mission among Hindus, but these attempts to find relevance in relation to classical Hindu traditions need to be understood in light of the fruitful propagation of Christianity among lower caste peoples.[13]

Robert de Nobili's pioneering work in Madurai is well known and almost iconic among those focused on the higher castes of Hindus. Nobili

---

[12] Herbert E. Hoefer, *Churchless Christianity*, (Pasadena: William Carey Library, 2001 [1991]), 151; Hoefer is discussing and commending Hindus who follow Jesus without formal alliance with Christianity or the church, on the lines (noted below) of Brahmabandhab Upadhyay and Manilal C. Parekh. There is of course vast diversity of church organization and practice in India.

[13] This paper juxtaposes the high castes and Dalits, each roughly 20% of the population of India. Half the population is the very diverse and hard to define "Other Backward Castes" (OBC, government of India official designation) or middle castes or Shudra castes, many of which are basically Dalit, many others basically high caste; all such rankings are severely contested in Indian social contexts.

distanced himself from Europeans and their foreign ways and religion and radically adapted to high caste religio-cultural ways until his work was halted in 1612 due to controversies surrounding his methods.[14]

Similar sentiments were expressed and experiments attempted at other times in Christian mission among Hindus. A striking example from a decidedly different theological perspective is from the Protestant decennial missionary gathering in 1892:

> The principle I contend for, then, is this: *that the books which we publish should be carefully related to Hindu thought, expressed in its terms, done in its style, adopting where it can its positions, and leading on, still in Hindu fashion and in its terminology, from points of agreement to essential points of difference*. In this way we may, perhaps, be able to furnish an effectual exhibition of legitimately 'Hinduized Christianity'.[15]

Christian higher education in India was developed in the mid-nineteenth century with a very different perspective. There was a clear focus on the evangelization of high caste Hindus, but with a simplistic understanding of Hinduism as a false religion. There was also a desire to undermine and destroy this ill-conceived "Hinduism," as indicated by the patriarch of Christian higher education, Alexander Duff:

> While you [evangelistic missionaries] engage in directly separating as many precious atoms from the mass as the stubborn resistance to ordinary appliances can admit, we shall, with the blessing of God, devote our time and strength to the preparing of a mine, and the setting of a train which shall one day explode and tear up the whole from its lowest depths.[16]

This negative, even cynical, view of Hinduism and of Christian mission among Hindus was prominently held and vigorously advocated for throughout mission history, and is by no means extinct even at the present time.[17] But in the development of Christian higher education, more liberal

---

[14] The controversies were not stirred by Hindu objections, but by objections from another European Catholic priest.

[15] H. Haigh, 'Vernacular Literature', in *Report of the Third Decennial Missionary Conference held at Bombay, 1892-93, vol. 2*, A. Mainwaring, Ed. (Bombay: Education Society's Steam Press. 1893), 667; italics in original

[16] George Smith, *The Life of Alexander Duff, D.D., LL.D.* (London: Hodder and Stoughton, 1881), 68.

[17] Duff wrote of Hinduism that "Of all the systems of false religion ever fabricated by the perverse ingenuity of fallen man, Hinduism is surely the most stupendous" (1988[1839]:204). Note a recent similar sentiment that stirred controversy in India: "More than 900 million people are lost in the hopeless darkness of Hinduism, worshipping 330 million gods and goddesses created by the imagination of men and women searching for a source of truth and strength" (International Mission Board 1999:1). Note that a later edition of this booklet, without any indication that a change had been made, altered this opening line to "More than 900 million people seek healing from disease, salvation from natural disasters, definition of their place and role in life, acceptance in their communities and meaning in life through the path of Hinduism" (International Mission Board 2000:1).

views came to dominate. There were some success stories of individuals coming to faith in Christ, but not to the extent that early educational missionaries had hoped. And, as John McKenzie well stated,

> It was not only the flow of converts to the Christian Church that was seriously checked; Hinduism was proved to be not a mass of rock that might be mined and blown up, but a living plant with many roots, that was capable of eluding the art of the sapper and miner.[18]

Christian higher education came to be commended for its suffusion of Christian principles into India and into Hinduism. There is no question that Christianity impacted Hinduism, and by the mid-twentieth century that reality became part of the focus of a new Christian approach to Hindus, dialogue.

But changes in Christian attitudes to Hinduism in the nineteenth century influenced more than just educational missions. A dominant new paradigm emerged, presenting Christianity as the crown or fulfillment of Hinduism. Fulfillment was a central idea at the Edinburgh 1910 gathering, as noted by Wesley Ariarajah:

> In summing up its findings, the Commission reiterated its conviction that the Christian attitude to Hinduism, notwithstanding the elements which the Christian must reject, should be one of understanding and sympathy. It said that the Christian should seek the noble elements in non-Christian religions and use them as steps to higher things, for Hinduism in its higher forms "plainly manifests the working of the Holy Spirit." The "merely iconoclastic attitude," the Commission said, was condemned by the majority of its correspondents as "radically unwise and unjust".[19]

The fulfillment motif came to dominance because it affirmed the centrality of Christ (or Christianity) while also being respectful towards other religious traditions. It was also, however, conveniently hazy, and there were a number of different angles by which to define exactly what was being fulfilled by what.[20]

In the heart of the fulfillment era another iconic figure appeared. Brahmabandhab Pathway was not noted at Edinburgh 1910, partly due to his not being Protestant and partly due to his having fallen from favor even with his Roman Catholic Church. But Upadhyay's radical adaptation of

---

[18] John McKenzie, 'Higher Education.' In *The Christian Task in India*, John McKenzie, Ed. (London: Macmillan, 1929), 91.

[19] Wesley Ariarajah, *Hindus and Christians: A Century of Protestant Ecumenical Thought* (Currents of Encounter, Grand Rapids: Eerdmans, 1991), 27; Ariarajah is quoting from *Commission on the Missionary Message: Hinduism*, II, (Bound Manuscripts, WCC Library), 267.

[20] Discussions of fulfilment theology point out this conundrum; note Paul Hedges' broader analysis of the haziness of fulfilment theology in his discussion which begins with this line: "The question as to what fulfilment theology is immediately encounters a very great problem, namely, the vast range of thought that has been classified under this title", *Preparation and Fulfilment, 26.*

Hindu forms (both cultural and intellectual) was powerfully influential in what has been called "the Calcutta School" in the 1930's and became yet more prominent when promoted by the founders of the Sacchidananda Ashram (1948; Jules Monchanin and Swami Abhishiktananda) in Trichy (south India). The fresh breezes welcomed into Roman Catholicism by the Vatican II Council allowed Upadhyay to be widely recognized as a prophetic forerunner in Christian mission among Hindus.

Upadhyay sought to maintain a Hindu identity while being Roman Catholic; troubles with the church, not entirely unlike those of Nobili centuries earlier, ushered him into full identity with Hindus. Protestant Manilal C. Parekh walked a similar path; into Christ and the church and then out of the church and into an ambivalent state as a Hindu lover of Christ. The missiological ferment that produced fulfillment theology and striking figures like Upadhyay and Parekh also sparked the growth of Christian ashrams, an attempt to alter the foreign face of Christianity in India.

E. Stanley Jones was among the enthusiastic promoters of Christian ashrams and made a clear distinction between Christ and Christianity in his evangelistic work among Hindus. But the Christian ashram movement failed to develop into the transformative force its proponents aimed towards. [21] The complexity of the Hindu-Christian encounter precludes simple solutions (such as a Christian ashram movement), and Christian mission among Hindus remains fraught with strains and struggles in many directions.

The last decades of the twentieth century brought transformations to the entire concept of Christian mission among Hindus. From the Indo-centric project outlined in this paper, globalization and its accompanying migrations brought mission to Hindus to the doorstep of churches across the world (though most still seem oblivious to this) while opening new channels for international Christian influence into rapidly urbanizing India.

Sensitive Christians alert to the complexities and challenges of this history and current reality have called for and engaged in interreligious dialogue, some seeing this as part of the Christian mission among Hindus while others would define it as parallel to mission. Dialogical efforts, however, remain marked by elitism and distrust. Let me again give two supporting quotations.

---

[21] The first Protestant Christian ashrams were established in the 1920s. Roman Catholic ashrams have proliferated since the 1960s. The failure to significantly impact either the church or Hindu society is often lamented by ashram advocates. For example, see Vandana, *Christian Ashrams: A Movement with a Future?* (Delhi: ISPCK, 1993).

> It seems to me that negative stereotypes, some deeply and almost unconsciously held, haunt both sides of most well-intentioned attempts at Hindu-Christian dialogue.[22]

> There are few Hindus who are interested in (contemporary) Christian theology, and there are fewer still that have a desire to enter into a dialogue with their Christian counterparts.... Celebrations and affirmations of dialogue notwithstanding, there seem to be few new ideas; there seems to be little progress.[23]

Christianity in its encounter with Hindus today is marked by theological diversity, if not conflict and confusion.[24] Mission among Dalits (and tribal peoples) proceeds with vigor, usually under Indian Christian initiative and leadership, creating massive controversy as many Hindus react against what they perceive to be proselytism.[25] Dialogical efforts continue between Hindu (high caste, generally) and Christian leaders, while Hindu discipleship to Jesus outside of Christianity is "increasingly pervasive and influential".[26] A century after Edinburgh 1910, vigorous debate and activity continues to mark Christian mission among Hindus.

---

[22] Richard Taylor, 'Current Hindu-Christian Dialogue in India,' In *Hindu-Christian Dialogue: Perspectives and Encounters*, Harold Coward, Ed. (Maryknoll: Orbis, 1989), 124.

[23] Klaus Klostermaier, 'The Future of Hindu-Christian Dialogue.' In *Hindu-Christian Dialogue: Perspectives and Encounters*. Harold Coward Ed. (Maryknoll, USA: Orbis Books. 1989), 265; For further examples on these lines see, Iswar Prasad, 'Preparation for Inter-Faith Dialogue.' In *Christian Ashrams: A Movement with a Future?* Vandana Mataji, Ed. (Delhi: ISPCK), 102-106; and Francis Clooney, 'Hindu-Christian Studies as a Necessary Luxury in the Context of Today's Pluralism.' *Hindu Christian Studies Bulletin* 7 (1994), 39-44; cf. Bob Robinson, "despite general Hindu reluctance to initiate dialogue, there are some exceptions" in *Christians Meeting Hindus: An Analysis and Theological Critique of the Hindu-Christian Encounter in India* (Regnum Studies in Mission, Carlisle, UK: Paternoster Press, 2004), 155.

[24] The rather simplistic categorization of exclusivist, inclusivist and pluralist Christian theologies at least clarifies the breadth and depth of the diversity.

[25] For an example of the negative reaction, note *Conversion is Violence* (Saraswati 1999). For a brief and balanced discussion of the issue, see Vempeny 1999.

[26] Frykenberg, *Christianity in India*, 465.

Mission Among Buddhists:

Mission to Buddhists

Notto R. Thelle

Mission and Roots

Many years ago I responded to a newspaper article accusing Christian mission for estranging people from their own culture, slicing through "roots that are absolutely essential, if life is to be lived in all its fullness. People become rootless and homeless. The deep sensation of belonging to a fellowship is put at risk, and people are left with a feeling of grief at the loss of something valuable and important". [1]

I had to admit that that Christian mission has often torn people out of the existential context in which they lived, making them foreigners vis-à-vis their own culture. The attempt to give them a new identity has detached them from their roots and made them homeless in their own hearts. If the Christian faith does not help people achieve a true relationship to their own selves, it will always be borrowed goods, a foreign body that can threaten personal development. Faith is meant to make people whole, not to make them spiritual refugees nourished on values borrowed from others.

On the other hand, I argued, to conclude that conversion from one religion to another is necessarily a bad thing, indicates a simplistic understanding of de facto historical processes. It also fails to appreciate the unease which always accompanies the religious search. Every people and culture experience periods of radical religious transformations, when religious allegiance changes: old ideas are discarded or lose their power, and are replaced by new ideas. The same is true of individuals. Some rebel against their parents' faith; or faith can quite simply die; or perhaps they encounter a faith which is more meaningful than their old faith. This leads to fear, pain, and grief, but this is often a necessary process in a healthy human life. One does not lose one's own identity when one rebels against inherited values, nor when one casts away something that has ceased to be meaningful.

I doubt whether there is anyone who can retain *all* his or her roots. Some roots are diseased; roots can be destroyed by lack of nutriments or water.

---

[1] See the chapter, 'Mission and Roots', in Notto R. Thelle, *Who Can Stop the Wind? Travels in the Borderland between East and West* (Collegeville, MN: Liturgical Press, 2010).

And roots can be cut by external circumstances. Sometimes, roots must be dug up and planted in new soil, if they are to have access to life-giving water. All this applies to religious faith as well. Many people have had to cut through Christian roots which had been destroyed in a diseased and acid soil, in order to discover their own true selves. Others again find that the Christian faith allows them, for the first time in their lives, to put down roots and connect with their own deepest longings.

But we must note that whatever the individual circumstances, it is difficult to have a whole relationship to oneself unless one has a living relationship to one's past. We can try to reject the past, suppress it, or forget it, but it does not go away: sooner or later, it will emerge with its demands. We must work on our past and integrate it – positively or negatively – into the life we live in the present and the future.

Christian mission is rightly criticized because it often demands a break with what went before, without recognizing that much of the past was good, that God may have been present in it, and that most of the roots were good. This is why it is not surprising to meet Japanese Christians who, after some years as Christians, begin to look to their past, in search of connections. They have received a Christian identity, but they discover that the faith cannot be wholly their own unless they establish a genuine relationship to their past. In some cases, this leads them away from the Christian faith, which had never really been more than borrowed goods. But if their faith is genuine, the rediscovery of their roots leads to a new richness and freedom – freedom for a new integration of the past. Some of this will indeed be rejected, but all that is "true, good, and honorable" takes on a new meaning. The past is not an empty space, but a source of richness and joy.

I may sharpen my position with a few questions: Is the Christian church entitled to engage in mission, as long as it remains unable to preserve the good things in the cultures in which it works? Is it meaningful to work as a missionary without asking oneself in all seriousness what place the religions and cultures one encounters have in God's plan? What are the insights, the truth, and the goodness with which God has endowed them? How can other religions and cultures help to deepen our Christian insight and experience? And how can the Christian message be communicated in a way that preserves all that is valuable?

If Christian missionary work is to have the right to summon people to become Jesus' disciples, it must first learn to appreciate what is going on in the depths of other religions and cultures. This entails sensitivity to those roots which are necessary "if life is to be lived in all its fullness and meaning".

Mission to Buddhists – Dilemmas and Tensions

The above reflections suggest a general position, but it is not final, and does not solve all the dilemmas of Christian mission to people who are nurtured in other religious traditions. Let me, therefore, be somewhat more specific and clarify the background for my own reflections, and at the same time describe some historical developments that have contributed to changing attitudes in missionary thinking concerning other faiths. I will concentrate my investigation on Buddhism, but the reader may find that my experiences apply to other faiths as well.

I grew up in a missionary tradition that was developed by the Norwegian missionary Karl Ludvig Reichelt in his Christian Mission to Buddhists. His work was based on a classical inclusivistic understanding of other religions as a divine preparation for fulfillment in Christianity, a position which was gaining support by progressive Protestant missions in the late nineteenth and early twentieth century. The original contribution of Reichelt was to implement the vision as a concrete strategy of creating communities of dialogical encounter, where a deep appreciation of Buddhism went along with a consistent attempt to convert Buddhists monks and religious seekers. The strategy was tested out by establishing "Christian monasteries for Buddhist monks" in Nanjing in the 1920s and in Hong Kong from the early 1930s, and to some extent in other locations as well. Because these communities consistently tried to adapt Christian piety to Buddhist conventions in architecture, liturgies and spiritual life, thousands of Buddhist monks and religious lay people visited the places, and some were actually converted to Christian faith.[2]

My father, Notto Normann Thelle, was Reichelt's closest associate from the very beginning in 1922, and became the leader and spokesman of the mission for several decades after Reichelt's death in 1953. The Chinese revolution and communist takeover in 1949 made it impossible to continue

[2] The mission began in Nanjing in 1922, and is continued with a new name and radically changed circumstances in Areopagos Foundation. For a thorough investigation of the visions and strategies of the mission, see my articles 'Karl Ludvig Reichelt 1877-1952: Christian Pilgrim of Tao Fong Shan', in Gerald H Anderson et al. (ed), *Mission Legacies: Biographical Studies of Leaders of the Modern Missionary Movement* (Maryknoll, NY: Orbis Press, 1994; 'The Conversion of the Missionary: Changes in Buddhist-Christian Relations in the Early Twentieth Century', *Ching Feng,* New Series 4.2 (2003); 'A Christian Monastery for Buddhist Monks 1: Karl Ludvig Reichelt's Sacred Mountains,' *Ching Feng* New Series 6.1 (2005); and 'A Christian Monastery for Buddhist Monks 2: Buddhist Rhetoric in Karl Ludvig Reichelt's Christian Liturgies', *Ching Feng*, New Series 6.2 (2005); 'Changed by the East: Notes on Missionary Communication and Transformation', *International Bulletin of Missionary Research*, 30.3 (July 2006); 'Crossing Religious Boundaries: Christian Mission and Global Transformation,' in Sturla S. Stålsett (ed), *Religion in a Globalised Age: Transfers & Transformations, Integration & Resistance* (Oslo: Novus Press, 2008), 21-36.

the original intentions of mission to Buddhist monks, and it proved almost impossible to realize the idea of creating spiritual communities of dialogue and mission in Hong Kong, Taiwan, or Japan. Apart from the so-called "Houses of Friendship" established with some initial success by Sverre Holth in Hong Kong and Taiwan in the late 1970s, the only work that to some extent maintained the vision of the mission to Buddhists was the establishment of Christian Study Centers in Hong Kong and in Kyoto, Japan. With my roots in the original mission, and later involvement as Associate Director of the NCC Center for the Study of Japanese Religions in Kyoto in the 1970s and 1980s, I have registered the inherent tensions in the combined commitment to mission and to dialogue, and will share a few observations about the inevitable changes such tensions stimulate.

The Christian Mission to Buddhists came as a refreshing missionary adventure, for Buddhists as well as Christians: finally there was a missionary work that broke the pattern of wholesale condemnation. Reichelt not only wanted to respect Buddhism and write learned books, as some missionaries had done before him, but he evidently felt a strong attraction to its piety. Holmes Welch describes him as "the first successful apologist" for Mahayana among Christian missionaries.[3] He was changed by the encounter with Buddhism and became a "converted missionary" who gave his own home constituency a new appreciation of the greatness of Buddhist piety.[4] With all his fascination with Buddhism, however, Reichelt was driven by an intense missionary calling and consistently tried to convert Buddhist monks to Christianity. With hindsight it is tempting to regard Reichelt merely as a "Bible-waving missionary who fraudulently adopted Buddhist guise",[5] or to brand his venture as naïve and uncritical, even crude and offensive. The fact that the mission neither in China nor in Japan used the official name of the mission, Christian Mission to Buddhists, but presented itself as The Society of Friends in Dao/the Way (Chin. *Daoyouhui*, Jap. *Dôyûkai*), is a clear indication that the missionary purpose was extremely sensitive. The inevitable result has been to downplay or reinterpret the missionary aspect, and to emphasize the mutual openness for change and transformation.

My own experiences from the NCC Study Center in Kyoto also reveal some of the characteristic changes which tend to follow serious contact with committed representatives of other religions. When the center began its work in 1959, the missionary and apologetic concern was unmistakable, "to promote the study of non-Christian religions for the sake of an effective witness". The experiences with study and dialogue, however, inevitably made such simplistic aims inadequate, and opened the center for a more

[3] Holmes Welch, *The Buddhist Revival in China* (Cambridge, Mass.: Harvard University Press, 1968), 240.

[4] See further discussion of the expression below.

[5] See Whalen Lai, 'Why is there not a Buddha-Christian Dialogue in China?' *Buddhist-Christian Studies* 6 (1986), 93.

dialogical posture. Summing up my own position after many years of active participation, I described a process which was not only mine but quite representative of committed Christians who for various reasons become exposed to the dialogical encounter:

> It often begins with a concern for true witness–in order to transmit the gospel in a meaningful way one has to be in dialogue–and becomes a pilgrimage which has two significant directions: journeying into another faith and at the same time searching into one's own faith. The one-way search becomes a two-way process; it still involves witness, but this is inevitably modified by a transformation from within.[6]

One important aspect of such a mutual process is the challenge to find a language of faith that at least to some extent communicates and makes sense to Buddhists. The two traditions are so different that one might say with S. Mark Heim that they seek different "salvations"[7] and develop two basically different types of religions language.[8] The Gospel stories about the life and message of Jesus Christ are able to transcend religious and cultural barriers and often make a strong impression on Buddhists; but Christian preaching and doctrines are easily rejected because they sound like strange or even absurd propositions about a revengeful God who cannot love unless he may punish and torture his own son.[9] There is no easy way to transcend such barriers.

In the 1990s The Christian Mission to Buddhists (now: Areopagos Foundation) initiated a process of reflection on missionary principles, and came up with a moderate but still quite open position concerning mission and dialogue, with Buddhism as the unmentioned object. Its understanding of mission is

> based on an expectant vision of the universal salvific will of God and his presence throughout the history of humankind. The proclamation of the

---

[6] Notto R. Thelle, 'Reflections on Dialogue as a Spiritual Pilgrimage', *Japanese Religions* 13.4 (1985), 20; see also my article, 'Dialogue – Study – Friendship', *Japanese Religions* 25.1-2 (2000) 8-14; '*In Memoriam* Harry Thomsen (1928-2008): Dialogical Missionary and Research Facilitator', *Japanese Religions* 34.1 (2009), 1-6; Martin Repp, 'The NCC Center for the Study of Japanese Religions: Forty Years of Research and Dialogue', *Japanese Religions* 25.1-2 (2000), 135-153.

[7] S. Mark Heim, *Salvations: Truth and Difference in Religion* (Maryknoll, NY: Orbis Books, 1995).

[8] I have discussed this in some detail in 'Relation, Awareness, and Energy – Three Languages, Three Worlds? An Approach to Mutual Understanding', *Japanese Religions* 30.1(2005), 113-127; also published in Werner G. Jeanrond & Aasulv Lande (eds), *The Concept of God in Global Dialogue* (Maryknoll, NY: Orbis Books, 2005).

[9] See my article, 'Foe and friend: The Changing Image of Christ in Japanese Buddhism', *Japanese Religions* 12.2 (1982); I have tried to find Buddhist categories for understanding the cross of Jesus in 'God's Vow: A Pure land Perspective on the Cross of Christ', in *Ching Feng*, New Series 7.1-2 (2006), 153-163.

> Christ event as the central event in God's history with the world goes along with faith in the creative and salvific work of the triune God even where Christ's name is not known. God is the God of the world, not only the God of Israel or the God of the church. The world is created in Christ, by Christ, and for Christ, and hence it is not (Christian) mission that first brings God to non-Christian cultures. God is there already, and the call of mission is to contribute to interpret his presence. Hence any proclamation of Christ will be accompanied by a humble expectation that God has made himself known, and in various ways may be traced in the wisdom and religious experiences in all cultures. Therefore, mission is not only a one-way proclamation of Christ and his salvation, but involves an attentive listening to the presence of the triune God already there. All mission must, consequently, be dialogical: what is said and done must take place in an attentive and trusting dialogue, and with a deep respect for the cultures to which the message is communicated, and with an expectation that God also has something to say to the church and its theology through these cultures.[10]

The Conversion of the Missionaries 1910-2010

I borrow the expression "the conversion of the missionaries" in order to suggest the radical changes in missionary motivations and principles that have taken place the last hundred years. "He had gone out to change the East and was returning, himself a changed man," observed Earl H. Cressy in 1919 about the new generation of missionaries who came to China around 1900. Himself a missionary, Cressy commented that "the conversion of the missionary by the Far East results in his being not only a missionary but an internationalist, an intermediary between the two great civilizations that inherit the earth".[11]

The background was the almost unanimous contempt for China's culture and religion in nineteenth-century Europe and America. The admiration once felt for China in the seventeenth and eighteenth centuries was forgotten. The Romantic reaction in Europe had rejected China in favor of India as the homeland of the mysteries. China was humiliated by the Opium Wars (1839-1840) and series of unjust trade agreements, and was regarded as stagnated, complacent, and without vitality. Confucianism had moral ideals, but lacked life. Daoism and Buddhism were merely empty rituals or "orgies of idolatry". A few missionaries had found noble and positive elements in Buddhism, but they still rejected it as "a science

---

[10] The translation is based on my own notes.

[11] Earl H. Cressy, ‚Converting the Missionary', *Asia: Journal of the American Asiatic Association* 19.6 (June 1919), 553-556. The theme is analyzed in great detail by Lian Xi, *Missionaries Distracted: The Rise of Syncretism in American Protestant Missions in China, 1907-1932,* doctoral dissertation (State University of New York at Albany, 1993). I refer here to this thesis. See also Lian's revised version, *The Conversion of the Missionary: Liberalism in American Protestant Missions in China, 1907-1932* (Pennsylvania: Pennsylvania State University, 1997).

without inspiration, a religion without God, a body without a spirit, unable to regenerate, cheerless, cold, dead, and deplorably barren of results". It might be useful to study paganism, some argued, but only in order to demonstrate the self-contradictions and absurdities of those religions so that the truth would shine forth.[12]

After 1900 a new generation of missionaries was prepared for change, and some were overwhelmed by China. They had come to the Far East with an ardent vocation to proclaim the Christian message, but in the process they discovered that the East had proclaimed its own message to them. Abroad, they represented a universal religion which wanted to change the society they had come to serve. At home, they changed people's attitudes by widening their horizon and helping them to appreciate better the greatness in the civilizations of the East. They did not convert to Buddhism or Eastern ways, but somehow had to integrate Eastern wisdom and insights in their own understanding of Christianity.

The new openness and willingness to appreciate Eastern wisdom can to some extent be seen in the documents from Edinburgh in 1910. The speeches and commission reports on the relationship to non-Christian religions reflect a change from exclusivistic rhetoric towards more inclusivistic statements, describing other religions as preparatory stages for fulfillment in Christianity.[13] But this went along with an overwhelming triumphalism that anticipated the triumph of Christianity and the demise of other religions within a short span of time. One might say that "the conversion of mission" took more time than "the conversion of the missionaries" described above, but the hundred years since Edinburgh 1910 have brought about changes in missionary experience and theological reflection that are so radical that one sometimes hesitates to realize their implications.

I will in the following mention a few changes that have contributed to a revised understanding of mission in general, and of Buddhism in particular.

The torment of hell. Like it or not, one of the strongest drives to foreign mission was the conviction that without the church or knowledge of Christ the millions of pagans were doomed to perdition and the torment of hell. Hudson Taylor, one of the most influential Christian missionaries to China, made a tremendous impact with his appeal about Chinas millions who died without knowing Christ, daily pouring into hell like a Niagara of unsaved souls.[14] Alternative voices could be heard, but evangelization of the world

---

[12] Se my detailed analysis in "Crossing Religious Boundaries" (n. 2 above).

[13] *World Missionary Conference Edinburgh 1910, Commission 4: The Missionary Message in Relation to Non-Christian Religions* (Edinburgh: World Missionary Conference Office, 1910). Such expectations of fulfilment were clearly reflected in many of the detailed reports from Japan that were submitted as preparation for Commission 4.

[14] Alvyn J. Austin, *China's Millions: The China Inland Mission and the Late Qing Dynasty, 1832-1905* (Grand Rapids MI: Eerdmans, 2007).

was to a great extent motivated by the need to save people from perdition and hell.

The rhetoric still exists to some extent in missionary circles, especially among evangelical and charismatic Christians, but every time I have tried to test the reality behind the rhetoric, even ardent proponents of eternal punishment in hell (with literal or symbolic meaning) come up with some explanation that God may have other ways. It seems unbearable or even impossible for modern Christians to imagine that the Father of Jesus Christ should reserve an eternal suffering for those who for various reasons rejected Christ or failed to know him. The fear of hell or the threat of hell no longer seems to be a motivation for mission.

The eschatological urge. Christian mission has to a great extent been driven by an eschatological urge, the expectation that the end will come when the gospel has been proclaimed to all nations (Matt 24:14). In 1910 such an eschatological urge went along with an optimistic expectation that the world would be evangelized "in this generation". The rhetoric of eschatology still exists, but is seldom heard in mainstream churches and missions.

Triumphalism. Edinburgh 1910 was characterized by a triumphalistic expectation that Christianity would conquer the world and defeat other religions. Missionary rhetoric was still characterized by images of struggle, warfare, occupation, and colonial expansion. The consequent history of the twentieth century undermined the validity of such triumphalism, and has given church and mission a radically different position in relation to other religions and cultures. In some cases triumphalism has been replaced by self-contempt and loss of nerve, but in general a positive affirmation of mission goes along with humility and open appreciation of other religions.

A new awareness of the East. While the early "conversion of the missionaries" took place in China and other Eastern countries, Buddhism and Eastern religions have established themselves also in the West. Buddhism is not merely an attraction for eccentric seekers or romantics on a literal or symbolic journey to the East, but is represented in the West by masters and teachers, journals and well-organized communities; and an increasing number of Christians are involved in dialogue and sharing of spiritual practices. The result of such contact is that Buddhists sometimes convert to Christianity, or that Christians decide to follow the Buddha way. Sharing of one's faith and experience with Buddhists is an inevitable part of the encounter, but it seems increasingly strange to single out Buddhism and Buddhists as a special target for Christian mission and conversion. Dalai Lama, Thich Nhat Hanh, and other Buddhist leaders argue that Christians should not become Buddhists, but return to their Christian roots. The fact that an increasing number of Westerners with background in Christianity have taken refuge in Buddhism, introduces a new dimension to

Christian witness. Christians, on their part, will have to realize that many Buddhists will come close to Christ and somehow belong to the fellowship of his disciples without converting to Christianity.

Acceptance of pluralism. In contrast to the expectation in 1910 that Christian mission would conquer the world and render other religions obsolete, other religions have regained their self-confidence, and are more widespread and powerful than ever before. It is true that Christian mission during the twentieth century has been extremely successful and changed the religious map of the world. While established churches in the West are declining, Christianity has spread to the rest of the world with new centers of power and expansive potential in the South and the East. Some of these new expansive Christian movements carry on visions of conquering the world, but the mainstream churches and missions have abandoned the dreams of world dominion and accepted the fact of religious plurality. This is not only a reluctant acceptance of a sad fact, but a realization that the Gospel of Jesus never envisioned that the world should be or would be "conquered" by Christ.

Theological transformations. There is no room here for discussing theologies of religion, but it is relevant to observe the dramatic changes in Christian reflection about other religions over the last hundred years. In 1910 the entire variety of positions already existed as theological options, from traditional forms of exclusivism to extreme relativism, but missionary thinking at that time was still dominated by exclusivist positions with openings towards various forms of inclusivism. Now the dominant trend seems to be inclusivistic, with remnants of exclusivism and openings toward various forms of pluralism. "Dominant" here refers to mainstream churches and missions, represented primarily by the World Council of Churches, the Lausanne Movement, and the Vatican. Some may object that the Lausanne Movement adheres to exclusivist positions, but it seems to me that its affirmation of dialogue and its interest in anthropology and cross-cultural studies have forced Lausanne people to abandon traditional exclusivism in favor of a more open awareness of the divine presence in other religions and cultures. The present Lausanne movement in many ways seems to favor positions that are closer to what the WCC advocated thirty or forty years ago than to its own initial exclusivism.

Others may describe the situation in different ways and emphasize other aspects. But one does not have to agree in order to realize that the situation has radically changed and poses new challenges to Christian mission. The numerous suggestions in the guidelines for study under the heading "The 2010 Mission Themes"[15] indicate a clear awareness of these challenges, with such themes as religious and cultural plurality, escalation of conflict, questions of conversion and proselytism, dialogue and encounter, secret and churchless believers, post-modernity and institutional religion, post-

[15] www.edinburgh2010.org

colonialism and asymmetries of power, liberation movements, contextualization, subaltern voices and ecology. None of these themes were formulated in a similar way in 1910.

Implications for Mission Among Buddhists

It is difficult to spell out the implications of my observations for the Christian community in relationship to Buddhists and Buddhist cultures. I am well aware that I have only touched a few aspects of the encounter with Buddhism, leaving out a number of potential tensions and conflicts, related to doctrinal and philosophical disagreements, and perhaps even the ways to deal with social and moral evils. I will, nevertheless, conclude my observations concerning mission to Buddhists with a few theses for further reflection:

- Mission is to share one's faith and conviction with other people, inviting them to discipleship whether they adhere to other religious traditions or not. Such sharing is to take place with confidence and humility: confidence, because Christ invites and empowers people to turn to God and to their true humanity; humility, because God "is not far from each one of us" (Acts 17:27), and has touched all creatures with his loving power.
- Mission to Buddhists should be accompanied by a deep respect for and understanding of the Buddhist way, with sensitivity about the wisdom and insight God may have revealed in the Buddhist tradition. Such a sharing of faith should also go along with a willingness to listen to what God wants to teach the church through Buddhism.
- Mission to Buddhists should not primarily be focused on conversion, baptism, and inclusion in the Christian church, but on discipleship. Discipleship–to follow the Jesus way–will as a rule lead to baptism and church membership, but does not necessarily involve a break with the Buddhist community. In some cases Buddhists will prefer to follow the Jesus way without abandoning the Buddha way, just as there are committed Christians who want to follow the Buddha way as Christians.
- In many cases the mission of the church would primarily be to establish dialogue and cooperation with Buddhists communities in order to deal with common moral and social challenges, such as conflicts, violence, discrimination, political oppression, disasters and health problems, poverty and injustice.
- Missionary and pastoral education for people who are expected to be in touch with Buddhist communities should take the study of Buddhism seriously in order to formulate Christianity in a way that is relevant and meaningful in a Buddhist context. The

purpose of such a study should not only be to formulate an "effective witness", but to open for mutual appreciation and sharing of spiritual gifts.

- Unless the church is able to embrace and nurture what is true, good, and honorable in Buddhism, it may not be desirable to engage in mission or to expect conversion.

Mission Among Buddhists:

Christian Mission Among Chinese Buddhists: A Centennial Reflection

Lai Pan-chiu

Introduction

1910 is an important year for the history of Christian mission in general and the Christian mission among the Buddhists in Asia particularly. It saw the World Missionary Conference successfully held in Edinburgh and also the publication of *The New Testament of Higher Buddhism* (Edinburgh: T & T Clark, 1910) authored by Timothy Richard (1845–1919), a Baptist missionary to China who shared his view on the relationship between Christianity and other religions at the Edinburgh Conference. Before considering the proper missionary strategy among the Chinese Buddhists in the 21st century, one must note first the dramatic change Buddhism in Asia has undergone in the last few decades. This essay will offer a focused historical survey on the Christian missions among the Chinese Buddhists in the last one hundred years or so and a more general reflection on the Christian mission among the Buddhists in Asia.

Timothy Richard at the Edinburgh Conference

Timothy Richard is particularly remembered for his contributions to the social and political reforms in China, especially his efforts in disseminating various Western social and political thoughts which inspired many Chinese intellectuals. Other than promoting the "Western learning" through publications, Richard himself also engaged in relief work for famine and the founding of a university in the heartland of China. Interestingly, on top of his rather busy missionary, educational and political activities, he took the initiatives to contact people of other religions, including Buddhist leaders.[1]

At that time many other Christian missionaries despised Chinese Buddhism which was admittedly rather weak and in disarray. However,

[1] For a biography of Timothy Richard, see: William Edward Soothill's *Timothy Richard of China: Seer, Statesman, Missionary and the Most Disinterested Adviser to China* (London: Seeley Service, 1926).

through reading some Buddhist scriptures and personal encounters with some Chinese Buddhists, especially the influential Buddhist reformer Yang Wen-hui (1837–1911), Richard became aware of not only the significant similarities between Christianity and Mahayana Buddhism, which is the dominant form of Buddhism in China, but also the emerging revival of Buddhism in China. Richard did not only help Yang to form partnership with Buddhist reformers from other countries, Richard also worked with Yang to translate some Buddhist texts into English.[2]

Richard's translation of the Buddhist texts was criticized on the ground that he used a lot of Christian expressions to translate the Buddhist terms. However, it is very important to note that Richard's intention was not to convert Buddhists to Christianity. Underlying his "theological" translation was his expectation that through demonstrating the similarities between Buddhism and Christianity, Buddhists and Christians "no longer feared each other as foes, but helped each other as friends." [3] In other words, Richard's translation aimed at establishing the common ground for the cooperation or "brotherhood" between Buddhists and Christians.[4] However, Richard's concern was not restricted to the so-called inter or intra religious relationship between Buddhism and Christianity as such. For him, an even more important goal of promoting Buddhist-Christian dialogue was to "strengthen the forces struggling against the selfish materialism of this age."[5]

As Andrew F. Walls correctly points out, Richard started his mission with a strictly evangelistic understanding of mission, but his experience in China expanded as well as deepened his understanding of mission – first to include feeding the hungry, and then to consider measures to eliminate the hunger, and at last to address the deeper or wider issues of justice and peace, including the oppressions throughout Asia and the race of armaments among the nations in the West.[6] It is obvious that what concerned Richard most was not the relationship among religions, but how to liberate the world from oppression, poverty and violence and to deliver humankind from ignorance, superstition, selfishness and sin.[7] For Richard, the ultimate aim of missionary work is the establishment of the kingdom of God on earth rather than the salvation of individual souls. And this missionary vision is to materialize through the cooperation between

[2] Timothy Richard (tr.), *The Awakening of Faith in the Mahayana Doctrine: The New Buddhism* (Shanghai: Christian Literature Society, 1907).

[3] Timothy Richard, *The New Testament of Higher Buddhism* (Edinburgh: T & T Clark, 1910), 49.

[4] Richard, *NTHB*, 47.

[5] Richard, *NTHB*, 142.

[6] Andrew F. Walls, *The Cross-Cultural Process in Christian History* (Maryknoll, NY: Orbis Books, 2002), 257.

[7] Richard, *NTHB*, 35–6.

Christians and non-Christians in the promotion of social justice, international peace, etc.

Given Richard's Kingdom-centered understanding of mission, one may not be surprised to find that when he spoke on the question concerning the relationship between Christianity and other religions at the Edinburgh Conference, the focus of his discussion actually shifted from inter-religious relationship to the issues of the poor and oppressed.[8] Similarly, after the outbreak of the First World War, Richard authored *An Epistle to All Buddhists*, a small bilingual (in Chinese and English) book published in China. In stead of encouraging the Buddhists to convert to Christianity, the book urged them to form partnership with Christians to work together for the poor, the oppressed, and to build up a new world civilization of justice and peace.[9]

Perhaps one may summarize that Richard's approach to Christian mission and inter-religious dialogue, which is reminiscent of the Kingdom-centered approach in the contemporary discussion concerning theology of religions, makes him not only a critic of colonialism, militarism as well as consumerism but also an active proponent for inter-religious dialogue and cooperation.[10]

Revival of Chinese Buddhism and the Christian Responses

During the Republican period (1911-1949), partially due to Yang Wen-hui's efforts, Buddhist philosophy became an important source of ideas for many Chinese intellectuals. Some of the Buddhist thinkers, e.g. Zhang Tai-yan (1868-1936), even made use of modern scientific theories to criticize Christian theology. Some of the Buddhists trained by the Buddhist seminaries established by Yang or influenced by his model of Buddhist education, which Yang learnt from Christianity, became influential leaders of the Buddhist reform. The best known of them is probably Ven. Tai Xu (1890-1947), who made a lot of efforts to modernize Buddhist education and organizations, to engage in various social and political activities, and to reinterpret the Buddhist doctrines creatively in response to the contemporary social and political contexts.[11] It is important to note that Taixu had a relatively friendly relationship with Christianity and even frankly admitted that the Buddhist reforms launched by him were partially

---

[8] Walls, *CCPCH*, 256–7.

[9] Richard, *An Epistle to All Buddhists* (Shanghai: Christian Literature Society, 1916), 11.

[10] A more detailed discussion on Timothy Richard, see: Lai Pan-chiu, 'Timothy Richard's Buddhist-Christian Studies', *Buddhist-Christian Studies* 29 (2009), 23-37.

[11] See for details: Don A. Pittman, *Toward a Modern Chinese Buddhism: Taixu's Reforms* (Honolulu: University of Hawaii Press, 2001).

inspired by Christianity, especially the missionary activities in China in education, social welfare, and medical service.[12]

Due to the recognizable revival of Chinese Buddhism, some Christian missionaries began to take a more positive view on Chinese Buddhism. Other than the Chinese Christians who were attracted to and then even converted to Buddhism, some Chinese Christian intellectuals proposed to learn from Chinese Buddhism concerning its successful experience in indigenization into the Chinese soil. Some Christian churches even began to adopt some Buddhist styles in their worship.[13]

Among the Christian missionaries working among the Chinese Buddhists, the best known is probably Karl Ludvig Reichelt (1877–1952).[14] Though he shared Richard's interests in Chinese Buddhism, Reichelt's approach to mission among the Buddhists is quite different from that of Richard. Reichelt's approach places greater emphasis on the idea that Christianity is the fulfillment of other religions. His endeavours in establishing meeting places in Buddhist architectural style for Buddhists and Christians, adopting some Buddhist terms and practices in Christian worship, etc. aimed at providing a friendly environment which might attract Buddhist monks to visit or even stay for spiritual cultivation. These meeting places included the Jing Feng Shan in Nanjing, Tien Feng Shan in Hangzhou and then Dao Feng Shan (Tao Fong Shan) in Hong Kong, which remains rather active in promoting Buddhist-Christian dialogue.[15] No matter whether this is Reichelt's intention, these efforts, including his generosity with financial assistance to the Buddhist monks escaping from Mainland China to Hong Kong around 1949, were considered by some as strategies for proselytizing or converting Buddhist monks to Christianity and as a result angered many Buddhists. In fact, there were several polemical disputes between Buddhists and Christians in Hong Kong and Taiwan during the second half of the twentieth century.[16]

Modernization and Globalization of Chinese Buddhism

Though the reforms proposed by Taixu could not continue in Mainland China after 1949 due to the historical and political circumstances, his basic

---

[12] He Jian-ming & Lai Pan-chiu, 'Christianity and the Modern Chinese Buddhist Reform', *Dialogue & Alliance* 17.2 (Fall/ Winter 2003/4), 41-69.

[13] Lai Pan-chiu, 'Influence of Chinese Buddhism on the Indigenization of Christianity in Modern China', *Ching Feng* (New Series) 1.2 (2000), 143-160.

[14] See: Eric Sharpe's *Karl Ludwig Reichelt: Missionary, Scholar & Pilgrim* (Hong Kong: Tao Fong Shan Ecumenical Centre, 1984).

[15] Lai Pan-chiu, 'The Role of Hong Kong in the Buddhist-Christian Encounter in China', *Ching Feng* (New Series) 5.1 (2004), 119–33.

[16] See: Whalen Lai & Michael von Brück, *Christianity and Buddhism: A Multi-Cultural History of Their Dialogue*, translated by Phyllis Jestice (Maryknoll: Orbis Books, 2001), 94-96.

ideas, including his aspiration for establishing a humanistic Buddhism, which places emphasis on this-world rather than next life, have materialized and deepened primarily in Taiwan and to a lesser extent in Hong Kong and overseas. After undergoing certain twist and turn or ups and downs, Chinese Buddhism has become to a certain extent modernized and globalized. Today Buddhism is probably the biggest and most influential religion in Taiwan and possibly also in Hong Kong and Mainland China. In Taiwan, it has established a good number of universities, television channels, schools, hospitals, and relief work agencies. In addition to its cultural and social influences, Buddhism became rather influential in the political development in Taiwan as well.[17] An even more remarkable achievement is that many Chinese Buddhist missionaries have been sent to most of the major continents and they have successfully established Buddhist temples or organizations in other parts of Asia, USA, Europe, Australia and even Africa. In Mainland China, with the government's support, the first World Buddhist Forum, which was the biggest Buddhist conference in modern China with representatives from Theravada, Mahayana and Tibetan traditions, was held in Hangzhou in 2006. This event signifies the recognition of the government with regard to the possible contribution of Buddhism towards the enhancement of social harmony.[18]

Partially due to the rise of Buddhism in China, there have been some academic conferences on Buddhist-Christian dialogue held in China with some participants from overseas, including the international conferences held in Xi'an in 2003, in Hong Kong in 2006 and in Hangzhou in 2009.[19] Furthermore, there are many other occasions or examples of Buddhist-Christian dialogue in China.[20] The increase of these dialogues indicates that there are a lot of potentials for the future development of Buddhist-Christian dialogue.

---

[17] See for details: Richard Madsen, *Democracy's Dharma: Religious Renaissance and Political Development in Taiwan* (Berkeley: University of California Press, 2001).

[18] See for details: *A Harmonious World Begins in the Mind: Collected Works of the World Buddhist Forum: English Collection* (Beijing: Religious Culture Publishing House, 2006). The first forum generated two other volumes in Chinese.

[19] The papers presented at the first two conferences were published as books in Mainland China, with some papers in English published as special issues in *Ching Feng* (New Series), Vol. 4 No.2; Vol.5 No.1; and Vol. 7.

[20] For a recent example, see: He Jian-ming, 'The Modern Chan Society and the China Lutheran Seminary in Conversation: A Case Study of Buddhist-Christian Dialogue in Contemporary Taiwan', *Ching Feng* Vol. 4, No. 2 (2003), 203-239.

Humanistic Buddhism and Pure Land

The revival of Chinese Buddhism during the first half of the 20th century was accompanied by the formation of the idea of humanistic Buddhism, which involves some re-interpretations of the Buddhist doctrine of Pure Land. Admittedly, the traditional Buddhist doctrine of Pure Land tends to focus on one's own rebirth in the next life in a paradise established by the other-power of the Amitabha Buddha (Amida). This kind of eschatological hope might appear to be too individualistic, other-worldly and supernatural to be relevant to Buddhist social praxis. It seemed to have nothing to do with this world, except that one might call upon the name of Amida (pronounced as o-mi-to-fu in Chinese) at one's deathbed and as often as possible in one's daily life. However, many modern Chinese Buddhists reinterpreted this seemingly "other-worldly" concepts in relation to Buddhist social praxis, including environmental protection. Nowadays, the concept of Pure Land has become the doctrinal basis of the reforms and the resultant new forms of Buddhism.

A typical example of this Humanistic Buddhism and re-interpretation of the Pure Land can be found in the motto "to build the Pure Land in our midst" proposed by Master Hsing Yün (Xing-yun) of Buddha-Light Mountain (*Fo Guang Shan*) which is probably the most modernized or globalized example of Buddhism in Taiwan.[21] The Dharma Master states, "Where is the Pure Land for a Ch'an practitioner? It is in the performing of lowly tasks. It is in the love for and salvation of others. It is also in the transformation of one's surrounding."[22] He further explains,

> Humanistic Buddhism is not a new kind of Buddhism: it is simply a name used to emphasize the core teachings of the Buddha. The Buddha taught wisdom and compassion. These teachings always lead us back to the lives of other sentient beings. To not understand the unity of human nature and Buddha nature is not to understand the teachings of the Buddha. Humanistic Buddhism encourages us to participate in the world and be a source of energy that is beneficial to others.[23]

Similar interpretation of the Pure Land can be found in the writings of some other Buddhist leaders in Taiwan, including Ven. Cheng Yen, who established the Compassion Relief Tzu Chi Foundation (*ci ji gong de hui*), which has become one of the most influential relief agencies in Taiwan. Another important example is Venerable Chan Master Sheng-yen (1931-2009), founder of the Dharma Drum Mountain Buddhist Associate (*fa gu*

---

[21] The centrality of the motto is reflected in the title of a recent study of Foguangshan. See: Stuart Chandler, *Establishing a Pure Land on Earth: The Foguang Buddhist Perspective on Modernization and Globalization* (Honolulu: University of Hawaii Press, 2004).

[22] Cf.: Donald W. Mitchell, *Buddhism: Introducing the Buddhist Experience* (New York: Oxford University Press, 2002), 302.

[23] *BIBE*, 302.

shan) and promoter of Spiritual Environmental Protection (*xin ling huan bao*). Underlying the famous Movement of the Pure Land on Earth advocated by him is his understanding that "when seen through the Buddha's eye of wisdom and compassion, every place in the world *is* a Pure Land."[24]

One may find that in modern Chinese Buddhism, the doctrine of Pure Land has changed rather dramatically from an "other-worldly" concept into a more "this-worldly" concept, from a Pure Land out there into a Pure Land in the human heart. Based on these re-interpretations, the doctrine of Pure Land becomes the major imagery inspiring the Buddhist participation in social praxis and also the doctrinal foundation for a balance between social praxis and spirituality. [25]

For the Kingdom of God

The case of Chinese Buddhism is by no means the only one. There are comparable movements in other countries in Asia. For example, there was a revival as well as resistant Buddhist movement called Protestant Buddhism formed in Sri Lanka.[26] Cases of globalized Buddhism and Buddhist Humanism can also be found in Japanese Buddhism.[27] There are many Buddhist liberation movements, which are collectively called Engaged Buddhism, formed in various countries in Asia.[28] These revival and liberation movements in Buddhism in Asia make it rather necessary for the Christian mission among the Buddhists to take seriously the task of Buddhist-Christian dialogue. The rise of Humanistic Buddhism and Engaged Buddhism, together with the "this worldly" re-interpretations of the Pure Land and other doctrines, may make the dialogue between Christianity and Buddhism on the relevant concepts, e.g. Pure Land and Kingdom of God, desirable and fruitful.[29]

At this juncture, one may recall Timothy Richard's Kingdom-centered approach to mission and Buddhist-Christian dialogue. Though the concept

[24] Sheng-yen, 'A Pure Land on Earth', in: *Buddhist Peace Word: Creating Cultures of Peace*, edited by David Chappell (Boston: Wisdom Publications, 1999), 179.

[25] Lai Pan-chiu, 'The Kingdom of God and the Pure Land: A Dialogical Study of Eschatology and Praxis', *Ching Feng* (New Series) 7.1-2 (2006), 183-210, esp. 200-208.

[26] Richard Gombrich, *Theravada Buddhism: A Social History from Ancient Benares to modern Colombo* (London: Routledge & Kegan Paul, 1988), 172-97.

[27] The best known example is probably Soka Gakkai, see: Richard Hughes Seager, *Encountering the Dharma: Daisaku Ikeda, Soka Gakkai, and the Globalization of Buddhist Humanism* (Berkeley: University of California Press, 2006).

[28] Christopher S. Queen and Sallie B. King (eds.) *Engaged Buddhism: Buddhist Liberation Movements in Asia* (Albany: State University of New York, 1996).

[29] See: Lai Pan-chiu and Xue Yu (eds.), *The Kingdom of God, the Pure Land and the Human World*, Special Issue of *Ching Feng* (New Series) 7.1-2 (2006), 1-246.

of the Kingdom of God was conventionally thought to be an eschatological doctrine related primarily if not exclusively to the individual's final destiny after death, Richard's interpretation of the Kingdom of God illustrates a trend in modern Christian theology, which tended to interpret the Kingdom of God as an ideal society to be actualized or established on earth in history through human efforts, rather than a trans-historical, super-natural reality to be established by God alone. Although this kind of interpretation of the Kingdom of God has been criticized by many biblical scholars and systematic theologians as being too one-sided and overlooking the transcendent or futuristic dimension of the Kingdom of God, it remains a key concept in the contemporary understanding of Christian mission.

In hindsight, some of Timothy Richard's ideas are questionable and his Kingdom-centered approach to Christian mission might be too ahead of his time. At that period, Buddhism in Asia might not be ready to form any viable or sustainable partnership with Christianity to work for a just and peaceful world. However, after one hundred years, with its doctrinal development as well as social, political and cultural influences, Buddhism has become one of the most important rivals as well as allies of Christianity. [30] Considering also the urgency of today's pressing issues concerning environmental crisis, human rights, rise of nihilism, conflicts among religions or races, etc., it is perhaps high time for Christians to further explore the Kingdom-centered approach to the Christian mission among the Buddhists, to have more in-depth dialogue with Buddhism, and to form partnership with Buddhism for the realisation of the Kingdom of God.[31]

---

[30] See: Ninian Smart, *Buddhism and Christianity: Rivals and Allies* (Honolulu: University of Hawaii Press, 1993).

[31] The research work published here is sponsored by a Direct Grant for Research (project no. 2010327) gratefully received from the Chinese University of Hong Kong.

Mission and New Religious Movements: The Church's Encounter with New Spiritualities

Ole Skjerbæk Madsen

From New Religious Movements to New Spiritualities / Spiritualities of Life

New Religious Movements (NRM), New Religions (NR) or Cults, as they were often called, received a massive publicity when The Beatles in the 1960s turned to Maharishi Mahesh Yogi (Transcendental Meditation) for spiritual guidance.

NR are not necessarily new; they may have a long history and may be new only because of a new context or be changed in and adapted to a new cultural situation as when Hindu and Buddhist religion and spiritual practices found their way to Western societies; this influx of Eastern spirituality and religious thoughts was promulgated by *the Theosophical movement* founded in 1875 and *the Parliament of the World's Religions* in Chicago 1893. But new religions exploded in the 1960s and the following decades.

In the 1970s NR were sometimes called "Jugendreligionen" (youth religions), because young people were attracted to them. The new religions often gathered their followers around a "charismatic" leader, offered an intimate and dedicated fellowship and a clear message which was understood as a panacea for the evils of our culture.

The new religious world of the 1970s and the 1980s was characterized inter alia by yoga-courses, Hindu gurus (Maharishi Mahesh Yogi, Osho, and Sathya Sai Baba), zen-meditation, Scientology, The Unification Church, and The Family of Love (Children of God). Also alternative healing practices appeared in the old Christendom world, among other things inspired from traditional Chinese medicine and other practices linked up with an energetic worldview. Many of the "old" new religions or cults have diminished in influence since the 1990s where "new" new religions began to appear with a less authoritarian character and a more fluid membership or affiliation. The "new" religions sometimes are part of the new spirituality milieu (cf. the following) or have grown out of it. Also a westernised Buddhism attracts many Westerners, and neo-pagan groups arise sometimes linked up with feminist and ecological spirituality.

Since the late 1970s a broader spiritual movement has been in the focus. This was not a new religion, but borrowed insights and practices from many religious and spiritual sources. Defining these new spiritualities is almost impossible, just as finding the right name for the phenomenon is difficult. In the 1980s and 1990s many people were satisfied with "New Age" and later on with "Holistic Movement".[1] We suggest the terms "new spiritualities" or "neo-spiritual milieus" because "New Age" does not cover for instance neo-pagan movements which do not understand themselves as New Age, yet have an important role in today's spiritual world. New spirituality (NS), however, may also be a difficult term since spirituality is a very broad term covering Christian spiritual practices, the practices of other religions as well as non-religious spirituality in the culture of wellbeing and wellness. The non-religious spiritualities have recently also been called "Spiritualities of Life".[2] At least in Scandinavia also humanistic atheism should be understood as a non-religious spirituality, e.g. creating its own rites of transition.[3]

NS might be understood in the light of the history of *Western Esotericism*.[4] The rise of neo-spiritual milieus may be understood as a part of *a spiritual revolution* and a drifting away from traditional, dogmatic religion to a non-sectarian spirituality.[5] New spiritualities thus may be seen as *a reaction against Christianity or at least Churchianity* as is the case in some forms of neo-paganism.[6]

The world view involved in the neo-spiritual milieus may be only vaguely implied or find more consciously elaborated expressions as in many neo-pagan groups and among practitioners of complementary medicine / alternative healing and spiritualities of life. In theosophical/neo-theosophical groups and among trendsetters and teachers the world view is expressed in more or less developed philosophies.

Significant features of the new spiritualities may be expressed in these statements:

- Spirituality is being in touch with the divine, which may have many names such as the Source, Love, Father-Mother-God, all

---

[1] Cf. William Bloom (ed), *Holistic Revolution. The Essential New Age Reader*. (Allen Lane / The Penguin Press, London 2000).

[2] Cf. Paul Heelas, *Spiritualities of Life. New Age Romanticism and Consumptive Capitalism*. (Blackwell Publishing, MA/Oxford 2008).

[3] Human-Etisk Forbund, www.human.no; Humanisterne in Sweden; Humanistisk Forbund in Denmark

[4] Wouter J. Hanegraaff, *New Age Religion and Western Culture. Esotericism in the Mirror of Secular Thought*. (E.J. Brill. Leiden. New York. Köln, 1996).

[5] Paul Heelas and Linda Woodhead et al. *The Spiritual Revolution. Why Religion is giving Way to Spirituality*. (Blackwell Publishing, MA/Oxford 2005).

[6] An example is Asatrofællesskabet, cf. www.asatrofaellesskabet.dk which sees the old religion as more suitable to Norse people.

that is, the Universe; often adherents speak of energy transmitted from the Universe.

- Spirituality concerns personal development, transformation of consciousness and spiritual experience as a process; some speak of finding the inner guru and being in contact with one's higher Self, which often is seen as a divine spark or a part of God. Spirituality is experiential and experimental and truth is not accepted unless personally experienced.
- Humans need tools for growth and for discovering and developing their spiritual, psychic or energetic potentials.
- Authenticity is valued above the authority of institutions, of dogmatic religion and reductionist science. Spiritual counsellors and teachers shall be authentic and be living examples of what they teach.
- Spirituality shall be relevant on the personal as well as the global level

NS have a holistic understanding of life; body, mind and spirit interact. In many parts of the neo-spiritual milieus holism tends to be monistic or non-dual, seeing the conditions of human life as illusionary; one might speak of a *monistic* or *non-dual holism*. Yet NS adherents care for the planet and the ecological environment; there is a sense of responsibility for the healing of nature and the protection of all life; one might speak of *a planetary holism*. At the same time it is an *individual* or *personal holism* – being concerned with personal wholeness, wellness and well being, personal development, and the transformation of consciousness.

From Demonization and Stigmatization to Dialogue and Contextual Mission

The contact between Christians and adherents of NR and NS has been marred by mutual suspicion and prejudice. The emphasis of many Christian expositions on New Religions and Spiritualities is on explaining how the *New Age* movement differs from Christian faith. It is the spiritual conflict and the view of New Age as a catalogue of heresies all the way back to Gnosticism that prevails. The main concern is pastoral, warning Christians to engage in a spirituality which eventually will lead them away from Christ and the Church. This approach may be important to help believers discern what is true and what is not, but it is not helpful for a dialogical evangelism and mission or for the inculturation of the Church in the holistic and neo-spiritual subcultures. This apologetical and heresy hunting attitude may even lead to a demonization of the new religions and spiritualities.

Even if Christian documents on New Age may state, "It is indeed our conviction that through many of our contemporaries who are searching, we can discover true thirst for God," they will not point at bridges between

Christian and New Age spirituality or areas of affinity and mutual concerns.[7]

An honest dialogue of course includes talking of differences, but if it shall open the other person to what we have received and experienced as truth we also have to recognize the *logoi spermatikoi* within NS.

There is a need for a new paradigm[8] for the Church's encounter with NRM, NR and NS. Such a paradigm calls for an abandonment of the atmosphere of fear in the relationship with adherents of the NRM, of the automatic demonization of their spiritual practices, and of the typecasting of them as spiritual enemies.

The new paradigm looks upon the adherents of NRM and practitioners of NS as people whom God loves and as potential disciples of Jesus Christ. This does not mean that the discernment of spirits is abandoned in relation to NRM and NS, but it means that Christians should not be afraid of establishing friendships, of studying and understanding their beliefs, their practices, their hopes, their hurts, and their fears. We recognize in and among ourselves similar beliefs, hopes, and fears sharing a common humanity and being created in the image of God.

In ministering among the people who comprise the NRM and NS, we are dealing with a group of people who often have been deeply hurt by Christians, and who have suffered from rejection and suspicion from Christians. For this reason a sincere asking forgiveness is a condition sine qua non for the enculturation of the Church in the NS milieus and for a contextual proclamation of the Gospel. Among adherents of the NRM and NS we also find many people who have misunderstood Christian teachings and practices, and who are unaware of the message and viability of Christianity in the post-modern world. Many spiritual seekers however have found inspiration in new expressions of East Asian religions, in nature-based spiritualities such as Contemporary Paganism, Neo-Pagan movements, Wicca ((modern movement of witchcraft) and in various esoteric traditions.

A new paradigm includes learning from the NRM and NS, since their practice and beliefs may reflect the unpaid bills of the Church, or failures of the church in engaging significant issues on a personal, spiritual, moral, social or global level, and in so doing, creating a vacuum filled by NRM

---

[7] Cf. *'Jesus Christ the Bearer of the Water of Life. A Christian Reflection on the "New Age"'* from the Pontifical Council for Culture / Pontifical council for Interreligious Dialogue. 2003. The same split has been prevalent in evangelical Christendom, e.g. the *Thailand Report on New Religious Movements*, published 1980 by the Lausanne Committee for World Evangelism. Here the acknowledgement that Cults and New Religious Movements are unreached people groups contrasts the spiritual warfare approach towards the occult.

[8] Cf. the consultation in Hong Kong 2006 of *the Lausanne network on Christian encounter with the new spiritualities*, http://www.lausanne.org/new-spiritualities-2006/overview.html

and NS. This reflection, as well as discerning the points of contact and areas of potential conflict, may help the Church to understand the questions of post-modern men and women, and this in turn may help Christians to proclaim the gospel by meeting actual concerns instead of answering questions which may be of interest to the Church but which are often not raised by the people we seek to meet.

The recognition of these unpaid bills and points of contact may help the Church to find new expressions of its life and spiritual practice, which may contribute to the creation of a revitalized Christian community where the spiritual seeker and the new follower of Christ may feel at home in the Church and accepted in the Christian fellowship.

A Christian Theological Response to the New Spiritualities

A Christian theological reflection answering the new spiritual concerns might find points of contact and a common background in the roots of Western esotericism,[9] and may be summarized in the following way:

What is needed is a Trinitarian theology of creation. God creates the world through God's *Logos* breathing the life-giving Holy Spirit into the created world. The original nature of the created world reflects the Logos and the Spirit. The Logos reflects the order of the created world, that law of servant love which is the condition of life and the unity of the world. The original nature of humankind as created in the image of God in a microcosmic way serves, reveals and establishes this *logos* of earthly creation. Thus humankind is closely linked to nature and all fellow creatures of the Earth. And everything lives, breathes and moves in the Spirit or Breath of God. So far a Christian theology of creation *affirms a planetary and personal holism* in the understanding of the role of humans and in the understanding of the human person. It also affirms the idea of nature as a book of revelation, proclaiming the glory or presence of the Lord. The created world was thus meant to be a sacrament. It *does not however affirm a monistic or non-dual holism*. Christian theology does not see the created world as *maya* (illusion), but as real and understands the network of right relations between humans and between all creatures as a reflection of the servant love of God.

Christian theology takes the fact of sin into account. The original nature of humans and of nature is disturbed by original sin which distorts the revelation of God in creation, breaks the relationship between God and humans and uproots the loving network of relations between all earthly creatures. The incarnation of the Logos of God restores the original nature

---

[9] Ole Skjerbæk Madsen, 'Theology in Dialogue with New Age or the Neospiritual Milieu' in Viggo Mortensen (ed), *Theology and the Religions: A Dialogue.* (William B. Eerdmans Publishing Company, Grand Rapids, Michigan 2003), 257-258, 264-285.

of humans. Christian theology *affirms the individual/personal way of transformation / sanctification*, preparing for the kingdom of God to be fully established among humans, and fulfilling the longing of all earthly creatures for the freedom of the children of God. Through the Holy Spirit Christians recognise the original sacramental nature of their fellow creatures, and restored to their own original nature in Christ they call their fellow creatures into a renewed relationship to God. As microcosmic beings humans reveal to nature, the Earth and their fellow creatures what is the nature of the created world. If humans live in original sin and a distorted relationship to God and one another, this is reflected to the world and submits creation to corruption and death. If humans are restored in the image of God, this is the restored image of what the world is meant to be.

A Christian Liturgical Response (Servants / Stewards)

Christian liturgy may reveal its inner meaning to the esoteric neo-spiritual groups if it is experienced as a microcosmic event, referring to the sign character of creation (nature as a book of revelation). The Church's sacraments and blessings are honouring the sacramental character of all of creation, and are founded in the sign character of nature and will thus provide for a Christian interpretation of the re-enchantment of nature which is happening in the neo-spiritual milieu. They are an antidote to consumerism, because they acknowledge the created world and its elements as gifts. This is most clearly established in the Eucharist, giving thanks for creation and its restoration and salvation through Christ. The Eucharist is an anticipatory reunion of the created world with the Creator in Christ.

The Church may in this way understand the role of its sacraments and spiritual practices in light of sanctification, prefiguring the transformation of humankind and the reestablishment of the balance/harmony of nature. Partaking in liturgy is partaking in a process of mediation: "Through Jesus Christ, God is persuading the Church in the direction of greater union with God self. Through the Church and the liturgy, Jesus Christ is luring the world in the direction of greater humanization."[10]

In developing a spiritual practice in the context of NS, Christians acknowledge that new rituals and liturgies will only be a full answer to spiritual seekers if they are also able to address individual concerns of spiritual growth and be seen as means towards achieving a higher consciousness. The priesthood of all believers may thus involve their privilege to create their own rituals as part of their disciple relationship to Jesus. New liturgies meeting the holistic spirituality may thus find much more room for the body and the bodily expressions in the liturgy such as

[10] James Empereur, *Models of Liturgical Theology* (Grove Booklets, Nottingham 1987), 33.

dancing, healing touch, foot washing, incense, aromatic oils and fragrances, and healing music.

Christians could on the basis of their own spiritual and liturgical tradition create liturgies, which express the concern for the Earth and the human race, which NS adherents and Christians have in common.[11] Such liturgies may express solidarity in concern and uniqueness in faith.

A Christian Pastoral Response

Soul care and spiritual direction as well as a healing ministry including prayer for the sick, inner healing and deliverance of demonised persons are very important if the Gospel should meet the needs of post modern spiritual seekers and the broader well-being culture. The Church has a rich experience and tradition. In praying for a sick or suffering person the Church's healing ministry focuses on the re-establishing of the *logos* (the created order) of the malfunctioning organs of the body in asking the *Logos* (Word) of God once more to call the organs back into their natural order. But more than that, at its deepest level it reminds the spiritual seeker of his/her original nature as a child of God. Where God has been reduced to an impersonal energy or force, God is now experienced in an I-You-relationship.

One of the recurring themes in the counselling situation and in dialogue with holistic and neo-spiritual seekers is the idea of reincarnation. The Church has to consider, how are we to deal with the past life experiences and the belief in reincarnation?

A condition *sine qua non* for the pastoral care for spiritual seekers and adherents of the NS is the Christian presence in the neo-spiritual milieus as such. Booth ministry at NS fairs and festivals like the Body Mind Spirit festival and alternative health festivals has proven successful in ministering to NS adherents and seekers. Also a co-wandering with to-days' pilgrims and the establishing of hostels and shelters along pilgrim routes make the healing and loving presence of Jesus manifest and provide opportunities for both soul care and Christian witness to Christ.

The Christian understanding of creation and of the role of humans as stewards of the planet, nature and fellow creatures as well as the celebration of the creative and restoring work of God in liturgy should be followed up by a "green *diakonia*", a practical environmental engagement and a less consumerist life style.

---

[11] How to use the principles of inculturation, dynamic equivalence and creative assimilation in relation to new spiritualities, cf. Ole Skjerbæk Madsen, 'Kontekstuel liturgy', in: *ΙΧΘΥΣ Dansk Tidsskrift for Teologi og Kirke* (May, 2008), 39-49.

MISSION AND JUDAISM:
BACK TO THE FUTURE: NINETEENTH CENTURY FOUNDATIONS OF MESSIANIC JUDAISM

Matt Friedman

> A youth named Lederer was converted in Budapest. Glowing with fresh enthusiasm, he went to New York. There he met a young, able, and accomplished student, Schereschewszky by name, and led him to Christ. Schereschewszky went to China, acquired the language, and translated for the first time the Old Testament into Chinese, direct from the original Hebrew, of which he was absolute master. His translation is the standard Chinese version to-day – the instrument used by every missionary in the land. By the blessing of God the conversion of a Jewish youth in Budapest was the means of giving the Bible to the vast Empire of China. This one fact surely sheds a vivid light upon that word of the great Jewish Christian missionary "If the casting away of them be the reconciling of the world, what shall the receiving of them be but life from the dead?" --Rev. William Ewing, in a discussion at the World Missionary Conference, Edinburgh 1910[1]

The gathering of missionaries and scholars in Edinburgh in 1910 for the World Missionary Conference was one of the pivotal moments in the history of Christian mission; indeed, in the history of the Church itself. For just over a week in June, delegates from throughout the Christian world discussed and debated, assessing the previous "Great Century" of mission (to use Kenneth Scott Latourette's phrase) as well as charting the course forward. Often overlooked amid the great swath of missional territory surveyed has been mission in the Jewish context. This brief paper will consider the lives of two representative figures from the nineteenth as well as in the subsequent century, before concluding with some brief remarks regarding mission in the Jewish context in the twentieth century

After centuries of mostly hostility and neglect by the Christian community, a fresh hope for witness to the Jews was to dawn with the nineteenth century, over the course of which about 205,000[2] Jewish people

---

[1] World Missionary Conference, *Report of Commission I: Carrying the Gospel to All the Non-Christian World* (Edinburgh and London: Oliphant, Anderson and Ferrier, 1910), 416-417.

[2] Arthur Ruppen, *The Jews of To-day* (Trans. Margery Bentwich; New York: Henry Holt and Company, 1913), 183-184, citing baptismal statistics compiled by J. F. De

would profess faith in Jesus as the Messiah of Israel. This movement featured a colorful cast of characters, two of whom we will briefly examine here: Joseph Samuel Frey and Joseph Rabinowitz. The lives of these two individuals serve as "bookends" to the century chronologically, and, in a way, serve to contrast two perspectives on mission in the Jewish context: what Arnold Fructenbaum refers to as a policy of "assimilation" as opposed to a policy of "distinction",[3] or to paraphrase Jakób Jocz, the difference between "Jewish converts to Christianity" and "Messianic Jews".[4] Of course, all of this should be understood in the context of the issues of identity and assimilation which were important from the beginning of the eighteenth century.[5]

Joseph Samuel Frey is sometimes called the "Father of Modern Jewish Missions".[6] According to his autobiographical account, he was born in Germany in 1771 to a fairly devout Jewish family. His maternal uncle had embraced the faith in Jesus, as a result of which Frey's mother had become embittered against Christianity. Frey notes that as a family they studied literature which was designed to refute Christian teaching as a means of being fortified against the Christian faith. He learned to read Hebrew from a very young age, and by the time he was six years old, he could read the Torah and was soon studying the commentaries as well as Talmud and other traditional writings in preparation for a career as a Jewish religious leader. As his studies continued, he was successively ordained as a *chazan* (cantor), as a *shochet* (ritual slaughterer) and finally as a rabbi. It is interesting that while Frey's autobiographical account unfortunately does not convey a very positive view of his Jewish upbringing, his narrative nonetheless includes an anecdote of his own father's prayers reviving his sister from what had appeared to be death.[7]

Frey's journey to faith in Messiah came about after a series of circumstances. Having received some misinformation about some possible employment in another town, he was impacted en route by a discussion in the stage coach in which he was traveling, between a man who was a serious Christian and a Jewish man who was non-observant. He ended up

---

le Roi. See also Israel Cohen, *Jewish Life in Modern Times* (London: Methuen & Co. Ltd, 1929), 268-284, for a non-sympathetic use of De le Roi's figures.

[3] Arnold G. Fructenbaum, *Hebrew Christianity: Its Theology, History and Philosophy* (Washington, D. C.: Canon Press, 1974), 48.

[4] Jakób Jocz, *The Jewish People and Jesus Christ* (London: SPCK, 1962), 233.

[5] The late eighteenth century onwards saw the rise of the *Haskalah*, or Jewish Enlightenment. See Mark Kinzer, *Post-Missionary Messianic Judaism: Redefining Christian Engagement with Jewish People* (Grand Rapids, MI: Brazos Press. 2005), 269-270.

[6] Meyer, Louis. 1983. *Louis Meyer's Eminent Hebrew Christians of the Nineteenth Century: Brief Biographical Sketches* (Ed. David A. Rausch; New York and Toronto: The Edwin Mellen Press, 1983), 113.

[7] Joseph S. C. F. Frey, *Judah and Israel* (Fourth Edition; New York: D. Fanshaw, 1841), 1-14.

traveling to Rostock, the town in which the Christian lived, in order to find him. To his dismay, he discovered that Jewish people were not allowed to stay overnight in this town. Having been intrigued, however, by the conversation in the coach, Frey declared himself an inquirer into the Gospel. He was subsequently shuttled around by Christians who were suspicious of his motives. In spite of this, he became convinced of the truth of the Gospel and was baptized by a Lutheran pastor.[8] It would, nonetheless, be some time before he entered into what he considered a living faith in Jesus, after coming into further contact with more devout Christians in another town.[9]

It was following this that Frey concluded that he should prepare for full-time ministry, and entered a missionary college.[10] Finding a place and group with which to serve was difficult; the Danish Missionary Society, for example, asked the college for potential candidates, but specifically rejected Frey, because he was Jewish.[11] Later, an opportunity arose for him to go with two other colleagues to Africa via England. They faced discouraging delays, but it was there that he felt guided by the Lord to remain in England and serve there among his own people.[12]

Initially working with the London Missionary Society, it was following difficulties with them that he left in 1809 to join and help establish what would then become known as the "London Society for Promoting Christianity Amongst the Jews", or the "London Jews' Society".[13] He worked with this group in London for the next six years, engaged in evangelism and helping the poor. They acquired the use of a chapel for what was mainly a "preaching point" in a largely Jewish area, with evangelistic messages by Frey and "ministers of the various denominations." The goal at that point was extraction, rather than the establishment of a community of Jewish believers.[14] This was not an easy ministry; often viewed as apostates and traitors, Frey and those who inquired at the chapel sometimes faced physical threats and intimidation.[15] When the society was brought under the Church of England in 1815 for financial reasons, it was no longer possible for Frey to remain working

---

[8] Frey, *Judah and Israel*, 15-21.

[9] Meyer, *Eminent Hebrew Christians*, 116.

[10] Meyer, *Eminent Hebrew Christians*, 116.

[11] Frey, *Judah and Israel*, 42.

[12] Frey, *Judah and Israel*, 49.

[13] A. E. Thompson, *A Century of Jewish Missions* (Chicago: Fleming H. Revell Company, 1902), 94.

[14] W. T. Gidney, *The History of the London Society for Promoting Christianity Amongst the Jews, 1809-1908* (London: London Society for Promoting Christianity Amongst the Jews, 1908), 39.

[15] Todd M. Endelman, *The Jews of Georgian England: 1714-1830* (Ann Arbor: University of Michigan Press, 1999), 286.

under their auspices due to denominational restrictions.[16] It was at this time that he left to work among the Jews in America.[17]

In America, Frey initially worked under a small mission to the Jewish community in New York shortly after his arrival. It wasn't long afterward, however, that he received a letter from one D. Marc, who was working among the impoverished Jews in parts of Europe. Marc urged Frey to establish a colony for these Christian Jews to which they could come in the United States.[18] This eventually led to the initiation of another new society, the "American Society for the Meliorating the Condition of the Jews" (A.S.M.C.J.). Their goals included resettling these European Jewish believers in Jesus as well as contributing to the evangelization of the Jewish community in the United States, which was still fairly small. They also published a paper called *Israel's Advocate*. The work was not without opposition, with a periodical called *The Jew* published in polemic response to *Israel's Advocate* by one Solomon Jackson.[19] Nonetheless, a farm was rented and outfitted for the immigrants, and a small society began to meet together as these Jewish believers from Europe trickled in.[20] Within a few years, however, the farm had collapsed financially and had to be sold off.[21]

Eventually, Frey withdrew from a primary focus on Jewish mission, and for the last several years of his life, he served as the pastor of several Baptist churches in New York and Michigan. He continued, however, to write about his life and about subjects which were related to mission among the Jews until his death in 1850. Meyer notes that, "God honored him exceedingly by making him the father of Christian work among the Jews on both sides of the Atlantic".[22] To be sure, Frey was a pioneer in that he was genuinely advocating and involved with focused mission to the Jewish population, both in England and in America. It bears repeating, however, that the essential goal was more to see Jews become assimilated Christians rather than bringing into being a community of Jewish believers. This remained the usual pattern throughout the nineteenth century. It was towards the end of the century that another model began to emerge, an example of which is found in the life and work of Joseph Rabinowitz.

---

[16] It is worth noting, however, that even many years later, Frey expressed satisfaction that the society which he had established ("my *child*," he wrote) had continued in the work among in the Jewish community; Frey, *Judah and Israel* 1841, 71.

[17] Frey, *Judah and Israel*, 72.

[18] *Minutes of the First Hebrew-Christian Conference of the United States* (Pittsburgh: Maurice Ruben, 1903), 18-19.

[19] S. H. Jackson, *The Jew: Being a Defense of Judaism Against All Adversaries, Particularly Against the Insidious Attacks of Israel's Advocate* (New York: Johnstone & Van Norden, 1824).

[20] *Minutes*, 20-21.

[21] Leo Shpall, Leo. 'Jewish Agricultural Colonies in the United States'. *Agricultural History* 24:3 (July 1950), 120-146.

[22] Meyer, *Eminent Hebrew Christians*, 119.

Joseph Rabinowitz was born in 1837 in what is now Moldova. Following his mother's death, he was sent to be raised by his maternal grandparents, who were devout Hasidic Jews, and at an early age he had committed to memory a significant amount of Jewish religious teaching.[23] It was at this time that he acquired a Hebrew New Testament from a Jewish acquaintance, who remarked that "possibly Jesus of Nazareth was the Messiah".[24] Married at eighteen, he became involved in Jewish community life, practicing law, lecturing for reform, contributing to Jewish newspapers, and seeking the welfare of the large Jewish community of the city of Kishinev[25] (now Chişinău), which had suffered anti-Semitic violence.[26]

In response to this wave of persecution, Rabinowitz made a visit to Palestine in 1882 to investigate the possibility of finding a location in which he could establish a Jewish settlement.[27] Discouraged by the condition of the Jewish community which he observed in Jerusalem, he climbed the Mount of Olives and, in view of the Dome of the Rock standing in the place where once stood Solomon's Temple, he sought to understand the cause of Jewish suffering throughout history.[28] The words came to his mind from the New Testament he had read, and which he had carried with him to Palestine: "Without me you can do nothing;" it was then that he concluded that Jesus of Nazareth truly *was* the Messiah, and that the restoration of his people could come only through him. "The key to the Holy Land," it came to his mind, "is in the hands of our brother Jesus".[29]

Once back in Kishinev, he began to share his beliefs with the general population, working towards the emergence of a congregation of Jewish believers in Jesus who would worship *as Jews*. Rabinowitz named the congregation *Bèney Israel, Beney Brit Chadashah* ("the People of Israel; the People of the New Covenant"),[30] and they continued practicing traditions such as Shabbat observance and circumcision. They worshipped in Hebrew with preaching in the Jewish-German vernacular of Yiddish.[31] Although the pastor of a Lutheran congregation in Kishinev, Rudolf Faltin,

---

[23] Meyer, *Eminent Hebrew Christians*, 89.

[24] Dan Cohn-Sherbok, *Messianic Judaism* (London: Cassell, 2000), 18.

[25] World Missionary Conference, *Report*, 269, n. 1, notes that half of the population of Kishenev was Jewish at that time.

[26] Cohn-Sherbok, *Messianic Judaism*, 18.

[27] Meyer, *Eminent Hebrew Christians*, 92.

[28] Hugh J. Schonfield, *The History of Jewish Christianity* (London: Duckworth, 1936), 224.

[29] Meyer, *Eminent Hebrew Christians*, 92.

[30] Kinzer, *Post-Missionary*, 274.

[31] Schonfield, *History*, 225.

had hoped to baptize Rabinowitz into the Lutheran Church,[32] Rabinowitz ultimately decided to travel to Berlin for a baptism ceremony which included ministers from a number of traditions; this would thus leave him free, not fully identified with any of them.[33] Although some Christian leaders still had questions regarding Rabinowitz's desire to encourage Jewish believers to maintain their Jewish identity and customs, generally there was a willingness to accept Rabinowitz's stance as at least a temporary measure.[34]

While Rabinowitz helped bring many Jewish people to faith in Jesus,[35] he was unable to baptize many of them as he was never able to receive the required legal permission to do so from the Russian authorities. When Rabinowitz died in 1899, he left no successor, and the congregation was quickly scattered. This may have been partly due to a devastating pogrom which broke out against the Jewish community of Kishinev in 1903 in which many were killed.[36]

Although the long-term results from Rabinowitz's work are difficult to calculate, his was one of several truly pioneering efforts at the end of the nineteenth century to birth a movement of Jewish believers in Jesus which would be genuinely indigenous in theology, practice and identity. Such movements sometimes faced opposition from Christian leaders who were concerned that they were going over into "legalism" or in danger of starting a "sect".[37] Rabinowitz himself was accused by Faltin of "Ebionitism"

---

[32] Kai Kjær-Hansen, *Joseph Rabinowitz and the Messianic Movement* (Grand Rapids, MI: Wm. B. Eerdmans Publishing Company, 1995), 79.
[33] Kinzer, *Post-Missionary*, 274.
[34] Kinzer, *Post-Missionary*, 274-275.
[35] Meyer, *Eminent Hebrew Christians*, 93-94.
[36] Kjær-Hansen, *Joseph Rabinowitz*, 204-205.
[37] Karl F. Heman, 'Missions to the Jews', in Samuel M. Jackson, ed., *The New Schaff-Herzog Encyclopedia of Religious Knowledge* (13 vols; New York: Funk and Wagnalls Company, 1910), Vol. VI, 181. Heman is worth quoting at length on this. This was published in English translation in 1910, the same year as the World Missionary Conference, and based on the original German article by the author published in 1903 in the *Realencyklopeie* (Karl F. Heman, 'Missionen unter den Juden', in Albert Hauck, ed., *Realencyklopädie für Protestantiche Theologie und Kirche* [24 vols; Leipzig: J.C. Hinrichs, 1903], Vol. 13, 171-192). "The proper persons to be employed in converting the Jews are Christian clergymen; although it is much more difficult to prepare born Christians for work of that kind than born Jews, who can more easily adapt themselves to the mode of thinking of their brethren. But it would be entirely wrong to gather the Jews into a separate Judæo-Christian Church, since that would lead only to a new sect; and, on the other hand, extreme caution must be observed that baptism may not be granted too hastily or to unworthy recipients. Methods of missionary work differ according to the various conditions of the Jews. While the Jews lived almost without any legal rights among the Christians the State and the Church could force them to hear the preaching of the Gospel in their own synagogues or in churches. Since the emancipation of the Jews, this method has become impossible, and they have accordingly been visited in

(though curiously, Faltin nonetheless praised his effective evangelistic preaching!).[38] Others suggested that Hebrew Christians were violating the principle of being "one in Christ",[39] and were "giving rise to increased cleavage within the Church".[40] Perhaps most ironic in the late nineteenth and early twentieth centuries was one group insisting that the formation of congregations of Jewish believers was somehow going against the grain of "dispensational truth".[41]

Such opposition notwithstanding, it can truly be said that Rabinowitz and others like him in his era helped pave the way for the emerging Messianic Judaism which continues to grow to this day. At the beginning of the nineteenth century we observed the initial step of a ministry focused on mission to the Jewish population, under Joseph Samuel Frey and those working with him. From this work developed the emergence of the first Hebrew-Christian fellowships by the middle of the nineteenth century, though without much which would be considered culturally or religiously Jewish.[42] By the end of the century we can see the first steps towards the re-emergence of an indigenous Messianic Jewish community, though it would still be much later before this would come more fully into fruition.

Where did the movement go from there? Particularly in Europe, the influx of thousands of Jews continued from where it had left off in the nineteenth century. It has been estimated that more than 200,000 Jewish people in Europe came to faith in Jesus in the years between the first and second world wars.[43] This movement, like so much else of beauty in the Jewish world, was swept away by the tide of death that was the Holocaust. Misconceptions aside, faith in Jesus offered no protection against those who sought to kill Jewish people regardless of their beliefs; most of the Jewish believers in Jesus in Europe perished among the millions of other Jewish people.[44] Following the Holocaust, many Jewish missions ceased to

---

their homes, and the Gospel has been announced to them by the distribution of tracts and books." (Heman, 'Missions', 181). Startlingly, the English article was republished without revision in 1950.

[38] Kjær-Hansen, *Joseph Rabinowitz*, 142.

[39] Schonfield, *History*, 210.

[40] B. Z. Sobel, *Hebrew Christianity: The Thirteenth Tribe* (New York: John Wiley & Sons, 1974), 311.

[41] Schonfield, *History*, 220.

[42] Cohn-Sherbok, *Messianic Judaism*, 16-17.

[43] Mitchell L. Glaser, 'Jewish Missions in Hungary, Poland and Czechoslovakia, 1900-1950' (Paper Presented to Lausanne Consultation on Jewish Evangelism North America, March 2-4, 1998), 69.

[44] Gavriel Gefen, 'Re-Contextualization: Restoring the Biblical Message to a Jewish-Israeli Context', *International Journal of Frontier Missiology* 25:2 (Summer 2008), 99-108; see also Cohn-Sherbok, *Messianic Judaism*, 42-43. For several particularly moving accounts of the martyrdom of Isaac Feinstein, a Jewish believing evangelist in Romania, at the hands of the Nazis, see Glaser, 'Jewish Missions', 51-57.

function, especially in areas where the Jewish population had been decimated, and many of the churches which had earlier supported evangelism in the Jewish community began to focus entirely on Christian-Jewish dialogue.[45]

Over the course of the next several decades, especially in the United States, a slow trickle of Jewish people continued to come to faith in Jesus. It was the "Jesus Movement" of the late 1960's and 1970's which would revive the fortunes of ministry among the Jews in a number of directions. This period saw thousands of Jewish young people once again embracing faith in Jesus. Many of them flocked into the churches, continuing the general process of assimilation with the surrounding culture which had already been taking place in the Jewish community. Others sought to develop a more authentically Jewish expression of faith in Jesus, and this led further in the direction of a Messianic Judaism along the lines envisioned and practiced by Joseph Rabinowitz many decades earlier. This led to the development of an increasingly robust congregational movement.[46]

Now, in the early twenty-first century, and in the midst of the centenary celebration and renewal of the World Missionary Conference, let us look at how mission in the Jewish context is progressing on three levels: mission *to* the Jewish community, mission *within* the Jewish community, and finally, mission *from* the community of Jewish believers in Jesus to the nations beyond, participating in the worldwide *missio Dei*.

While there is an increasing focus on Jewish authenticity of the sort exemplified by Joseph Rabinowitz, it is important to remember that the role of the Gentile church in mission *to* the Jewish community remains crucial; indeed, as Susan Perlman has pointed out, "the majority of Jews coming to Christ today are still coming to know the Messiah as a result of the witness of Gentile Christians".[47] It cannot be overestimated how crucial mission to the Jewish people is through the wider body of Christ in word, deed and life example. Indeed, the original report from Edinburgh 1910 had noted how the work of Jewish missions in aiding those in need had helped in reducing prejudice against the Gospel in that age.[48] It needs to be understood that Jewish society continues to see changes which are as dynamic as is the case within broader societies especially in the West. Thus, we must not fall into the fallacy of attempting to use the same strategy for all Jewish people everywhere. The Jewish community is not

---

[45] Cohn-Sherbok, *Messianic Judaism*, 46. See, however, Glaser, 'Jewish Missions', 31 (on Hungary) and 59-60 (on Romania) concerning some post-War efforts by indigenous churches.

[46] Cohn-Sherbok, *Messianic Judaism*, 65.

[47] Susan Perlman, 'Missiological Issues in the Encounter with Emerging Judaism'. *Missiology* 28:1 (January 2000), 79.

[48] World Missionary Conference, *Report*, 276.

monolithic, and strategies must be prayerfully developed for mission in all segments of the Jewish community.[49]

At the same time, the importance of mission *within* the Jewish community has grown as a number of different streams of Messianic Jewish congregational life have emerged. These streams vary considerably in terms of the degree of Jewish ritual and lifestyle practiced in services as well as in the personal lives of the members. There is an awareness, however, of the need for authenticity and for an identity which will be understandable to, if not always necessarily accepted by, the broader Jewish community. Stuart Dauermann, in an adaptation of a similar illustration by the Indian Christian figure Sadhu Sundar Singh, offers the "Yahrzeit Glass Principle": a yahrzeit candle is a candle in a small glass which one burns as a memorial on the anniversary of the death of an immediate relative. The glasses are often saved and used in serving drinks, often tea. To be served tea in a yahrzeit glass, Dauermann observes, demonstrates that "at least someone in that home honors Jewish traditions" and that one is being "treated like a member of the family".[50] Even as tea served in such a glass is more easily received, so the Gospel ought to be presented in a manner consistent with indigenous traditions insofar as this is possible without compromising the Gospel itself. Interestingly, one rather fascinating corollary to the deepening level of identification of some Messianic Jews with the Jewish tradition has been a slowly growing, albeit still fairly marginal, degree of acceptance by some of Messianic Judaism as a valid form of Judaism;[51] indeed, in one startling account, Israeli writer Gavriel Gefen describes hearing one unnamed Jewish scholar who is not an adherent to Messianic Judaism suggesting publicly that faith in Jesus as the Messiah may in the near future no longer be considered a "boundary issue" for inclusion within or exclusion from the Jewish community.[52]

Forums for developing (and indeed, arguing about) an indigenous Messianic Jewish theology have emerged, such as the Lausanne Consultation on Jewish Evangelism and the Hashivenu forum.[53] These have had their share of controversies, but representatives of several of the streams of Messianic Jewish theological and missiological thought have come together to present papers and discuss key issues in a search for greater depth as well as unity.[54] All of these streams have had their place, deepening the mission of discipleship and witness in the Jewish community.

---

[49] Perlman, 'Missiological Issues', 77.

[50] Faña Spielberg and Stuart Dauermann, 'Contextualization: Witness and Reflection. Messianic Jews as a Case', *Missiology* 25:1 (January 1997), 23.

[51] See, for example, Cohn-Sherbok, *Messianic Jews*, 210-213.

[52] Gefen, 'Re-Contextualization', 108.

[53] Gefen, 'Re-Contextualization', 102.

[54] The papers presented at this 2007 conclave, the "Borough Park Symposium," are available online at http://www.boroughparksymposium.com

Finally, there is the developing dimension of mission *from* the Jewish community to the nations This is where we began this paper, with the quote from the documents of the original 1910 World Missionary Conference. On the one hand, as long as there have been Jewish followers of Jesus, there have been those such as Schereschewszky who have felt a call on their lives to be involved in mission among the nations of the world. With the advent of a more robust congregational movement, however, this has extended into at least one Messianic Jewish mission agency, sending Israeli Jewish believers out to the nations.[55] It is certainly hoped that this kind of trend will continue, and that people from all segments of the Messianic Jewish world will become more involved in mission to the nations. In this, Messianic Judaism is coming full circle. Even as a genuinely indigenous movement to and in Jesus the Messiah has continued to grow, members of this movement will begin moving out, bearing witness to the presence of the Messiah in their midst, partnering with him in the initiation of indigenous movements to faith in this same Messiah among those who still have not heard.

---

[55] On the history of this movement, see Gavriel Gefen, 'Restoring Mission from Israel to the Nations'. *International Journal of Frontier Missions* 21:3 (Fall 2004), 103-109.

Mission and Judaism: The Scandal of Jewish Evangelism From Edinburgh 1910 to Edinburgh 2010

Kai Kjær-Hansen

According to Paul 'the message of the cross' is a *skandalon* to Jews and 'foolishness' to non-Jews. God, however, decided to save those who believe 'through the foolishness of what was preached,' namely Christ, the crucified and risen one (1 Cor 1:18-23).

Whether or not it is compatible with contemporary theology and missiology, the question needs to be asked: Does an apostolic concept like this have anything to say to Christian theology and mission in the 21st century? And does it still apply to Jewish people?

First: Which stand did they take on Jewish evangelism in Edinburgh in 1910 and in the subsequent decades?

Edinburgh 1910 and Amsterdam 1948 – and the Jewish People

In *Edinburgh 1910* there was a clear affirmation of Jewish evangelism:

> Followers of the Lord Jesus Christ – Himself after the flesh a Jew – should give to the presentation of Christ to the Jew its rightful place in the Great Commission. It is not a task to be left to a few enthusiastic believers, but the obligation and responsibility of the whole Christian Church. The Gospel must be preached to the Jew wherever he may be found.[1]

In *Amsterdam 1948* – only three years after the war in which six million Jews had been killed in concentration camps in so-called Christian countries – the Jewish question could, of course, not be ignored by the World Council of Churches (WCC). It is stated that anti-Semitism 'is a sin against God and man'. In the first paragraph of *The Church's Commission to preach the Gospel to all men*, there is still a clear call to Jewish evangelism:

> All of our churches stand under the commission of our common Lord, 'Go ye into all the world and preach the Gospel to every creature'. The fulfilment of

[1] World Missionary Conference, 1910. *Report of Commission I: Carrying the Gospel to All the Non-Christian World,* vol I (Edinburgh and London: Oliphant, Anderson & Ferrier, 1910), 276-77.

> this commission requires that we include the Jewish people in our evangelistic task.[2]

And by the International Missionary Council in 1957 it was proclaimed:

> Judaism is as much without Christ as Mohammedanism and Hinduism, Buddhism and Confucianism. Either all people need Christ or none.[3]

Do such words still apply to those who celebrate Edinburgh 2010? If *yes*, then it implies a *no* to the idea that religious plurality is a God-given plurality. If *no*, then the door is wide open for a religious plurality where the *biblical* insistence on the uniqueness of Christ and salvation in him has been reduced to theological and missiological anachronisms.

This short article does not allow long explanations and references.[4]. The call to Jewish evangelism has, not least within the last 50 years, become increasingly weak in the framework of ecumenical theology and missiology; in some cases there has even been a strong dissociation from it.[5] In the evangelical world there are still groups that advocate it. A case in point is the full-page ad which the World Evangelical Alliance (WEA) inserted in the New York Times on March 28, 2008.[6] In content there is a clear continuity between this and Edinburgh 1910. The question is: Will Edinburgh 2010 be able to produce a *comparable* statement with a clear affirmation of Jewish evangelism, which implies support for and solidarity with the Jesus-believing Jews of our time? The Messianic Jews have practically been made losers in the Jewish-Christian dialogue.

The Gospel and the Jewish People – An Evangelical Statement

The WEA statement from 2008 speaks of love for the Jewish people, and it dissociates itself from anti-Semitism. In this way the statement does not differ from the many hundred similar statements or documents that have

---

[2] Online, http://www.jcrelations.net/en/?item=1489

[3] Göte Hedenquist, *Twenty-five Years of the International Missionary Council's Committee on the Christian Approach to the Jews* (Uppsala: Almquist & Wiksells, 1957), 5.

[4] See Tuvya Zaretsky (ed), *Jewish Evangelism: A Call to the Church*, Lausanne Occasional Paper (LOP) no. 60 (Lausanne Committee for World Evangelization, 2005). Online, http://www.lausanne.org/documents/2004forum/LOP60_IG31.pdf

[5] See e.g. *Mishkan* 36 (2002), whose theme is 'The Church and Israel – Dialogue and Witness'.

[6] Online, http://www.worldevangelicals.org/news/article.htm?id=1732 – In August 2008 an international task force of the Theological Commission of the WEA drew up the document 'The Berlin Declaration on the Uniqueness of Christ and Jewish Evangelism in Europe Today'. Online, http://www.worldevangelicals.org/commissions/tc/berlin.htm – Expected publication of all papers in 2011 by Koorong Books, Australia.

been issued since World War II.[7] But it is nonetheless maintained that Jews need the gospel for salvation. This salvation is determined as eternal life. And with a reference to the well-known words in Acts 4:12, it is stressed that only Jesus can grant this salvation: 'Salvation is found in no one else, for there is no other name under heaven given to men by which we must be saved' – words said *about* the Jew Jesus, words said *by* Jesus-believing Jews, and words directed *to* the Jewish leaders in Jerusalem shortly after Jesus' death. The statement, moreover, validates the existence of a purposive mission to Jewish people while it distances itself from the use of deception and coercion. It is also asserted that it is not dishonest for Jesus-believing Jews to continue to see themselves as Jews.

In the current dialogue between Jews and Christians the principal perception is the opposite. Because of the church's history with the Jewish people – often characterized by hatred, coercion, persecution and a theologically motivated contempt resulting in anti-Judaism and anti-Semitism – the church has reconsidered its attitude, something which has often resulted in a rejection of Jewish evangelism, which the church has regarded as not only irrelevant but also unethical and theologically unnecessary. There should no longer be an active and organized proclamation of the gospel of Jesus to Jews. And, it is often concluded, Jews who come to faith in Jesus should no longer insist on seeing themselves as Jews.

Jewish reactions to the WEA advertisement came promptly.[8] Here is just one example. Abraham H. Foxman, National Director of the Anti-Defamation League, pronounced:

> The World Evangelical Alliance Statement defending the targeting of Jews for conversion is offensive and insulting to the Jewish people and brazenly dismisses Jewish self-definition. Instead of validating God's irrevocable covenant with the Jewish people, and ongoing Jewish covenantal life, themes also found in their Scripture, this group of religious leaders does the opposite.
>
> It is especially odious to defend the duplicitous proselytizing of Jews by groups such as Jews for Jesus and so-called 'Messianic Jews.' While they claim to deplore the use of deception and coercion, they 'reject the notion that it is deceptive for followers of Jesus Christ who were born Jewish to continue to identify as Jews,' thus turning the meaning of deception on its head.[9]

---

[7] For a huge collection of documents, see (1) Rolf Rendtorff and Hans Herman Henrix (eds), *Die Kirchen und das Judentum: Dokumente von 1945 bis 1985* (Padderborn/München: Bonifatius Verlag/Christian Kaiser, 1988. (2) Hans Herman Henrix and Wolfgang Krauss (eds), *Die Kirchen und das Judentum: Dokumente von 1986 bis 2000* (Paderborn: Gütersloher Verlagshaus/Christian Kaiser/Bonifatius Verlag, 2001).

[8] Cf. also Susan Perlman, 'A Look at the Response to The Gospel and the Jewish People – An Evangelical Statement', *LCJE Bulletin* 93 (2008), 4-6.

[9] Online, http://pjmiller.wordpress.com/2008/04/01/evangelical-leaders-jews-need-jesus-christ-brings-rebuke-from-adl/

This rejection from Jewish quarters is similar, also in the language used, to the reaction to *The Willowbank Declaration on the Christian Gospel and the Jewish People* (1989), which with more theological arguments voices the same viewpoints as the WEA ad.[10] Rabbi A. Rudin, then National Director of Inter-Religious Affairs for the American Jewish Committee, called the Declaration a 'blueprint for spiritual genocide that is shot through with the ancient Christian "teaching of contempt" for Jews and Judaism.' Rabbi Alexander Schindler, then President of the Union of American Hebrew Congregations, described the Declaration as 'retrograde and primitive'. Schindler is quoted as labelling the Declaration 'a desperate attempt to stop the clock of progress in inter-religious relations.' Rudin calls the Declaration 'the worst kind of Christian imperialism'.[11]

God's Covenant with Israel and Supersessionism

One of the central pivotal points for the theological conversation between Jews and Christians for more than half a century has been the concept of 'covenant'. The classical Christian position has been that God in Christ has annulled his covenant with his people Israel and that the church has *replaced* Israel. Although many have rejected this notion, it has not resulted in agreement concerning the question of Jewish evangelism. The fact that God still honours his covenant with the Jewish people has made many people reject the idea of Jewish evangelism. However, people who are involved in Jewish evangelism maintain that even if Israel continues to be the chosen people, it does not mean that they do not need the gospel about Jesus.

Modern covenant thinking within the framework of the Jewish-Christian dialogue is often some brand of two-covenant theology in which Jews via Sinai – but without Jesus – and non-Jews via Calvary – but with Jesus – reach the same God, Israel's God. In such a context it is not appropriate to say that Jews need Jesus for salvation. If this happens, nonetheless, it is because one's Christian theology is permeated with *supersessionism*, a word which is filled with contempt and in dialogue circles sometimes seems to be a synonym for anti-Semitism.

Theologically it is used against those who believe that Christianity replaces and supersedes Judaism. The most extreme form of supersessionism is found in second-century Marcion. He did not believe that Israel's God was identical with Jesus' father. The God of the Old Testament was the God of vengeance and wrath, whereas the New Testament portrayed a loving God. Although the church as such, and rightly so, dissociated itself from Marcion and proclaimed him a heretic,

---

[10] http://www.worldevangelicals.org/commissions/tc/willowbankdeclaration.htm

[11] Concerning references, see Kai Kjær-Hansen, 'The Problem of the Two-Covenant Theology', *Mishkan* 21 (1994), 56-57.

Marcionism seems to be hale and hearty in Christian circles today, but it is based on a poor reading of the Old as well as the New Testament.

But even if a Christian today distances himself from Marcion and a 'Christian' neo-Marcionism, it does not mean that he becomes *kosher* in the Jewish-Christian dialogue or among Jewish theologians. For if you insist that with Christ came 'something more', 'something which was not there before' but which has been 'fulfilled' in Jesus, something with an existential and crucial significance also for Jewish people today, you will nonetheless be denounced as a supersessionist, which Jewish Orthodox scholar Professor Jon D. Levenson, among others, has made abundantly clear: 'This claim of a fuller revelation is the foundation of what has come to be known as Christian "supersessionism", the theology that sees the putative new revelation as transcending and surpassing the old, rendering it obsolete.'[12]

Christianity is not for Jews but for Non-Jews

In 2000 five professors of Jewish studies published the document *Dabru Emet* (Speak [the] Truth), with a reference to the words of Zechariah 8:16. By way of introduction it is said that 'there has been a dramatic and unprecedented shift in Jewish and Christian relations'. An increasing number of Church bodies 'acknowledge God's enduring covenant with the Jewish people and celebrate the contribution of Judaism to world civilization and to Christian faith itself'. Since Christians have changed their view of Judaism in a positive direction, the time has come for Jews to come to terms with the misunderstanding that Christianity should be an erroneous religion for non-Jews.[13] *Dabru Emet's* first point, of a total of eight, has the heading: 'Jews and Christians worship the same God.' Here it is said:

> While Christian worship is not a viable religious choice for Jews, as Jewish theologians we rejoice that, through Christianity, hundreds of millions of people have entered into relationship with the God of Israel.

It is easy to ignore the sentence 'Christian worship is not a viable religious choice for Jews' in sheer joy at the words that Jewish theologians rejoice that 'hundreds of millions of people have entered into relationship with the God of Israel'. What is implied by this sentence?

Up to around 1300 it was a dominant Jewish viewpoint that Christianity with its doctrines of the Trinity and Jesus' divinity, etc., constituted idolatry

---

[12] See Jon D. Levenson: 'Did God Forgive Adam? An Exercise in Comparative Midrash', in Carl E. Braten and Robert W. Jenson (eds), *Jews and Christians. Peoples of God* (Grand Rapids, Michigan/Cambridge, UK: Eerdmans Publishing Company, 2003), 152.

[13] Written by Tikva Frymer-Kensky, David Novak, Peter Ochs, David Fox Sandmel and Michael A. Signer. Online, http://www.jcrelations.net

for non-Jews. This viewpoint was revised so that Christian worship was no longer seen as idolatry for non-Jews.[14] At the same time it was said that *for Jews* faith in Jesus was idolatry, and it is this understanding which seems to be underlying the somewhat polished sentence in *Dabru Emet.*

A similar claim is expressed in a modern refutation of Christianity. The book *Jews and 'Jewish Christianity'* appeals to Jews who have come in contact with Messianic Jews and who feel attracted to their faith. But the authors are not in doubt that, in *Dabru Emet's* words, 'Christian worship is not a viable religious choice for Jews'. The concluding words in the book are:

> Furthermore, every form of 'Jewish Christianity' in existence today teaches Jesus as God and not only as the Messiah. Any Jew who embraces this belief commits idolatry. While he does not thereby cease to be a Jew, since a Jew always remains a Jew, he commits one of the gravest sins of which a Jew is capable. It is imperative that Jews know this.[15]

Dabru Emet and the current Jewish-Christian dialogue thus challenge the Christian church to rediscover its Jewish roots, which is positive and should be welcomed. On the other hand, Christians are called on to dissociate themselves from Jews who have come to faith in Jesus, something Christians most certainly cannot do. How should one be able to dissociate oneself from messianic Jews who like oneself confess faith in the crucified and risen Lord – and agree with those Jews who regard them as idolaters?

Then it is preferable to live with the *accusation* of supersessionism and vigorously *fight* anti-Semitism and religious triumphalism and in *loyalty* to the Lord of the church continue to point to the triumph of the gospel as it is found in the crucified and risen Jesus, and accept that both Judaism and Christianity make truth claims. The Jewish professor Jon D. Levenson has pointed this out in his severe criticism of *Dabru Emet.* He says, among other things: "For classical Judaism, there is no covenant between God and the Church."[16] And he continues:

> *Dabru Emet* is not wrong to draw attention to common scriptures and "similar lessons." The problem is that it reduces what is not common to mere differences of opinion – as if the two traditions make no truth claims. This easygoing relativism profoundly impedes any sophisticated understanding of the two millennia of Jewish-Christian dialogue and dispute over the meaning of the Scripture. A more accurate statement would note that it is precisely the

[14] See Jacob Katz, *Exclusiveness and Tolerance. Studies in Jewish-Gentile Relations in Medieval and Modern Times* (New York: Schocken Books, 1962), 114-28.

[15] David Berger and Michael Wyschogrod, *Jews and 'Jewish Christianity'* (USA: Ktav Publishing House, 1978), 66. – Both authors have for many years been influential Jewish theologians in North America.

[16] Jon D. Levenson, 'How Not to Conduct Jewish-Christian Dialogue', *Commentary* (December 2001), 34.

points of commonality that make disputation over the differences inevitable – at least within communities committed to the idea of religious truth and not simply to the theological equivalent of "I'm OK, you're OK."[17]

Theological and Missiological Absurdities

It is beyond all doubt that Jesus is portrayed as the Messiah and the Son of God for Jews in the New Testament. Whether or not he was it, and is it, is a question that can only be answered in the realm of faith. The claim that Jesus was a false or failed Jewish Messiah – and thereby really an irrelevance for Jews – is not to me a theological absurdity. Anyone has the right to assert it. That is also a question to be answered in the realm of faith.

But for me it is an absurdity to assert that this Jewish irrelevance, Jesus, who is without importance for Jews today, should nevertheless have decisive importance for us non-Jews! How is it possible to assert that the Jesus who met his own Jewish people with a demand to be heard and obeyed as they heard and obeyed God – indeed volunteered his own life for it – is without importance for the Jewish people, all the while it is said that his radical message is of decisive importance for all other people?

Jesus can only have this importance for non-Jews if he has it for Jews. It is a biblical absurdity to claim that the Jesus who allegedly is not the Messiah for Jews should nevertheless be the Christ for non-Jews when practically everything this Jesus did was done for Jews and practically everything he proclaimed was proclaimed for Jews. Jesus is either nothing for all, or he is everything for all, for all that Jesus according to the New Testament means for non-Jews is *derived* from what he means for Jews. And it is a missiological absurdity to give one's consent to the idea that belief in Jesus, whom non-Jews confess as Lord, should be idolatry for a Jew confessing the same belief.

Likewise it is an absurdity to reject "organized" mission to the Jewish people, as if truth claims can only be made in "unorganized" way; just imagine what would happen if such a principle was applied to world evangelization!

If it is maintained that Jews need the gospel for salvation, it has significant missiological implications, and world mission has been rendered a service! For when the Jewish people, which historically speaking is closest to God, needs the gospel for salvation, then it follows that all other peoples also do. We included. And vice versa: If Christian mission to the Jewish people is rejected, the road is open to a rejection of Christian mission to other peoples.

Already at the WCC's second assembly in Evanston, August 1954, significant contrasts were voiced concerning these questions. Swedish Göte Hedenqvist, then Director of the International Missionary Council's

---

[17] Levenson, 'How Not to Conduct', 35.

Committee on the Christian Approach to the Jews, cannot hide his disappointment in a report from the meeting.

> The experience from Evanston has made it clear that there are still many men of the Church who believe that the difference between Jewish and Christian faith is so insignificant (after all, it is only Christ who is the subject of discord) that we should instead devote ourselves to more important mission work.[18]

To this can be added: Experience also shows that when mission to the people of Israel is disregarded, it often has a negative impact on Christian mission to other peoples. Now it is often said: the difference between Christian faith and other faiths is so insignificant – "after all, it is only Christ who is the subject of discord" – that we should refrain from evangelizing and instead focus on building a better world together.

People of different faiths should indeed go on building a better world together. Shared values concerning our lives as human beings charge us to do so. In such contexts it should be possible to work together without fear of being "missionized" by the other party. But this is a different, and important, matter and not the subject matter of this article.

As the "intended outcomes" of Edinburgh 2010 the organizers first of all list *celebration* of the past and an affirmed *biblical call* to mission with particular focus on *evangelization.* This sounds promising. And this must naturally also include the Jewish people.

Translated from Danish by Birger Petterson

---

[18] Göte Hedenquist, 'Evanston og Israels Haab' ['Evanston and the Hope of Israel'], *Israelsmissionen* (Denmark) (1955), 56-57. Translated from Danish.

MISSION AND PRIMAL RELIGIONS: A NEO-PENTECOSTAL EXPERIENCE OF BOLIVIAN AIMARA PEOPLE

Marcelo Vargas

Background to the Case Study

The capital La Paz is the most culturally indigenous Latin American capital. Of the Andean nations, Bolivia preserves the most indigenous identity inherited from the two most influential pre-colonial cultures of the region: Aimara and Quechua. Herbert S. Klein says: 'It is also the most Indian in the American republics: as late as the census of 1976 only a minority of the population were monolingual speakers of Spanish'.[1] These cultures remain despite a systematic opposition to their existence from the colonizing Spaniards and the Creoles of the Republican era. The invaders used the sword and the cross as their weapons to subdue the people and with them they pursued and fought the natives. However, even if their intention had been peaceful and respectful – which was obviously not the case – they brought an exogenous, cultural system from foreign lands. This system represented very different political, economic, religious and social realities that could not substitute the strong Aimaran identity and related lifestyles.

In addition to all this background, the Aimaras have been affected by new and numerous impacts during the last century. They have been moulded by political, social, economic and religious influences and changes. Modernity and globalization have hit them with all their force via education, democracy, legislation, trade unions, and non-Catholic religious groups. The proliferation of new forms of Christianity has brought new sources of tension and profound changes. Evangelical or Protestant denominations have made inroads into Aimara indigenous communities, none with more success than the Neopentecostals, although these, just like previous invasions, have failed to erase the fundamental components of their ethnic identity.

At first sight, Neopentecostals are blazing a trail for indigenous women to play leadership roles within a context of gender equity. They are also

---

[1] Herbert S. Klein, *Bolivia: The Evolution of a Multi-Ethnic Society* (New York: Oxford University, 1982), vii.

using their own language for services and adopting symbols and rituals that come from their own indigenous identity rather than Protestant tradition. When it is recognised or not, the Aimara identity proposes new ways of living and representing the Christian faith. It is, therefore, important to learn to read and interpret these languages. The urgent task is to listen to what people are feeling and understanding about their decision to join a Neopentecostal congregation. To share with people who possibly have very little theoretical or theological knowledge about what they think and believe even when this does not coincide with the official position of the church that represents their newfound faith.

It is the purpose of this analysis to concentrate our attention on the identity and mission of Neopentecostals from the city of La Paz, Bolivia's administrative capital, where the Aimaras are the largest, dominant ethnic group, particularly those who belong to the 'Power of God' (PoG) Church.

The Distinctive Nature of Aimara Culture

This section will take different aspects of the Aimara imaginary, including their worldview, indigenous spirituality, language, multi-ethnic sense, three-dimensional logic, and integral epistemology as the basis for the analysis of Neopentecostals.

Worldview and Spirituality

What makes the Aimara culture distinctive? What do the Aimaras think about themselves and about the world? How do they perceive who they are and the world around? How do they conceive the spiritual and material worlds? The great obstacle when trying to respond to these questions is that our effort to understand these issues tends to be monocultural, in other words we try to mould our understanding based on the western modern paradigm. Our mind tends to conceive life divided into separate, independent compartments. We automatically dichotomize and by doing so impoverish the reality. The mind of the native Aimara conceives life in a way that is different and often, contradictory way to the westernized mindset. Life and the world for them are an integrated whole that is fundamentally spiritual and in harmony with the cosmos. What makes the Aimara culture different is its vision of life as something complete and integrated, something which is essentially spiritual and in harmony with the cosmos.

How does the Aimara understand their world and how does she/he fit into it? With the arrival of Christian spirituality and morality, a foreign worldview was incorporated into the Aimara metaphysical outlines. It was an adaptation that, on the one hand, left their own continuities alive and, on the other hand, strengthened them. However, inevitably, changes and modifications occurred which, in turn, became apparent in their own discontinuities. For example, the western worldview makes a clear distinction between the opposition and separation between heaven and earth, while, for the Aimara, even today, the '*alajj pacha*' (heaven) and the '*manqha pacha*' (hell) have mixed elements of wickedness and kindness. Not all the bad is in the '*manqha pacha*' not all the pure is in the '*alajj pacha*'. Although there are forces that work for wrong, these same forces can work for good and this is part of the framework of the belief and morality of the ancient Aimara.[2]

Social Life: Multicultural and Intercultural

The interrelationships found in each event and in the Aimara personality are a vital foundation for their identity and this aspect is utterly contrary to the individualism prevailing in globalized societies, where relationships and events have a marked anthropocentric character. In the Aimara conscience, however, the human being is not the centre. Man and woman are not taken into account in an isolated or individualized form. Nature and the cosmos coexist, they feed each other, and they protect and mutually respect each other. Community life is where needs, preferences and a sense to life are generated. The human being is inserted into the physical and spiritual atmosphere that surrounds him, to form one indivisible, integral whole. It is impossible to live without the diverse fabric and multifaceted nature of interdependent cosmic relationships.

However, not everything is perfect in the Aimara '*ayllu*' (the community life as an ancestral base of coexistence). Community life, be it in the rural areas or urban context, combines values that are highly human and integrating with reproducer anti-values of domination, perversion and discrimination. The historic context of marginalisation, poverty and suffering influences many aspects of Aimara life. Their creativity is expressed with a sense of originality; their sense of festiveness in the imaginary of celebration; interdependence in reciprocity and complementarity. However, there are also shadows of fatalism, where fate is stained with pessimism; accommodation to the belief that natural and supernatural forces are pigheaded and unavoidable. Frivolity, cheating and vengeance are seen as acceptable forms of behaviour and despair is commonplace because life is seen only in terms of the present, with few positive roots in the past or indications of a better future.[3]

---

[2] O. Harris & T. Bouysse-Cassagne, 'Pacha: En Torno al Pensamiento Aymara' in Xavier Albo, ed., *Raices de America: El mundo Aymara* (Madrid: Alianza Editorial & UNESCO,1988), 246.

[3] Juan J. Tancara, *Teologia Pentecostal: Propuesta Desde Comunidades Pentecostales de la Ciudad del Alto* La Paz (ISEAT, 2005), 5.

Language

The Aimara culture is a spoken relational culture. Its channels, its sources are not written documents produced by isolated individuals. There are no illuminated individuals who apply a discursive rationality. The Aimara do not determine tradition by conceptualizing or idealizing their utopias in written texts. The Aimaras' main 'text' is a colourful fabric of live 'perceptions' in minds and hearts. It is a treasure of accumulated community wisdom shared by means of an oral ancestral traditional that manifests itself in beliefs, customs and forms of life. Rather than being textual, Aimara communication has been and still is a living experience. Language, as a result, is central. The Aimara language gives its speakers an abundance of linguistic resources to be use. It is enough to know some of the grammatical system to have a clear idea of the wealth and complexity of this language. The extensive demarcation of the sources of information, the affirmation of humanity and its differentiation from the non-human by means of language, and the dynamic interaction between language, culture and the perception of the world are also aspects of the Aimara language. Neither the Aimara culture nor the language is sexist as the Spanish and English languages are. When the Aimara speaks about human beings, he or she does not exclude half the human race by referring to someone only in masculine terms.[4] The language gives the Aimara woman an equal social level in a way that could serve as a model for the contemporary world, with its glaring inequities in terms of gender and justice.

Three-Dimensional Logic

Implicit within the cultural Aimara language is a trivalent logic.[5] The logic of its beliefs, for example, is not bipolar. In other words, it is not conclusive or absolutist on one hand, and static and individualistic on the other. It does not have the binary logic of belief or non-belief, of the legitimization of a unique, exclusive, closed system of beliefs. This trivalent logic implies the compassionate submission to its imaginary religious community and its syncretistic practices, but at the same time, the construction of elements that modifies the established 'pantheon'.

The Aimara worldview starts, in the same way as the Vedic tradition of India, in the non-duality of reality.[6] Reality is not conceived in dimensions that are in conflict or opposed to each other – good and bad, sacred and

---

[4] M. J. Hardman, 'Jaqi Aru: La Lengua Humana' in Xavier Albo, ed., *Raices de America: El mundo Aymara* (Madrid: Alianza Editorial & UNESCO,1988), 155-216.

[5] Blithz Lozada, 'Identidad y Vision del Mundo Aymara' (II Seminário Internacional del Pensamiento Andino, Cuenca:UNESCO, 2005), 10.

[6] Josef Estermann, *La Filosofia Andina Como Alteralidad Que Interpela: Una Critica Intercultural del Androcentrismo y Etnocentrismo Occidental* (La Paz: ISEAT, 2004), 6.

profane; masculine and feminine, visible and invisible, true and false. Neither one nor the other can exist without the possibility of there being a third alternative. God exists and so does the Devil; human beings and Nature; spirit and body. In the Aimara concept of cosmos, there is room for a third alternative of equal importance. The parts do not counterattack each other; on the contrary, they are complementary, inclusive. This three-dimensional – and sometimes more – Aimara logic is sustained by the relational cosmic system mentioned earlier with its principles of reciprocity and solidarity.

Is the Neopentecostal experience at PoG Church specifically and profoundly Aimara? Is its vital identity moulded by the singularity of this culture? Do their principles, values, sacred holism, their cosmic interrelationship, orality and linguistic inclusivity, their three-dimensional logic and thirst for the unknown, place them outside inadequate overseas moulds?

Analysis and Findings

The Aimara people have their own operating system and ways of representing their religion. For example, their rituals are not simply religious acts, but expressions of social procedures, political realities, economic intentions, felt emotions, and physical movements. These features should be understood together as a complete package, a united whole that not only concerns the spirit – or just the mind or the soul – but every part of life, and this is reflected in the loud, ostentatious, mass meetings in the 'Power of God' Church. Aimara believers, on attending church, do not do so for reasons that are merely doctrinal, but also with holistic expectations and understanding. Conversion to Neopentecostal faith, therefore, has a profound affect on several aspects of daily life and family relationships while mirroring several deep-rooted aspects of their cultural tradition. Church members participate in civic organizations, which can be compared with the role of the traditional '*ayllu*' in rural areas. On facing crisis situations, indigenous urban dwellers may continue to recur to Aimara religious performances and performers, revealing the strength of old links with ancestors and rural life. Also, in their understanding of conversion or motivations for church membership, piety practices or perceptions concerning leadership, there is no room for doubt – the church's solid, active platform is evidently primal, religious substructure.

The Neopentecostal believer is someone who believes and – like any other human being – can act based on false beliefs or in contradiction to the beliefs he or she holds dear. Religious rituals guide his or her existence in this world, but by no means hold the monopoly in that realm. Believing is not only or emphatically a mental occurrence or a mere psychological state. The complete existential condition does not include the prior assumption, found in intellectualism, that reasoning comes first, leading to actions that respond to and reflect that reasoning, where the former determines the latter in a dominant hierarchy. Different objects of belief can determine different areas of possible responses. For the Neopentecostal believer, belief in divine healing does not rule out the use of scientific or natural medicine. Balance is achieved via the subtle combination of compatible and opposing elements, implying that the trivalent logic of language and Aimara worldview is at stake. The relativity of absolutes has outlasted the test of time and remains to be an important element of Aimara thinking and identity for Aimaras in general. We believe that case study findings and analysis reveal that the same is true for Aimara Neopentecostals. Just as Einstein's theory of relativity with rest and motion as a relative dimensions in relation to the speed of light; how and what people believe or do not believe are relative factors in relation to the whole indigenous cosmology. Whereas the bipolar Western logic that creates in interminable conflicts of opposites, the three-dimensional logic system tends towards the conciliation and coexistence of elements, some of which are contradictory. Good and evil live side by side, the future is the past and the past is the future in the present. The nutrient of indigenous trivalent logic is the relational cosmic system rooted in reciprocity and solidarity.

The religiosity practiced by Neopentecostals does not start with a list of dogmas in a tightly defined creed that must be understood, nor is it based on what individuals believe. If it were so, we would be entering the dangerous, partial terrain of undecipherable mental events submitting us to the merely rational. Their religiosity is based on visible, ritual acts where people make a public commitment to adhere to their new faith within their own cultural tradition, acting in line with collective group representations.

The Aimara Neopentecostal faith, like most indigenous religions, has no creed, but is composed of institutions and practices. The purpose of their beliefs and religious practices is not theological discussion or proselytism using rational arguments, but the survival and wellbeing of the community. The goal of the PoG Neopentecostal Aimaras is not only to save souls but the survival and continuity of their community in the urban world. Just like the Catholics who landed in Latin America with their Spanish form of Christianity, the Pentecostals and evangelicals in general combine old and new, collective and individual elements of salvation where everything rests on the foundation of an already-existing cosmology. Indigenous Aimara rituals have an expressive, symbolic meaning. They symbolize the shared feelings of group solidarity, of appreciation for and inevitable reference to the past, of a break with and loyalty to coactive tradition. Much of this has been inserted, adopted and adapted in Neopentecostal churches like PoG.

So why are Neopentecostals so attractive? Instead of a structured, logical system of ideas and thought, they issue a persuasive offer to experience God intensely. They are capable of offering a road to the solution. This experience of God involves no bureaucratic intermediaries and is communicated in a familiar, easy-to-understand language by someone the listener can identify with – usually from the same people group and social class. The experience is even more attractive because it involves becoming part of a community of people who share the same experience and celebrate it warmly and enthusiastically with their new brothers and sisters in the faith.

The symbolic group universe centres on the magic of the word. If for the Aimara people in general, their culture is a spoken relational culture, the Aimara Neopentecostal emphasizes its rituals via spoken relational aspects. The word 'ritual' is valued, not 'rational'. Oral rather than written communication is important. Testimony is appreciated more than preaching. It is vital and crucial the symbolic efficacy of Pastor Guachalla dramatized sermons. The focus is on feelings rather than intellectual understanding. The pastor effusively communicates oral, narrative thought. It is vital in the PoG church services to hear the pastor's moving speeches, a simple, intentionally narrative orality transmitted in such a way as to be perceived, not with the sole purpose of making rational arguments, but to clearly communicate emotions, feelings. The focus is on the 'heart' rather than the mind. The spell cast by the pastor's words creates holds such strong power that some people never want to miss a church meeting and can be found in church every day of the week. The growing use of the Aimara language in the pastor's sermons and healing testimonies given by church members adds to the emotional charge of the rituals practiced in church services. An interpreter who does an excellent job of capturing exactly the dramatic tone used by Pastor Guachalla is simultaneously translating more and more messages into Aimara and the result is neuralgic for his listeners. The television programs broadcast by PoG also reflect this effusive, Aimara love of the narrative and the almost total absence of written material also found in the church. To outline the church's history, we had to collect information from the historic narrations shared by the founder during his sermons after failing in a formal attempt to obtain written material in what could be referred to as the church's 'hypothetical' archives. The emotional symbolism of the oral word is one of the most anxiously awaited highpoints in the church service when people are invited up to the platform to give testimony of recent miracles. The pastor interviews them asking questions, which gradually lead the interviewee and the congregation into a climax of ecstasy.

Just as it is possible to speak a language without fully understanding its grammar, Neopentecostal believers can participate in a religious activity without grasping its 'grammar'. The delight of the experience within the sacred place, the former Roby Cinema, and at home or on the street is the powerhouse for the actions and aspirations. The deeper meaning of the church services is understood only partially or not at all, not because the people are insensitive or unintelligent, but because it is symbolic, imposed by the '*caudillo*' (strong, charismatic leader) or indigenous tradition.

The Bible is the principle of totality, the visible symbol of salvation as a moral and behavioural code. However, Neopentecostal discourse and practice are related – in the complex dynamic of continuity and discontinuity – with orality, with popular culture and the indigenous, religious-animist form of expression. Neopentecostal religious discourse and practice are related to the popular culture, specifically the people's form of religious expression. As a result, Neopentecostalism can propose new religious feelings using an oral language and religious practices that evoke the indigenous world, are familiar to the people, and can be assimilated by them in a natural manner.

The Neopentecostal experience in the La Paz PoG Church is first and foremost Aimara. Its core identity is defined by that particular culture – its values, cosmic integrality, orality and linguistic equity, its spirituality focused on the transcendental, its three-dimensional logic system. All this and so much more form the character of the Aimara Neopentecostals, what they are today and what motivates them in their mission. It is worth making the observation that contemporary Aimara Neopentecostals have a great deal in common with the first Old Testament believers and their history, people groups and identity. There is also significant analogy with New Testament Christianity, its cultures, people and world vision. The differences, on the other hand, are enormous when comparing Aimara Neopentecostalism with westernized Christianity – with either Roman Catholic or European or North American Protestant roots – with its egocentric value system and individualistic religiosity.

Conclusion

The indigenous worldview, so essentially different from the globalized one, exercises a powerful influence in Bolivian society and defining the religious and social behaviour of the majority. The advance of Neopentecostalism is taking place specifically in the Aimara cultural context in the city of La Paz, without completely eliminating or replacing indigenous religiosity.[7] The indigenous Aimara identity still builds values, behaviour and spirituality in Bolivia. All evangelicals and Neopentecostals in particular, are strongly influenced by this indigenous worldview.

There is a lack of wholeness in the church witness and mission in relation to cases like the Aimara people. Instead of having an attitude of making the kingdom of God established in each culture with the purpose of home-grown wholeness and redemption the most common experience has been prejudice in imported forms, contents and spirit.

[7] Kwame Bediako, *Christianity in Africa: The Renewal of a Non-western Religion* (Edinburgh: Edinburgh University Press & Orbis Books 1995), 215.

Mission and Primal Religions: Case Study on Contextual Mission, Indigenous Context

Terry LeBlanc and Jeanine LeBlanc Lowe

Introduction

In the late1980s and early 1990s, increasing numbers of Native North American men and women began asking questions like, "Why shouldn't we express our faith walk with Jesus in specifically Native North American ways? Why should we have to become like white people to be authentic followers of the Jesus Way?" Some among us compared it to leaving our own sin-stained culture just to enter another equally sin-stained one. On top of this concern lay the roller-coaster of Native Christian faith, evident for all to see: one-day people were walking life well and the next it seemed they could be found in all the negative social statistics of our society.

Was it simply that we were spiritually obstinate people of a dark spirituality – what many mission methods and theologies in the past (and some even today) seemed to imply? We had to find answers to these questions. As if to respond to our queries, two significant movements were inaugurated, each of which would contribute part of the answer.

Inculturative Foundations

The World Christian Gathering on Indigenous People (WCGIP) erupted onto the world indigenous stage in 1996. This movement, not particularly theologically driven, was a simple expression of faith in indigenous garb. Its inauguration witnessed a number of North American Native leaders attend, seeking a deeper understanding of culture's role in their faith. Ezekiel 37 was a reference point for the experience – the dry bones of their people being fashioned into living beings and, not without clear Native symbolism apparent, the wind of the Spirit blowing from the four directions to animate them to life.

In reflecting on the initial event, Terry LeBlanc noted, "Pentecost lit the flame of cultural diversity, the Jerusalem Council fanned that flame and the

WCGIP provided it with a contemporary vessel."[1] For most within the WCGIP Christian unity was moot without diversity – the same Creator enjoying human variety in worship along with the many-splendored realm of the rest of creation.

During this period of time a second, separate movement, took note of the dearth of theological and biblical materials available written by and from the perspective of Native North Americans. Testimonial books, in limited quantities, existed but theological materials were almost entirely absent as were language-rooted materials. And so, in the late 90s, a small group set about to establish a writers group to develop materials for publication from Native points of view.

Opposition, meanwhile, continued its focus on the specter of syncretism and idolatry inherent in contextualization. In an effort to head-off what some perceived to be a growing attempt to blend Native religious traditions with Christian faith, three traditionally-focused mission organizations – the Native District of the Christian & Missionary Alliance, USA, (C& MA),Christian Hope Indian Eskimo Fellowship (CHIEF) and, the Native American Fellowship (NAF) of the Assemblies of God in the USA) – produced "statements" and brief papers on the subject. Following a short preamble, the CHIEF document outlined a shopping list of scriptures, which the authors believed condemned the use of any physical object or traditional practice where such a thing might have been used in 'idolatrous' fashion in the past. <u>*Boundary Lines*</u>,[2] the C&MA USA document,[3] as the title itself suggests, sketched out strict cultural parameters, articulating more carefully than the CHIEF document, concerns with material culture and the specter of syncretism. The NAF document[4], the shortest and most open of the three, reiterated a long-standing position that culture must be subject to scripture and the Holy Spirit – and that its use should have as its primary if not singular consideration, use in evangelism.

By this time, many Native men and women were tiring of the messages condemning indigenous culture that simultaneously turned a blind eye to the West. That western cultures were matchless receptacles for Christian

[1] Taken from a personal conversation by the author with Doug Koop, editor, *Christian Week*, June 12, 2009.

[2] Craig S. Smith, *Boundary Lines: The Issue of Christ, Indigenous Worship and Native American Culture.* (Glendale, AZ: The Native American District of the Christian and Missionary Alliance, 2000).

[3] It is important to note that the US document of the Native C&MA and its concern was in no way paralleled in the Native part of the C&MA work in Canada nor was it supported by the C&MA denominational leadership or their theological training facilities anywhere in North America.

[4] 'A Biblical Position by the Native American Fellowship of the Assemblies of God on the presentation of the Gospel within the context of Native Cultures' in *Journal of The North American Institute for Indigenous Theological Studies*, ed. by Wendy Peterson, vol. 1, (2003), 99-146.

faith and Native cultures uniquely reprobate was vacuous for its absurdity. It seemed logical then to host a symposium and invite scholars and practitioners from a broad cross-section of the Christian community to reflect on this using the documents above as points of reference. The originators of the documents were invited to make personal presentations of their views. All declined or ignored the invitation.[5]

NAIITS emerged from this intersection of trends and movements, presenting its initial symposium, a "First Nations Missiological Symposium," November 29 – December 1, 2001. Both the symposium and the subsequently published journal included three important presentations: Douglas Hayward's *Foundations for Critical Contextualization*,[6] Ray Aldred's *Us Talking to Us,*[7] and Randy Woodley's *Hard Questions Concerning Structure and Values in the New North American Aboriginal Church.*[8]

During the conference the newly emerged NAIITS community, supported by a significant number of seminaries, universities and mission organizations,[9] shored up its position on the necessity of contextualized mission and theological education in the Native community. What's more, the potential of and need for the "redemption" of culture through Christ was significantly bolstered with an included paper, *Culture, Faith and Mission: Creating the Future*,[10] by LeBlanc as well as the joint work of Jacobs, Twiss and LeBlanc in *Culture, Christian Faith and Error.*[11] While the phrase "redeeming culture" was subsequently discontinued, the concepts it evoked remain active in the heart of the work of NAIITS today.

---

[5] Reprinted verbatim in the first volume of the NAIITS journal, the three papers provided the focus for discussion at the first symposium of the North American Institute for Indigenous Theological Studies (NAIITS) in 2001.

[6] Douglas Hayward, 'Foundations for Critical Contextualization,' in *Journal of The North American Institute for Indigenous Theological Studies*, ed. by Wendy Peterson, vol. 1 (2003), 37-52.

[7] Raymond Aldred, 'Us Talking to Us,' in *Journal of The North American Institute for Indigenous Theological Studies*, ed. by Wendy Peterson, vol. 1 (2003), 79-93.

[8] Randy Woodley, 'Hard Questions Concerning Structure and Values in the New North American Aboriginal Church' in *Journal of The North American Institute for Indigenous Theological Studies*, ed. by Wendy Peterson, vol. 1 (2003), 67-71.

[9] See *Journal of The North American Institute for Indigenous Theological Studies*, ed. by Wendy Peterson, vol. 1 (2003) for a partial listing of those providing initial support for NAIITS and the symposium.

[10] Terry L. LeBlanc, 'Culture, Faith and Mission: Creating the Future' in *Journal of The North American Institute for Indigenous Theological Studies*, ed. by Wendy Peterson, vol. 1 (2003), 149-166.

[11] Originally published as an occasional paper, this article appeared in expanded form in *Journal of The North American Institute for Indigenous Theological Studies*, ed. by Wendy Peterson, vol. 1 (2003), 5-35.

Moving the Vision Along: Next Steps

The year was now 2002. For perhaps the first time since mission began in North America, Native peoples were boldly suggesting that theological education be specifically designed to meet the cultural and learning needs of the Native North American community. Theological education to date had been non-contextual in its approach, in fact in many cases anti-contextual. It seemed obvious that for a truly indigenous church, something different needed to be done to train its leaders. Movement between community and classroom would need to be an integral part of any and all education. As we weighed this with the traditional requirements of Seminary we realized it was anything but inculturative!

Flexible method adhering to recognized standards was our concern; training Native men and women to the same level as those in the rest of the church, in a culturally affirming way, our goal – moving for extended periods from our communities, cultures and people, our apprehension. Maintaining academic rigor, clear standards and ensuring meaningful participation in the academy was the seminary's concern. How could these be married together if at all? And, what kinds of risks and challenges would it entail?

In the fall of 2002, Terry LeBlanc enrolled, embarking on a modified attendance plan that retained academic and timeline requirements. In the year that followed, four more students enrolled in individualized plans of study – three at the doctoral and one in graduate level of study. The first learning cohort was formed and contextualized education was beginning to emerge.

Early on, Adrian Jacobs, Richard Twiss and Terry LeBlanc's aforementioned paper, *Culture, Christian Faith and Error* was an early attempt as was Richard Twiss's self-published *Christ, Culture and the Kingdom of God* were apologetically focused. As time went on however, we became more emboldened and realized we had something more significant to explore. Reflecting on this need for greater depth of scholarly exploration LeBlanc noted in his opening address to the second symposium, "Contextual theology must no longer be restricted to tinkering at the edges of the *'Textus Receptus'*[12] of Western theology, making things fit for us, pointing us to the appropriation of a culture and theology not our own. Instead, it must open new horizons where church tradition and the scriptures act as our guide but, where pre-contact histories, cultures and worldviews are not simply footnotes to someone else's story!"

Thereafter, NAIITS' members stretched themselves to write about such things as might begin to capture more of the thought and context of our people. In the years that followed, Ray Aldred addressed himself to *The*

[12] The reader will, it is hoped, forgive the intentional allusion to the Greek manuscripts!

Resurrection of Story,[13] Edith Woodley, offered a way forward in Native mission with her and Randy Woodley's *Ministry in a Good Way*[14] – a missiology where the socio-cultural context is not peripheral but central to the way in which the Gospel of Jesus is lived in ministry.

Other papers followed in subsequent symposia dealing with the Missio Dei, theological education and a widening array of topics in mission and theology. Anita Keith and Miriam Adeney spoke on education and the tension between competence and credential; Karen Hoeft and Cheryl Barnetson worked the edges of an Inuit communal theology and a First Nations theology of mystery respectively. In each symposium that followed, topics ranging from a theology of indigenous education to the unfolding of the Indigenous Church were explored for the first time.

As per the founding philosophy of NAIITS, topics of discussion are always rooted in the indigenous perspective; intercultural contributions however, are actively and consistently invited. One of the best received of these was Damian Costello's re-appropriation of the story of Black Elk. In *Black Elk: Colonialism and Lakota Catholicism,*[15] Costello offered a stirring reinterpretation of the deep Christian contextualization evident in Black Elk's life and teaching.

Addressing the Myths, Moving Forward

On other similar issues, NAIITS scholars have sought to address themselves to what seem to be theological starting points in Western thought. As noted above, Ray Aldred, appointed Assistant Professor of Theology at Ambrose Seminary in 2008, has offered a different place of departure for evangelism – the Gospel Story. Aldred asserts that unless the story is clearly identifiable from beginning to end, it cannot function as an appropriate point of departure in Cree thinking. "Children," Aldred would go on to say, "know intuitively when the story has been modified or parts have been replaced. It ceases to be the story when the Big Bad Wolf uses a pirated computer key card to unlock the door of the high-rise apartment of the Three Little Pigs!"[16]

Randy Woodley, now Distinguished Associate Professor of Faith and Culture at George Fox University and Seminary, found himself asking pragmatic questions about the intention of God for all peoples. Eloheh, or

---

[13] Ray Aldred, 'The Resurrection of Story,' in *Journal of The North American Institute for Indigenous Theological Studies*, ed. by Wendy Peterson, vol. 2 (2004) 5-14.

[14] Edith Woodley and Randy Woodley, 'Ministry in a Good Way,' in *Journal of The North American Institute for Indigenous Theological Studies*, ed. by Wendy Peterson, vol. 2 (2004) 16-27.

[15] Damian Costello, *Black Elk: Colonialism and Lakota Catholicism*, (Maryknoll, N.Y.: Orbis Books, 2005).

[16] Aldred, 'The Resurrection of Story,' 5-14.

the "Harmony Way" has been the result of long investigation into the traditions of many Native peoples who knew of the need for restoration of loss of balance in creation. More than simply the absence of conflict and the presence of peace, Woodley views this impartation in Native peoples as the fullest sense of the Hebrew concept of shalom.

Métis people are well represented in the work of Wendy Peterson – not only as NAIITS' journal editor, and adjunct faculty in World Religions at Providence Seminary, but also as competent researcher and writer focusing her efforts on revitalization within the church. Her work, presented at conferences in the past several years, is being recognized by Native scholars as crucial to a full understanding of the role that social stressors within culture play in the emergence of new forms of Church.

Two wrong-headed perceptions in contact history have continued to play out over the centuries – the fairy tale of "The New World" as Eden and its polar opposite – the lie of the godless heathen land. Terry LeBlanc has argued forcefully for two different starting points to address this. First, he has suggested holism versus dualism as a philosophical foundation more consonant with the clear sense of Scripture and the culture of its writers. Second, he contends that theology must move its place of departure out of Genesis chapter three, the depravity of humanity and the fall of creation, into Genesis chapter one and two – the plan and intent of God. This means asking different questions about the nature of the breech, the impact of sin and the outcome of its expiation.

Twiss's work has reawakened us to the realization that God has in all times and all places been seeking to reconcile God's creation to the community, which is God. His work emphasizes the fact it is God at work in and through us – now and, then. We have a valid spiritual history that predates European contact! The recovery of the Missio Dei in the native world has meant we are no longer an afterthought – we have always been fully in the heart and mind of God.

Elumeaak: The Future

Since the first symposium, NAIITS' focus has been on contextualizing the message of the Gospel. In its human-focused transmission, we have come to describe this Good News as restoration to right relationship with the Creator, right relationship with one another and, right relatedness to the rest of creation.[17] It is the exploration of this simple news that takes our attention as we simultaneously ensure that training of Indigenous leaders is undertaken in a culturally engaged way. In so doing, we believe we will be better able to involve the wider church in discussions of importance to both indigenous and non-indigenous peoples who follow Jesus.

[17] Terry LeBlanc and Ray Aldred; remarks from the opening of the 2006 symposium held at Asbury Theological Seminary, Wilmore, KY

And, the impact of it all is without question. As Terry LeBlanc observed at the signing of the agreement with George Fox in June of 2010, "In just over seven years, NAIITS has accomplished more within the evangelical Native Christian world in respect of contextual higher education and theological development than the previous 120 years combined!"[18] Perhaps this is an overstatement of the reality – but then again, perhaps not. As of the date of this writing, NAIITS is printing the eighth volume of its academic journal, establishing the grass roots educational initiatives noted above, extending the reach of its symposium and, enrolling and graduating more students.

As NAIITS' literature says, it is a mission-focused institution seeking to provide for the mentoring and training of indigenous leaders in the area of contextualized evangelical missions. We are a partnership-based consortium of people and institutions convened for training, and for dialogue on methods and means of mission in the indigenous world, by and for Indigenous people and for impact in the wider church and our world. [19]

In an era where the social liberal value of individual autonomy seems paramount even in the church, NAIITS' ability to live as a complex community is a much needed and refreshing presentation of what it might look like to be faithful followers of the Jesus Way. The wider church experiments in post-modernity and its efforts at community rediscovery could benefit greatly from the pre-modern ideas that continue to inform the Native men and women of NAIITS.

NAIITS has opened the door for innovative and unique Native expressions, bringing the issues of contextualization, academic mobility and an indigenous First Nations worldview to the forefront. This has created a previously unknown freedom for Native people to participate and be more fully welcomed into the church. In addition, NAIITS has promoted indigenous leadership in mission by engaging Native North Americans and other indigenous peoples within their own global contexts and communities in inter-cultural approaches to mission.

Pragmatically, and theologically this has suggested many changes for the way we do mission. Just a few include: where European mission among us saw godlessness, we see the presence of God in people and their circumstance; where the effects of the fall were at the surface for Anglo-American/Canadian missionaries, the plans and intention of God – albeit distorted by human weakness and broken relationship – are visible to us; rather than start in the middle of the story – someone else's story at that – we start, as the story does, "In the beginning."[20] In so doing we find ways

---

[18] Excerpted from a speech given at the signing of the *NAIITS GFES Memorandum of Agreement*, signed June 12, 2010 at George Fox University following the conclusion of NAIITS 7th annual symposium.

[19] Statement of Purpose taken from the NAIITS website, http://www.naiits.com/ accessed July 12, 2010.

[20] Genesis 1:1.

to weave the histories of our own peoples into the broader narrative of the Creator's work among all peoples which finds its climax in Jesus.

Conclusion

That is the story of NAIITS' efforts at educational contextualization to the present. But it must not stop there. The new generations need to take it up. In the words of Jeanine LeBlanc Lowe,

> NAIITS became an organization dedicated to introducing change into the education and practice of evangelical Christian mission and theology. They pressed forward believing that the Christian evangelical community had essentially written them (and their culture) out of the story centuries ago during colonization. They did so believing that the post-colonial Christian church had continued to ignore its irrelevance to Native North American people and their culture. They desired to introduce change through emphasizing the inclusion of a First Nations indigenous worldview, especially as it relates to training future First Nations people. And we are they!

Ten years ago, the controversial issue of contextualization of Christian mission and theology by and for Native North Americans prompted a group of us to create an organization to address this issue. And, in response, on a frosty December day in 2001, NAIITS facilitated its first Missiological Symposium in Winnipeg, Manitoba, Canada.

We now begin to see ourselves in the church in its fullest, though culturally contextual sense. The future is brighter as a result. What's more, the vital contribution of indigenous people in theological development and mission is being ushered into its rightful place in the Missio Dei.

Bibliography

Abdulahugli, Hasan. 'Factors Leading to Conversion Among Central Asian Muslims'. In *From the Straight Path to the Narrow Way: Journeys of Faith*. David Greenlee, Ed. Waynesboro GA: Authentic Media, 2006. 157-166.

Abhedānanda, Swami. *Complete Works of Swami Abhedananda, Vol. 1-10*. Calcutta: Ramakrishna Vedanta Math, 1967.

Abhishiktananda, Swami. *Hindu-Christian Meeting Point Within the Cave of the Heart*. Bangalore: The Christian Institute for the Study of Religion and Society, 1969.

-----------. *Saccidānanda: A Christian Approach to Advaitic Experience*. Delhi: I.S.P.C.K., 1974.

Abimbola, 'Wande, and Ivor Miller. *Ifá Will Mend Our Broken World: Thoughts on Yoruba Religion and Culture in Africa and the Diaspora*. Roxbury: Aim Books, 2003.

Abu-Nimer, Mohammed, and David Augsburger. *Peace-Building by, Between, and Beyond Muslims and Evangelical Christians*. Lanham: Lexington Books, 2009.

Addison, James. *The Christian Approach to the Moslem: A Historical Study*. New York: Columbia University Press, 1942.

Aghamkar, Pramod. 'Building Church on Holy Ground: Proposals to Contextualize Church Buildings in India'. PhD Dissertation. Asbury Theological Seminary, 2002.

Ahonen, Tiina. *Transformation Through Compassionate Mission: David J. Bosch's Theology of Contextualization*. Helsinki: Luther-Agricola-Society, 2003.

Akhilananda, Swami. *Hindu View of Christ*. New York: Philosophical Library, 1949.

Albó, Xavier. *Raíces De América: El Mundo Aymara*. Madrid: Alianza Editorial and UNESCO, 1988.

Aldred, Raymond. 'The Resurrection of Story'. Wendy Peterson, Ed. *Journal of the North American Institute for Indigenous Theological Studies* 2 (2004), 5-14.

-----------. 'Us Talking to Us'. Wendy Peterson, Ed. *Journal of the North American Institute for Indigenous Theological Studies* 1 (2003), 79-93.

Aleaz, K. P. *An Indian Jesus from Śaṅkara's Thought*. Calcutta: Punthi Pustak, 1997.

-----------. *Christian Thought Through Advaita Vedānta*. Delhi: ISPCK, 1996.

-----------. *Dialogical Theologies: Hartford Papers and Other Essays*. Kolkata: Punthi Pustak, 2004.

-----------. *From Exclusivism to Inclusivism: The Theological Writings of Krishna Mohn Banerjea (1813-1885)*. Delhi: ISPCK, 1998.

-----------. *Jesus in Neo-Vedānta: A Meeting of Hinduism and Christianity*. Delhi India: Kant Publications, 1995.

-----------. *Religions in Christian Theology*. Kolkata: Punthi Pustak, 2001.

-----------. *Some Indian Theological Reflections*. Kolkata: Punthi Pustak, 2007.

-----------. *The Gospel of Indian Culture*. Calcutta: Punthi Pustak, 1994.

-----------. *The Role of Pramāṇas in Hindu Christian Epistemology*. Calcutta: Punthi-Pustak, 1991.

-----------. *Theology of Religions: Birmingham Papers and Other Essays*. Calcutta: Moumita Publishers & Distributors, 1998.

Ambedkar, Bhimrao. *The Buddha and His Dhamma*. Bombay: Siddharth, 1974.

Ananyananda, Swami. *Complete Works of Swami Vivekananda, Vol. 1-7*. Calcutta: Advaita Ashrama, 1968.

Anderson, J. N. D. *Christianity and Comparative Religion*. Downers Grove IL: Inter-Varsity Press, 1970.

-----------. 'Christianity and the World's Religions'. In *The Expositor's Bible Commentary, Vol 1*. Frank Gaebelein, Ed. Grand Rapids MI: Zondervan, 1979. 143-157.

-----------. *Christianity and World Religions: The Challenge of Pluralism*. Downers Grove IL: InterVarsity Press, 1984.

-----------. 'The Gospel: A Story to Tell to the Nations'. In *Evangelical Roots: A Tribute to Wilbur Smith*. Kenneth Kantzer, Ed. Nashville TN: Thomas Nelson, 1978. 173-83.

-----------. *The World's Religions*. 4th ed. London: InterVarsity Press, 1975.

Appasamy, A. *The Gospel and India's Heritage*. London: Society for Promoting Christian Knowledge, 1942.

Arapura, J. G. 'The Use of Indian Philosophical Traditions in Christian Thought'. *The Indian Journal of Theology* 29.2 April-June (1980), 68-71.

Ariarajah, Wesley. *Hindus and Christians: A Century of Protestant Ecumenical Thought*. Amsterdam/ Grand Rapids MI: Rodopi/ William B. Eerdmans Pub. Co., 1991.

Asamoah-Gyadu, J. Kwabena. '"Get on the Internet!" Says the Lord': Religion, Cyberspace and Christianity in Contemporary Africa'. *Studies in World Christianity* 13 (2007), 225-242.

Aśvaghoṣa. *The Awakening of Faith in the Mahayana Doctrine – the New Buddhism*. Trans. Timothy Richard. Shanghai: Christian Literature Society, 1907.

Austin, Alvyn. *China's Millions: The China Inland Mission and Late Qing Society, 1832-1905*. Grand Rapids MI: William B. Eerdmans Pub., 2007.

Baker, David, Ed. *Biblical Faith and Other Religions: An Evangelical Assessment*. Grand Rapids MI: Kregel Academic & Professional, 2004.

Barrett, David B., Todd M. Johnson, and Peter F. Crossing. 'Missiometrics 2008: Reality Checks for Christian World Communions'. *International Bulletin of Missionary Research*. 32.1 (2008), 27-30.

Batty, David, and Ethan Campbell. *Teen Challenge: 50 Years of Miracles*. Springfield MO: Teen Challenge Inc., 2008.

Bediako, Kwame. *Christianity in Africa: The Renewal of a Non-Western Religion*. Edinburgh/Maryknoll NY: Edinburgh University Press/Orbis Books, 1995.

Berger, David, and M. Wyschogrod. *Jews and 'Jewish Christianity'*. New York: Ktav, 1978.

Bharill, Hukamchand. *Tirthankara Mahavira and His Sarvodaya Tirtha*. Bombay: Shri Kundkund-Kahan Digambar Jain Tirtha Suraksha Trust, 1981.

Bloom, William, Ed. *Holistic Revolution: The Essential New Age Reader*. London, New York: Allen Lane, The Penguin Press, 2000.

Bosch, David Jacobus. *Transforming Mission: Paradigm Shifts in Theology of Mission*. Maryknoll, NY: Orbis Books, 1991.

Braaten, Carl, and Philip Clayton, eds. *The Theology of Wolfhart Pannenberg: Twelve American Critiques, with an Autobiographical Essay and Response*. Minneapolis: Augsburg Publ. House, 1988.

Brück, Michael, and Whalen Lai. *Christianity and Buddhism: A Multi-Cultural History of Their Dialogue*. Maryknoll NY: Orbis Books, 2001.

Brueggemann, Walter. *The Covenanted Self: Explorations in Law and Covenant*. Minneapolis MN: Fortress Press, 1999.

Bugge, Henriette. *Mission and Tamil Society: Social and Religious Change in South India (1840-1900)*. Richmond Surrey: Curzon Press, 1994.

Bunt, Gary. *iMuslims: Rewiring the House of Islam*. Chapel Hill: University of North Carolina Press, 2009.

Burrows, William, Ed. *Redemption and Dialogue: Reading 'Redemptoris Missio' and 'Dialogue and Proclamation'*. Maryknoll NY: Orbis Books, 1993.

Bush, Andrew. 'The Implications of Christian Zionism for Mission'. *International Bulletin of Missionary Research* 33.3 (2009), 144-150.

Carson, D. *The Gagging of God: Christianity Confronts Pluralism*. Grand Rapids MI: Zondervan Pub. House, 1996.

Chakkarai, V. *Jesus the Avatar*. Madras: Christ. Lit. Soc. for India, 1930.

Chambésy Dialogue Consultation. *Christian Mission and Islamic Da'wah : Proceedings of the Chambésy Dialogue Consultation*. Leicester: The Islamic Foundation, 1982.

Chamorro, Graciela. *Auf Dem Weg Zur Vollkommenheit: Theologie Des Wortes Unter Den Guaraní in Südamerika*. Münster: LIT Verlag, 2003.

Chandler, Stuart. *Establishing a Pure Land on Earth: The Foguang Buddhist Perspective on Modernization and Globalization*. Honolulu: University of Hawai'i Press, 2004.

Chenchiah, P. 'Jesus and Non-Christian Faith'. In *Rethinking Christianity in India*. G. V. Job, Ed. [Madras: Sudarisanam, 1938. 49-60.

Chowdhury, Bhawani. *The New Wine of Jesus: Christ Taught Vedanta*. Calcutta: One World Pub., 1982.

Clark, David. 'Is Special Revelation Necessary for Salvation?' In *Through No Fault of Their Own?: The Fate of Those Who Have Never Heard*. William Crockett & James Sigountos, Eds. Grand Rapids MI: Baker Book House, 1991. 40-41.

Clarke, Andrew, and Bruce Winter. *One God, One Lord: Christianity in a World of Religious Pluralism*. 2nd ed. Grand Rapids MI: Baker Book House, 1992.

Clooney, Francis. 'Hindu-Christian Studies as a Necessary Luxury in the Context of Today's Pluralism'. *Hindu Christian Studies Bulletin* 7 (1994), 39-44.

Cobb, John. *Beyond Dialogue: Toward a Mutual Transformation of Christianity and Buddhism*. Philadelphia: Fortress Press, 1982.

Cohen, Israel. *Jewish Life in Modern Times*. London: Methuen, 1929.

Cohn-Sherbok, Dan. *Messianic Judaism*. London: Cassell, 2000.

Cole, Owen W. *The Guru in Sikhism*. London: Darton, Longman and Todd, 1982.

Congregation for the Doctrine of the Faith. 'Dominus Iesus: "Declaration on the Unicity and Salvific Universality of Jesus Christ and the Church"'. 2000. <http://www.vatican.va/roman_curia/congregations/cfaith/documents/rc_con_cfaith_doc_20000806_dominus-iesus_en.html>.

Corduan, Winfried. *A Tapestry of Faiths: The Common Threads Between Christianity & World Religions*. Downers Grove IL: InterVarsity Press, 2002.

Costello, Damian. *Black Elk: Colonialism and Lakota Catholicism*. Maryknoll NY: Orbis Books, 2005.

Covell, Ralph. 'Jesus Christ and World Religions: Current Evangelical Viewpoints'. In *The Good News of the Kingdom: Mission Theology for the Third Millennium*. Charles E. Van Engen et al, Eds. Maryknoll NY: Orbis Books, 1993.

Cox, Harvey. *Fire from Heaven: The Rise of Pentecostal Spirituality and the Reshaping of Religion in the Twenty-First Century*. London: Cassell, 1996.

Cragg, Kenneth. *The Call of the Minaret*. Maryknoll NY: Orbis, 1985.

-----------. *The Qur'an and the West*. Washington DC: Georgetown University Press, 2006.

Cressy, Earl H. 'Converting the Missionary'. *Asia: Journal of the American Asiatic Association* 19.6 (1919), 553-56.

Cunningham, David. *These Three Are One: The Practice of Trinitarian Theology*. Malden MA: Blackwell Publishers, 1998.

D'Costa, Gavin. *The Meeting of Religions and the Trinity*. Maryknoll NY: Orbis Books, 2000.

De Smet, R. V. 'Categories of Indian Philosophy and Communication of the Gospel'. *Religion and Society* 10.3 (1963), 20-26.

-----------. 'Materials for an Indian Christology'. *Religion and Society* 12.4 December (1965), 11-13.

DeJong, Lowell. 'An Insider Movement Among Fulbe Muslims'. In *From the Straight Path to the Narrow Way: Journeys of Faith*. David Greenlee, Ed. Waynesboro GA: Authentic Media, 2006. 215-228.

Deming, Will. *Rethinking Religion: A Concise Introduction*. New York: Oxford University Press, 2005.

Derrida, Jacques. 'Force of Law: The Mystical Foundation of Authority'. In *Deconstruction and the Possibility of Justice*. D. Cornell, M. Rosenfeld, & D.G. Carlson, Ed. New York: Routledge, 1992.

Dharmaraj, Jacob. *Colonialism and Christian Mission: Postcolonial Reflections*. Delhi: Indian Society for Promoting Christian Knowledge, 1993.

Donaldson, Hal. *Huldah Buntain: A Woman of Courage*. Wheaton IL: Tyndale House, 1984.

Dotolo, Carmelo. *Un Cristianesimo Possibile: Tra Postmodernità E Ricerca Religiosa*. Brescia: Queriniana, 2007.

Duff, Alexander. *India and Indian Missions*. Delhi: Swati Publications, 1988.

Dulles, Avery. *A History of Apologetics*. New York: Corpus, 1971.

Dupuis, Jacques. *Toward a Christian Theology of Religious Pluralism*. Maryknoll N.Y.: Orbis Books, 1997.

Duraisingh, Christopher. 'Reflection on Theological Hermeneutics in the Indian Context'. *The Indian Journal of Theology* 34.3-4 (1982), 271-75.

Duran, Abraham. 'The Beauty of Jesus as an Evangelistic Factor'. In *From the Straight Path to the Narrow Way: Journeys of Faith*. David Greenlee, Ed. Waynesboro GA: Authentic Media, 2006. 265-74.

Edwards, Jonathan. *Treatise on the Religious Affections*. Reprint. New Haven: Yale Univ. Press, 1978.

Ellul, Jacques. *Islam Et Judéo-Christianisme: Texte Inédit*. Paris: Presses Universitaires de France, 2004.

Empereur, James. *Models of Liturgical Theology*. Bramcote Nottingham: Grove Books, 1987.

Endelman, Todd. *The Jews of Georgian England, 1714-1830: Tradition and Change in a Liberal Society*. Ann Arbor: University of Michigan Press, 1999.

Erickson, Millard. 'Hope for Those Who Haven't Heard? Yes, But...'. *Evangelical Missions Quarterly* 11 (1975), 122-26.

Estermann, Josef. *La Filosofía Andina Como Alteralidad Que Interpela: Una Critica Intercultural Del Androcentrismo Y Etnocentrismo Occidental*. La Paz: ISEAT, 2004.

Farrer, Austin. 'The Christian Apologist'. In *Light on C. S. Lewis*. Jocelyn Gibb, Ed. London: Geoffrey Bles, 1965.

Fee, Gordon D. 'The Kingdom of God and the Church's Global Mission'. In *Called & Empowered: Global Mission in Pentecostal Perspective*. Murray Dempster, B. Klaus, & D. Peterson, Eds. Peabody MA: Hendrickson, 1991. 7-21.

Fernando, Ajith. *Sharing the Truth in Love: How to Relate to People of Other Faiths*. Grand Rapids MI: Discovery House, 2001.

Flemming, Dean E. *Contextualization in the New Testament: Patterns for Theology and Mission*. Downers Grove IL: InterVarsity Press, 2005.

Frederiks, Martha T. *We Have Toiled All Night: Christianity in the Gambia, 1456-2000*. Zoetermeer, The Netherlands: Uitgeverij Boekencentrum, 2003.

Frey, Joseph S. C. F. *Judah and Israel*. 4th ed. New York: D. Fanshaw, 1841.

Friesen, J. Stanley. *Missionary Responses to Tribal Religions at Edinburgh, 1910*. New York: P. Lang, 1996.

Frodsham, Stanley H. *With Signs Following: The Story of the Pentecostal Revival in the Twentieth Century*. Springfield MO: Gospel Pub. House, 1946.

Fruchtenbaum, Arnold. *Hebrew Christianity: Its Theology, History, and Philosophy*. Washington: Canon Press, 1974.

Frykenberg, Robert. *Christianity in India: From Beginnings to the Present*. Oxford, New York: Oxford University Press, 2008.

Gallagher, Robert, and Paul Hertig, eds. *Landmark Essays in Mission and World Christianity*. Maryknoll N.Y.: Orbis Books, 2009.

Gandhi, M. *My God*. Ahemdabad: Navajivan Pub. House, 1962.

Gärtner, Bertil. *The Areopagus Speech and Natural Revelation*. Uppsala: Gleerup, 1955.

Gaudeul, Jean-Marie. *Called from Islam to Christ: Why Muslims Become Christian*. Crowborough: Monarch, 1999.

-----------. *Encounters & Clashes: Islam and Christianity in History*. Roma: P. I. S. A. I., 2000.

Gaustad, Edwin, and Philip Barlow, eds. *New Historical Atlas of Religion in America*. New York: Oxford University Press, 2000.

Gefen, Gavriel. 'Re-Contextualization: Restoring the Biblical Message to a Jewish-Israeli Context'. *International Journal of Frontier Missions* 25.2 (2008), 99-108.

-----------. 'Restoring Mission from Israel to the Nations'. *International Journal of Frontier Missions* 21.3 (2004), 103-9.

George, S. K. *Gandhi's Challenge to Christianity: With Foreword by S. Radhakrishnan and Horace Alexander*. Ahmedabad: Navajivan Publishing House, 1947.

Gidney, W. *The History of the London Society for Promoting Christianity Amongst the Jews: From 1809 to 1908*. London: London Society for Promoting Christianity Amongst the Jews, 1908.

Glaser, Ida. *The Bible and Other Faiths: Christian Responsibility in a World of Religions*. Downers Grove IL: InterVarsity Press, 2005.

Gnanakan, Ken. *The Pluralist Predicament*. Bangalore India: Theological Book Trust, 1992.

Goel, Sita. *History of Hindu-Christian Encounters*. New Delhi: Voice of India, 1989.

Goff, James R., Jr. *Fields White Unto Harvest: Charles F. Parham and the Missionary Origins of Pentecostalism*. Fayetteville AR: University of Arkansas, 1987.

Gombrich, Richard. *Theravāda Buddhism: A Social History from Ancient Benares to Modern Colombo*. London, New York: Routledge & Kegan Paul, 1988.

Grant, Sara. *Towards an Alternative Theology: Confessions of a Non-Dualist Christian*. Bangalore: Asian Pub. House, 1991.

Great Britain. Dept. of the Environment. *This Common Inheritance: Britain's Environmental Strategy*. London: HMSO, 1990.

Greenham, Anthony. 'Muslim Conversions to Christ: An Investigation of Palestinian Converts Living in the Holy Land'. PhD Dissertation. Southeastern Baptist Theological Seminary, 2004.

Greenlee, David. 'Christian Conversion from Islam: Social, Cultural, Communication, and Supernatural Factors in the Process of Conversion and Faithful Church Participation'. PhD Dissertation. Trinity Evangelical Divinity School, 1996.

Grenz, Stanley J. 'Toward an Evangelical Theology of Religions'. *Journal of Ecumenical Studies* 31 (1994), 49-65.

Griffith, Sidney. *The Church in the Shadow of the Mosque: Christians and Muslims in the World of Islam*. Princeton N.J.: Princeton University Press, 2008.

Griffiths, Bede. *Return to the Centre*. London: Fount paperbacks, 1978.

Guder, Darrell. *The Continuing Conversion of the Church*. Grand Rapids MI: W.B. Eerdmans Pub., 2000.

Haigh, H. 'Vernacular Literature'. In *Report of the Third Decennial Missionary Conference Held at Bombay, 1892-1893*. Alfred Mainwaring, Ed. Bombay: Education Society's Steam Press, 1893. 664-674.

Hanegraaff, Wouter. *New Age Religion and Western Culture: Esotericism in the Mirror of Secular Thought*. Leiden, New York: E.J. Brill, 1996.

Hardman, M. J. 'Jaqi Aru: La Lengua Humana'. In *Raíces De América: El Mundo Aymara*. Xavier Albó, Ed. Madrid: Alianza Editorial and UNESCO, 1988. 155-216.

Harper, Susan Billington. *In the Shadow of the Mahatma: Bishop V.s. Azariah and the Travails of Christianity in British India*. Grand Rapids MI: W.B. Eerdmans Pub. Co., 2000.

Harris, O., and T. Bouysse-Cassagne. 'Pacha: En Torno Al Pensamiento Aymara'. In *Raíces De América: El Mundo Aymara*. Xavier Albó, Ed. Madrid: Alianza Editorial and UNESCO, 1988. 226.

Hayward, Douglass. 'Foundations for Critical Contextualization'. Wendy Peterson, Ed. *Journal of the North American Institute for Indigenous Theological Studies* 1 (2003), 37-52.

He, Jian-ming. 'The Modern Chan Society and the China Luthern Seminary in Conversation: A Case Study of Buddhist-Christian Dialogue in Contemporary Taiwan'. *Ching Feng* 4.2 (2003).

He, Jian-ming, and Pan-Chiu Lai. 'Christianity and the Modern Chinese Buddhist Reform'. *Dialogue & Alliance* 17.2 (2003).

Hebrew-Christian Conference of the United States. *Minutes of the First Hebrew-Christian Conference of the United States. Held at Mountain Lake Park, Md. July 28-30, 1903*. Pittsburgh: M. Ruben, 1903.

Hedenquist, Göte. 'Evanston Og Iraels Haab [Evanston and the Hope of Israel]'. *Israelsmissionen (Denmark)* (1955), 56-7.

Hedenquist, Göte, and International Missionary Council. *Twenty-Five Years of the International Missionary Council's Committee on the Christian Approach to the Jews: 1932 – 1957*. Uppsala: Almquist & Wiksells, 1957.

Hedges, Paul. *Preparation and Fulfilment: A History and Study of Fulfilment Theology in Modern British Thought in the Indian Context*. Frankfurt am Main: Peter Lang, 2001.

Hedlund, Roger. *Mission to Man in the Bible*. Madras: Evangelical Literature Service, 1985.

Heelas, Paul. *Spiritualities of Life: New Age Romanticism and Consumptive Capitalism*. Malden MA: Blackwell Pub., 2008.

Heelas, Paul, and Linda Woodhead. *The Spiritual Revolution: Why Religion Is Giving Way to Spirituality*. Malden MA: Blackwell Pub, 2005.

Hefner, Robert. 'Of Faith and Commitment: Christian Conversion in Muslim Java'. In *Conversion to Christianity Historical and Anthropological Perspectives on a Great Transformation*. Robert Hefner, Ed. Berkeley: University of California Press, 1993.

Heim, S. Mark. *Salvations: Truth and Difference in Religion*. Maryknoll, NY: Orbis Books, 1995.

Heman, Karl F. 'Missionen Unter Den Juden'. In *Realencyklopädie Für Protestantische Theologie Und Kirche*. Albert Hauck, Ed. Leipzig: Hinrichs, 1903. 171-192.

-----------. 'Missions to the Jews'. In *The New Schaff-Herzog Encyclopedia of Religious Knowledge*. S. M. Jackson, Ed. New York: Funk and Wagnalls, 1910. 177-181.

Henrix, H. H., and W. Krauss, eds. *Die Kirchen Und Das Judentum: Dokumente Von 1986 Bis 2000*. Paderborn: Bonifatius [u.a.], 2001.

Henrix, H. H., and R. R. Rendtorff, eds. *Die Kirchen Und Das Judentum: Dokumente Von 1945 Bis 1985*. Paderborn/München: Bonifatius/Chr. Kaiser, 1988.

Henry, Carl. *God, Revelation, and Authority*. Waco TX: Word Books, 1983.

Hick, John. *God Has Many Names*. 1st ed. Philadelphia: Westminster Press, 1982.

Hick, John, and Paul F Knitter, eds. *The Myth of Christian Uniqueness: Toward a Pluralistic Theology of Religions*. Maryknoll NY: Orbis Books, 1987.

Hick, John, Dennis Okholm, and Timothy Phillips. *More Than One Way?: Four Views on Salvation in a Pluralistic World*. Grand Rapids MI: Zondervan Pub. House, 1995.

Hiebert, Paul G. 'Critical Contextualization'. *International Bulletin of Missionary Research* 11.3 (1987), 104-112.

-----------. 'Worldview Transformation'. In *From the Straight Path to the Narrow Way: Journeys of Faith*. David Greenlee, Ed. Waynesboro GA: Authentic Media, 2006. 23-24.

Hill, C. E., and F. A. James, eds. *The Glory of the Atonement: Biblical, Historical & Practical Perspectives: Essays in Honor of Roger R. Nicole*. Downers Grove IL: InterVarsity Press, 2004.

Hocking, William, Ed. *Re-Thinking Missions: A Laymen's Inquiry After One Hundred Years*. New York: Harper & Brothers, 1932.

Hoefer, Herbert. *Churchless Christianity*. Pasadena CA: W. Carey Library, 2001.

Hudson, Dennis. 'Hindu and Christian Theological Parallels in the Conversion of H. A. Kṛṣṇa Piḷḷai, 1857-1859'. *Journal of the American Academy of Religion* 40.2 (1972), 191-206.

Hughes, Philip. 'The Use of Actual Beliefs on Contextualizing Theology'. *East Asia Journal of Theology* 2.2 (1984), 251-258.

International Mission Board. *Divali: Festival of Lights, Prayer for Hindus*. Richmond VA: International Mission Board Southern Baptist Convention, 1999.

Jackson, S. M. *The Jew: Being a Defence of Judaism Against All Adversaries, and Particularly Against the Insidious Attacks of Israel's Advocate*. New York: Johnstone & Van Norden, 1824.

Jacobs, Adrian. 'A History of Slaughter: Embracing Our Martyrdom at the Margins of Encounter'. Wendy Peterson, Ed. *Journal of the North American Institute for Indigenous Theological Studies* 2 (2008), 159-72.

Jansen, Gabriel. 'Reaching Moroccans in Amsterdam (the Netherlands) with the Gospel'. Master of Arts in Religion Thesis. Tyndale Theological Seminary, 2000.

Jathanna, O. V. *The Decisiveness of the Christ-Event and the Universality of Christianity in a World of Religious Plurality: With Special Reference to Hendrik Kraemer and Alfred George Hogg, as Well as to William Ernest Hocking and Pandipeddi Chenchiah*. Frankfurt: P. Lang, 1981.

Jeanrond, Werner, and Aasulv Lande, eds. *The Concept of God in Global Dialogue*. Maryknoll NY: Orbis Books, 2005.

Jenkins, Philip. *The Next Christendom: The Rise of Global Christianity*. Oxford/New York: Oxford University Press, 2002.

Jeyaraj, Dasan. *Followers of Christ Outside the Church in Chennai, India: A Socio-Historical Study of a Non-Church Movement*. Zoetermeer: Boekencentrum Academic, 2010.

Jocz, Jakob. *The Jewish People and Jesus Christ: A Study in the Controversy Between Church and Synagogue*. London: S.P.C.K., 1962.

John Paul II. 'Ecclesia in Asia: Post-Synodal Apostolic Exhortation (November 6, 1999)'. 1999. <http://www.vatican.va/holy_father/john_paul_ii/apost_exhortations/documents/hf_jp-ii_exh_06111999_ecclesia-in-asia_en.html>.

-----------. 'Redemptor Hominis: Encyclical Letter'. 1979. <http://www.vatican.va/holy_father/john_paul_ii/encyclicals/documents/hf_jp-ii_enc_04031979_redemptor-hominis_en.html>.

-----------. 'Redemptoris Missio 'On the Permanent Validity of the Church's Missionary Mandate''. 1990. <http://www.vatican.va/holy_father/john_paul_ii/encyclicals/documents/hf_jp-ii_enc_07121990_redemptoris-missio_en.html>.

Jørgensen, Jonas A. 'Global Christianity, Contextual Religious Identity and Local Theologies: Īsā Imandars and Khrist Bhaktas in South Asia'. *Lausanne World Pulse* (2008) <http://www.lausanneworldpulse.com/themedarticles.php/895/02-2008>.

-----------. *Jesus Imandars and Christ Bhaktas: Two Case Studies of Interreligious Hermeneutics and Identity in Global Christianity*. Frankfurt: Peter Lang, 2008.

Kalliath, Antony. 'Retelling the Story of Jesus Through Stories of People'. *Vidya Jyoti* 74.3 (2010), 55-74.

Kärkkäinen, Veli-Matti. *An Introduction to the Theology of Religions: Biblical, Historical, and Contemporary Perspectives*. Downers Grove, Ill.: InterVarsity Press, 2003.

-----------. 'Doing Christ's Mission in the Pluralistic Context of Asia: A Critical Dialogue with Some Asian Christologies'. In *Asian Church and God's Mission: Studies Presented in the International Symposium on Asian Mission in Manila, January 2002*. Wonsuk Ma & Julie Ma, Eds. Manila Philippines: OMF Literature, 2003. 109-126.

-----------. *Trinity and Religious Pluralism: The Doctrine of the Trinity in Christian Theology of Religions*. Burlington VT: Ashgate, 2004.

Katz, Jacob. *Exclusiveness and Tolerance Studies in Jewish-Gentile Relations in Medieval and Modern Times*. New York: Schocken Books, 1962.

Keller, Carl. 'The Vedanta Philosophy and the Message of Christ'. *International Review of Mission* 42 (1953), 377-89.

Khalil, M. H., and M. Bilici. 'Conversion Out of Islam: A Study of Conversion Narratives of Former Muslims'. *The Muslim World* 90.1 (2007), 111-24.

Kim, Kirsteen. 'Ethereal Christianity: Reading Korean Mega-Church Websites'. *Studies in World Christianity* 13 (2007), 208-224.

-----------. *The Holy Spirit in the World: A Global Conversation*. Maryknoll NY: SPCK ;;Orbis Books, 2007.

Kinzer, Mark S. *Post-Missionary Messianic Judaism: Redefining Christian Engagement with Jewish People*. Grand Rapids MI: Brazos Press.

Kjaer-Hansen, Kai. *Joseph Rabinowitz and the Messianic Movement: The Herzl of Jewish Christianity*. Grand Rapids MI: Wm. B. Eerdmans Pub., 1995.

-----------. 'The Problem of the Two-Covenant Theology'. *Mishkan* 21 (1994), 56-7.

Klein, Herbert. *Bolivia, the Evolution of a Multi-Ethnic Society*. New York: Oxford University Press, 1982.

Klostermaier, Klaus. 'The Future of Hindu-Christian Dialogue'. In *Hindu-Christian Dialogue: Perspectives and Encounters*. Harold Coward, Ed. Maryknoll NY: Orbis Books, 1989. 262-274.

Knitter, Paul F. *Jesus and the Other Names: Christian Mission and Global Responsibility*. Maryknoll N.Y.: Orbis Books, 1996.

-----------. *No Other Name?: A Critical Survey of Christian Attitudes Toward the World Religions*. Maryknoll NY: Orbis Books, 1985.

-----------. *One Earth, Many Religions: Multifaith Dialogue and Global Responsibility*. Maryknoll NY: Orbis Books, 1995.

Kraemer, Hendrik. *The Christian Message in a Non-Christian World*. London: Edinburgh House Press, 1938.

Kraft, Kathryn A. 'Community and Identity Among Arabs of a Muslim Background Who Choose to Follow a Christian Faith'. PhD Dissertation. University of Bristol, 2007.

Kraft, Kathryn A., and Abu Atallah. 'The Lives of Arab Muslims Who Choose the Christian Faith'. *Mishkan* 54 (2008), 16-24.

Kronk, Richard. 'Non-Literary Personal Revelation the Role of Dreams and Visions in Muslim Conversion'. MA Thesis. Dallas Theological Seminary, 1993.

Lai, Pan-Chiu. 'Influence of Chinese Buddhism on the Indigenization of Christianity in Modern China'. *Ching Feng* New Series 1.2 (2000).

-----------. 'Mahayana Interpretation of Christianity: A Case Study of Zhang Chunyi (1871-1955)'. *Buddhist-Christian Studies* 27.1 (2007), 67-87.

-----------. 'The Kingdom of God and the Pure Land: A Dialogical Study of Eschatology and Praxis'. *Ching Feng* New Series 7.1-2 (2006).

-----------. 'The Role of Hong Kong in the Buddhist-Christian Encounter in China'. *Ching Feng* New Series 5.1 (2004).

-----------. 'Timothy Richard's Buddhist-Christian Studies'. *Buddhist-Christian Studies* 29 (2009).

Lai, Pan-Chiu, and Yu Xue, eds. 'The Kingdom of God, The Pure Land and the Human World'. *Ching Feng* New Series 7.1-2 (2006).

Lai, Whalen. 'Why Is There Not a Buddho-Christian Dialogue in China?' *Buddhist-Christian Studies* 6 (1986), 81-96.

Larsen, Timothy. 'Defining and Locating Evangelicalism'. In *The Cambridge Companion to Evangelical Theology*. Timothy Larsen & Trier, Ed. Cambridge: Cambridge University Press, 2007. 1-14.

Lausanne Committee for World Evangelism. 'LOP 11: Christian Witness to New Religious Movements'. 1980. <http://www.lausanne.org/all-documents/lop-11.html>.

-----------. 'LOP 60: Jewish Evangelism: A Call to the Church'. 2005. <http://www.lausanne.org/documents/2004forum/LOP60_IG31.pdf>.

Lausanne Movement. 'The Lausanne Covenant'. 1974. <http://www.lausanne.org/covenant>.

-----------. 'The Manila Manifesto'. 1989. <http://www.lausanne.org/all-documents/manila-manifesto.html>.

-----------. 'The Manila Manifesto'. In *Basic Statements 1974-1991*. James A. Scherer & Stephen Bevans, Eds. Maryknoll N.Y: Orbis Books, 1992.

LeBlanc, Terry L. 'Culture, Faith and Mission: Creating the Future'. Wendy Peterson, Ed. *Journal of the North American Institute for Indigenous Theological Studies* 1 (2003), 149-66.

LeBlanc, Terry L., Adrian Jacobs, and Richard Twiss. 'Culture, Christian Faith and Error'. Wendy Peterson, Ed. *Journal of the North American Institute for Indigenous Theological Studies* 1 (2003), 5-35.

Leonard, John. 'Oasis: An Ethnography of a Muslim Convert Group in France'. PhD Dissertation. Trinity International University, 2006.

Levenson, Jon D. 'Did God Forgive Adam? An Exercise in Comparative Midrash'. In *Jews and Christians: People of God*. Carl Braaten & R. W. Jensen, Eds. Grand Rapids MI: William B. Eerdmans Pub. Co., 2003.

-----------. 'How Not to Conduct Jewish-Christian Dialogue'. *Commentary* 112.5 (2001), 31-34.

Lewis, Rebecca. 'Insider Movements: Honoring God-given Identity and Community'. *International Journal of Frontier Missions* 26.1 (2009), 16-19.

Lian, Xi. 'Missionaries Distracted: The Rise of Syncretism in American Protestant Missions in China, 1907-1932'. Doctor of Arts Dissertation. State University of New York as Albany, 1993.

-----------. *The Conversion of Missionaries: Liberalism in American Protestant Missions in China, 1907-1932*. University Park PA: Pennsylvania State University Press, 1997.

Loewen, Jacob A. 'The Gospel: Its Content and Communication: An Anthropological Perspective'. In *Gospel & Culture: The Papers of a Consultation on the Gospel and Culture*. John R W Stott & Robert T. Coote, Eds. Pasadena Calif.: William Carey Library, 1979.

Lokhaṇḍe, Bhāū. *Boudhanche San,Utsav Ani Mansikta [Buddhist Festivals, Celebrations and Manners]*. Wardha, India: Sudhir Prakashan, 2009.

Love, Rick. *Muslims, Magic and the Kingdom of God: Church Planting Among Folk Muslims*. Pasadena CA: William Carey Library, 2000.

Lozada Pereira, Blithz. *Identidad Y Vision Del Mundo Aymara*. Seminário Internacional del Pensamiento Andino Cuenca: UNESCO, 2005.

Ludwig, Theodore, and Hance Mwakabana. *Explorations in Love and Wisdom: Christians and Buddhists in Conversation*. Geneva: Lutheran World Federation, 2002.

Ma, Julie. 'Pentecostalism and Asian Mission'. *Missiology* 35.1 (2007), 22-37.

Ma, Wonsuk. 'God's Creation: The Source for Mission in the Spirit'. In *Med Kristus Til Jordens Ender: Festskrift Til Tormod Engelsviken*. K. O. Sannes et al, Eds. Trondheim: Tapir Akademisk Forlag, 2008. 65-76.

-----------. 'The Spirit and Mission: Two Ripples of Pentecostal Mission'. *Lausanne World Pulse* (2008). <http://www.lausanneworldpulse.com/themedarticles.php/925>.

Madsen, Richard. *Democracy's Dharma: Religious Renaissance and Political Development in Taiwan*. Berkeley: University of California press, 2007.

Madson, Ole Skjerbaek. 'Kontekstuel Liturgy'. In *ΙΧΘΥΣ Dansk Tidsskrift for Teologi Og Kirke* May (2008), 39-49.

-----------. 'Theology in Dialogue with New Age or the Spiritual Milieu'. *Theology and the Religions: A Dialogue*. Viggo Mortensen, Ed. Grand Rapids MI: W.B. Eerdmans Pub. Co., 2003. 257-285.

Martin, David. *Tongues of Fire: The Explosion of Protestantism in Latin America*. Oxford UK and Cambridge MA: B. Blackwell, 1990.

Maurer, Andreas. 'In Search of a New Life: Conversion Motives of Christians and Muslims'. Th.D. Thesis. University of South Africa, 1999.

-----------. 'In Search of a New Life: Conversion Motives of Christians and Muslims'. In *From the Straight Path to the Narrow Way: Journeys of Faith*. David Greenlee, Ed. Waynesboro GA: Authentic Media, 2006. 93-106.

Maximov, Yurij. 'A History of Orthodox Missions Among the Muslims'. 2004. <http://www.orthodoxytoday.org/articles4/MaximovMuslims.php>.

McClung, Grant. *Azusa Street and Beyond: 100 Years of Commentary on the Global Pentecostal and Charismatic Movemnt*. Gainesville FL: Bridge-Logos, 2006.

McDermott, Gerald. *Can Evangelicals Learn from World Religions?: Jesus, Revelation & Religious Traditions*. Downers Grove IL: InterVarsity Press, 2000.

-----------. *God's Rivals: Why Has God Allowed Different Religions?: Insights from the Bible and the Early Church*. Downers Grove IL: IVP Academic, 2007.

McGee, Gary. *This Gospel Shall Be Preached: A History and Theology of Assemblies of God Foreign Missions to 1959--Volume 1*. Springfield MO: Gospel Publishing House, 1989.

McGrath, Alister. *Evangelicalism and the Future of Christianity*. Downers Grove IL: InterVarsity Press, 1995.

-----------. *Intellectuals Don't Need God & Other Modern Myths: Building Bridges to Faith Through Apologetics*. Grand Rapids MI: Zondervan Pub. House, 1993.

McKenzie, John. 'Higher Education'. In *The Christian Task in India*. John McKenzie, Ed. London: Macmillan, 1929. 85-102.

McVey, Dan. 'Hindrances to Evangelistic Growth Among Muslim Background Believer Churches of the 'Jijimba' People of West Africa'. In *From the Straight Path to the Narrow Way: Journeys of Faith*. David Greenlee, Ed. Waynesboro GA: Authentic Media, 2006. 199-214.

McVicker, Mary. 'Experiencing Jesus: Reflections of South Asian Women'. In *From the Straight Path to the Narrow Way: Journeys of Faith*. David Greenlee, Ed. Waynesboro GA: Authentic Media, 2006. 125-36.

Meyer, Louis. *Louis Meyer's Eminent Hebrew Christians of the Nineteenth Century: Brief Biographical Sketches*. David A. Rausch, Ed. New York: E. Mellen Press, 1983.

Miller, Donald, and Tetsunao Yamamori. *Global Pentecostalism: The New Face of Christian Social Engagement*. Berkeley: University of California Press, 2007.

Miller, Harold F. 'Closure for an African Century'. In *Exploring the Wisdom of Africa*. Akron, PA: Mennonite Central Committee, 1999. <http://www.worldcat.org/title/exploring-the-wisdom-of-africa/oclc/42885287&referer=brief_results>.

Mitchell, Donald. *Buddhism: Introducing the Buddhist Experience*. New York: Oxford University Press, 2002.

Mogensen, Mogens S. 'Contextual Communication of the Gospel to Pastoral Fulbe in Northern Nigeria'. PhD Dissertation. Fuller Theological Seminary, 2000.

-----------. 'Migration and Conversion: The Conversion of Immigrants to Christianity in a Danish Context'. In *Mission to the World: Communicating the Gospel in the 21st Century: Essays in Honour of Knud Jørgensen*. T. Engelsviken & T. Strandenaes, Eds. Oxford: Regnum Books International, 2008.

Montgomery, Robert. 'The Spread of Religions and Macrosocial Relations'. *Sociological Analysis* 52.1 (1991), 37-53.

Morgan, Christopher, and Robert Peterson, eds. *Faith Comes by Hearing: A Response to Inclusivism*. Downers Grove IL: IVP Academic, 2008.

Mott, John R. *Addresses and Papers of John R. Mott*. New York: Association Press, 1947.

Muck, Terry C., and Francis S. Adeney. *Christianity Encountering World Religions: The Practice of Mission in the Twenty-First Century*. Grand Rapids, MI: Baker Academic, 2009.

Nash, Ronald. *Is Jesus the Only Savior?* Grand Rapids MI: Zondervan, 1994.

Netland, Harold. *Encountering Religious Pluralism: The Challenge to Christian Faith & Mission*. Downers Grove IL: InterVarsity Press, 2001.

-----------. 'Theology of Religions, Missiology, and Evangelicals: Some Reflections'. *Missiology* 33.2 (2005), 142-158.

Newbigin, Lesslie. *Foolishness to the Greeks: The Gospel and Western Culture*. Grand Rapids MI: W.B. Eerdmans Pub. Co., 1986.

-----------. *The Gospel in a Pluralist Society*. Grand Rapids, MI: W.B. Eerdmans, 1989.

-----------. *The Open Secret: An Introduction to the Theology of Mission*. Rev. ed. Grand Rapids MI: W.B. Eerdmans, 1995.

Nicholls, Bruce, Ed. 'The WEF Manila Declaration'. In *The Unique Christ in Our Pluralist World*. Grand Rapids MI: Baker Books, 1994.

Nirmal, A. P. 'Celebrations of Indian Festivals'. In *Primal World-Views: Christian Involvement in Dialogue with Traditional Thought Forms*. John B. Taylor, Ed. Ibadan, Nigeria: Daystar Press, 1976.

O'Brien, Joanne, and Martin Palmer. *The Atlas of Religion*. Berkeley: University of California Press, 2007.

Oddie, Geoffrey. *Imagined Hinduism: British Protestant Missionary Constructions of Hinduism, 1793-1900*. New Delhi: Sage, 2006.

Osei-Bonsu, Joseph. 'Biblically/Theologically Based Inculturation'. *Afer* 32.348 (2009).

Packer, J. I. 'Evangelicals and the Way of Salvation'. In *Evangelical Affirmations*. Kenneth Kantzer & Carl Henry, Ed. Grand Rapids MI: Academie Books, 1990.

Panikkar, Raimundo. *The Unknown Christ of Hinduism: Towards an Ecumenical Christophany*. London: Darton, Longman and Todd, 1981.

Pannenberg, Wolfhart. *Anthropology in Theological Perspective*. Philadelphia: Westminster Press, 1985.

Paolucci, Giorgio, and Camille Eid. *Cristianos Venidos Del Islam: Historias De Musulmanes Convertidos Al Catolicismo*. Madrid: Libroslibres, 2007.

Perlman, Susan. 'A Look at the Response To the Gospel and the Jewish People: An Evangelical Statement'. *LCJE Bulletin* 93 (2008), 4-6.

-----------. 'Missiological Issues in the Encounter with Emerging Judaism'. *Missiology* 28 (2000), 65-84.

Petersen, Douglas. *Not by Might, nor by Power: A Pentecostal Theology of Social Concern in Latin America*. Oxford: Regnum Books International, 1996.

Peterson, Wendy. 'An Aboriginal Missiology of Identity Reclamation: Towards Revitalization for Canada's Indigenous Peoples Through Healing of Identity'. Terry C. Muck, Ed. *The Asbury Journal* 65.1 (2010), 48-64.

-----------. 'Jesuits and Indigenous Canada'. Wendy Peterson, Ed. *Journal of the North American Institute for Indigenous Theological Studies* 5 (2007), 115-135.

Philip, T. V. *Edinburgh to Salvador: Twentieth Century Ecumenical Missiology: A Historical Study of the Ecumenical Discussions on Mission*. Delhi: ISPCK, 1999.

Pierard, Richard V., and Walter A. Elwell. 'Evangelicalism'. Walter A. Elwell, Ed. *Evangelical Dictionary of Theology*, 2001.

Pieris, Aloysius. *Love Meets Wisdom: A Christian Experience of Buddhism*. Maryknoll NY: Orbis Books, 1988.

Pinnock, Clark. *A Wideness in God's Mercy: The Finality of Jesus Christ in a World of Religions*. Grand Rapids MI: Zondervan, 1992.

Piper, John. *Let the Nations Be Glad! The Supremacy of God in Missions*. Grand Rapids MI: Baker Books, 1993.

Pittman, Don. *Toward a Modern Chinese Buddhism: Taixu's Reforms*. Honolulu: University of Hawai'i Press, 2001.

Pontifical Council for Inter-Religious Dialogue. *Dialogo Interreligioso: Nell'insegnamento Ufficiale Della Chiesa Cattolica: Dal Concilio Vaticano Ii a Giovanni Paolo Ii (1963-2005)*. 2nd ed. Francesco Gioia, Ed. Vatican City: LEV, 2006.

-----------. 'Dialogue and Proclamation: Reflections and Orientations on Interreligious Dialogue and the Proclamation of the Gospel of Jesus Christ'. 1991.
<http://www.vatican.va/roman_curia/pontifical_councils/interelg/docu

ments/rc_pc_interelg_doc_19051991_dialogue-and-proclamatio_en.html>.

-----------. 'Jesus Christ the Bearer of the Water of Life – a Christian Reflection on the New Age'. 2003. <http://www.vatican.va/roman_curia/pontifical_councils/interelg/documents/rc_pc_interelg_doc_20030203_new-age_en.html>.

Prabhavananda, Swami. *The Sermon on the Mount According to Vedanta*. Madras: Sri Ramakrishna Math, 1979.

Prasad, Iswar. 'Preparation for Inter-Faith Dialogue'. In *Christian Ashrams: A Movement with a Future?* Mataji Vandana, Ed. Delhi: Indian Society for Promoting Christian Knowledge, 1993. 102-106.

Pries, Ludger. *Die Transnationalisierung Der Sozialen Welt: Sozialräume Jenseits Von Nationalgesellschaften*. Frankfurt am Main: Suhrkamp, 2008.

Prill, Thorsten. *Global Mission on Our Doorstep: Forced Migration and the Future of the Church*. Münster: Monsenstein und Vannerdat, 2008.

Queen, Christopher, and Sallie King. *Engaged Buddhism: Buddhist Liberation Movements in Asia*. Albany: State University of New York Press, 1996.

Radhakrishnan, S. 'Reply to Critics'. In *The Philosophy of Sarvepalli Radhakrishnan*. Paul Schilpp, Ed. New York: Tudor Pub. Co., 1952.

Rajashekar, J. Paul, Ed. *Religious Pluralism and Lutheran Theology: Papers and Report from an LWF-Sponsored Working Group, Geneva, Switzerland, October-November 1986*. Geneva: Lutheran World Federation, 1988.

Ramachandra, Vinoth. *The Recovery of Mission: Beyond the Pluralist Paradigm*. Grand Rapids MI: W.B. Eerdmans, 1997.

Rambo, Lewis. *Understanding Religious Conversion*. New Haven: Yale University Press, 1993.

Randeria, Shalini, and A. Eckert, eds. *Vom Imperialismus Zum Empire: Nicht-Westliche Perspektiven Auf Globalisierung*. Orig.-Ausg. Frankfurt am Main: Suhrkamp, 2009.

Ranganathananda, Swami. *The Christ We Adore*. 4th ed. Calcutta: Ramakrishna Mission Institute of Culture, 1969.

Rao, Kalagara Subba. *The Outpouring of My Heart [English Translation of the Telugu Compositions by C. D. Airan, Ed.]*. Guntur: Shrimathy Parripati Sita Mahalakshmi Satya Narayan, 1964.

Rao, P. N., K. Gopalaswami, and S. Ramakrishnan, eds. *Radhakrishnan Reader an Anthology: Selections from the World-Famous Philosopher-Statesman's 40 and Odd Books Written Over a Period of 60 Years*. Bombay: Bharatiya Vidya Bhavan, 1969.

Rasjidi, Muhammad. 'The Role of Christian Missions: The Indonesian Experience'. In *Christian Mission and Islamic Da'wah : Proceedings of the Chambésy Dialogue Consultation*. Leicester: The Islamic Foundation, 1982. 80.

Reisacher, Evelyne. 'North African Women and Conversion: Specifics of Female Faith and Experience'. In *From the Straight Path to the Narrow Way: Journeys of Faith*. David Greenlee, Ed. Waynesboro GA: Authentic Media, 2006. 109-23.

Renou, Louis. *Hinduism*. New York: G. Braziller, 1962.

Repp, Martin. 'The NCC Center for the Study of Japanese Religions: Forty Years of Research and Dialogue'. *Japanese Religions* 25.1-2 (2000), 135-154.

Richard, H. L., Ed. *R. C. Das: Evangelical Prophet for Contextual Christianity*. Delhi: ISPCK, 1995.

Richard, Timothy. *The New Testament of Higher Buddhism,*. Edinburgh: T. & T. Clark, 1910.

Rink, Tobias. 'Eine Multidimensionale Methodik Zur Analyse Von Bekehrungsmotiven'. Master of Theology Thesis. University of South Africa, 2006.

Robinson, Bob. *Christians Meeting Hindus: An Analysis and Theological Critique of the Hindu-Christian Encounter in India*. Oxford UK: Regnum Books International in association with Paternoster Press, 2004.

Rommen, Edward, and Harold Netland, eds. *Christianity and the Religions: A Biblical Theology of World Religions*. Pasadena CA: William Carey Library, 1995.

Ruppin, Arthur. *The Jews of To-Day*. Trans. Margery Bentwich. New York: Holt, 1913.

Sacks, Jonathan. *To Heal a Fractured World: The Ethics of Responsibility*. London, New York: Continuum, 2005.

Salgaonkar, Jayant, Ed. *Kalanirnaya*. Mumbai, India: ABC Prakashan, 2009.

Samartha, Stanley J. *Between Two Cultures: Ecumenical Ministry in a Pluralist World*. Geneva: WCC Publications, 1996.

-----------. *One Christ, Many Religions: Toward a Revised Christology*. Maryknoll NY: Orbis Books, 1991.

-----------. *The Lordship of Jesus Christ and Religious Pluralism: (with Responses by Arthur Glasser and Robert Schreiter and a Reply by the Author)*. Madras, India: Christian Literature Society, 1981.

Sanders, John. *No Other Name: An Investigation into the Destiny of the Unevangelized*. Grand Rapids MI: W.B. Eerdmans, 1992.

Sanneh, Lamin O. *Translating the Message: The Missionary Impact on Culture*. Maryknoll NY: Orbis Books, 1992.

-----------. *Whose Religion Is Christianity?: The Gospel Beyond the West*. Grand Rapids MI: W.B. Eerdmans Pub., 2003.

Saraswati, Dayanand. *Conversion in Violence*. Coimbatore, India: Sruti Seva Trust, 1999.

Satprakashananda, Swami. *Hinduism and Christianity: Jesus Christ and His Teachings in the Light of Vedanta*. St. Louis: Vedanta Society of St. Louis, 1975.

Scherer, James A. *Gospel, Church & Kingdom: Comparative Studies in World Mission Theology*. Minneapolis: Augsburg Publishing House, 1987.

Schmidt-Leukel, Perry, Ed. *Buddhist Attitudes to Other Religions*. St. Ottilien: EOS, 2008.

Schonfield, Hugh. *The History of Jewish Christianity: From the First to the Twentieth Century*. London: Duckworth, 1936.

Seager, Richard. *Encountering the Dharma: Daisaku Ikeda, Soka Gakkai, and the Globalization of Buddhist Humanism*. Berkeley: University of California Press, 2006.

Senior, Donald, and Carroll Stuhlmueller. *The Biblical Foundations for Mission*. Maryknoll NY: Orbis Books, 1984.

Sharkey, Heather. *American Evangelicals in Egypt: Missionary Encounters in an Age of Empire*. Princeton: Princeton University Press, 2008.

Sharpe, Eric. *Karl Ludwig Reichelt: Missionary, Scholar and Pilgrim*. Hong Kong: Tao Fong Shan Ecumenical Centre, 1984.

Sheng-yen. 'A Pure Land on Earth'. In *Buddhist Peacework: Creating Cultures of Peace*. David Chappell, Ed. Somerville MA: Wisdom Publications, 1999.

Sherwin, Byron, and Harold Kasimow, eds. *John Paul II and Interreligious Dialogue*. Maryknoll NY: Orbis Books, 1999.

Shourie, Arun. *Missionaries in India: Continuities, Changes, Dilemmas*. New Delhi: ASA Publications, 1994.

Shpall, Leo. 'Jewish Agricultural Colonies in the United States'. *Agricultural History* 24.3 (1950), 120-146.

Sider, Ronald. *Evangelicalism and Social Action in a Lost and Broken World*. London: Hodder and Stoughton, 1993.

Singh, Brig. Hardit. 'Review of 'Guru Hargobindji: His Life and Times''. *Abstracts of Sikh Studies* Oct-Dec (1996), 76-80.

Singh, Ranbir. *The Sikhs and Their Religion*. Dublin: Sikh Education and Religious Foundation, 1999.

Sivananda, Swami. *The Bhagavad Gita: Text Translation, and Commentary by Swami Sivananda*. Shivanandanagar, India: Divine Life Society, 1995.

Smart, Ninian. *Buddhism and Christianity: Rivals and Allies*. Honolulu: University of Hawaii Press, 1993.

Smith, Craig S. *Boundary Lines: The Issue of Christ, Indigenous Worship, and Native American Culture*. Glendale AZ: Native American District of the Christian and Missionary Alliance, 2000.

Smith, David. 'Looking Ahead'. In *From the Straight Path to the Narrow Way: Journeys of Faith*. David Greenlee, Ed. Waynesboro GA: Authentic Media, 2006. 285-304.

Smith, George. *The Life of Alexander Duff*. London: Hodder and Stoughton, 1881.

Smith, W. C. *Faith and Belief*. Princeton N.J.: Princeton University Press, 1979.

-----------. *Towards a World Theology: Faith and the Comparative History of Religion*. London: Macmillan, 1981.

Sobel, B. Z. *Hebrew Christianity: The Thirteenth Tribe*. New York: John Wiley, 1974.

Soothill, William E. *Timothy Richard of China, Seer, Statesman, Missionary & the Most Disinterested Adviser the Chinese Ever Had*. London: Seeley Service, 1926.

Spielberg, F, and S Dauermann. 'Contextualization: Witness and Reflection Messianic Jews as a Case'. *Missiology* 25.1 (1997), 15-36.

Stackhouse, John G., Ed. *No Other Gods Before Me? Evangelicals and the Challenge of World Religions*. Grand Rapids MI: Baker Academic, 2001.

Stanley, Brian. *The World Missionary Conference, Edinburgh 1910*. Grand Rapids, MI: Wm. B. Eerdmans Publishing, 2009.

Stott, John R W. *Christian Mission in the Modern World*. Downers Grove IL: InterVarsity Press, 1975.

-----------. *The Authentic Jesus*. London: Marshall Morgan and Scott, 1985.

-----------. *The Cross of Christ*. Leicester: InterVarsity Press, 1985.

Stott, John R W, and Robert T. Coote. *Gospel & Culture: The Papers of a Consultation on the Gospel and Culture*. Pasadena CA: William Carey Library, 1979.

Straehler, Reinhold. 'Conversion from Islam to Christianity in the Sudan'. Master of Theology Thesis. University of South Africa, 2005.

Sugden, Chris. 'Fair Trade and Christian Mission: An Overview of Further Steps in Christian Witness in International Trade'. *Transformation* 17.3 (2000), 118.

Sumner, George. *The First and the Last: The Claim of Jesus Christ and the Claims of Other Religious Traditions*. Grand Rapids MI: William B. Eerdmans Pub., 2004.

Sundar Raj, Ebe. *Sat Guru Aradhana*. Mussoorie, India: Nivedit Good Books, 2007.

Synan, Vinson. *The Spirit Said 'Grow': The Astounding Worldwide Expansion of Pentecostal and Charismatic Churches*. Monrovia CA: MARC, 1992.

Syrjänen, Seppo. *In Search of Meaning and Identity: Conversion to Christianity in Pakistani Muslim Culture*. Helsinki: Finnish Society for Missiology and Ecumenics, 1984.

Tan, Kang San. 'Evangelical Missiology From an East Asian Perspective: A Study on Christian Encounter With People of Other Faiths'. In *Global Missiology for the 21st Century: The Iguassu Dialogue*.

William Taylor, Ed. Grand Rapids MI: Baker Academic, 2000. 295-306.

Tancara, Juan J. *Teologia Pentecostal: Propuesta Desde Comunidades Pentecostales De La Ciudad Del Alto*. La Paz: ISEAT, 2005.

Taylor, Richard. 'Current Hindu-Christian Dialogue in India'. In *Hindu-Christian Dialogue: Perspectives and Encounters*. Harold Coward, Ed. Maryknoll NY: Orbis Books, 1989. 119-128.

Tennent, Timothy C. *Christianity at the Religious Roundtable: Evangelicalism in Conversation with Hinduism, Buddhism, and Islam*. Grand Rapids, MI: Baker Academic, 2002.

-----------. 'Followers of Jesus (Isa) in Islamic Mosques: A Closer Examination of C-5 'High Spectrum' Contextualization'. *International Journal of Frontier Missions* 23.3 (2006), 113.

-----------. *Theology in the Context of World Christianity: How the Global Church Is Influencing the Way We Think About and Discuss Theology*. Grand Rapids, MI: Zondervan, 2007.

Thelle, Notto. 'A Christian Monastery for Buddhist Monks, Part 1: Karl Ludvig Reichelt's Sacred Mountains'. *Ching Feng* New Series 6.1 (2005).

-----------. 'A Christian Monastery for Buddhist Monks, Part 2: Buddhist Rhetoric in Karl Ludvig Reichelt's Christian Liturgies'. *Ching Feng* New Series 6.2 (2005).

-----------. 'Changed by the East: Notes on Missionary Communication and Transformation'. *International Bulletin of Missionary Research* 30.3 (2006), 115.

-----------. 'Crossing Religious Boundaries: Christian Mission and Global Transformation'. In *Religion in a Globalised Age: Transfers & Transformations, Integration & Resistance*. Sturla Stålsett, Ed. Oslo: Novus Press, 2008.

-----------. 'Dialogue – Study – Friendship'. *Japanese Religions* 25.1-2 (2000).

-----------. 'Foe and Friend: The Changing Image of Christ in Japanese Buddhism'. *Japanese Religions* 12.2 (1982).

-----------. 'God's Vow: A Pure Land Perspective on the Cross of Christ'. *Ching Feng* New Series 7.1-2 (2006).

-----------. 'In Memoriam Harry Thomsen (1928-2008): Dialogical Missionary and Research Facilitator'. *Japanese Religions* 34.1 (2009).

-----------. 'Karl Ludvig Reichelt 1877-1952: Christian Pilgrim of Tao Fong Shan'. In *Mission Legacies: Biographical Studies of Leaders of the Modern Missionary Movement*. Gerald Anderson, Ed. Maryknoll NY: Orbis Books, 1994.

-----------. 'Reflections on Dialogue as a Spiritual Journey'. *Japanese Religions* 13.4 (1985).

-----------. 'Relation, Awareness, and Energy -- Three Languages, Three Worlds?: An Approach to Mutual Understanding'. *Japanese Religions* 30.1 (2005), 113.

-----------. 'The Conversion of the Missionary: Changes in Buddhist-Christian Relations in the Early Twentieth Century'. *Ching Feng* New Series 4.2 (2003).

-----------. *Who Can Stop the Wind?: Travels in the Borderland Between East and West*. Collegeville MN: Liturgical Press, 2010.

Thomas, Joe M. 'Continuity, Discontinuity, and the Finality of Christ: A Theological Essay on the Thought of Leslie Newbigin and Hendrik Kraemer'. *Dharma Deepika: A South Asian Journal of Missiological Research* 29.1 (2009), 28.

Thomas, M. M. *The Acknowledged Christ of the Indian Renaissance*. Bangalore/ Madras: The Christian Institute for the Study of Religion and Society/ The C. L. S, 1970.

Thompson, A. E. *A Century of Jewish Missions*. Chicago: Fleming H. Revell Co., 1902.

Tiessen, Terrance. *Who Can Be Saved?: Reassessing Salvation in Christ and World Religions*. Downers Grove Ill.: InterVarsity Press, 2004.

Travis, John, and Anna Travis. 'Appropriate Approaches in Muslim Contexts'. In *Appropriate Christianity*. Charles Kraft, Ed. Pasadena CA: William Carey Library, 2005. 397-414.

-----------. 'Factors Affecting the Identity That Jesus-Followers Choose'. In *From Seed to Fruit: Global Trends, Fruitful Practices, and Emerging Issues Among Muslims*. J. Dudley Woodberry, Ed. Pasadena CA: William Carey Library, 2008. 193-205.

Trimingham, J Spencer. *The Christian Approach to Islam in the Sudan*. London, New York: Oxford Univ. Press, 1948.

Twiss, Richard. *One Church, Many Tribes*. Ventura CA: Regal, 2000.

Van Engen, Charles E. *Mission on the Way: Issues in Mission Theology*. Grand Rapids, MI: Baker Academic, 1996.

-----------. 'The Uniqueness of Christ in Mission Theology'. In *Landmark Essays in Mission and World Christianity*. Robert Gallagher & Paul Hertig, Eds. Maryknoll NY: Orbis Books, 2009. 160-75.

Vanhoozer, Kevin, Ed. *The Trinity in a Pluralistic Age: Theological Essays on Culture and Religion*. Grand Rapids MI: W.B. Eerdmans Pub., 1996.

Vatican II. '*Ad Gentes*: Decree on the Mission Activity of the Church'. 1965. <http://www.vatican.va/archive/hist_councils/ii_vatican_council/documents/vat-ii_decree_19651207_ad-gentes_en.html>.

-----------. '*Dignitatis Humanae*: Declaration on Religious Freedom'. 1965. <http://www.vatican.va/archive/hist_councils/ii_vatican_council/documents/vat-ii_decl_19651207_dignitatis-humanae_en.html>.

-----------. '*Gaudium Et Spes*: Pastoral Constitution on the Church in the Modern Word'. 1965. <http://www.vatican.va/archive/hist_councils/ii_vatican_council/documents/vat-ii_cons_19651207_gaudium-et-spes_en.html>.

-----------. '*Lumen Gentium*: Dogmatic Constitution on the Church'. 1964. <http://www.vatican.va/archive/hist_councils/ii_vatican_council/documents/vat-ii_const_19641121_lumen-gentium_en.html>.

-----------. '*Nostra Aetate*: Declaration on the Relation of the Church to Non-Christian Religions'. 1965. <http://www.vatican.va/archive/hist_councils/ii_vatican_council/documents/vat-ii_decl_19651028_nostra-aetate_en.html>.

Vempeny, Ishanand. *Conversion: National Debate or Dialogue*. Anand: Gujarat Sahitya Prakash, 1999.

Wagner, C, and F. D. Pennoyer. *Wrestling with Dark Angels: Toward a Deeper Understanding of the Supernatural Forces in Spiritual Warfare*. Ventura CA: Regal Books, 1990.

Walls, Andrew F, and Cathy Ross. *Mission in the Twenty-First Century: Exploring the Five Marks of Global Mission*. Maryknoll, NY: Orbis Books, 2008.

Walls, Andrew F. 'Converts or Proselytes? The Crisis over Conversion in the Early Church'. *International Bulletin of Missionary Research* 28.1 (2004), 2-6.

-----------. *The Cross-Cultural Process in Christian History: Studies in the Transmission and Appropriation of Faith*. Maryknoll, NY: Orbis Books, 2002.

-----------. *The Missionary Movement in Christian History: Studies in the Transmission of Faith*. Maryknoll, NY: Orbis Books, 1996.

Webster, John. 'Dalits and Christianity in Colnial Punjab: Cultural Interactions'. In *Christians, Cultural Interactions, and India's Religious Traditions*. Judith Brown & Robert Frykenberg, Eds. Grand Rapids MI: W.B. Eerdmans ;;RoutledgeCurzon, 2002. 92-118.

-----------. *The Dalit Christians: A History*. Delhi: Indian Society for Promoting Christian Knowledge, 1992.

Welch, Holmes. *The Buddhist Revival in China*. Cambridge MA: Harvard University Press, 1968.

Wesley, Ariarajah. *Hindus and Christians: A Century of Protestant Ecumenical Thought*. Grand Rapids MI: William B. Eerdmans Pub. Co., 1991.

White, Ellen. *Our High Calling*. Washington D.C.: Review and Herald Pub. Association, 1961.

-----------. *The Desire of Ages: The Conflict of the Ages Illustrated in the Life of Christ*. Mountain View Calif.: Pacific Press, 1956.

White, L. 'The Historical Roots of Our Ecologic Crisis'. *Science (New York, N.Y.)* 155.3767 (1967), 1203-7.

Wiher, Hannes. *Shame and Guilt: A Key to Cross-Cultural Ministry*. Edition IWG, Mission academics, Bd. 10. Bonn: Verlag für Kultur und Wissenschaft, 2003.

Wink, Walter. *Engaging the Powers: Discernment and Resistance in a World of Domination*. Minneapolis MN: Fortress Press, 1992.

Winter, Bruce. 'Official Proceedings and the Forensic Speeches in Acts 24-26'. In *The Book of Acts in Its Ancient Literary Setting*. Bruce Winter & Andrew Clarke, Eds. Grand Rapids MI: W.B. Eerdmans Pub. Co., 1993.

Woodley, Edith, and Randy Woodley. 'Ministry in a Good Way'. Wendy Peterson, Ed. *Journal of the North American Institute for Indigenous Theological Studies* 2 (2004), 16-27.

Woodley, Randy. 'Hard Questions Concerning Structure and Values in the New North American Aboriginal Church'. Wendy Peterson, Ed. *Journal of the North American Institute for Indigenous Theological Studies* 1 (2003), 67-71.

-----------. *Living in Color: Embracing God's Passion for Ethnic Diversity*. Downers Grove IL: InterVarsity Press, 2004.

-----------. 'North American Native Theologies'. William Dyrness & Veli-Matti Kärkkäinen, Eds. *Global Dictionary of Theology: A Resource for the Worldwide Church*, 2008.

World Council of Churches. 'Baar Statement: Theological Perspectives on Plurality'. 1990. <http://www.oikoumene.org/en/resources/documents/wcc-programmes/interreligious-dialogue-and-cooperation/christian-identity-in-pluralistic-societies/baar-statement-theological-perspectives-on-plurality.html>.

-----------. 'Religious Plurality and Christian Self-Understanding: Preparatory Document for the WCC Assembly, Porto Alegre, 2006, Document No. PB-14'. 2006. <http://www.oikoumene.org/en/resources/documents/assembly/porto-alegre-2006/3-preparatory-and-background-documents/religious-plurality-and-christian-self-understanding.html>.

-----------. 'Report from Inter-Religious Consultation on 'Conversion – Assessing the Reality': Organized by the Pontifical Council for Interreligious Dialogue, Vatican City, and the Office on Interreligious Relations & Dialogue of the World Council of Churches, Geneva'. 2006. <http://www.oikoumene.org/en/resources/documents/wcc-programmes/interreligious-dialogue-and-cooperation/interreligious-trust-and-respect/report-from-inter-religious-consultation-on-conversion.html>.

-----------. *The San Antonio Report: Your Will Be Done Mission in Christ's Way*. Frederick Wilson, Ed. Geneva: WCC Publications, 1990.

-----------. 'Towards a Code of Conduct on Conversion'. 2006. <http://www.oikoumene.org/en/programmes/interreligiousdialogue/christian-self-understanding/code-of-conduct-on-conversion.html>.

World Missionary Conference, Edinburgh 1910. *Report of Commission I: Carrying the Gospel to All the Non-Christian World*. Edinburgh and London: Oliphant, Anderson & Ferrier, 1910.

-----------. *Report of Commission IV: The Missionary Message in Relation to Non-Christian Religions*. Edinburgh and London: Oliphant, Anderson & Ferrier, 1910.

Wright, Christopher J.H. 'The Christian and Other Religions: The Biblical Evidence'. *Themelios* 9.2 (1984), 4-15.

-----------. *The Mission of God: Unlocking the Bible's Grand Narrative*. Downers Grove IL: IVP Academic, 2006.

-----------. *Thinking Clearly About the Uniqueness of Jesus*. Crowborough England: Monarch, 1997.

-----------. *What's so Unique About Jesus?* Eastbourne, England: Monarch, 1990.

Yandell, Keith. *Philosophy of Religion: A Contemporary Introduction*. New York: Routledge, 2002.

Yong, Amos. '"As the Spirit Gives Utterance": Pentecost, Intra-Christian Ecumenism and the Wider Oikoumene'. *International Review of Mission* 92.366 (2003), 299.

-----------. *Beyond the Impasse: Toward a Pneumatological Theology of Religions*. Grand Rapids MI: Baker Academic, 2003.

-----------. *Discerning the Spirit(s): A Pentecostal-Charismatic Contribution to Christian Theology of Religions*. Sheffield: Sheffield Academic Press, 2000.

-----------. 'The Spirit, World Pentecostalism, and the Renewal of Theology and Praxis in the 21st Century'. *Journal for the Interdisciplinary Study of Pentecostal Charismatic Movement* 8.1 (2009), 15.

Young, Richard F. 'Seeking India's Christ-Bearing Word: Some Reflections--Historical, Indological and Theological on the Quest for a 'Christian' Vedanta'. *International Journal of Frontier Missions* 19.3 (2002), 19-29.

Zehnle, Richard. *Peter's Pentecost Discourse: Tradition and Lukan Reinterpretation in Peter's Speeches of Acts 2 and 3*. Nashville: Abingdon Press, 1971.

LIST OF CONTRIBUTORS

Editors

Lalsangkima Pachuau is professor of the History and Theology of Mission and dean of Advanced Research Programs at Asbury Theological Seminary, Kentucky, USA. Ordained by the Presbyterian Church of India (Mizoram Synod), he has taught at the United Theological College, Bangalore, India, and served as the Mission Coordinator of the New Brunswick Presbytery (PCUSA). Currently, Parish Associate Pastor of Nicholasville Presbyterian Church, the editor of Mission Studies: Journal of IAMS, a member of the executive of the International Association for Mission Studies (IAMS), and a member of the steering committee for the World Christianities forum of the American Academy of Religion. Authored and edited several books, including *Ethnic Identity and Christianity* (Peter Lang, 2002); *Ecumenical Missiology* (Bangalore: UTC, 2002), and *News of Boundless Riches* (Delhi: ISPCK, 2007).

Knud Jørgensen, 1942, journalist, MTh from The University of Copenhagen in 1970, Ph.D. in missiology from Fuller Theological Seminary 1985, has been programme director at Radio Voice of the Gospel in Ethiopia, executive secretary for communication within the Lutheran World Federation in Geneva, director of the International Mass Media Institute in Kristiansand, principal of the Go Out Centre in Hurdal, director of information within Norwegian Church Aid, dean of the leadership department at the Mekane Yesus Seminary in Addis Ababa, director for the mission foundation Areopagos, and since 2008 dean of Tao Fong Shan in Hong Kong. He is now retired but continues as adjunct professor at the Norwegian School of Theology and the Lutheran Theological Seminary, Hong Kong. Publications: *The role and function of the media in the mission of the Church (with particular reference to Africa).* Arbor, Mich: University Microfilms International, 1986; *Visjon og hverdag : lederskap i misjon og menighet.* – Oslo : Verbum, 1991; *Missiology i dag*, J-M. Berentsen, Tormod Engelsviken / Knud Jørgensen (ed.), Oslo: Universitetsforlaget, 2004, “Communication – the future. Where to go from here?” in *Festschrift for Charles H. Kraft.* Maryknoll, NY: Orbis, 2007.

Contributors

Pramod Aghamkar: Founder and executive director of Satsang Ministries; a culturally sensitive ministry to reach Asian communities. He has a Ph.D. from Asbury Theological Seminary in Intercultural Studies with a specialization in contextualization. His wife Ranjana and Pramod have started an indigenous ministry High Path to reach tribal communities in

India. He is an ordained minister with the Christian & Missionary Alliance. They live in Mumbai and Dayton, Ohio, with their two children.

***Kalarikkal Poulose Aleaz*:** Professor of Religions at Bishop's College as well as Professor and Dean of Doctoral Programme of North India Institute of Post-Graduate Theological Studies, Kolkata, India. He guides doctoral candidates of South Asia Theological Research Institute, Bangalore, India as well. Author of 21 books and more than 200 articles, he was William Patton Fellow of the Selly Oak Colleges, Birmingham, in 1977, Visiting Professor at Hartford Seminary, USA, as well as University of South Africa, Pretoria, in 2002 and Teape Lecturer, in the Universities of Cambridge, Birmingham, Bristol and Edinburgh, in 2005.

Charles Amjad-Ali is the Martin Luther King Jr. Professor for Justice and Christian Community and the Director of the Islamic Studies Program at Luther Seminary. He was the Director of the Christian Study Centre in Rawalpindi, Pakistan, and has taught around the world. His many publications include *Islamophobia or Restorative Justice: Tearing the Veil of Ignorance* (2006), *Leaving the Shadows?: Pakistani Christian and the Search for Orientation in an Overwhelmingly Muslim Society* (2008), *Dreaming a Different World: Globalization and Justice of Humanity and the Earth* (2010).

John Azumah is originally from Ghana. He did his doctoral work with the University of Birmingham, UK, on Islam in Africa and Christian-Muslim Relations. He is currently a Lecturer in Islamics and Mission Studies and Director of the Centre for Islamic Studies at the London School of Theology. He has taught in seminaries in India, South Africa and Ghana and was a Research Fellow at the Akrofi-Christaller Institute in Ghana. John is author of *The Legacy of Arab-Islam in Africa: A Quest for Inter-Religious Dialogue* (2001) and *My Neighbour's Faith: Islam Explained for Christian* (2008).

Nikos Dimitriadis, born in Greece in 1974, Ph.D. from Thessaloniki Theological School in Inter-Faith Dialogue 2009, and M.Th. in Religious History 2003. Administrator of *Globethics.net,* advisor of the Athens 2005 World Mission Conference, and Organiser of a Mutirao in the General Assembly of WCC at Porto Alegre 2006. Author of *"Religious responsible leadership. An Orthodox Perspective"*, Geneva 2007, 129-138; *"Dialogue with non believers in a secular society,"* Porto Allegre (2006); *"Fundamentalism and Religion,"* Huissen (2006); "*Deepening the AGAPE process and follow up,*" Geneva (2006); *"Acting Together for Transformation: Christians in the Technical and Social Revolutions of Our Time. An Orthodox Perspective"*, Geneva (2006); *"Religion and Society. Partners or Competitors. Interfaith Perspectives on Human Rights,"*

Copenhagen (2006); *"Migration and the integration of young migrants into Society. An Interreligious Perspective,"* Rome (2007);*"Religion and Democracy in Europe,"*Brussels (2007);*"Care and Compassion. Ensuring a Successful Interreligious Dialogue on Ethics,"* Nairobi (2009).

Ganoune Diop, born in Dakar, Senegal in 1957, Ph.D. in Old Testament exegesis and theology from Andrews University, 1995, MA in NT Theology in Collonges, France, MA in Ancient Near Eastern Languages and Civilizations at ELCOA, in Paris, France. He has taught at two Adventist universities in the USA. Prior to serving in the USA, he taught at the Adventist Seminary in Collonges sous Saleve near Geneva. Currently, director of global mission study centers on world religions and contemporary cultures, at the General Conference of Seventh day Adventist and the world headquarters in Maryland. He has also served as cross-cultural pastor for many years in France represented the SDA church at major interdenominational and interfaith conferences and dialogues.

Carmelo Dotolo, Th.D. on Fundamental Theology at Pontifical Gregorian University. He is extraordinary professor of Theology of Religion at Pontifical Urbaniana University and visiting professor at Pontifical Gregorian University. He is president of Italian Society for Theological Research (SIRT) and member of European Group of Theological Research (GERT) of Comboni Missionaries. For other information and his publications, see www.carmelodotolo.eu.

Matt Friedman was born in 1965, and came to faith in Jesus at the age of seventeen. He has been engaged in relationship and inter-religious dialogue in South Asia for over 20 years. Currently a PhD candidate at Asbury Seminary, his dissertation work is focused on early Christian interaction with Jewish apocalyptic mysticism as a model for interaction with Islamic mysticism.

David Greenlee, raised of missionary parents in Colombia, has served with Operation Mobilisation for over 30 years including many years with OM's ships Logos, Doulos, and Logos II, as well as in ministries based in Spain, England, and Cyprus. Since 1998 he has served as the mission's International Research Associate and currently resides in his wife's homeland, Switzerland. He holds an MS in electrical engineering (University of Colorado, Boulder) and a Ph.D. in Intercultural Studies (Trinity International University, Deerfield). He serves as an adjunct faculty member at Tyndale Theological Seminary, Badhoevedorp, the Netherlands and frequently lectures as a guest at Bible colleges and seminaries in South and Southeast Asia.

Antony Kalliath, CMI, born in Kerala, India is a Carmelite Catholic priest. He took the PhD in systematic theology from the Gregorian University, Rome. He had been the Dean of Theology, Pontifical Athenaeum Dharmaram Vidya Kshetram, Bangalore, India. He was the director of *Centre for World Religions* at Dharmaram. He is currently on the faculty of *National Biblical and Catechetical Centre*, a research institute of the Indian Bishops Conference of India. He is the present Executive Secretary of *Indian Theological Association* and the Board Member o f *the Christian Chair*, Madras University, India.

Veli-Matti Kärkkäinen (Dr.Theol.Habil. University of Helsinki) is Professor of Systematic Theology at Fuller Theological Seminary, Pasadena, California and Docent of Ecumenics at the University of Helsinki. A native of Finland, he has also lived and taught theology in Thailand. Author of over 150 articles and more than ten books, including *Trinity and Religious Pluralism* (Ashgate) and *The Trinity. Global Perspectives* (WJKP). He is also the co-editor of *The Global Dictionary of Theology* (IVP). He has participated widely in the ecumenical, theological, and interreligious work of the World Council of Churches, Faith and Order, as well as two international bi-lateral dialogues.

Kai Kjær-Hansen, born in Denmark in 1945, Master of Theology from The University of Copenhagen in 1972, Doctor of Divinity in the New Testament from Lund University, Sweden, 1982; has lectured at the Lutheran School of Theology in Aarhus, served as pastor in Jerusalem; Bible translator for the Danish Bible Society, and author of a number of books. Since 1991, International Coordinator of the Lausanne Consultation on Jewish Evangelism and editor of the LCJE Bulletin; from 1997 chairman of the Danish Israel Mission. In the period 1995-2009, General Editor of *Mishkan.*

Terry LeBlanc (Gi'tpoolg), a Mi'kmaq/Acadian, is the founding chair and director of NAIITS (North American Institute for Indigenous Theological Studies). As a sessional and guest lecturer at various colleges, seminaries and universities he has worked with indigenous peoples throughout the world.

Jennifer LeBlanc (Demi'k), also a Mi'kmaq/Acadian, has recently completed her MDiv degree and is engaged in indigenous ministry with iEmergence, a mission of My People International connecting youth and young adults globally. She will be pursuing her PhD in linguistics with an emphasis on the Mi'kmaq language in the next years.

Julie C. Ma (Ph.D., Fuller) serves as Research Tutor of Missiology at Oxford Centre for Mission Studies, Oxford, UK. She represented the world

Pentecostal Church in the General Council of Edinburgh 2010. She is author of four books and has written numerous academic articles. She also edited *Journal of Asian Mission.*

Alister McGrath is a former atheist who converted to Christianity while a student at Oxford University. He has a long-standing interest in communicating the faith in secular and non-Christian cultural contexts. At present, he is Professor of Theology, Ministry and Education at King's College London, and President of the Oxford Centre for Christian Apologetics. His most recent books include *Mere Theology* (2010) and *The Dawkins Delusion?* (2007).

Harold Netland is Professor of Philosophy of Religion and Intercultural Studies at Trinity Evangelical Divinity School, in Deerfield, Illinois. Much of his life has been spent in Japan, where he was born and where he served as a missionary educator from 1984-93. Among his publications are *Dissonant Voices: Religious Pluralism and the Question of Truth* (1991); *Encountering Religious Pluralism* (2001); *Globalizing Theology: Belief and Practice in an Era of World Christianity* (2006) co-edited with Craig Ott; and *Buddhism: A Christian Exploration and Appraisal* (2009) co-authored with Keith Yandell.

LAI Pan-chiu, born in Hong Kong in 1963, received his B.A in 1985 and M.Div. in 1987 from The Chinese University of Hong Kong, and Ph.D. in Theology and Religious Studies from King's College, London in 1991. He had been pastor of the Rhenish Church in the United Kingdom and lecturer at the Middlesex University. Since 1996, he has been teaching at The Chinese University of Hong Kong. Currently he is Associate Dean of the Faculty of Arts and Professor of the Department of Cultural and Religious Studies of the University. In addition to his publications in Chinese, he has published the following in English: *Towards a Trinitarian Theology of Religions: A Study of Paul Tillich's Thought* (1994), *Sino-Christian Theology: A Theological Qua Cultural Movement in Contemporary China* (2010, co-edited with Jason Lam) and numerous journal articles.

H. L. Richard was involved in grass roots Christian ministry in India for ten years before devoting another ten years to study of Hinduism and Christian work among Hindus. As a result of his studies he published "A Survey of Protestant Christian Evangelistic Efforts among High Caste Hindus in the Twentieth Century" (Missiology 25:4, Oct. 1997), "Following Jesus in the Hindu Context: The Intriguing Implications of N. V. Tilak's Life and Thought" (William Carey Library, 1998), "R. C. Das: Evangelical Prophet for Contextual Christianity" (ISPCK, 1995), "Exploring the Depths of the Mystery of Christ: K. Subba Rao's Eclectic Praxis of Hindu Discipleship to Jesus" (Centre for Contemporary

Christianity, 2005) and "Hinduism: A Brief Look at Theology, History, Scriptures and Social System with Comments on the Gospel in India" (William Carey Library, 2007) as well as other articles in Missiology, the Evangelical Missions Quarterly, the Evangelical Dictionary of World Missions, A Dictionary of Asian Christianity, etc. He is a contributing editor with the International Journal of Frontier Missiology and is one of the founders of the Rethinking Forum and HiS Friends (Hindu Student Friendship Network).

Ole Skjerbæk Madsen, born in Denmark 1947, graduated in theology from the University of Copenhagen 1975 with a thesis on Coptic Eucharistic Prayers. He served as an Evangelical-Lutheran parish pastor in Copenhagen 1975-1999; since 2000 he has been a mission pastor in the mission foundation Areopagos. He has started the bridge building project "In the Master's Light" which since 1975 has created a Christian presence in the new spiritualities milieus. He has published several books and articles on new religions, Church renewal and charismatic renewal, and liturgical studies

Notto R. Thelle (1941) is senior professor at The Faculty of Theology, University of Oslo, where he was professor of Ecumenics and Missiology (1986-2006). He served as an Areopagos missionary in Japan (1969-1985), most of the time as Associate Director of the NCC Center for the Study of Japanese Religions in Kyoto. He has written extensively on Buddhism, Buddhist-Christian dialogue, and Christian spirituality. Among publications in English are *Buddhism and Christianity in Japan: From Conflict to Dialogue* (Hawaii University Press, 1987), *Seeking God's Face: Faith in an Age of Perplexity* (Paulist Press, 2008), and *Who Can Stop the Wind? Travels in the Borderland between East and West* (Pilgrim Press, 2010).

Hans Ucko, born in Lund, Sweden in 1946, theologian, M.Th. from the University of Lund in 1971, D.Th. in systematic theology from Senate of Serampore College, Calcutta, India 2000, has pursued studies in France, India and Israel, has inter alia served as minister of the Church of Sweden in the diocese of Lund and in Paris, France, been the Director of the "Institut Eglise et Monde Juif" in Paris, the Secretary for Jewish-Christian and interfaith relations in Uppsala, Secretary for East Asia of the Church of Sweden Mission, Uppsala, and Program Executive for interreligious relations and dialogue of the World Council of Churches (WCC) in Geneva. He is now the President of Religions for Peace (WCRP) Europe, an interfaith advisor to the Japanese Buddhist Foundation Arigatou International, Tokyo and the co-chair of its interreligious campaign "A Day of Prayer and Action for Children" in cooperation with UNICEF and the Secretary of the Board of Trustees, Hartford Seminary, Hartford. He lives in Switzerland and Sweden.

Petros Vassiliadis, born in Greece in 1945, professor of N.T., Missiology and Inter-Faith Dialogue at the University of Thessaloniki, Ph.D. from Athens Theological School 1977. Visiting professor at various Universities of Geneva, USA, Copenhagen, Lund, Oslo, Joensuu, Bologna, and Reykjavik. One of the translators of the Bible into modern Greek, he served as a Consultant for UBS-Orthodox Relations of the United Bible Societies (1981-1982), and Editor-in-chief for Eastern and South-Eastern Europe of the monograph series *International Studies in Formative Christianity and Judaism* and *Ecclesia-Koinonia-Oikoumene* and co-editor of *Commentaries of the N.T.* and *Bibliotheca Biblica.* Founding member of the Society for Ecumenical Studies and Inter-Orthodox Relations and member of the Synodical Commissions on Liturgical Renewal, and on Inter-Orthodox and Inter-Christian Relations of the Church of Greece, and her Commissioner for 8 years (1998-2005) of CWME/WCC. Author of *Eucharist and Unity. Orthodox Perspectives on Unity and Mission of the Church,* 1998 (website:users.auth.gr/pv).

INDEX

REGNUM EDINBURGH 2010 SERIES
Series Listing

David A. Kerr, Kenneth R. Ross (eds.)
Edinburgh 2010
Mission Then and Now
2009 / 978-1-870345-73-6 / xiv + 343pp (paperback)
2009 / 978-1-870345-76-7 / xiv + 343pp (hardback)

No one can hope to fully understand the modern Christian missionary movement without engaging substantially with the World Missionary Conference, held at Edinburgh in 1910. As the centenary of the Conference approaches, the time is ripe to examine its meaning in light of the past century and the questions facing Christian witness today. This book is the first to systematically examine the eight Commissions which reported to Edinburgh 1910 and gave the conference much of its substance and enduring value. It will deepen and extend the reflection being stimulated by the upcoming centenary and will kindle the missionary imagination for 2010 and beyond.

Daryl M. Balia, Kirsteen Kim (eds.)
Edinburgh 2010
Witnessing to Christ Today
2010 / 978-1-870345-77-4 / xiv +301pp

This volume, the second in the Edinburgh 2010 series, includes reports of the nine main study groups working on different themes for the celebration of the centenary of the World Missionary Conference, Edinburgh 1910. Their collaborative work brings together perspectives that are as inclusive as possible of contemporary world Christianity and helps readers to grasp what it means in different contexts to be 'witnessing to Christ today'.

Claudia Währisch-Oblau, Fidon Mwombeki (eds.)
Mission Continues
Global Impulses for the 21st Century
2010 / 978-1-870345-82-8 / 271pp

In May 2009, 35 theologians from Asia, Africa and Europe met in Wuppertal, Germany, for a consultation on mission theology organized by the United Evangelical Mission: Communion of 35 Churches in Three Continents. The aim was to participate in the 100th anniversary of the Edinburgh conference through a study process and reflect on the challenges for mission in the 21st century. This book brings together these papers written by experienced practitioners from around the world.

Brian Woolnough and Wonsuk Ma (Eds)

Holistic Mission

God's plan for God's people 2010 / 978-1-870345-85-9

Holistic mission, or integral mission, implies God is concerned with the whole person, the whole community, body, mind and spirit. This book discusses the meaning of the holistic gospel, how it has developed, and implications for the the church. . It takes a global, eclectic approach, with 19 writers, all of whom have much experience in, and commitment to, holistic mission. It addresses critically and honestly one of the most exciting, and challenging, issues facing the church today. To be part of God's plan for God's people, the church must take holistic mission to the world.

Kirsteen Kim and Andrew Anderson (Eds)

Mission Today and Tomorrow

2011/978-1-870345-91-0

The centenary of the historic and influential World Missionary Conference held in Edinburgh 1910 presented a unique opportunity for the whole church worldwide to come together in celebration, reflection and recommitment to witnessing to Christ today. Edinburgh 2010 also engaged in serious study and reflection on the current state of world mission and the challenges facing all those who seek to witness Christ today. The results of this research was presented and debated within the context of Christian fellowship and worship at the conference in June 2010. This record of that conference is intended to give the background to that Call, to share the spirit of the conference, and to stimulate informed and focused participation in God's mission in Christ for the world's salvation.

Tormod Engelsviken, Erling Lundeby and Dagfinn Solheim (Eds)

The Church Going Glocal

Mission and Globalisation 2011/978-1-870345-93-4

This book provides thought-provoking and inspiring reading for all concerned with mission in the 21st century. I have been challenged by its contributors to re-think our Gospel ministries in our new local contexts marked by globalisation and migration. With its biblical foundation, its missiological reflection and interaction with contemporary society I warmly recommend this volume for study and pray that it will renew our passion for the Gospel and compassion for people.

REGNUM Studies in Global Christianity

(Previously GLOBAL THEOLOGICAL VOICES series)

Series Listing

David Emmanuuel Singh (ed.)
Jesus and the Cross
Reflections of Christians from Islamic Contexts
2008 / 978-1-870345-65-1 / x + 226pp

The Cross reminds us that the sins of the world are not borne through the exercise of power but through Jesus Christ's submission to the will of the Father. The papers in this volume are organised in three parts: scriptural, contextual and theological. The central question being addressed is: how do Christians living in contexts, where Islam is a majority or minority religion, experience, express or think of the Cross? This is, therefore, an exercise in listening. As the contexts from where these engagements arise are varied, the papers in drawing scriptural, contextual and theological reflections offer a cross-section of Christian thinking about Jesus and the Cross.

David Emmanuuel Singh (ed.)
Jesus and the Incarnation
Reflections of Christians from Islamic Contexts
2011/978-1-870345-90-3

In the dialogue of Christians with Muslims nothing is more fundamental than the Cross, the Incarnation and the Resurrection of Jesus. This book contains voices of Christians living in various 'Islamic contexts' and reflecting on the Incarnation of Jesus. The aim of these reflections is constructive and the hope is that the papers weaved around the notion of 'the Word' will not only promote dialogue among Christians on the roles of the Person and the Book, but, also, create a positive environment for their conversations with Muslim neighbours.

Sung-wook Hong
Naming God in Korea
The Case of Protestant Christianity
2008 / 978-1-870345-66-8 / xiv + 170pp

Since Christianity was introduced to Korea more than a century ago, one of the most controversial issue has been the Korean term for the Christian 'God'. This issue is not merely about naming the Christian God in Korean language, but it relates to the question of theological contextualization—the relationship between the gospel and culture—and the question of Korean Christian identity. This book examines the theological contextualization of the concept of 'God' in the contemporary Korean context and applies the translatability of Christianity to that context. It also demonstrates the nature of the gospel in relation to cultures, i.e., the universality of the gospel expressed in all human cultures.

Hubert van Beek (ed.)
Revisioning Christian Unity
The Global Christian Forum
2009 / 978-1-870345-74-3 / xx + 288pp

This book contains the records of the Global Christian Forum gathering held in Limuru near Nairobi, Kenya, on 6 – 9 November 2007 as well as the papers presented at that historic event. Also included are a summary of the Global Christian Forum process from its inception until the 2007 gathering and the reports of the evaluation of the process that was carried out in 2008.

Paul Hang-Sik Cho
Eschatology and Ecology
Experiences of the Korean Church
2010 / 978-1-870345-75-0/ 260pp (approx)

This book raises the question of why Korean people, and Korean Protestant Christians in particular, pay so little attention (in theory or practice) to ecological issues. The author argues that there is an important connection (or elective affinity) between this lack of attention and the other-worldly eschatology that is so dominant within Korean Protestant Christianity. Dispensational premillennialism, originally imported by American missionaries, resonated with traditional religious beliefs in Korea and soon came to dominate much of Korean Protestantism. This book argues that this, of all forms of millennialism, is the most damaging to ecological concerns.

Dietrich Werner, David Esterline, Namsoon Kang, Joshva Raja (eds.)
The Handbook of Theological Education in World Christianity
Theological Perspectives, Ecumenical Trends, Regional Surveys
2010 / 978-1-870345-80-4/ 759pp

This major reference work is the first ever comprehensive study of Theological Education in Christianity of its kind. With contributions from over 90 international scholars and church leaders, it aims to be easily accessible across denominational, cultural, educational, and geographic boundaries. The Handbook will aid international dialogue and networking among theological educators, institutions, and agencies. The major objectives of the text are (1) to provide introductory surveys on selected issues and themes in global theological education; (2) to provide regional surveys on key developments, achievements, and challenges in theological education; (3) to provide an overview of theological education for each of the major denominational / confessional traditions; and (4) to provide a reference section with an up-to-date list of the regional associations of theological institutions and other resources.

David Emmanuel Singh & Bernard C Farr (eds.)

Christianity and Education

Shaping of Christian Context in Thinking

2010 / 978-1-870345-81-1/ 244pp (approx)

Christianity and Education is a collection of papers published in *Transformation: An International Journal of Holistic Mission Studies* over a period of 15 years. It brings to life some of the papers that lay buried in shelves and in disparate volumes of *Transformation,* under a single volume for theological libraries, students and teachers. The articles here represent a spectrum of Christian thinking addressing issues of institutional development for theological education, theological studies in the context of global mission, contextually aware/informed education, and academies which deliver such education, methodologies and personal reflections.

J.Andrew Kirk

Civilisations in Conflict?

Islam, the West and Christian Faith 2011- 978-1-870345-71-2

Samuel Huntington's thesis, which argues that there appear to be aspects of Islam that could be on a collision course with the politics and values of Western societies, has provoked much controversy. The purpose of this study is to offer a particular response to Huntington's thesis by making a comparison between the origins of Islam and Christianity; the two religions that can be said to have shaped, in contrasting ways, the history of the Western world. The early history of each faith continues to have a profound impact on the way in which their respective followers have interpreted the relationship between faith and political life. The book draws significant, critical and creative conclusions from the analysis for contemporary intercultural understanding, and in particular for the debate about the justification of violence for political and religious ends.

REGNUM STUDIES IN MISSION
Series Listing

Kwame Bediako

Theology and Identity

The Impact of Culture upon Christian Thought in the Second Century and in Modern Africa

1992 / 1-870345-10-X / xviii + 508pp

The author examines the question of Christian identity in the context of the Graeco–Roman culture of the early Roman Empire. He then addresses the modern African predicament of quests for identity and integration.

Christopher Sugden

Seeking the Asian Face of Jesus

The Practice and Theology of Christian Social Witness in Indonesia and India 1974–1996

1997 / 1-870345-26-6 / xx + 496pp

This study focuses on contemporary holistic mission with the poor in India and Indonesia combined with the call to transformation of all life in Christ with micro-credit enterprise schemes. 'The literature on contextual theology now has a new standard to rise to' – Lamin Sanneh (Yale University, USA).

Hwa Yung

Mangoes or Bananas?

The Quest for an Authentic Asian Christian Theology

1997 / 1-870345-25-8 / xii + 274pp

Asian Christian thought remains largely captive to Greek dualism and Enlightenment rationalism because of the overwhelming dominance of Western culture. Authentic contextual Christian theologies will emerge within Asian Christianity with a dual recovery of confidence in culture and the gospel.

Keith E. Eitel

Paradigm Wars

The Southern Baptist International Mission Board Faces the Third Millennium

1999 / 1-870345-12-6 / x + 140pp

The International Mission Board of the Southern Baptist Convention is the largest denominational mission agency in North America. This volume chronicles the historic and contemporary forces that led to the IMB's recent extensive reorganization, providing the most comprehensive case study to date of a historic mission agency restructuring to continue its mission purpose into the twenty-first century more effectively.

Samuel Jayakumar

Dalit Consciousness and Christian Conversion

Historical Resources for a Contemporary Debate

1999 / 81-7214-497-0 / xxiv + 434pp

(Published jointly with ISPCK)

The main focus of this historical study is social change and transformation among the Dalit Christian communities in India. Historiography tests the evidence in the light of the conclusions of the modern Dalit liberation theologians.

Vinay Samuel and Christopher Sugden (eds.)

Mission as Transformation

A Theology of the Whole Gospel

1999 / 0870345133/ 522pp

This book brings together in one volume twenty five years of biblical reflection on mission practice with the poor from around the world. The approach of holistic mission, which integrates proclamation, evangelism, church planting and social transformation seamlessly as a whole, has been adopted since 1983 by most evangelical development agencies, most indigenous mission agencies and many Pentecostal churches. This volume helps anyone understand how evangelicals, struggling to unite evangelism and social action, found their way in the last twenty five years to the biblical view of mission in which God calls all human beings to love God and their neighbour; never creating a separation between the two.

Christopher Sugden

Gospel, Culture and Transformation

2000 / 1-870345-32-0 / viii + 152pp

A Reprint, with a New Introduction, of Part Two of Seeking the Asian Face of Jesus

Gospel, Culture and Transformation explores the practice of mission especially in relation to transforming cultures and communities. - 'Transformation is to enable God's vision of society to be actualised in all relationships: social, economic and spiritual, so that God's will may be reflected in human society and his love experienced by all communities, especially the poor.'

Bernhard Ott

Beyond Fragmentation: Integrating Mission and Theological Education

A Critical Assessment of some Recent Developments in Evangelical Theological Education

2001 / 1-870345-14-2 / xxviii + 382pp

Beyond Fragmentation is an enquiry into the development of Mission Studies in evangelical theological education in Germany and German-speaking Switzerland between 1960 and 1995. The author undertakes a detailed examination of the paradigm shifts which have taken place in recent years in both the theology of mission and the understanding of theological education.

Gideon Githiga

The Church as the Bulwark against Authoritarianism

Development of Church and State Relations in Kenya, with Particular Reference to the Years after Political Independence 1963-1992

2002 / 1-870345-38-x / xviii + 218pp

'All who care for love, peace and unity in Kenyan society will want to read this careful history by Bishop Githiga of how Kenyan Christians, drawing on the Bible, have sought to share the love of God, bring his peace and build up the unity of the nation, often in the face of great difficulties and opposition.' Canon Dr Chris Sugden, Oxford Centre for Mission Studies.

Myung Sung-Hoon, Hong Young-Gi (eds.)

Charis and Charisma

David Yonggi Cho and the Growth of Yoido Full Gospel Church

2003 / 1-870345-45-2 / xxii + 218pp

This book discusses the factors responsible for the growth of the world's largest church. It expounds the role of the Holy Spirit, the leadership, prayer, preaching, cell groups and creativity in promoting church growth. It focuses on God's grace (charis) and inspiring leadership (charisma) as the two essential factors and the book's purpose is to present a model for church growth worldwide.

Samuel Jayakumar

Mission Reader

Historical Models for Wholistic Mission in the Indian Context

2003 / 1-870345-42-8 / x + 250pp

(Published jointly with ISPCK)

This book is written from an evangelical point of view revalidating and reaffirming the Christian commitment to wholistic mission. The roots of the 'wholistic mission' combining 'evangelism and social concerns' are to be located in the history and tradition of Christian evangelism in the past; and the civilizing purpose of evangelism is compatible with modernity as an instrument in nation building.

Bob Robinson

Christians Meeting Hindus

An Analysis and Theological Critique of the Hindu-Christian Encounter in India

2004 / 1-870345-39-8 / xviii + 392pp

This book focuses on the Hindu-Christian encounter, especially the intentional meeting called dialogue, mainly during the last four decades of the twentieth century, and specifically in India itself.

Gene Early

Leadership Expectations

How Executive Expectations are Created and Used in a Non-Profit Setting

2005 / 1-870345-30-4 / xxiv + 276pp

The author creates an Expectation Enactment Analysis to study the role of the Chancellor of the University of the Nations-Kona, Hawaii. This study is grounded in the field of managerial work, jobs, and behaviour and draws on symbolic interactionism, role theory, role identity theory and enactment theory. The result is a conceptual framework for developing an understanding of managerial roles.

Tharcisse Gatwa

The Churches and Ethnic Ideology in the Rwandan Crises 1900-1994

2005 / 1-870345-24-X / approx 300pp

Since the early years of the twentieth century Christianity has become a new factor in Rwandan society. This book investigates the role Christian churches played in the formulation and development of the racial ideology that culminated in the 1994 genocide.

Julie Ma

Mission Possible

Biblical Strategies for Reaching the Lost

2005 / 1-870345-37-1 / xvi + 142pp

This is a missiology book for the church which liberates missiology from the specialists for the benefit of every believer. It also serves as a textbook that is simple and friendly, and yet solid in biblical interpretation. This book links the biblical teaching to the actual and contemporary missiological settings with examples, making the Bible come alive to the reader.

Allan Anderson, Edmond Tang (eds.)

Asian and Pentecostal

The Charismatic Face of Christianity in Asia

2005 / 1-870345-43-6 / xiv + 596pp

(Published jointly with APTS Press)

This book provides a thematic discussion and pioneering case studies on the history and development of Pentecostal and Charismatic churches in the countries of South Asia, South East Asia and East Asia.

I. Mark Beaumont

Christology in Dialogue with Muslims

A Critical Analysis of Christian Presentations of Christ for Muslims from the Ninth and Twentieth Centuries

2005 / 1-870345-46-0 / xxvi + 228pp

This book analyses Christian presentations of Christ for Muslims in the most creative periods of Christian-Muslim dialogue, the first half of the ninth century and the second half of the twentieth century. In these two periods, Christians made serious attempts to present their faith in Christ in terms that take into account Muslim perceptions of him, with a view to bridging the gap between Muslim and Christian convictions.

Thomas Czövek,

Three Seasons of Charismatic Leadership

A Literary-Critical and Theological Interpretation of the Narrative of Saul, David and Solomon

2006 / 978-1-870345484 / 272pp

This book investigates the charismatic leadership of Saul, David and Solomon. It suggests that charismatic leaders emerge in crisis situations in order to resolve the crisis by the charisma granted by God. Czovek argues that Saul proved himself as a charismatic leader as long as he acted resolutely and independently from his mentor Samuel. In the author's eyes, Saul's failure to establish himself as a charismatic leader is caused by his inability to step out from Samuel's shadow.

Jemima Atieno Oluoch

The Christian Political Theology of Dr. John Henry Okullu

2006 / 1-870345-51-7 / xx + 137pp

This book reconstructs the Christian political theology of Bishop John Henry Okullu, DD, through establishing what motivated him and the biblical basis for his socio-political activities. It also attempts to reconstruct the socio-political environment that nurtured Dr Okullu's prophetic ministry.

Richard Burgess

Nigeria's Christian Revolution

The Civil War Revival and Its Pentecostal Progeny (1967-2006)

2008 / 978-1-870345-63-7 / xxii + 347pp

This book describes the revival that occurred among the Igbo people of Eastern Nigeria and the new Pentecostal churches it generated, and documents the changes that have occurred as the movement has responded to global flows and local demands. As such, it explores the nature of revivalist and Pentecostal experience, but does so against the backdrop of local socio-political and economic developments, such as decolonisation and civil war, as well as broader processes, such as modernisation and globalisation.

David Emmanuel Singh & Bernard C Farr (eds.)
Christianity and Cultures
Shaping Christian Thinking in Context
2008 / 978-1-870345-69-9 / x + 260pp

This volume marks an important milestone, the 25th anniversary of the Oxford Centre for Mission Studies (OCMS). The papers here have been exclusively sourced from Transformation, a quarterly journal of OCMS, and seek to provide a tripartite view of Christianity's engagement with cultures by focusing on the question: how is Christian thinking being formed or reformed through its interaction with the varied contexts it encounters? The subject matters include different strands of theological-missiological thinking, socio-political engagements and forms of family relationships in interaction with the host cultures.

Tormod Engelsviken, Ernst Harbakk, Rolv Olsen, Thor Strandenæs (eds.)
Mission to the World
Communicating the Gospel in the 21st Century:
Essays in Honour of Knud Jørgensen
2008 / 978-1-870345-64-4 / 472pp

Knud Jørgensen is Director of Areopagos and Associate Professor of Missiology at MF Norwegian School of Theology. This book reflects on the main areas of Jørgensen's commitment to mission. At the same time it focuses on the main frontier of mission, the world, the content of mission, the Gospel, the fact that the Gospel has to be communicated, and the context of contemporary mission in the 21st century.

Al Tizon
Transformation after Lausanne
Radical Evangelical Mission in Global-Local Perspective
2008 / 978-1-870345-68-2 / xx + 281pp

After Lausanne '74, a worldwide network of radical evangelical mission theologians and practitioners use the notion of "Mission as Transformation" to integrate evangelism and social concern together, thus lifting theological voices from the Two Thirds World to places of prominence. This book documents the definitive gatherings, theological tensions, and social forces within and without evangelicalism that led up to Mission as Transformation. And it does so through a global-local grid that points the way toward greater holistic mission in the 21st century.

Bambang Budijanto

Values and Participation

Development in Rural Indonesia

2009 / 978-1-870345-70-5 / x + 237pp

Socio-religious values and socio-economic development are inter-dependant, inter-related and are constantly changing in the context of macro political structures, economic policy, religious organizations and globalization; and micro influences such as local affinities, identity, politics, leadership and beliefs. The three Lopait communities in Central Java, Indonesia provide an excellent model of the rich and complex negotiations and interactions among all the above factors. The book argues that the comprehensive approach in understanding the socio-religious values of each local community is essential to accurately describing their respective identity which will help institutions and agencies, both governmental and non-governmental, to relate to these communities with dignity and respect.

Young-hoon Lee

The Holy Spirit Movement in Korea

Its Historical and Theological Development

2009 / 978-1-870345-67-5 / x + 174pp

This book traces the historical and theological development of the Holy Spirit Movement in Korea through six successive periods (from 1900 to the present time). These periods are characterized by repentance and revival (1900-20), persecution and suffering under Japanese occupation (1920-40), confusion and division (1940-60), explosive revival in which the Pentecostal movement played a major role in the rapid growth of Korean churches (1960-80), the movement reaching out to all denominations (1980-2000), and the new context demanding the Holy Spirit movement to open new horizons in its mission engagement (2000-). The volume also discusses the relationship between this movement and other religions such as shamanism, and looks forward to further engagement with issues of concern in wider society.

Alan R. Johnson

Leadership in a Slum

A Bangkok Case Study

2009 / 978-1-870345-71-2 xx + 238pp

This book looks at leadership in the social context of a slum in Bangkok from an angle different from traditional studies which measure well educated Thais on leadership scales derived in the West. Using both systematic data collection and participant observation, it develops a culturally preferred model as well as a set of models based in Thai concepts that reflect on-the-ground realities. This work challenges the dominance of the patron-client rubric for understanding all forms of Thai leadership and offers a view for understanding leadership rooted in local social systems, contrary to approaches that assume the universal applicability of leadership research findings across all cultural settings. It concludes by looking at the implications of the anthropological approach for those who are involved in leadership training in Thai settings and beyond.

Titre Ande

Leadership and Authority

Bula Matari and Life - Community Ecclesiology in Congo

2010 / 978-1-870345-72-9 xvii + 189pp

This book proposes that Christian theology in Africa can make significant developments if a critical understanding of the socio-political context in contemporary Africa is taken seriously. The Christian leadership in post-colonial Africa has cloned its understanding and use of authority on the Bula Matari model, which was issued from the brutality of colonialism and political absolutism in post-colonial Africa. This model has caused many problems in churches, including dysfunction, conflicts, divisions and a lack of prophetic ministry. Titre proposes a Life-Community ecclesiology for liberating authority, where leadership is a function, not a status, and 'apostolic succession' belongs to all the people of God.

Frank Kwesi Adams

Odwira and the Gospel

A Study of the Asante Odwira Festival and its Significance for Christianity in Ghana

2010 /978-1-870345-59-0

The study of the Odwira festival is the key to the understanding of Asante religious and political life in Ghana. The book explores the nature of the Odwira festival longitudinally - in pre-colonial, colonial and post-independence Ghana - and examines the Odwira ideology and its implications for understanding the Asante self-identity. The book also discusses how some elements of faith portrayed in the Odwira festival could provide a framework for Christianity to engage with Asante culture at a greater depth. Theological themes in Asante belief that have emerged from this study include the theology of sacrament, ecclesiology, eschatology, Christology and a complex concept of time. The author argues that Asante cultural identity lies at the heart of the process by which the Asante Christian faith is carried forward.

Bruce Carlton

Strategy Coordinator

Changing the Course of Southern Baptist Missions

2010 / 978-1-870345-78-1 xvii + 268pp

In 1976, the Southern Baptist Convention adopted its Bold New Thrusts in Foreign Missions with the overarching goal of sharing the gospel with every person in the world by the year 2000. The formation of Cooperative Services International (CSI) in 1985 and the assigning of the first non-residential missionary (NRM) in 1987 demonstrated the Foreign Mission Board's (now International Mission Board) commitment to take the gospel message to countries that restricted traditional missionary presence and to people groups identified as having little or no access to the gospel. Carlton traces the historical development along with an analysis of the key components of the paradigm and its significant impact on Southern Baptists' missiology.

Julie Ma & Wonsuk Ma

Mission in the Spirit:

Towards a Pentecostal/Charismatic Missiology

2010 / 978-1-870345-84-2 xx + 312pp

The book explores the unique contribution of Pentecostal/Charismatic mission from the beginning of the twentieth century. The first part considers the theological basis of Pentecostal/Charismatic mission thinking and practice. Special attention is paid to the Old Testament, which has been regularly overlooked by the modern Pentecostal/Charismatic movements. The second part discusses major mission topics with contributions and challenges unique to Pentecostal/Charismatic mission. The book concludes with a reflection on the future of this powerful missionary movement. As the authors served as Korean missionaries in Asia, often their missionary experiences in Asia are reflected in their discussions.

S. Hun Kim & Wonsuk Ma (eds.)

Korean Diaspora and Christian Mission

2011-978-1-870345-89-7

As a 'divine conspiracy' for Missio Dei, the global phenomenon of people on the move has shown itself to be invaluable. In 2004 two significant documents concerning Diaspora were introduced, one by the Filipino International Network and the other by the Lausanne Committee for World Evangelization. These have created awareness of the importance of people on the move for Christian mission. Since then, Korean Diaspora has conducted similar research among Korean missions, resulting in this book. It is unique as the first volume researching Korean missions in Diasporic contexts, appraising and evaluating these missions with practical illustrations, and drawing on a wide diversity of researchers.

GENERAL REGNUM TITLES

Vinay Samuel, Chris Sugden (eds.)
The Church in Response to Human Need
1987 / 1870345045 / xii+268pp

Philip Sampson, Vinay Samuel, Chris Sugden (eds.)
Faith and Modernity
Essays in modernity and post-modernity
1994 / 1870345177 / 352pp

Klaus Fiedler
The Story of Faith Missions
1994 / 0745926878 / 428pp

Douglas Peterson
Not by Might nor by Power
A Pentecostal Theology of Social Concern in Latin America
1996 / 1870345207 / xvi+260pp

David Gitari
In Season and Out of Season
Sermons to a Nation
1996 / 1870345118 / 155pp

David. W. Virtue
A Vision of Hope
The Story of Samuel Habib
1996 / 1870345169 / xiv+137pp

Everett A Wilson
Strategy of the Spirit
J.Philip Hogan and the Growth of the Assemblies of God Worldwide, 1960 - 1990
1997 /1870345231/214

Murray Dempster, Byron Klaus, Douglas Petersen (eds.)
The Globalization of Pentecostalism
A Religion Made to Travel
1999 / 1870345290 / xvii+406pp

Peter Johnson, Chris Sugden (eds.)
Markets, Fair Trade and the Kingdom of God
Essays to Celebrate Traidcraft's 21st Birthday
2001 / 1870345193 / xii+155pp

Robert Hillman, Coral Chamberlain, Linda Harding
Healing & Wholeness
Reflections on the Healing Ministry
2002 / 978-1- 870345-35- 4 / xvii+283pp

David Bussau, Russell Mask
Christian Microenterprise Development
An Introduction
2003 / 1870345282 / xiii+142pp

David Singh
Sainthood and Revelatory Discourse
An Examination of the Basis for the Authority of Bayan in Mahdawi Islam
2003 / 8172147285 / xxiv+485pp

For the up-to-date listing of the Regnum books see www.ocms.ac.uk/regnum

regnum

Regnum Books International

Regnum is an Imprint of The Oxford Centre for Mission Studies
St. Philip and St. James Church
Woodstock Road
Oxford, OX2 6HR
Web: www.ocms.ac.uk/regnum